Cyberpl@y

New Technologies/New Cultures Series

General Editor: Don Slater, London School of Economics

New Technologies/New Cultures will draw together the best scholarship, across the social science disciplines, that addresses emergent technologies in relation to cultural transformation. While much contemporary literature is caught up in wild utopian or dystopian pronouncements about the scale and implications of change, this series invites more grounded and modulated work with a clear conceptual and empirical focus. The series draws on a wealth of dynamic research agendas, from Internet and new media scholarship to research into bio-sciences, environmentalism and the sociology of consumption.

Cyberpl@y

communicating online

brenda danet

BERG

Oxford • New York

First published in 2001 by
Berg
Editorial offices:
150 Cowley Road, Oxford, OX4 1JJ, UK
838 Broadway, Third Floor, New York, NY 10003-4812, USA

Berg is an imprint of Oxford International Publishers Ltd.

Library of Congress Cataloging-in-Publication Data
A catalogue record for this book is available from the Library of Congress.

British Library Cataloguing-in-Publication Data
A catalogue record for this book is available from the British Library.

ISBN   1 85973 419 7 (Cloth)
       1 85973 424 3 (Paper)

Typeset by JS Typesetting, Wellingborough, Northants.
Printed in the United Kingdom by Biddles Ltd, Guildford and King's Lynn.

For Walter

Contents

Additional resources, illustrations and links are available at:
http://atar.mscc.huji.ac.il/~msdanet/cyberpl@y/.

Acknowledgment

Publication of this book and its companion Website was made possible through the generosity of Donna Arnold, widow of the founder of The Danny Arnold Chair in Communications at the Hebrew University of Jerusalem, with additional funding from the Research and Development Authority of the Hebrew University of Jerusalem.

Preface

This book is the culmination of nine years of research and experience on the Internet. I first began to use email at the Hebrew University in the summer of 1991. Sensing that there are distinctive aspects to this new form of letter-writing, for a while I kept a journal of my observations on the language of email and the experience of using it. I had had an interest in letters and letter-writing from the early days of my Ph.D. dissertation in sociology at the University of Chicago, an analysis of letters to the Israel customs authorities. Then, however, the focus was on issues of substance, not the form of letters.

Research in sociolinguistics and discourse analysis, with an emphasis on the intersection of law and language, had led me in the mid-1980s to undertake a study of the transitional language of Old English wills, together with Bryna Bogoch. At the time, I was interested in aspects of the transition from oral to literate culture. In the fall of 1991 I taught a graduate seminar at the Hebrew University on "Communication in Times of Technological Transition." Like the research, the seminar focused on medieval times.

A doctoral student at New York University in Jerusalem at the time, Lucia Ruedenberg-Wright (later to become my collaborator), had contacted me, knowing that her supervisor, Barbara Kirshenblatt-Gimblett, and I were friends and colleagues. Originally, Lucia had discovered Internet Relay Chat (IRC) as a means for Barbara and her to be in touch while she worked on her dissertation in Jerusalem. But Lucia noticed that there were fascinating things going on in this new form of communication. She began sending Barbara interesting sequences of chat on IRC. Knowing my interests, Barbara, then on leave at the Getty Center in California, sent them flying back to me in Jerusalem. So great was the impact of what I saw that I felt that my seminar students and I could no longer discuss "communication in times of techno-logical transition" without talking about the Internet. I proposed to them, midway through the semester, that we abandon the course structure as presented at the beginning, and start again (only because I had tenure at the university did I dare to take such a radical step). Eleven out of 12 students agreed to make this startling change, and so we started over. There was little to read, as the literature was mainly about instrumental, rather than expressive aspects of communication on the Internet. Still, it was a beginning.

The textual case studies in this book, of the language of email (Chapter 2) and of writing as playful performance on IRC (Chapter 3) draw directly on my emerging research interests in those early years. The studies focusing on visual aspects of communication on the Net came later. The work on digital greetings (Chapter 4) and on ASCII art and IRC art (Chapters 5 and 6) was undertaken while I was on sabbatical leave and a Visiting Scholar at the Center for Folklife Programs and Cultural Heritage of the Smithsonian Institution, September 1996–January 1998. I thank Richard Kurin, Director of the Center, along with Marc Pachter, Amy Horowitz, and especially Zahava Doering for several forms of help and encouragement while at the Smithsonian.

Twice it happened that, just when I thought I knew what the structure of this book would be, I discovered a new phenomenon which I immediately decided just *had* to be in the book. The first such unsettling experience occurred in May 1997 when I discovered the brilliantly colored and patterned form of text-based art displayed on IRC (Chapter 6). Then, in the fall of 1998, when I was back in Jerusalem, I began to recognize what I call "font frenzy," having become something of a font addict myself (Chapter 7). Once again, I had to restructure the book. These unsettling but exciting experiences are illustrative of the difficulties any researcher studying a volatile phenomenon like the Internet must face.

Like most social scientists I used to be a "text" person. To study visual aspects of communication on the Internet, I had to acquire many new skills, including how to capture, store and manage thousands of images, as well as to develop modes of analyzing them. In general, writing the book and producing its illustrations have been a self-reflexive task, a playful performance in its own right.

I have had to invest extra time and effort to make sure that the book would be heavily illustrated. To some extent, it intentionally breaks down conventional distinctions between an academic prose monograph in which "text is all," an art book, and the often denigrated "coffee table book." Aiming for a book that would be an ambitious academic monograph, yet fun to read and look at, I have trod a delicate path, running the risk of not being taken seriously.

Color plates are indeed unusual in a social science book. I could not imagine the book without them, but there were formidable obstacles to their inclusion, mainly financial. Only through a generous contribution from Donna Arnold, widow of the man who established the Danny Arnold Chair in Communications, which I have held at the Hebrew University of Jerusalem, with additional support from the Research and Development Authority of the university, did this become possible. I am grateful to Jonathan Davis, Director of the Division for Development and Public Relations at the Hebrew University, and to Joan Maslansky, Director of Development, Los Angeles office of the American

Friends of the Hebrew University, for their invaluable help in raising this subvention.

Most of the illustrations are screen captures, by either Tsameret Wachenhauser, my former research assistant, or me. Preparation of images for inclusion in the book was itself a very time-consuming task, including the cropping of unsightly edges and adjusting the contrast when a colored image was changed to grayscale. If some of the illustrations fail to look "professional," it is because they were produced by an amateur, myself, working "on the fly." Ethnographic authenticity will have to make up for aesthetic deficiencies. Readers should be aware that, in general, these screenshots look far better when viewed online than in print – on a computer screen the backlit colors seem to glow.

My work in this area was supported by a grant from the Israel Science Foundation during 1994–96. A team of five people worked with me during that period, mainly on the studies of writing as playful performance – the typographic simulation of smoking marihuana and the parodies of *Hamlet* and *Macbeth*, both presented in Chapter 3. Members of my research team included Lucia Ruedenberg-Wright, co-principal investigator, and Haya Bechar-Israeli, Amos Cividalli, Yehudit Rosenbaum-Tamari, and Tsameret Wachenhauser.

Tsameret Wachenhauser went on to become an invaluable partner in many technical aspects of this research, as well as an important sounding board for ideas and a source of helpful information of various kinds. She co-authored with me a working paper on the Hamnet Players' performances of "PCbeth," parts of which were incorporated in Chapter 3, and served as research assistant in the work on IRC art, spending many hours, even without pay when the money ran out, capturing images for our database. She was always at least five steps ahead of me in acquiring new computer equipment and learning new tricks. Most of the technical skills I acquired for this book I learned from her. She helped with the editing of images for illustrations in this book. Finally, she created the companion Website for this book, in partnership with me.

More than any other person, Barbara Kirshenblatt-Gimblett influenced the shape and substance of the book. She saw immediately that my work focused on what is, in effect, an extension of the notion of "speech play," the subject of a book she had edited in 1976. Now, the focus was not just on words and the sounds of spoken language, but on play with the "look" of inscribed communication too. She also read nearly the entire manuscript at several stages, and made many important and useful comments and suggestions. Daniel Miller and Don Slater also read and commented on the entire manuscript. I am indebted to Miller for arranging my appointment as Visiting Fellow in anthropology at University College London in the spring of 2000, and especially for putting me in touch with Kathryn Earle, Editorial and Managing Director of Berg Publishers.

In a book as interdisciplinary as this one, the help of many people of varied training and experience is unusually important. Naomi Baron offered a linguist's helpful comments on a draft of Chapter 2, about the language of email. Earlier versions of this chapter were presented at a conference, "Attending to Technology: Implications for Humanities Teaching and Research," University of Maryland, College Park, November 1996, and at the Annual Meeting of the International Pragmatics Association in Budapest, July 2000, as well as in the 1999–2000 Annual Hugo Mueller Lecture, Department of Language and Foreign Studies and The School of Communication, American University, Washington DC, October 1999; and at Stockholm University, May 2000.

As for my discussion of online writing as playful performance in Chapter 3, I am indebted to Stuart Harris and his companion Gayle Kidder for making materials related to the activities of the Hamnet Players available to me, for allowing members of my research team to play small roles in Hamnet performances, and for granting permission to incorporate extensive materials in the chapter. Members of my research group made many contributions to the analysis of Hamnet performances. In the summer of 1994 we met for regular, often hilarious marathon sessions to analyze logs of performances. Barbara Kirshenblatt-Gimblett put me in touch with Richard Schechner, her colleague in performance studies at New York University, a practicing theater director, and editor of *TDR – The Drama Review.* An email dialogue with him greatly benefited this chapter too. Communication with other individuals experimenting with virtual theater, including Antoinette LaFarge, Steve Schrum, and Monika Wunderer, was also helpful. Earlier versions of this chapter were presented at a conference I organized, "Science Fiction or Reality? Culture, Society and Communication on the Internet," Smart Family Foundation Institute of Communications, Hebrew University, June 1995, and at a conference on "Crossroads in Cultural Studies," Tampere, Finland, July 1998. The wonderful Villa Serbelloni, run by the Rockefeller Foundation in Bellagio, Italy, a kind of "academic heaven," provided a superb setting in which to draft the writing on the Hamnet Players and their performances, in July 1995.

The index at Cardcentral.Net maintained by Margaret Collins was an invaluable source of information for my chapter on digital greetings (Chapter 4). This study was enriched by access to the archives of the National Museum of American History at the Smithsonian Institution, John Flecker, Director. At the Archives Center I was able to view the Norcross Greeting Card Collection, which contains greeting cards from 1800 through 1981, the Victor A. Blenkle Postcard Collection, and the Olive Leavister 19th Century Antique Valentine Collection. Goldie Rivkin commented on a draft of this chapter.

Chapter 5, on ASCII art and its antecedents, benefitted from the assistance of many people. I learned a great deal from extensive email correspondence with Joan Stark, an ASCII artist featured in Chapter 5, and from material on her Website. Others providing information, assistance and examples include Andrew Belsey, practitioner of typewriter art (Figure 5.4) as well as an academic; George Hutchinson, John Foust, director of the Computer Museum in Jefferson, Wisconsin, and John Sheetz, formerly of Bell Laboratories, all involved in the preservation of RTTY ("radio teletype") art; and Elisheva Revel-Neher, an art historian who directed me to the medieval Jewish prayer book from which the example of micrography in Figure 5.6 comes. Bryan Meadan, a former student, presented me with a 1960s printout of a teletype art work, an image of John F. Kennedy, another version of which appears in Figure 5.8, and John Sheetz kindly made new prints of several early teletype art works for me (Figure 5.7).

The work on the IRC variety of text-based art (Chapter 6) could not have been carried out without the extensive cooperation and assistance over several years of the leaders of the two channels studied, <patches> and <texxy> of *#mirc_rainbow* and <elusive>of *#mirc_colors*. In particular, I would like to thank <patches> for granting permission on behalf of *rainbow* players and artists to reproduce the illustrations in the chapter, and for investing much time and effort in identifying the artists wherever possible. Both <texxy> and <patches> also took the time to write important memos summing up their views on *rainbow* activities. This chapter also benefited from the insights and suggestions of Walter Cahn, an art historian. I received useful feedback from colleagues and others in the Dean's Forum, Social Science Faculty, Hebrew University of Jerusalem, February, 1999; a conference on "The Arts and the Wonders of Technology at the End of the Millennium," Van Leer Institute, Jerusalem, Rachel Bilski-Cohen, convenor, May 1999; colloquia at the Open University and Tel Aviv University, Israel, April–May 1999; the conference "Digital Borderlands: A Cybercultural Symposium," Department of Journalism, Media and Communication, Stockholm University and Institute of Working Life, Norrköping, Sweden, May 2000; and two presentations while in London on sabbatical leave in the spring of 2000, to the "Material Culture Work Group," Department of Anthropology, University College London, Daniel Miller, convenor, and the Seminar in Design History, Royal College of Art and Victoria and Albert Museum, Alison Clarke, convenor, both in May 2000.

While previous to the ASCII art and IRC art studies I had had an avocational interest in folk art, the subject of Chapter 7 – typography and how the digital revolution is changing it – was completely new territory for me. I was therefore particularly glad to have important comments and suggestions from Anthony Crouch and Steve Renick, book design professionals, and Miriam Shein, a specialist in publications in the field of education, on an earlier version of this chapter. "Absinth," former administrator of Fonts Anon~, enabled me to use the facilities of her site to gather information about attitudes toward typefaces.

The "TrueType Resource" Index, managed by Jami Reed, provided useful information and links. This research was presented for the first time at the inaugural conference of the Association of Internet Researchers, University of Kansas, September 2000.

Among the many others whom I would like to thank for help and encouragement of various kinds are Daniela Anzarout, Dave Goldman, Stanley Holwitz, Terry Suzanne Hoppenworth, Barbro Klein, Bryan Meadan, Marian Peña, Terry Winfield, and the scores of individuals, too numerous to mention, who gave permission to use email letters, material from Websites, etc. in the analysis and in illustrations. The book has also benefited from discussions with students in my courses at the Hebrew University, "Introduction to Communication and Culture on the Internet" and "Virtual Culture." The following institutions provided access to useful resources: the Smithsonian Institution libraries and collections, the Arts of the Book Collection at Sterling Memorial Library and general collections at Yale University, the British Library, and the library of the Victoria and Albert Museum.

Portions of material in this book have appeared a different form in *EJC – the Electronic Journal of Communication* (1995), the *Journal of Computer-mediated Communication* (1995, 1997), *Cybersociety 2.0: Revisiting Computer-mediated Communication and Community* (1998), edited by Steven G. Jones, and *Network and Netplay: Virtual Groups on the Internet*, edited by Fay Sudweeks, Margaret McLaughlin and Sheizaf Rafaeli (1998). Most of the material is original, however.

I am grateful to Kathryn Earle, Editorial and Managing Director of Berg Publishers, for taking a chance on an unconventional book. Sara Everett's role in supervising the production of this book is much appreciated. In particular, I thank her for allowing me to participate in decisions about the design of the book. I also thank David E. Michael for his careful copy editing of the manuscript, and Kim Clayson for an excellent job of typesetting. The handsome jacket design is by Richard Baker of Wilson Harvey Limited (London).

Finally, special thanks from <doremi> to Walter Cahn, *aka* <hazmat> online, for his patience, help, and encouragement.

All URLs cited in this book were checked and updated during the first week of January 2001. If a source is not given in captions accompanying illustrations containing screen captures from the Web, it means that the source was no longer available. For further updates, as well as additional illustrations, links and resources, please visit the companion Website to this book, at http://atar.mscc.huji.ac.il/~msdanet/cyberpl@y/.

Brenda Danet
New Haven and Jerusalem

1

Introduction

This book is about playfulness in communication on the Internet in the mid-to late 1990s. The cover of the book is a fine example of play with digital typography, one of the central topics of the book. An @ ("at") symbol, ubiquitous in email, has been substituted for the letter "a" in the title. By 2001 this had become a commonplace in discourse relating to the Internet. Note also that the title is surrounded by 10 "smileys," little icons composed of clusters of typographic symbols. Only the first one in the top row at the left is likely to be familiar to some readers – a "wink" composed of a semi-colon, a dash and an end-parenthesis – though it is far less commonly used online than the basic smiley (smiling face) composed of a colon, a dash and an end-parenthesis. If you are unfamiliar with these icons, tilt your head toward your left shoulder and you should be able to see the wink. The rest of these clusters of symbols are typical of humorous collections of smileys that have circulated on the Internet for 20 years, but are not much used in communication on the Internet.[1] If you happen to dislike smileys, don't put this book aside. It is about much much more than these symbols.

In the past we often encountered play with typography in advertising, as in the name of the chain of toy stores, *TOYS R US* with the *R* backwards. In such contexts, signage was typically rendered in what professional typographers and designers call a display typeface. The texts of scientific prose and newspapers, on the other hand, were set in text typefaces – those that enhance readability and legibility, that appear to be "transparent."[2]

In the late 1990s, developments in online communication and culture increasingly blurred the boundaries between genres of communication in which play with typography and spelling was conventionally practiced and those where it was not. There was a riot of experimentation with typography on the Internet and in relation to computers. For instance, as we will see in Chapter 7, people without formal training in design or typography became "fontaholics," collecting and displaying their favorite fonts on the World Wide Web, and even designing their own.

Texts that had long been published in sober black and white were bursting into color. Thus, in the fall of 1997, the *New York Times* introduced color into its pages, in advertisements and photographs. Around the same time, emailers who had formerly been restricted to black and white plain text began to send each other graphic and sound files as email attachments, and to vary the size and shape of fonts and even font color in messages.

The @ symbol, which replaces the letter "a" in my title, has been a standard component of all email addresses since 1972, when an engineer called Ray Tomlinson chose it to separate the names of users from the machine where their accounts were located (Hafner and Lyon 1996: 191–192). The history of this symbol is an intriguing microcosm of developments in the history of writing. It migrated from medieval scribal calligraphy to 19th-century handwriting to the typewriter, and finally to the computer keyboard. It may have begun as a medieval ligature or contraction of the Latin *ad*, ("to, toward, at").[3] In the 19th century it was used in cursive, commercial handwriting to represent the notion of "price," as in "3 apples @ 10 cents an apple".[4] Eventually, it became a standard feature of the typewriter keyboard, and was pronounced "commercial A" or "commercial at," in English, French, Italian and Russian. Today, @ is one of the 128 7-bit ASCII (American Standard Code for Information Interchange) characters in digital plain text, which are used in communication between all types of computers, regardless of operating system.[5]

In the 1990s typographic characters became central expressive symbols of emergent cyber-culture, as in the title of a novel, *back slash: a cyber thriller*.[6] On the jacket, the title was set in all lower case, a common practice in textual communication online. Another popular symbol was the ubiquitous "smiley" icon :-), a sideways smiling face[7] composed of a colon, dash and end-parenthesis, often used in online communication to indicate a smile or that one is joking. Thus, in 1998 the Wells Fargo Bank promoted its online services with a paper prospectus containing a giant smiley. The continuing popularity of smileys drew on that of the conventional "happy face" :). The @ symbol was the most popular of all. We saw it everywhere, online and offline: on T-shirts, in online and print journalism and advertising (e.g., a Gap ad for children's clothes containing the expression *gap@school*) and in book titles (e.g., *Modest_Witness@Second.Millennium* by Donna Haraway),[8] as well as in the logos of many cybercafés (Figure 1.1). The second example in Figure 1.1 is particularly clever: @ is vocalized as *strudel* in Hebrew;[9] thus, the name of this Jerusalem Internet café and wine bar cleverly unites strudel the cake and its rolled shape with the Internet and the double functions of cybercafés.[10]

Expressivity was particularly evident when @ was substituted gratuitously for the plain letter "a," or when the symbol was graphically over-large. The cover of the program of a 1997 conference in performance studies featured a

Figure 1.1. Logos of three cybercafés.

huge @ symbol. In December, 1998 the Swatch Corporation, makers of stylish watches for young people, announced the arrival of *@Internet Time*, a global time something like Greenwich Mean Time.[11] Internet time was represented on its Website as, e.g., *@634*, for the 634th "beat" in an Internet day containing 1000 "beats." Other examples were *Cyberst@tion*, the Internet department of the branch of Waterstone's bookstore opposite University College, London, and *meg@*, the Saturday youth supplement to the London Times. Gratuitous uses also occurred in other languages. *F@ites de l'Internet* was the title of an evening of programs broadcast on the French-German Arte cable television channel on March 19, 1998.[12]

Subject of the Book

As my title indicates, this book is a series of studies of playfulness in communication and culture on the Internet. Its focus is on play with form of various kinds in online communication. Quite a few authors, e.g., Michael Heim (1987), Jay David Bolter (1991), Richard Lanham (1993), Sherry Turkle (1995), Allucquère Rosanne Stone (1996), and Malcolm McCullough (1996), comment generally on the playfulness of the medium. The approaches of these authors are philosophical (Heim), literary (Bolter, Lanham), or otherwise treat the medium in a general, mainly non-empirical manner (Stone, McCullough). Sherry Turkle's (1995) *Life on the Screen, Identity in the Age of the Internet* is an empirical study but deals with play with identity, not with the new medium per se, and she focuses primarily on psychological, rather than cultural, social or linguistic aspects.

Two book-length studies of the language of online communication are Murray (1991) and Davis and Brewer (1997). Neither is about playfulness. Some post-1995 articles and book chapters that are reviewed below[13] do focus on aspects of playfulness with the medium. However, to my knowledge, this is the first detailed, empirical, book-length study of specific forms of playfulness, focusing primarily on actual messages exchanged in specific settings. Moreover, this is the first book to accommodate linguistic, typographic and multimedia phenomena within the same theoretical framework. I am interested both in linguistic/textual (Chapters 2 and 3) and visual-graphic and multimedia phenomena (Chapters 4–7).

The title of the book also reflects the spirit of adventure, fun and experimentation that accompanied explorations in a new medium, and the ways that it shook up old norms and expectations. Millions of serious email messages were sent and received every day, and people wrote serious articles and books with word-processors. At the same time, play with writing was distinctive enough and frequent enough in the many modes of this new medium as we approached the millennium to warrant a book-length treatment.

Online communicators played with many other aspects of communication besides language and writing, including their own identities, the frames of interaction and the conventions of pre-digital genres of communication. The visual "look" of communication on the Internet became increasingly important, not only on the World Wide Web, but also in other modes. For example, mIRC, a Windows 95-based version of the IRC software, enabled players to vary the color of both the font used during chat and the background of the chat window. Moreover, players could now incorporate colored images and sound in their messages. Chapter 6 is a case study of two IRC channels that specialized in primarily visual communication.[14]

The late 1990s also saw the development of a variety of chat modes incorporating a graphical interface. Thus, in "The Palace" players chose visual avatars to represent themselves, or even designed their own, and could add virtual props to enhance their online identities.[15] While players could animate their avatar if they had the skills to do so, the graphic background of "The Palace" was static. Like the Palace, "Dreamscape" and "Vzones" offered a third-person perspective on a two-dimensional world.[16] By mid-1999, another company, Worlds, Inc., offered a dynamic, three-dimensional graphical interface with music.[17]

In *The Second Self: Computers and the Human Spirit*, Sherry Turkle (1984) had suggested that computers serve as important "objects to think with" – evocative objects for thinking through questions about who we are. In the 1990s the computer became a key cultural symbol and metaphor, and not just a medium for the transfer of information. With the rise of networks of computers which could exchange messages with one another, the computer became an expressive communication medium, going beyond the isolation of the person-machine dyad. Designers of virtual environments came to understand that their systems were shaped as much, if not more, by interaction among participants as by technology per se (Laurel 1991: 4).

Interest in the expressive aspects of online communication was slow to develop among social scientists, because they had a primarily instrumental orientation toward computers themselves. Early research between 1975 and 1990 had focused on such issues as how email affected communication in work settings. Terms like "teleconferencing" and "conferences" were frequently used in research published during that period.[18] The Internet was originally developed for defense purposes in the late 1960's and early 1970's by the United States Department of Defense (Hafner and Lyon 1996). In its early applications beyond defense needs it was primarily used in work settings, at first by programmers themselves, and later by others.[19] Thus, people expected the frame of messages exchanged to be serious. The medium was perceived as cold, anonymous, and lacking in "social presence" because of the absence of non-verbal cues such as facial expression.[20]

The commonly used metaphor "the Information Highway" perpetuated perception of the new media as mere conduits for the transfer of bits and bytes. Today we know that cyberspace is as much about people and their activities as about information. By the mid- to late 1990s, cyberspace was a buzzing hive of social and cultural activity. Expressive aspects of the new forms of communication are likely to have at least as profound consequences for the future of human culture as work-related ones. As the millennium approached, the older paradigm of computers as rational tools competed with the newer one of computers as arenas for play, social experience and dramatic interaction.[21]

Theoretical Approach

The Bi-stable Text

In text-based digital communication the need to say in writing what we have been used to saying in speech calls attention to the communicative means employed in formulating the message. Reduced transparency of messages heightens meta-linguistic awareness, and leads us to treat words, letters and other typographic symbols as objects, and to play with them (Cazden 1976).[22]

Richard Lanham (1993) speaks of the bi-stability of the textual surface in digital writing, as opposed to the goal of transparency in literate culture. Recapitulating the history of writing, he notes that it took a long time for writing to become "transparent" in the manner to which we have been accustomed in print culture. In Eric Havelock's (1982) work on the Greek alphabet he had stressed that an efficient writing system "would become a transparent window into conceptual thought. The shape of the letters, the written surface, was not to be read aesthetically; that could. . . interfere with purely literate transparency" (Lanham 1993: 4).

According to Johanna Drucker (1994), the notion of the transparent text came into its own with the invention of printing in the 15th century:

> The basic distinction between marked and unmarked typography occurred simultaneously with the invention of printing. Gutenberg printed two distinctly different kinds of documents. . . . . On the one hand, he printed bibles, with their perfectly uniform gray pages, their uninterrupted blocks of text, without heading or subheadings or any distraction beyond the occasional initial letter. These bibles are the archetype of the unmarked text, the text in which the words on the page "appear to speak for themselves" . . . . By contrast, the Indulgences which he printed displayed the embryonic features of a marked typography. Different sizes of type were used to hierarchize information, to create an order in the text so that different parts of it appear to "speak" differently. (Drucker 1994: 94–95)

With its prime goal of legibility, the typographically unmarked text has been the dominant model for works of literature and authoritative scholarly prose in our own times. Since the Renaissance, the marked text flourished in only two domains, modern advertising and visual poetry. Late 19th- and early 20th-century advertising began to put type on the diagonal, mixed type faces, sizes, and styles all in one line or even one word (Drucker 1994: 96). All of these practices are commonplace in advertising today.

In visual poetry, sometimes called concrete or pattern poetry, the text of a poem is shaped into a visual image. As I will report in greater detail in Chapter 5, this practice dates back to ancient Greece. In the early 20th century, avant-garde movements such as Dada and Futurism experimented with typography. In the 1960s there was again a revival of interest in poetry whose visual form is important.[23]

With the advent of the computer, conventional thinking about the marked versus the unmarked text was seriously challenged. Lanham suggests that when we read a digital text,

> We are always looking first AT it [the text] and then THROUGH it, and this oscillation creates a different implied ideal of decorum, both stylistic and behavioral. Look THROUGH a text a you are in the familiar world of the Newtonian interlude, where facts were facts, the world was really "out there," folks had sincere central selves, and the best writing style dropped from the writer as "simply and directly as a stone falls to the round". . . . Look AT a text, however, and we have deconstructed the Newtonian world into Pirandello's and yearn to "act naturally." (Lanham 1993: 5)

Lanham adds, "As literary scholars above all should know, where the. . . creative spirit has room to play, play it will" (Lanham 1993: 5).

Cyberspace as a Space for Play

As Johan Huizinga's classic *Homo Ludens* (1955) so eloquently expounded, play has always been an important component in human culture. In a reworked version of Huizinga's formulation, Roger Caillois suggests that play is activity which is:

1. Free: in which playing is not obligatory. . .
2. Separate: circumscribed within limits of space and time, defined and fixed in advance
3. Uncertain: the course of which cannot be determined, nor the result attained before hand and some latitude for innovations being left to the player's initiative
4. Unproductive: creating neither goods, nor wealth. . .
5. Governed by rules: under conventions that suspend ordinary laws, and for the moment establish new legislation, which alone counts
6. Make-believe: accompanied by a special awareness of a second reality, or of a free unreality, as against real life (Caillois 1961: 9–10).

All of these features except the second fit playful activity in cyberspace. Actually, Huizinga was not quite so categorical, noting that "All play moves and has its being within a playground marked off beforehand *either materially or ideally*, deliberately, or as a matter of course" (Huizinga 1955: 10; italics added). Objectively, cyberspace is marked off by connections between objects having a definite physicality – computers and the bodies that activate them.

But phenomenologically, the space for play in cyberspace is abstract, held in the mind.

Among forms of online communication, chat modes are especially conducive to the activation of a play frame. Because identity is disguised, participants enjoy reduced accountability for their actions, and can engage in "pretend" or "make-believe" behavior of all kinds (Bateson 1972; Goffman 1974; Handelman 1976). In this frame, process is more important than outcome (Kirshenblatt-Gimblett 1976).

Cyberspace is often anarchic, playful and even carnivalesque, despite the absence of the body, or at least a radical transformation of its role (Bakhtin 1968; Slater 1998; Stone 1996).[24] In Victor Turner's (1969; 1974; 1986) terms it is a liminal space,[25] "betwixt and between," freed from the rules and expectations that normally govern daily life, governed by the subjunctive mode of possibility and experiment. This is so both because in the late 20th century it was new and still relatively uncharted culturally, and because, at least in its textual forms, it frequently masked identity and reduced accountability as efficiently as all-enveloping costumes and masks worn at carnival time (Figure 1.2). I will have more to say about these factors and others fostering playfulness later in the chapter. At the same time, we should not over-use the carnival metaphor. Already in the concluding years of the 20th century, there were many signs of normalization and institutionalization, processes that curtailed the carnivalesque flavor of cyberspace in many contexts.

It makes no sense to ask what time it is in an online chatroom since each person is located in his or her own space/time matrix. Similarly, the space for online play is not a matter of geography or fences, though one does have a strong sense of "place," particularly in chat modes but even in listserv discussion groups and Usenet newsgroups. Barbara Kirshenblatt-Gimblett (1996) suggested that this sense of "place" is constructed through focus on topic. As she points out, "topic" and "topography" both come from the Greek "topos" for "place."[26]

Play versus Playfulness

According to the *Shorter Oxford English Dictionary*, to be playful is to be "full of play, frolicsome, sportive; also pleasantly humorous or jocular, merry." A caper is "a frolicsome leap, as of a kid; a frisky movement." Too often, the myriad theories of play that have circulated in the 20th century and earlier have not distinguished between play and playfulness. Brian Sutton-Smith (1997: 147) notes that

Figure 1.2. Masked participants, Carnival, 1996, Venice. Photograph by Brenda Danet.

> Play is sometimes defined in terms of the content of the forms it takes, such as children's play, games, sports, festivals, and so on, most of which are well-organized entities within human culture and are pursued with great earnestness, while playful refers more to a mood of frolicsomeness, lightheartedness, and wit. (Sutton-Smith 1997: 147)

Thus, a golfer may plan and execute his or her moves with the utmost seriousness, and an amateur pianist may experience little fun practicing a difficult Beethoven sonata for hours. Sutton-Smith suggests that we reserve the concept of playfulness for

> that which is meta-play, that which plays with normal expectations of play itself. . . . Playful would be that which plays with the frames of play. Play, by contrast, would that which plays with the frames of the mundane and sticks to its purpose of being a stylized form of [play] in which the expected routines or rules guide and frame the action in a steady way throughout. (Sutton-Smith 1997: 148)

An additional source of confusion in theorizing about play is the tendency to confound activity and emotional state. We have just seen evidence of this in the two passages from Sutton-Smith. The expression "lightheartedness" highlights the emotional state of the player, while "frolicsomeness" and "wit" are observable by another person. The second passage invites us to focus only on observable features of activity. In a study of playfulness as a personality trait, J. Nina Lieberman ascribed three components to playfulness: spontaneity, manifest joy, and a sense of humor (Lieberman 1977: 6). Here too one can discern a potential mixture of observable behavior and emotional state.

Suffice it to say that in the five studies reported in this book, I focus primarily on overt manifestations of more or less spontaneous playfulness on the computer screen. In the coming chapters, I analyze some of the ways that people frolicked and gamboled and capered about with, or experimented with, the stuff of speech and writing, as well as with graphics and color. I also refer secondarily to evidence for the fun that people had, the joy and exhilaration that they experienced, and the humor that accompanied or characterized their activities.

Speech Play and the Ethnography of Speaking

The concept of "speech play" is particularly relevant for the conceptual framework of this book. It is "The creative disposition of language resources; the manipulation of formal features and processes of language to achieve a striking restructuring of familiar discourse alignments. . . . Speech play highlights relationships that tend to remain latent in the more reference-oriented uses of linguistic codes" (McDowell 1992: 139).

In instances where speech play is present the poetic function of language is dominant (Jakobson 1960). Obviously, the term "speech play" is normally used to refer to play with language in spoken face-to-face encounters. The study of play with written language, on the other hand, is normally relegated to the field of literary stylistics.[27] Speech play and its close cousin, verbal art[28] (again, spoken, not written), have been studied by sociolinguists, linguistic anthropologists, folklorists, and ethnographers of communication. The ethnography of speaking[29] is a description in cultural terms of the patterned uses of language and speech in a particular group, institution, community, or society that includes native theories and practices of speaking, both as overtly articulated by individuals and as enacted by them in a range of activities, situations, and interactions (Sherzer 1992: 76).

To play with speech or writing is to be artful in formulating a message. The *Oxford English Dictionary* offers several pertinent definitions: (1) skillful in adapting means to ends, adroit; (2) performed according to rules of art; (3)

of actions, skillfully adapted for a purpose. In Chapter 2 we will see rare glimpses of artful, playful language even in primarily serious email. Chapter 3 celebrates its flowering in online typed performances of parodies of *Hamlet* and *Macbeth* on IRC. Artful use or treatment of letters and other typographic symbols is the theme common to Chapters 5–7, all of which deal with visual aspects of aestheticized writing.

The Ethnography of Writing

The ethnography of writing is a much less developed field than the ethnography of speaking, though some important contributions were made in the last 15 years before the millennium.[30] This research investigates shared knowledge and norms for culture-specific genres of written texts, produced in specific media. The emphasis is on everyday uses of writing, in school, at home, or in the office. Researchers ask: who uses writing for what purposes? What genres and subgenres of texts are recognized, and how do they develop? What media are considered appropriate for which kinds of messages, and what are the norms governing usage in the various genres?

Dealing as it does with an anomalous medium lying between speaking and writing, this book will show that in the novel circumstances of online communication, our practice of separating the two is not useful. On the contrary, confrontation with it forces us to re-examine some of our most basic assumptions about what characterizes speech or writing and what the physical medium of each dictates.

Most broadly conceived, then, this book is an ethnography of play with communicative form on the Internet. By form I mean, depending on the topic at hand: linguistic form, typographic form, emergent conventions of genre or text type,[31] the mix and type of media considered appropriate for specific communicative functions, and even the formal features of a visual image.

Doubly Attenuated, Doubly Enhanced: Uniqueness of The Digital Medium

Although text-based online communication is written, it shares many qualities with oral communication. In interactive – synchronous – modes, it is dynamic, improvisational and sometimes even agonistically toned, most prominently in sequences of "flaming," the sudden flare-up of tempers.[32] These features make it anomalous and puzzling. Kathleen Ferrara and her associates (Ferrara et al. 1991) proposed to call it "Interactive Written Discourse." Christopher Werry (1996) adopted this term for his study of language and communication on IRC. In my preferred formulation, digital communication is paradoxically both doubly attenuated and doubly enhanced (Figure 1.3).

	"speech"	**"writing"**
Attenuated	absence of non-verbal cues	loss of text as object
Enhanced	ability to re-examine utterance	restoration of presence of interlocutor

Figure 1.3. The paradoxical nature of digital communication.

We can think of online typed communication as in some way less rich than either speech or writing, and therefore doubly attenuated. *The Shorter Oxford English Dictionary* defines "attenuate" as "1. To make thin or slender; 2. To make thin in consistency. 3. fig. To reduce in intensity, force, amount or value." Digital text is clearly a form of writing: pixels on the computer screen are formed into letters and words that we read and write. Digital writing is attenuated because the text is no longer a tangible physical object. Printing is optional even in email, and in synchronous modes of typed chat communication on the fly is the thing, not an optional textual log of what happened.

At the same time, online linguistic communication can also be viewed as attenuated speech. Because it is dynamic, interactive and ephemeral, it is like conversation: we can receive instant feedback to our message, and many messages can be exchanged in rapid-fire fashion, even in asynchronous email, if the parties both happen to be logged on. Thus, social psychologists such as Sara Kiesler and her collaborators (1984) see computer-mediated, typed communication as reduced (many speak of "reduced bandwidth," in information theory terms), because of the loss of the nonverbal and paralinguistic cues which contribute importantly to meaning in spoken encounters.

Paradoxically, it is, I believe, no less justified to speak of online linguistic communication as doubly enhanced as it is to claim that it is doubly attenuated. We can say that it is "enhanced speech," since, unlike ordinary speech, it leaves traces, and can therefore be re-examined as long as we are logged on, the program is open, and the text is retained in the computer's memory. We can reread what the other person or we have just written.

Similarly, we can speak of digital writing as enhanced writing, since in its real-time interactive modes, the medium restores the presence of one's interlocutor, long absent in the production of extensive texts. Moreover, it is far easier to establish immediate communication with the writer of an asynchronous message or text than in the past, making it more dialogic than in print culture. This curious condition of being both doubly attenuated and doubly enhanced means that typed online communication lies between speech and writing, yet is neither: in short, it is something new.[33]

Location of the Book in the Orality/Literacy Debate

To sharpen this outline of the theoretical framework of the book still further, one more issue must be clarified. The terms "oral" and "orality" are used in many different ways in the literature, often leading to confusion. Sociolinguists, specialists in discourse analysis, and ethnographers of communication sometimes speak of an "oral" style in writing, meaning that it is "speech-like" linguistically.

The terms "oral" and "orality" often bring to mind the work of Walter Ong (1982), Marshall McLuhan (1965), Eric Havelock (1986), Jack Goody (1986; 1987; 1963) and others on oral, written, and electronic media. Although I may sometimes speak of the "oral" or "speech-like" nature of digital writing, my research is not addressed to issues typically associated with this group.

In his book, *The Muse Learns to Write: Reflections on Orality and Literacy from Antiquity to the Present*, Eric Havelock (1986) identified four different aspects of the "Orality Problem," as he put it, which had been debated and investigated in the preceding 25 years:

> There is the historical dimension: What has it meant for societies and their cultures in the past to discard oral means of communication in favor of literate ones of various sorts? There is the contemporary one: What precisely is the relationship between the spoken word of today (or yesterday) and the written text? There is the linguistic one: What happens to the structure of a spoken language when it becomes a written artifact?. . . From this, one can proceed to the philosophical (or psychological) level and ask: Is oral communication the instrument of an oral state of mind, a type of consciousness quite different from the literate state of mind? (Havelock 1986: 24)

The central issue in this book can be formulated as a light paraphrase of the third dimension or question, and this one only: what happens to patterns of usage when writing loses its artifactual nature and becomes digital? Broadening the scope even further, to take account of the shift from pure text to multimedia, we can reformulate the question somewhat awkwardly but more precisely: what happens to patterns of inscribed communication when it loses its artifactual nature and becomes digital and multimedia?

Types of Online Communication

Interpreted broadly, "online communication" includes not only person-to-person and person-to-group communication, but also person-to-remote-computer contacts, as when individuals read or download documents on the World Wide Web. Global computerization is breaking down the traditional distinction in print culture between the solo-authored, decontextualized, written text and the face-to-face personal conversation. Within minutes of examining a document on the World Wide Web, a person can begin a dialog with the author by email. This dialog in turn can become part of a cluster of stored texts linked to the original.[34] Many Websites also offer instant access to a chat mode. In this book I am primarily concerned with direct person-to-person and person-to-group communication, rather than person–computer interaction, though some aspects of the latter type of communication, on the World Wide Web, will also be important.

Asynchronous Modes: Email, Listserv Lists, Usenet

For readers unfamiliar with the Internet I review briefly the main forms of communication in cyberspace. There are two main forms of online inter-personal communication, asynchronic, and synchronic (Figure 1.4). Basic, private email resembles ordinary letter-writing: the sender composes and sends the message at a time separate from that in which the recipient receives or reads it. However, whereas ordinary mail takes days to arrive, email arrives in seconds or minutes.

Person-to-person

Non-synchronous	Private email
	BBSs
	Listserv discussion lists (moderated or unmoderated)
	Usenet newsgroups
Synchronous	Two-party chat: @talk on UNIX, ICQ, etc.
	Multi-party chat: IRC channels, MUDs, ICQ, etc.
Person-machine	World Wide Web

Figure 1.4. Types of computer-mediated communication.

Group communication based on the basic email mode included listserv discussion groups, Usenet newsgroups, and electronic bulletin boards (BBSs) run by hobbyists, whether children, teenagers or adults. Hundreds of thousands of such groups were in intense daily interaction in the 1990s. Electronic groups discussed topics ranging from (1) the professional or academic (astronomy, computer matters) to (2) the recreational (e.g., StarTrek, soap operas) to (3) issues requiring group support (single fathers, dieters). Listserv messages posted to a central host address were automatically distributed to the personal accounts of all other subscribers.

In some groups, a moderator edits and distributes messages in batches. In Usenet newsgroups and BBSs, individuals read postings stored on a host computer, rather than receiving them in their individual accounts. When individuals exchanging email happen to be logged on at the same time, communication feels like chatting, even if technically they are exchanging asynchronous messages.

Synchronous Modes: Typed Chat

Synchronous modes of online communication enable individuals simultaneously logged on to chat in real time by typing. Just as face-to-face speakers hear their interlocutors formulating their messages as they are spoken, when the @*talk* function is activated on the UNIX computer, two individuals can read each other's contributions while they are being typed. The chat function in ICQ, a program that enables individuals to track others on the entire Internet, works the same way.[35] Other chat modes included Internet Relay Chat (IRC), MUDs (Multi-User Domains or Multi-User Domains),[36] the CB (Citizens' Band) Channel on Compuserve, and chatrooms on many commercial services, including America Online and New York's ECHO.[37] Chat modes were, of course no longer restricted to two parties, as they were in UNIX days.

The most popular chat program in the world in the late 1990s was probably IRC. This public domain program was created in 1988 by Jarkko Oikarinen, a Finnish student, to expand the possibilities for chat to three or more persons. At any hour of the day or night, many thousands of persons all over the world were logged on. As of July, 1998, the number of users of IRC had grown to an estimated 1,000,000–1,500,000 people, via well over 100 networks of host servers. [38] Remarkably, devotees ran the entire system on a volunteer basis.

Individuals divided up into channels (equivalent to "chat rooms") with names based on geography and cultural affinity (#*russia*, #*england*), professional interests (#*www*, #*macintosh*), playful fantasy and themes of popular culture (#*dragonrealm*, #*startrek*), or special needs (e.g., #*huggs*, a support group for women with gynecological cancer, their families and friends), and crises (#*rabin* and #*diana*, temporary channels created following the murder of Yitzhak Rabin in 1995 and the death of Princess Diana in 1997). In many other cases the name was constitutive of the channel's nature as a virtual café or pub, as in #*nicecafe*, #*friendly*, or #*tahitibar*.[39] Once logged on, individuals had only to type, e.g., /*join* #*cyberchat*, and they joined the players in the channel. It was possible to interact in more than one channel at a time, by opening up a window for each and moving back and forth between them.

MUDs evolved from the computer game Dragons and Dungeons. Most MUDs were text-based virtual realities, with a more structured environment than IRC channels. A MUD is

> a software program that permits multiple users (typically from widely dispersed sites) simultaneously to access a shared database and to communicate and interact in a virtual environment characterized by a spatial metaphor and an architectural motif. (Jacobson 1996: 464)

The database contains virtual rooms and objects, and users can manipulate and extend it. Interaction on MUDs was primarily rendered in the third person, thus resembling fiction, whereas IRC dialog was in the first person, like ordinary talk.

Like so many other aspects of the Internet, the number of MUDs grew enormously in a very few years. As of July 1998, 1,191 MUDs were listed in the MudConnect database on the World Wide Web. Of these, 55 were graphical rather than merely text-based.[40] There were three main types, primarily game-oriented MUDs, social or recreational ones, of which the best known was probably LambdaMOO, the original recreational one developed by Pavel Curtis (1996), and professionally or academically oriented MUDs like Media MOO, run for media researchers by Amy Bruckman.[41] MUDs could be quite large. LambdaMOO became the equivalent of a town, with a population of some 8,000 players by 1998, and its own internal email system.[42] ChibaMOO had more than 5,000 players (Jacobson 1996: 464).

Recreational MUDs featured extensive collective role-playing. Individuals developed elaborate fictional personae, and interacted in virtual rooms or outdoor spaces. One could play a dragon, a femme fatale or even a plural character, such as "Mutt&Jeff," and it was possible to change one's character at any time, even to play different characters in different MUDS simultaneously. The virtual environment might be a mansion, a town, a castle, and so on.

"Speech-like" versus "Writing-like" Online Communication

Depending on the technology used, different forms of online communication are located at different points along a continuum from situations which elicit or facilitate the most writing-like use of language at one end, to those which elicit or facilitate the most speech-like use at the other. Thus, asynchronous email composed offline is likely to be relatively writing-like in its linguistic features. There is time to edit, and one can even use a word-processor and import it into the email interface or enclose the edited text as an attachment.

In contrast, chat modes most resemble oral conversation; speed is all-important – we cannot type as fast as we speak, but we do our best to type fast – and editing virtually impossible. Finally, email written online with software that does not facilitate editing lies somewhere in between these two ends of the continuum; it is likely to resemble the language of chat modes to some degree.[43] Because interlocutors are virtually present to one another, individuals are aware of their audience, and interactive writing can become a stylized performance, particularly when a play frame is activated (Bateson 1972; Goffman 1974; Handelman 1976).

Common Features of Digital Writing

Many of the emergent practices and conventions of digital writing originated in hacker usage (Raymond 1996: 14–22). The first seven features in Figure 1.5 are devices to compensate for the nature of the medium as attenuated "speech."[44] The last two are devices to help convey the message as fast as possible, since we can't type as fast as we speak; thus, they are writing-specific.

---

(1)	Multiple punctuation	Type back soon!!!!!!
(2)	Eccentric spelling	Type back sooooooooon.
(3)	Capital letters	I'M REALLY ANGRY AT YOU!
(4)	Asterisks for emphasis	I'm really *angry* at you.
(5)	Written out laughter	hehehe hahahaha
(6)	Descriptions of action	*grins* <grin> <g>
(7)	"Smiley" icons	:-) ;-) :-(
		(smile) (wink) (frown)
(8)	Abbreviations	LOL BRB
(9)	All lower case	hi, how are you? did you hear about tom?

Figure 1.5. Common features of digital writing.

Multiple punctuation, some forms of eccentric spelling, asterisks and use of all capital letters for emphasis are strategies to enhance readers' and writers' ability to experience the words as if they were spoken. We rarely, if ever, encounter them in formal genres of paper-based writing such as business letters or reports, because people have been taught to avoid them. In the past, expressivity had been suppressed by the teaching of literacy in the schools. Children were taught that a written composition must differ in a host of ways from a spontaneous oral sequence of utterances (Britton 1982; Gundlach 1982). An exception in conventional writing practice is the use of underlining or italics, which may be used sparingly in formal genres.

Multiple punctuation and eccentric spelling were especially common in online writing of children, e.g., in letters to "keypals" by participants in Kidlink, a network for children,[45] but they also occurred in email by adults too. The use of all capital letters, as in "I REALLY LIKE THAT!" is familiar from the comics and street graffiti, especially when the word is a graphic representation of a sound.[46] In practice, however, writing in all caps was generally discouraged. "Newbies," newcomers to cyberspace, were told that such messages are interpreted as shouting and should only be used in small doses. Several of these features might come together, as when a writer types "UGGHHHHH!!!", thus reinventing conventions from the comics for inter-actional purposes. Typing "hehehe" is also obviously a device to convey a sound, in this case the sound of laughter.

Smiley icons and descriptions of action like *grins*[47] supply information about non-verbal aspects of communication which would have been discern-ible if the words had been uttered aloud in a face-to-face encounter. Detested by some and enjoyed by others, smiley icons were more formally called "emoti-cons" – a conflation of "emotion" and "icon" (Raymond 1996: 173–174). As we saw earlier, they are composed of clusters of ordinary typographic symbols such as commas, periods and parentheses. When viewed with the head tilted toward the left shoulder they form "faces". The three shown in Figure 1.5 were the best known and most widely used on the Internet. Besides the smile, they include a wink and a frown.[48]

Synchronous typed conversations, listserv and Usenet contributions, and even private email were often sprinkled with abbreviations, some of which were already in use before the advent of computers, e.g., FYI for "For Your Information." IRL is an example of one that emerged in digital culture, mean-ing "In Real Life." A partial listing of other frequently used abbreviations is shown in Figure 1.6. As in both oral and paper-based written communication, abbreviations promote efficiency. Online, they save valuable typing time.

Writing in all lower case is also efficient: it saves time and effort not to have to capitalize the first word of sentences, proper names, etc. However, writing in this manner probably also came to signal membership in the new culture. Normative issues raised by many of the practices listed in Figure 1.5 are discussed in Chapter 2.

AFK	away from keyboard
B4	before
BBL	be back later
BTDT	been there, done that
BTW	by the way
CU	see you
CUL	see you later
CYA	see ya
FAQ	frequently asked questions
FTF	face to face
FYI	for your information
GAL	get a life
IMO	in my opinion
IMHO	in my humble opinion
IRL	in real life
L8R	later
NRN	no reply necessary
OTOH	on the other hand
REHI	hi again
ROFL	rolling on the floor laughing
RTFM	read the f***ing manual
TIA	thanks in advance
TNX	thanks
WB	welcome back

*Compiled mainly from Angell and Heslop, *The Elements of E-mail Style* (1994), Stuart Harris, *The IRC Survival Guide* (1995); *The Internet Dictionary* (1996).

Figure 1.6. Commonly used abbreviations online.

Some Forms of Playfulness

The variety of forms of playfulness, both online and offline, was dazzling, and it is impossible to treat all of them in this book. Many of us encountered playful userids and names of computers and of domains on the World Wide Web.[49] Here are just a few examples of other types of playfulness that were common in the mid-to late 1990s.

Playfulness on the Desktop

People of all ages customized their computer desktop in a host of ways, e.g., with fancy screensavers,"[50] "wallpaper," icons and coordinated "themes" or

₁s."[51] With the profusion of screensavers available, one could collect ₁ change them often. Customizing computers was far more popular than ₁stomizing cars, a phenomenon that attracted attention in the 1960s (Wolfe 1965). The tremendous enthusiasm for customization was also a means for people to make themselves as home with the strange new world of computers and the Internet.

A related phenomenon was the care and "feeding" of virtual pets. I refer not to the small physical objects with computer chips, including some on keychains, for which there was a craze in 1997, an intriguing phenomenon in its own right, but to virtual creatures, "cats," "dogs" and others, which "live" on one's computer desktop.[52] Thus, software called "Petz" invited us to adopt a "dogz" (yes, "z" even in the singular) or a "catz." One could "feed," "pet" and play with the pet in a virtual playpen. The adopted pet grew over time, and also became the subject of a screensaver.[53] Petz owners not only cultivated their petz offline, but also created elaborate Websites for them, displaying "snapshots" of their beloved creatures, offering mock "stud" services and puppies and kittenz for adoption. In August, 1999 I discovered a Webring with over 100 such sites, no doubt run by teenagers and even young children, with a little help from their parents.[54]

There were other fascinating forms of playfulness on the World Wide Web. Several years ago, I followed a listserv list called "Words-L" briefly. Ostensibly a forum for discussion of the English language, this list became a kind of virtual pub, called "The Blue Moon Saloon." The listowner was Natalie Maynor, a professor of English at Mississippi State University. In 1994, 40 members of the group gathered in Rhode Island for a clambake, their first real-world meeting. Maynor drove from Mississippi to Rhode Island. Along the way, she sent email messages of her progress to the group, often mentioning her companion Bernard Chien, referring to him as "Bernard."

Only several years later, when visiting the Home Pages of "Words-L" and of Natalie Maynor herself did I discover that Bernard Chien, whose full name was Bernard Chien Perro, was a dog, and that he had his own Home Page (Figure 1.7)! Of course I now realized that *chien* means "dog" in French and *perro* is "dog" in Spanish.[55] On Bernard's Website we find this biography:

> Born in April 1982 in rural Oktibbeha County, Mississippi, I moved in with my Significant Human on 4 July 82 and have lived happily ever after. I discovered net life in March 1988 and was, I think, the only dog with his own e-mail address on our old Univac Bitnet. The New Yorker cartoonist was wrong a few years ago: On the Internet everybody knows I'm a dog. Among other net activities, I've been co-owner of WORDS-L for a long time now.

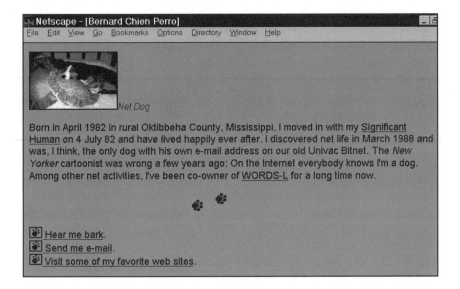

Figure 1.7. The home page of Bernard Chien Perro.

Revisiting the Website in September 1998, I learned that Bernard had left this world in June 1998. The title "In Memoriam, April 1982–June 1998" had been added to the Website. Visitors could still hear Bernard bark, and watch his animated paw prints cross the screen from left to right.[56]

Another example of play with our perceptions of, and expectations for the "human" and "non-human" was documented on the Home Page of the IRC channel #*CoffeeHouse* on Efnet.[57] When observed in 1997, the site invited visitors to view biographies of regulars. I was surprised to discover that the first two entries were images of computers, with the names "Caffiene" (sic) and "Nicotine":[58]

> Caffiene [sic] is our resident host robot. He serves many useful functions such as greeting our guests and being the gateway to the Party Line. Caffiene [sic] resides in the RAM of our provider Cyberenet, He is an eggdrop bot running version 0.9r compiled with TCL. He is normaly [sic] a very friendly chap but tends to be silent when the channel operators are not around. If you find #CoffeeHouse is empty, try the PartyLine.[59]

Still another form of playfulness was verbal and visual puns. One of my favorite sites on the Web was "TUCOWS," an acronym for "The Ultimate Collection of Winsock Software," a utilitarian site offering a comprehensive, annotated catalogue of software for the Internet, with ratings. The entire site was built around a "cow" motif.[60] Exploiting the word "cow" in the acronym,

Figure 1.8. The "cow" motif on the TUCOWS Website.

the creator of the site, Scott Swedorski, chose an image of pairs of black and white cows for the standard background of the site. For many months the cow motif filled the background, in a repeating pattern on pale lime green, and the eyes of the large cows' heads at the top of the page also blinked (Figure 1.8). As of fall, 1998, the cow motif was cut to only a column at the left, with the main window left white, apparently to enhance legibility.

Instead of giving various programs stars in the ratings, they earned one, two, three, four or five cows, or even four and a half. A subscription list for updates to the service was called "T-milk," an acronym for "TUCOWS Message Interchange List Kit," a silly name obviously chosen to fit the acronym. In the fall of 1997 there was a link to "What's MOO in TUCOWs?" Once one arrived there, the title changed to "What's New in TUCOWS?" Here is the sales pitch for their CD-ROM:

> all the best software, four or five cow rating. If you agree, that this is UDDERLY awesome. . . go straight to our order form. . . . If you like our CD but prefer the CREAM of the world's best software to be fresh and updated, check out the BEST of TUCOWS subscription. . . Get MOO-ving and order now.

I wrote to Scott Swedorski to find out how he came to develop the cow motif. Here is his reply:

> The site was created in 1992 as a hobby. All the graphics (except for the logo) were done by myself. We are still more or less a non-commercial site. We do sell advertising

and a CD-ROM product, but we currently have a very high overhead (10 servers and 4 T-1's) to run TUCOWS and the majority of the profits go into keeping the server(s) running.

The site was originally called The Ultimate Collection of Winsock Software. After the site was created I read some articles in usenet news about UCOWS and figured out it was talking about my site. Not liking UCOWS, but liking TUCOWS, I decided to go with it.[61]

From this correspondence I also discovered that Swedorski's personal signature file contained an image of a cow (Figure 1.9). This site is a marvelous example of how a site could be both playful and serious, and maintain a successful balance between the two. One could also download a free TUCOWS screensaver, with cows moving around the screen and the inevitable audio rendering of a cow mooing.

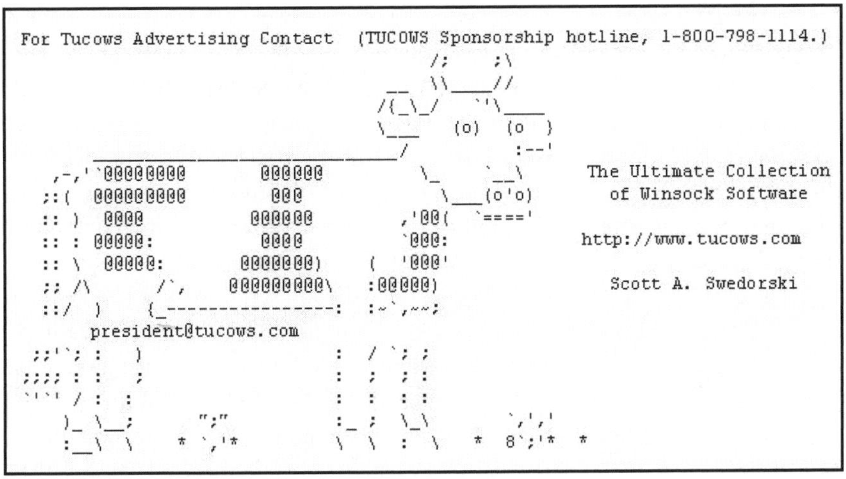

Figure 1.9. Scott Swedorski's signature file. Original by Bill Ames, Chris Johnson's ASCII Art Collection, http://www.chris.com/ascii.

As amusing, charming, or attention-catching all these phenomena are, they are not discussed at length in the book. Instead, for the most part, I have given priority to grass-roots forms of spontaneous playfulness and expressivity, in actual, direct communication with other people, in which no commercial interests are involved.[62] While demonstration programs to customize one's desktop or experiment with virtual pets are free, ultimately the companies offering these programs want to sell the full versions of their software. These forms of playfulness were created by professional programmers, not ordinary users.

There are two important forms of playful interaction with computers which are not treated in depth in the book: hypertext[63] and computer games.[64] These topics have already received a good deal of attention, in many cases book-length treatments; thus I do not deal with them. Two chapters do deal with the Web (Chapters 4 and 7), and thus inevitably attend to hypertext phenomena; however, hypertext per se is not at issue in my analyses.

Why So Playful?

Why was interaction involving computers so playful? There is no simple answer. Many factors work together to promote it. One factor – really a set of features – which must be included in any short list is what has come to be known as "interactivity."

Interactivity

There is little doubt that the nature of the computer as medium fosters playfulness, but just what is involved is a matter of some debate. Many people use the term "interactivity" in their attempts to elucidate what is unique about computers, but they understand the term differently. The dynamic nature of digital interaction is made possible by the shift "from atoms to bits," to use Nicholas Negroponte's (1995) apt phrase. Interaction of all kinds with computers is often felt to be totally absorbing; computers are experienced as an extension of the self (Belk 1988), even as a "second self" (Turkle 1984). Users have a sense of "flow" and lose track of time.[65] The "magical" quality of instant efficaciousness in interaction with the computer – even when no human partner is involved – enhances this sense of flow. We receive instant feedback to our choices. The sense of flow may be even greater when online than offline, and greatest of all when participating in synchronous modes. Chatting in these modes may be so absorbing that people begin to feel they are addicted.[66] The astonishing speed and ease with which formerly difficult, time-consuming tasks can now be done, and the ephemerality of the medium invite playfulness. We will see evidence of this, over and over again, in this book.

Sheizaf Rafaeli and Fay Sudweeks (1997: 175) argue instead that interactivity is an aspect of human communication, not of the medium per se. It is, in their view, the extent to which later messages in any sequence take into account not only immediately preceding messages, but earlier ones too. Because it focuses on emergent, shared interpretive contexts, their concept highlights interpersonal communication, not solo interaction with computers.

Another approach focuses on the metaphor of the theater, as in the work of Brenda Laurel (1991), Richard Lanham (1993) and Allucquère Stone (1996).

24

Thus, Brenda Laurel suggests that the more choices we have, the more often we can make them, the more they matter, and the more immersive the experience, the more interactive it is. This view can apply both to solo interaction with computers and to interpersonal communication mediated by them.

Richard Lanham (1993: 6) views the personal computer as "a device of intrinsic dramaticality." The speed, flexibility, interactivity, and richness of possibilities it offers – even in mere text, let alone when multimedia options are available – turn every user into a kind of "director" of his or her own show. Or, we become, as it were, the conductor of a vast orchestra with instruments of every kind waiting to do our bidding. But we are also the composer and the musicians. As Janet Murray (1997: 128) puts it, "When things are going right on the computer, we can be both the dancer and the caller of the dance. This is the feeling of agency."

Macintosh users were the first to experience and articulate computing as "flying," as extraordinarily liberating, in the mid-1980s. In his book, *Zen and the Art of the Macintosh: Discoveries on the Path to Computer Enlightenment*, designed entirely on a Macintosh, Michael Green (1986) celebrated the new experiences:

> MacPaint is so fast and so fun, it just leads you on and on. . . . I could snapshot and stash away any graphic idea. . . and continue playing around with a copy of it. . . This had a wonderfully liberating effect. The tendency to freeze up a design just as it starts looking good just dissolved away. Playful process took over. the logo became a movie, and I was both director and spectator (Green 1986: 30; italics in the original).[67]

Whatever one thinks of Microsoft's copying of the Macintosh interface or its marketing strategies, it is a fact that the general public began to experience this exhilaration only with the spread of Windows and the IBM-compatible PC.

Janet Murray suggests that digital environments have four essential properties; they are procedural, participatory, spatial, and encyclopedic (Murray 1997: 71). The first two properties pertain to interactivity. The fantasy environment in computer games such as *Dungeons and Dragons* uses literary and gaming conventions to script interactors and to provide a repertoire of actions, yet make virtual worlds as responsive as possible to every combination of available commands. The key term in her formulation is *immersion*, which we just encountered in Brenda Laurel's approach:

> The experience of being transported to an elaborately simulated place is pleasurable in itself . . . We refer to this experience as immersion. Immersion is a metaphorical term derived from the physical experience of being submerged in water. We seek the

same feeling from a psychologically immersive experience that we do from a plunge in the ocean or swimming pool: the sensation of being surrounded by a completely other reality, as different as water is from air . . . We enjoy the movement out of our familiar world, the feeling of alertness that comes from being in this new place, and the delight that comes from learning to move within it. (Murray 1997: 98–99)

We can take the immersion metaphor still further. Just as we feel lighter when in water than when on land, so, freed of our bodies, we feel light in cyberspace, in a novel form of "floating" produced at present by typing and clicking. While the sensation of immersion may be greatest in fantasy role-playing games, it can be considerable even in other kinds of interaction with computers, and with people via computers.

Hacker Culture

Hacker culture was another very important influence on emergent Net practices. Playfulness is absolutely central to what hackers do and how they perceive themselves. According to hackers' self-definition, a hacker is "A person who

---

hacker, n.

1. A person who enjoys exploring the details of programmable systems and how to stretch their capabilities, as opposed to most users, who prefer to learn only the minimum necessary.

2. One who programs enthusiastically (even obsessively) or who enjoys programming rather than just theorizing about programming.

3. A person capable of appreciating hack value.

4. A person who is good at programming quickly.

5. An expert at a particular program, or one who frequently does work using it or on it; as in "a UNIX hacker". (Definitions 1 through 5 are correlated, and people who fit them congregate.)

6. An expert or enthusiast of any kind. One might be an astronomy hacker, for example.

7. One who enjoys the intellectual challenge of creatively overcoming or circumventing limitations.

8. [deprecated] A malicious meddler who tries to discover sensitive information by poking around. Hence "password hacker", "network hacker". The correct term is cracker.

Raymond (1996), *The New Hackers' Dictionary*, pp. 233–234.

Figure 1.10. Definition of a hacker.

enjoys exploring the details of programmable systems and how to stret_ capabilities," or "one who enjoys the intellectual challenge of creatively overcoming or circumventing limitations" (Raymond, 1996: 233–234; Figure 1.10).[68] To "hack" is "to interact with a computer in a playful and exploratory rather than a goal-directed way" (Raymond 1996: 231).

Hackers love to play with words and symbols, and are known for punning and other clever, irreverent uses of language (Barlow 1996; Meyer and Thomas 1990; Raymond 1996), as in the popular "snail mail" for ordinary paper mail. With its apt metaphor and rhyme, this expression illustrates the condescending attitude of hackers toward ordinary mortals and old technologies, as well as their clever use of language.

"Dry humor, irony, puns, and a mildly flippant attitude are highly valued – but an underlying seriousness and intelligence are essential" (Raymond 1996: 22). Hackers "often make rhymes or puns in order to convert an ordinary phrase into something more interesting," as in "Boston Glob" for *Boston Globe* (Raymond 1996: 10), or "Macintrash" for the Apple Macintosh (Raymond 1996: 290). In January 1992 I encountered a wonderful Israeli example on the IL-Board, a local listserv list, a complaint about bad service from *Nezeq*. Literally, *nezeq* means "harm" or "trouble" in Hebrew. Only after a moment's thought, and with my new knowledge of hacker culture did I successfully decode the referent as *Bezeq*, Israel's telephone company!

Hackers love to play with typography and spelling. This tendency was especially pronounced among crackers, hackers who engage in criminal activities and run pirate bulletin boards, and conveyed subversiveness, if not downright aggressiveness and hostility to outsiders. Among the better known intentional misspellings is substitution of "f" for "ph," as in "fone" for "phone," or vice versa, as in "phreak" instead of "freak." Many substituted "z" for "s" in the plural. Another eccentricity was the substitution of "O" for "o," as in "rOdent." "A substantial subculture of crackers referred to themselves as "warez dOOdz" – "wares dudes," in plain English (Raymond 1996: 478).[69] Examples of hackers' nicknames containing this kind of play are "Phelix the Hack" and "Phiber Optik."[70] Sometimes playful or intentionally annoying eccentricity consisted only of alternating capital and lower-case letters, as in the opening screen of an issue of "The Hacker Brothers Newsletter" (Figure 1.11).[71] The only exception is the consistently upper-case "O". Like the rest of the text, the nicknames "HackerWang" and "hacker" are represented eccentrically and require effort to decode.[72]

Hackers cherish virtuoso, playful performance. A "neat hack" is "a clever technique" or "a brilliant practical joke, where neatness is correlated with cleverness, harmlessness, and surprise value" (Raymond 1996: 322). A collection of outstanding hacks was immortalized in a 1972 document known as

```
ÅÅÅÅÅÅÅÅÅÅÅÅÅÅÅÅÅÅÅÅÅÅÅÅÅÅÅÅÅÅÅÅÅÅÅÅÅÅÅÅÅÅÅÅÅÅÅÅÅÅÅÅÅÅÅÅÅÅÅÅÅÅÅÅÅÅÅÅÅÅÅÅÅÅÅÅÅÅÅ
ÅÅÅÅÅÅÅÅÅÅÅÅÅÅÅÅÅÅÅÅÅÅÅÅÅÅÅÅÅÅÅÅÅÅÅÅÅÅÅÅÅÅÅÅÅÅÅÅÅÅÅÅÅÅÅÅÅÅÅÅÅÅÅÅÅÅÅÅÅÅÅÅÅÅÅÅÅÅÅ
ÅÅÅÅÅÅÅÅÅÅÅÅÅÅÅÅÅÅÅÅÅÅ                                ÅÅÅÅÅÅÅÅÅÅÅÅÅÅÅÅÅÅÅÅÅÅÅÅ
ÅÅÅÅÅÅÅÅÅÅÅÅÅÅÅÅÅÅÅÅÅÅ  ThE HaXOR bRoThErS NeWzLetTeR  ÅÅÅÅÅÅÅÅÅÅÅÅÅÅÅÅÅÅÅÅÅÅÅÅÅ
ÅÅÅÅÅÅÅÅÅÅÅÅÅÅÅÅÅÅÅÅÅÅ  ------------------------------  ÅÅÅÅÅÅÅÅÅÅÅÅÅÅÅÅÅÅÅÅÅÅÅÅ
ÅÅÅÅÅÅÅÅÅÅÅÅÅÅÅÅÅÅÅÅÅÅ              By                ÅÅÅÅÅÅÅÅÅÅÅÅÅÅÅÅÅÅÅÅÅÅÅÅÅ
ÅÅÅÅÅÅÅÅÅÅÅÅÅÅÅÅÅÅÅÅÅÅ      HaxOrWang & |=|4xOr       ÅÅÅÅÅÅÅÅÅÅÅÅÅÅÅÅÅÅÅÅÅÅÅÅÅ
ÅÅÅÅÅÅÅÅÅÅÅÅÅÅÅÅÅÅÅÅÅÅ                                ÅÅÅÅÅÅÅÅÅÅÅÅÅÅÅÅÅÅÅÅÅÅÅÅ
ÅÅÅÅÅÅÅÅÅÅÅÅÅÅÅÅÅÅÅÅÅÅ           IsSuE #1             ÅÅÅÅÅÅÅÅÅÅÅÅÅÅÅÅÅÅÅÅÅÅÅÅÅ
ÅÅÅÅÅÅÅÅÅÅÅÅÅÅÅÅÅÅÅÅÅÅ                                ÅÅÅÅÅÅÅÅÅÅÅÅÅÅÅÅÅÅÅÅÅÅÅÅÅ
ÅÅÅÅÅÅÅÅÅÅÅÅÅÅÅÅÅÅÅÅÅÅÅÅÅÅÅÅÅÅÅÅÅÅÅÅÅÅÅÅÅÅÅÅÅÅÅÅÅÅÅÅÅÅÅÅÅÅÅÅÅÅÅÅÅÅÅÅÅÅÅÅÅÅÅÅÅÅÅ
ÅÅÅÅÅÅÅÅÅÅÅÅÅÅÅÅÅÅÅÅÅÅÅÅÅÅÅÅÅÅÅÅÅÅÅÅÅÅÅÅÅÅÅÅÅÅÅÅÅÅÅÅÅÅÅÅÅÅÅÅÅÅÅÅÅÅÅÅÅÅÅÅÅÅÅÅÅÅÅ


We ArE tHe HaXOR bRoThErZ, AnD SiNcE aLl oF yOo aRe LaYmOrS aNd WeRe k-RaD
HaXORz wE dEcIdEd To TeAcH yOu Of OuR k-RaD wAyZ. ThIs Is OuR fIrZT
NeWzLeTtEr, BuT eXpEct AlOt oF uS iN tHe NeAr FuTuRe yOu FuXiNg lAyMoRs!!
NoW rEeD oN tO bEcOmE a LeEt HaXOR!


CoNtEnTs:
uS HaXoRs In MiRc.........................................................1
The e1E3T haxOr b1Ble......................................................2
PhReAkInG.................................................................3
H4XORs DiCtIoNaRy.........................................................4
HoW I KnEW i WuZ a K-kEwL HaxOr whOrE.....................................5
MaIl-bOmBiNg..............................................................6
```

Figure 1.11 The HaXOR bRoThErS NeWzLetTeR (The Hacker Brothers Newsletter)

"HAKMEM" ("hacks memo") (Raymond 1996: 237).[73] One of the most famous "hacks" is a transformation of the M.I.T. Website (Figure 1.12).[74]

A fascinating expression of hacker culture is the phenomenon of "Easter Eggs." These are not eggs at all, despite the reference to eggs hidden in an Easter Egg hunt, but little jokes and secret messages hidden in programs by software developers (Figure 1.13). According to the Easter Egg Archive FAQ, an "Easter Egg" is a reproducible, unofficial feature of a product, accessible to every user if he or she knows how to activate it, intentionally put there by programmers, non-destructive (unlike a virus), and usually put there just for fun (Figure 1.14). Hackers and programmers engaged in this practice at least since the 1970s, and continued to do so in the 1990s.

I was amazed to discover, once I learned about Easter Eggs,[75] that the four programs I had been using regularly, Netscape, Eudora 3.0, Word 97, and mIRC (the Windows version of the IRC software), contained one.[76] Easter Eggs just listing credits are not as playful as those which are "pure fun" like the animated "aquarium" hidden in Netscape. In the same playful spirit, microchip designers have been burying minuscule, non-functional images like the owls in Figure 1.15 on silicon chips since the 1970s, visible only under a microscope. Sometimes developers' credits are buried in these images, just as software developers sometimes bury their credits in computer code.[77]

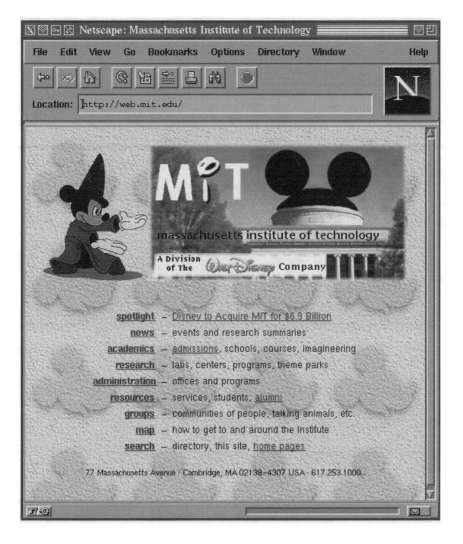

Figure 1.12. A virtuoso hack of the M.I.T. Website. http://hacks.mit.edu/Hacks/
by_year/1998/disney_buys_mit/snapshot/.

Cyberspace as a New Social and Cultural Frontier

A major factor fostering playfulness on the Internet was the frontier-like quality
of this new world in the 1980s and 1990s, highlighted in the titles of several
books, Howard Rheingold's (1993) *The Virtual Community: Homesteading
on the Electronic Frontier,* Katie Hafner and John Markoff's (1991) *Cyberpunk: Outlaws and Hackers on the Computer Frontier,* and Peter Ludlow's
(1996) *High Noon on the Electronic Frontier: Conceptual Issues in Cyber-*

Figure 1.13. "Easter Eggs" in software programs.

space.[78] The Electronic Frontier Foundation fights for civil rights in cyberspace. Hackers are sometimes called "computer cowboys" (Hafner and Markoff 1991: 10), or "digital explorers" (Levy 1984). Case, the main character in William Gibson's (1984) Neuromancer, is a "data cowboy."[79]

John Perry Barlow suggested that:

> Cyberspace, in its present condition, has a lot in common with the 19th century West. It is vast, unmapped, culturally and legally ambiguous, verbally terse[80] . . . hard to get around in, and up for grabs. Large institutions already claim to own the place, but most of the actual natives are solitary and independent, sometimes to the point of sociopathy. It is, of course, a perfect breeding ground for both outlaws and new ideas about liberty. (Barlow 1996: 460)

Already in the late 1990s one could take issue with the frontier metaphor, which Barlow had first used in the 1990 online version of his paper. There was much evidence of growing social organization in cyberspace. Usenet newsgroups and listserv lists were rapidly developing their own subcultures, including rules to govern interaction and sanctions for offenders, which they publicized in FAQs (Frequently Asked Questions files).[81] Home Pages of MUDs and IRC channels on the World Wide Web served as community bulletin

. . . a hidden feature or novelty that the programmers have put in their software. This can be anything from a hidden list of the developers, to hidden commands, to jokes, to funny animations . . . A true Easter Egg must satisfy the following criteria:

1. Undocumented

An Easter Egg can't be a legitimate feature of a product. Before you label something an Easter Egg, make sure it's not in any of the documentation or help files.

2. Reproducible

Every user with the same product or combination of products must be able to produce the same result given the instructions.

3. Put There by the Programmers

you can't get an Easter Egg by somehow "hacking" the program . . . You can change the startup files or command line parameters to reveal an Egg, but motifying the code itself is strictly forbidden.

4. Non-destructive

Easter Eggs are there for fun, not to do damage.

5. ENTERTAINING!

The most important element . . . if it's not there for entertaining, it's not an Egg.

*Source: Easter Egg Archive FAQ, URL http://www.eeggs.com/faq.html.

Figure 1.14. What is an Easter Egg?

boards, posting photographs of regulars, rules, and information about past and upcoming real-world and online social events. Ferment in the media and in emergent cyberspace law[82] in the late 1990s about the problematics of regulating pornography, racism, and libelous communication, and of preventing and punishing computer crime was part of the struggle to domesticate what was still largely a "Wild West." Certainly, the fact that there was no "Mr. Internet," no central governing body supervising the behavior of all participants, contributed to this sense of an open frontier. In a powerful critique of libertarianism, Lawrence Lessig (2000) advocated recognition of the need for regulation in cyberspace and an end to glorification of the frontier metaphor.

At the same time, Murray Melbin's (1987) analysis of night culture in the real world was highly suggestive for an understanding of emergent cyberculture

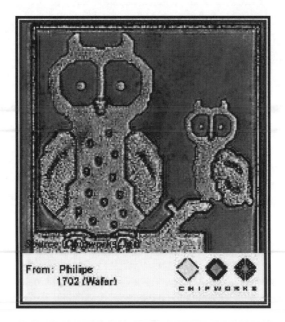

Figure 1.15. Miniature art on a computer microchip. "Chipworks-Silicon Art," http:/
/www.chipworks.com/home.html.

in the mid- to late 1990s. Like the American West, he found, night is characterized by uneven stages of advance, organized sponsorship rather than solo
activity of individuals, sparse and homogeneous population, chances for escape
and opportunity, a wider range of tolerated behavior than in daytime life, fewer
status distinctions, novel hardships, decentralization of authority, lawlessness
and peril. The similarities to the eternal "night" of cyberspace are striking.
Even the problem of novel hardships – in the present case, the fragility and
slowness of technology was present, and relationships created online were not
without peril, as was evident from cases of women raped or murdered by men
whom they met online, computer viruses, online fraud, etc. But in other
respects applicability of the analogy was weakening: with tens of millions of
people online, cyberspace was no longer sparsely populated.

The Masking of Identity

I have suggested that yet another factor promoting playfulness was the anonymity of the medium. Textual chat modes were especially carnivalesque because
they generally masked identity more completely than email. In these modes,
one's email address was not necessarily available to others. Not actual masks
and costumes, as in traditional carnivals, but the ephemeral medium and the

typed text provided the mask. This point was brought home in the famous New Yorker cartoon, "On the Internet, nobody knows you're a dog."[83]

The absence of non-verbal and other social or material cues to identity freed participants to behave in novel ways, or to explore aspects of their personality which had hitherto gone unexpressed, especially when participants adopted nicknames or developed elaborate fictive personas.[84] The effect was not unlike that of real-world masks:

> The mystique of the mask is powerful. One immediately feels different behind it. When an actor is responding to the commands of the mask, he experiences a sense of wholeness, relaxation, and well-being. There is a calm sensation of being taken over by it. If he is improvising he finds himself doing unexpected things, feeling impelled to obey the choices suggested by the mask. (Rolfe 1977: 14)

Nicknames were *de rigueur* on IRC and on chat modes generally. While IRC players could change their nick (IRCese for nickname) at any time, they generally chose one carefully and used it consistently over time. Ordinarily, one could not reconstruct an IRC player's email address, let alone his or her RL (real-world) identity – one could only identify the host computer via which he or she was logged on.[85] At the same time, at least some channels maintaining home pages often encouraged individuals to reveal aspects of their RL identity, including their real names.[86]

Play with identity was far more elaborate on MOOs than on IRC and probably more far-reaching in its consequences. When they joined a MOO, individuals created an elaborate "persona" or "character," whose description was registered and available for reading by anyone logged on to them.[87] After registering their character, players might role-play in this guise for months or years.

Textual "cross-dressing" was the most attention-getting form of play with identity on MOOs. The MOO software offered an amazing variety of genders from which to choose. Figure 1.16 lists the genders available on MediaMOO and LambdaMOO. Besides "male" and "female" one could choose "neuter," "either," "spivak," "splat," "plural," "egotistical," "royal" (as in the royal "we"), "2nd," and "person." Each gender had its own set of pronouns. Some are familiar from ordinary usage – for "neuter," the pronouns are "it, its, itself." In the case of "either," the player will be consistently represented with "s/he, him/her, his/her, his/hers/ (him/her)self, and so on.

MediaMOO added a gender choice not available on LambdaMOO: "person." This allowed players to say "Per reads per book perself." Such sentences are comprehensible when we take into account that much of the dialogue on MUDs and MOOs is, in fact, rendered in the third person: chatting on MOOs was more like writing collective fiction than the dialogue of a drama. The category

@gender male   Gender set to male.
Your pronouns: he, him, his, his, himself, He, Him, His, His, Himself
Example: He reads his book himself.

@gender female   Gender set to female.
Your pronouns: she, her, her, hers, herself, She, Her, Her, Hers, Herself
Example: She reads her book herself.

@gender neuter   Gender set to neuter.
Your pronouns: it, it, its, its, itself, It, It, Its, Its, Itself
Example: It reads its book itself

@gender either   Gender set to either.
Your pronouns: s/he, him/her, his/her, his/hers, (him/her)self, S/He Him/Her, His/Her, His/Hers, (Him/Her) self
Example: S/he reads his/her book him/herself.

@gender spivak   Gender set to Spivak.
Your pronouns: e, em, eir, eirs, eirself, E, Em, Eir, Eirs, Eirself
Example: E reads eir book eirself.

@gender splat   Gender set to splat.
Your pronouns: *e, h*, h*, h*s, h*self, *E, H*, H*, H*s, H*self
Example: *e reads h* book h*self.

@gender plural   Gender set to plural.
Your pronouns: they, them, their, theirs, themselves, They, Them, Their, Theirs, Themselves
Example: They read their book themselves.

@gender egotistical   Gender set to egotistical.
Your pronouns: I, me, my, mine, myself, I, Me, My, Mine, Myself
Example: I read my book myself.

@gender royal   Gender set to royal.
Your pronouns: we, us, our, ours, ourselves, We, Us, Our, Ours, Ourselves
Example: We read our book ourselves.

@gender 2nd   Gender set to 2nd.
Your pronouns: you, you, your, yours, yourself, You, You, Your, Yours, Yourself
Example: You read your book yourself.

@gender person*   Gender set to person.
Your pronouns: per, per, per, pers, perself, Per, Per, Per, Pers, Perself
Example: Per reads per book perself.

*MediaMOO only

Figure 1.16. Gender options on LambdaMOO and MediaMOO. Reprinted with permission from Danet (1998a), Fig. 5.2, p. 138. Copyright © 1998, Sage Publications, Inc.

"spivak" was added to the program after Michael Spivak, a mathematics professor who was known for having proposed various sets of gender-neutral pronouns, and for using them in his textbooks. As for "per," inspiration in this case apparently came from science fiction. In Marge Piercy's novel *Woman on the Edge of Time*, 21st- century individuals use it to refer to third persons, regardless of gender. "Splat" is the vocalization of the asterisk * in mathematics and computing.

The single most common choice was "male," followed by "female;" a substantial proportion chose a category other than these two (Table 1.1). On both MOOs, about half the players chose "male" genders, with the proportions choosing "female" and "unconventional" or "neuter" reversed on the two MOOs. On MediaMOO nearly a third chose an unconventional gender; on LambdaMOO it dropped to about a fifth. Thus, substantial numbers of people were experimenting with gender identity in cyberspace, over much longer periods of time than in once-a-year carnivals and masked balls.[88] Since there were more males than females in cyberspace in the late 1990s, more males than females were "cross-dressing" textually.[89]

The Need for a Comparative Approach

In some respects it was probably justified to speak in monolithic fashion of "Internet culture" or "virtual culture" in the late 1990s, as did the titles of three academic books (Jones 1997; Kiesler 1997; Porter 1997). "Netizens" came increasingly to share a common jargon, set of attitudes, skills, and practices. However, Dave Healy (1997: 65), one of the authors in the Porter volume, cautioned that in some respects the Internet was not monolithic at all.[90] Indeed, my own studies of IRC (Chapter 3 and particularly Chapter 6) reveal dramatically different worlds from that analyzed by Don Slater (1998; 2000). This book pursues a differentiated, comparative approach by including within the same framework case studies of three very different modes of communication: email, chat – IRC – and the World Wide Web. As readers will see, my case studies also involve quite different groups of people from the viewpoint of social background, although that was not originally a primary consideration in choosing the topics for study.

Compared with MUDs, IRC has been under-researched, despite its enormous popularity. Whereas MUDs received a great deal of attention in the popular media, e.g., Dibbell (1996), originally written for the Village Voice, as well as from social scientists,[91] fewer persons have studied IRC.[92] Over time, it became a locus not just of spontaneous small talk, but also of sustained, organized social activity of many kinds. Unlike earlier researchers who focused on spontaneous chat,[93] I look at two forms of organized activity on IRC (Chapters 3 and 6).[94]

Table 1.1. Conventional and unconventional genders actually chosen on MediaMOO and LambdaMOO. Reprinted with permission from Danet 1998a, Table 5.1, p. 142. Copyright © 1998, Sage Publications, Inc.

	*MediaMOO**	*LambdaMOO***
male	495	3651
female	197	2069
neuter	280	1162
spivak	10	74
either	9	15
plural	7	26
royal	6	30
splat	5	17
egotistical	2	16
2nd	2	5
person	2	–
Total	1015	7065
Percent male	48.8%	51.7%
Percent female	19.4	29.2
Percent unconventional	31.8	19.1
	100.0%	100.0%
	(1015)	(7065)

*Breakdown as of January 17, 1996.
**Breakdown as of February 9, 1996

Overview of Five Case Studies

Stated in the most global terms, this book has two complementary goals: (1) to document and analyze play with form in three modes of online communication, email, chat, and the World Wide Web, in an era which the Internet first became a mass medium; and (2) to document and analyze important aspects of the transition from text-only to multimedia communication, and to debate some of its implications. I will pursue these goals via five case studies.[95] My approach is empirical, qualitative and interpretive, and draws on nine years of intensive experience with online communication of all kinds. Below, I explain additional, specific goals of each case study. The five studies are independent of one another and may be read in any order, though there are important affinities between various combinations of them, and presentation of the two text-based studies before the three multimedia ones echoes chronological developments on the Internet.

Public Email in Transition

Empirically, playful language was less prominent in email than in other modes of digital communication, but even here it sometimes "bubbled up," even in primarily serious "business" or "official" letters. While I will give some examples of playfulness in this type of email, my main concern in Chapter 2 is not with playful language per se, but with experimentation with new text types as a form of playfulness. Because of the newness of the medium, even the most serious email business letter was experimental in the 1990s, I suggest.

Most research on the language of email tends to be ahistorical and to consist of statistical descriptions of the distribution of individual features.[96] In contrast, keeping in mind the history of letter-writing, I treat letters holistically,[97] emphasizing the ways in which the medium and its use challenge traditional norms of letter-writing, and the drift toward partially speech-like patterns, with consequent erosion of the traditional business letter template.

In Chapter 2, I offer preliminary evidence for two hypotheses about the changing language of public email, and debate some of the normative issues at stake. I examine linguistic and structural features of two corpora of email messages, mainly from my own correspondence. The analysis focuses on how people wrote to me, not my own writing style. One corpus consists of "first letters" by academics responding to a Call for Papers by a stranger in a position of authority, the guest editor of a prospective special issue of a journal (myself). The second corpus is a set of letters exchanged between a software developer and a customer, once again myself. The very specific, known set of circumstances in which these sets of letters were sent provides much-needed context for textual analysis.

Online Communication as Playful Performance

A second specific goal of the book is to analyze typed chat on IRC as playful performance. Chapter 3 summarizes two studies, an analysis of a typed simulation of smoking marihuana (!), that took place in December 1991, and a study of a group called the "Hamnet Players,"[98] who experimented with the idea of "virtual theater" on IRC in 1993–95. They performed hilarious typed parodies of Shakespeare's *Hamlet* and *Macbeth*, as well as of Tennessee Williams' *Streetcar Named Desire*. Though scripted, performances included many forms of improvisation. The founder of the Hamnet Players, Stuart Harris, kindly made available to me scripts and logs of all performances.[99] In addition, beginning with the second performance of "PCbeth," the parody of *Macbeth*, my research group and I were "present" at Hamnet performances and even played small roles. The analysis thus draws both on the texts of scripts and performances and on experiences during participant observation.

The chapter shows how participants in the 1991 simulation depicted the sequence of actions involved in smoking marihuana verbally and pictorially, using smiley icons and other typographic means. As for the Hamnet parodies, I analyze various forms of playfulness both in scripts and in actual performances, which included many kinds of clever individual and collective improvisation. The chapter also explains logistic aspects – how one mounts a performance among people who were geographically dispersed, had never met, could not see one another and could only communicate by typing. I propose theoretical grounds for accepting Hamnet activities as a form of virtual theater, despite the anomaly that actors and audience were not physically co-present. The chapter demonstrates that artful performance is not confined to person-to-person genres of oral communication, but can thrive in interactive writing online as well.

Digital Greetings

With Chapter 4, the book shifts from primarily textual to multimedia communication. The subject of this chapter is digital greetings on the World Wide Web – birthday and holiday greetings, etc. Many contain brilliantly colored graphics, animation and music. Either one sends them as an email attachment, or, more often, the recipient is invited to view the greeting at the Website. Other types of greetings are sometimes called "electronic postcards," all-purpose greetings which can be used just to say "hello," like ordinary postcards.

In the 1990s these greetings were a form of playful experimentation with a new mode of communication to meet familiar ritual needs, e.g., to celebrate life-cycle events such as births, weddings, and graduations. In the past such events were traditionally marked by sending someone a greeting card, or including one with a gift. Condolence at the death of a loved one was marked either by a handwritten note or a suitably subdued sympathy card. The treatment of condolence, or rather, the lack of it, in digital greetings is of special interest in the chapter.

In an apparent deviation from the primary focus of this book on grassroots behavior on the Net, this chapter discusses what was offered on the Web, not actual use of these greetings. However, the deviation is not as great as it seems: I will show that most of the sites offering greetings were created by amateurs.[100] They too were experimenting with a new medium – the World Wide Web. In the late 1990s there was an excess of playfulness in these sites. Digital greetings were too playful in their fledgling form. Most egregiously, the vast majority of sites lacked a category for condolence. The chapter asks: is there a contradiction in terms between this playful medium and certain important social and ritual needs? Can a digital greeting of no physical substance and featuring animation and music be considered appropriate to express sentiments of condolence? To pursue these and other questions, I created a database of approximately 300 images captured on the World Wide Web, using Paint Shop Pro and Image AXS Pro, programs for the collection of images, and for managing a database of them, respectively.[101]

ASCII Art and Beyond

One of the most prominent forms of play with digital writing in the period between 1960 or so and 2000 was ASCII art – visual images created from typographic symbols on the computer keyboard.[102] A typical example is the butterfly shown in Figure 1.17. In the early days (approximately 1960–1995) one either printed images out or viewed them as phosphorescent green or amber images on a black screen.[103] This book presents the first extended academic research on this phenomenon. I ask: what forms and styles of ASCII art were prominent, and who were their practitioners? Chapter 5 addresses these questions. Chapter 6 is about a form of post-1995, text-based art on IRC that draws on, but goes beyond ASCII art.

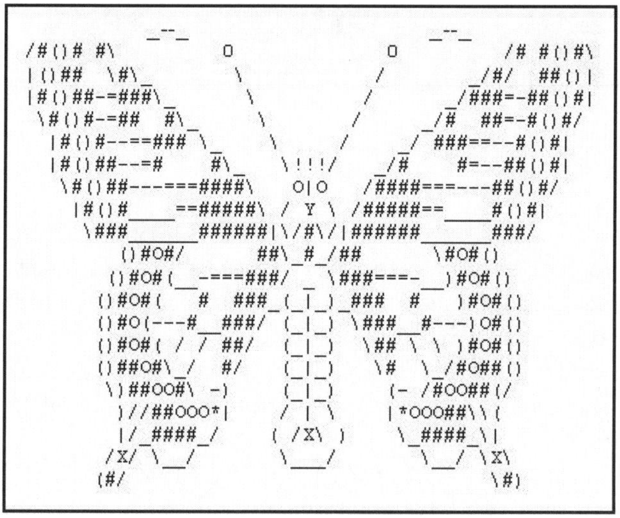

Figure 1.17. An ASCII butterfly.

The Windows version of the IRC program facilitated a new variety of text-based art. One could now incorporate up to 16 colors in images,[104] as well as unusual symbols such as the Japanese yen sign ¥ or the legal/ bureaucratic "double-S §. One could create brilliant decorative effects and abstract patterns (Figure 1.18).[105] Images often resembled needlepoint, embroidery, patchwork quilts, and weaving.

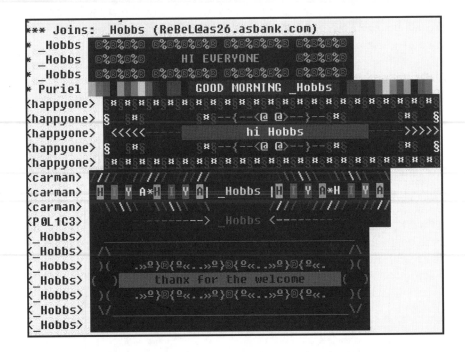

Figure 1.18. Interactive greetings on IRC.

In Chapter 5 I show how ASCII art blossomed on BBSs, Usenet and the World Wide Web in the 1990s. I offer an overview of its many antecedents over the centuries, including mosaics, micrography, and teletype art, which circulated by radio in the period 1950–1980. Chapter 6 is a detailed ethnographic study of the form and functions of interactive, text-based art displayed in real time on two channels on IRC. I demonstrate that this is both a form of "communication" and a form of "art."

To analyze the form of IRC images, I draw on concepts from the study of the visual arts such as pattern and symmetry, as well as the notion of *gestalt* in psychology. Images are both a source of aesthetic pleasure and a type of "visual speech act," via which players create an emergent virtual community.

Thus, in Figure 1.18 a player nicknamed <Hobbs> greets the others, and is greeted in turn by them. Images are experienced as "virtual hugs." The chapter argues that creating, viewing, and playing images were all ways to strive for a sense of closure or completion.

The art documented in Chapter 5 was collected mainly from the World Wide Web, in screen-captures via Paint Shop Pro. As for IRC images, over a period of two years, my research assistant, Tsameret Wachenhauser, and I monitored two channels on the Undernet network featuring this art. Via Paint Shop Pro and Image AXS Pro, we created a database of about 3,500 images. Analysis of images was supplemented with material from textual logs and from channel Websites, as well as from online interviews with many participants. I was also able to interview two of the three channel leaders personally, and an assistant conducted a telephone interview with the third.

"Font Frenzy"

The last case study (Chapter 7) is about "font frenzy" – a passion for digital typefaces among ordinary people – collecting and displaying fonts, and even designing one's own. In the late 1990s many thousands of individuals became preoccupied with the visual look of writing, downloading free or shareware fonts from the Web, or buying CD-ROMS full of them. Unlike collectors of material objects like dolls or Chinese porcelain, these individuals cultivated collections of no tangible substance. Yet, like them, they too invested heavily in their display – not on shelves or in cabinets, but on the Web. Figure 1.19 is the logo of a font collector's Website, called "Fred's Font Funhouse."[106] The elaborate multicolored graphic, the alliteration, and the animated pinwheels exuberantly conveyed this collector's enthusiasm for fonts. One sure sign of growing interest in fonts was a Website called "Fonts Anonymous."[107] This virtual gathering place for font devotees was founded in April 1998, and by December 1999 had over 900 members.

Many enthusiasts proudly displayed their own font designs on handsomely designed Websites, offering them to others for free or for a modest price. Basic font design had become so easy that even children could create respectable-looking ones.[108] An important topic in Chapter 7 is how these developments challenged the traditional mandate and values of design and typography professionals. The chapter argues that interest in fonts was an inevitable outcome of the shift from print to digital text, and that, by the millennium, font frenzy had become a part of popular culture.

Drawing mainly on screen-captures of Websites, this chapter also integrates material on fonts from many other sources: operating systems, word-processing software, applications such as programs to create greeting cards or enhance

Figure 1.19. "Fred's Font Funhouse."

typography, and CD-ROM collections sold in museum shops and elsewhere. I also interviewed selected informants by email.

Themes in the Book

Six themes crosscut the various studies. The language of text-based digital communication is treated in Chapters 2 and 3. Experimentation with new digital genres of communication is a theme common to Chapters 2–4 (email, virtual theater, digital greetings). Virtual theater and writing as playful, stylized performance are the theme of Chapter 3. Aspects of greetings are discussed in Chapters 4–6. Chapters 5 and 6 are devoted to ASCII art and IRC art, respectively. Finally, the more general topic of aestheticization of the visual aspects of writing includes Chapter 7, in addition to Chapters 5 and 6. Readers may pursue each of these themes independently.

Writing about a Dynamic Medium in a Static One

It has been a daunting task to write a book about such a volatile medium. Every writer about contemporary phenomena faces the problem of what to do about new developments that occur during the writing of a book. In the present case the rate of change is so great that any "take" on what is happening is bound to be seriously outdated by the time this book appears in print. Some of the phenomena studied may have either disappeared or become greatly transformed by the time this book appears.[109] Inevitably, as I completed this book, many URLs I had earlier visited or documented were no longer active, and, no doubt, many more that *were* still active when I completed it will be obsolete by the time it appears in print. Some readers may ask, then, why bother to publish this book?

First of all, research on text-based digital communication continues to be worthwhile in the early 2000s because these modes may not disappear so fast as some may think. While the advent of full multimedia technologies could make some forms of text-based communication obsolete, it is not self-evident that everyone will always opt for a multimedia option. There are times when typed chat will be more convenient or liberating than full video chat, and when people will prefer email to a phone call.

But there is a more important reason for publishing this book: with regard to both text-based and multimedia communication, the pioneering stages in their evolution documented here may be largely lost to memory in a few generations. My primary concern, then, is to provide a time capsule – a textual and visual "screenshot" – of forms of expression and experimentation in the mid- to late 1990s, to help future researchers and others, in 20, 50 or even 500 years, understand how they got from our times to theirs.

In February 1999, the Sloan School of Management at M.I.T. created such a time capsule, to be opened in 2004.[110] Predictably, it documented phenomena "from the top down." In contrast, this book highlights how things looked "from the bottom up" – how millions of ordinary people became involved with the Internet and made it a part of their daily lives. Despite the difficulties of writing about such a volatile medium, I concur with Michael Heim (1987) that it is important to write about our experiences and observations *while we are still surprised by them.* I hope this book conveys some of my own surprise and amazement at many of the phenomena it documents.

Notes

1. Some people love smileys and use them all the time. Others hate them. I will have more to say about them later in this book. For a typical collection of smileys in print, see Godin (1993). Introductory online collections include "The Canonical Smiley List," http://www.astro.umd.edu/~marshall/smileys.html; "The Unofficial Smiley FAQ,"

http://Newbie.NET/SmileyFAQ/; and "Internet Smileys," http://members.aol.com/bearpage/smileys.htm.

2. The distinction between text and display fonts, the concepts of "typeface" and "font," and the problematics of readability and legibility are all discussed in further detail in Chapter 7.

3. However, Olaf Plauta, an expert on medieval Latin abbreviations, believes its origins may be Middle English rather than Latin. Personal email from Olaf Plauta, April, 1997.

4. In 2000 an Italian scholar, Giorgio Stabile of the University of Rome, claimed to have documented commercial use of this symbol as early as the 16th century, in texts of Mediterranean merchants. Personal email from C. Luethy, September 15, 2000.

5. Strictly speaking, there are only 95 characters available for textual communication; the rest are devoted to hidden codes. "Seven-bit" means a series of seven 0s or 1s, each profile of which encodes a different symbol. See the brief discussion of ASCII characters toward the end of this chapter, and fuller discussions in Chapters 5 and 6.

6. Lovejoy (1997).

7. To view this icon and others similar to it, one tilts the head toward the left shoulder.

8. Haraway (1997).

9. There are fascinating differences in how the @ symbol is vocalized in different languages. As with Hebrew, speakers of many languages are influenced by the shape of the symbol, e.g., *escargot* ("snail") in French; *kammerklaffe* ("spider monkey") in German. See Danet (1997a) and the discussion of this topic on the Linguist listserv list, March 17–July 2, 1996, especially the summary by Karen S. Chung, available from the Linguist archives at http://www.ai.univie.ac.at/archives/Linguist/. .

10. There are other forms of play with language in the logos of many cybercafés, e.g., the pun of "bites" and "bytes" in "Gig@bites" (Figure 1.1).

11. Swatch announced that the zero-point for Internet time would be Biele, location of its headquarters. As this book was completed in 2000, there was little evidence that this innovation had caught on.

12. Beginning September 1998, I also documented many expressive uses of the @ in Israel's Hebrew media too.

13. See, e.g., Danet (1995); Werry (1996); Stivale (1997).

14. See Figure 1.18 and Chapter 6. For information on mIRC, see http://www.mirc.co.uk/.

15. See http://www.palacetools.com/ and http://www.dmoz.org/Computers/Internet/Chat/The_Palace/. For a study of "The Palace" employing participant observation, see Suler (1999b).

16. See Vzones/WorldsAway, http://www.avaterra.com/.

17. See Worlds, Inc., http://www.worlds.net/3dcd/index.html.

18. See, e.g., Short et al. (1976); Hiltz (1978; 1993); Johansen et al. (1979); Hiemstra (1982); Kiesler (1984).

19. Direct person-to-person communication via email or any form of conferencing was not the initial goal of developers, but rather, efficient sharing of intellectual resources among different computers in a distributed system. Development of networks

for person-to-person communication came later; see Campbell-Kelly and Aspray (1996: 288–293).

20. See Short et al. (1976); Kiesler (1984); Rice and Love (1987); Walther (1992).

21. See Laurel (1991); Turkle (1995); Stone (1996: 14–15); Murray (1997).

22. I am indebted to Yehudit Rosenbaum-Tamari for this point.

23. See Solt (1968); Higgins (1987); Drucker (1994; 1996).

24. On carnival, in addition to Bakhtin (1968), see Turner (1986); Stam (1989); Argyle (1996: 137–141). See also the discussion of carnivalesque wordplay in Chapter 3.

25. Time will tell to what extent and under what conditions the liminal quality of cyberspace will persist, as processes of institutionalization proceed in the 21st century.

26. In conversation we frequently say "Now where were we?" when we have digressed from the original topic. While people have thought a good deal about the Internet as a new kind of "place," far less attention had been given to "cybertime." One exception is a thoughtful paper by Lance Strate (1996).

27. See, e.g., van Dijk (1985); Mills (1995). Other aspects of written communication pertinent to this study, notably, the language and form of letter-writing and the history of the memo format, belong to the domain of business communication. See, e.g., Yates (1989a; 1989b; 1992) and Chapter 2.

28. The concept of speech play refers to phenomena occurring spontaneously during the flow of conversation, whereas the term verbal art is used for specific genres where stylization is expected, and tends to follow crystallized norms (Bauman 1975; 1977; 1990).

29. For general formulations, see, e.g., Hymes (1964); Gumperz (1972); Bauman and Sherzer (1974; 1989); Saville-Troike (1989); Bauman (1990). For case studies of spoken verbal art, see, e.g., Sherzer (1990); Briggs (1988).

30. See e.g., Basso (1974); Heath (1983); Shuman (1986); Besnier (1995); Street (1984; 1993).

31. For a discussion of the notion of text type, see Biber (1989).

32. See Lea (1992); Dery (1993a; 1993b); Thompsen (1996); Danet (1998a).

33. This formulation of its nature as both doubly attenuated and doubly enhanced is my own.

34. An example is William Mitchell's (1995) *City of Bits*. See http://mitpress.mit.edu/e-books/City_of_Bits/, and also the link to Mitchell's reflections on the experience of creating and maintaining this Website at http://mitpress.mit.edu/e-books/City_of_Bits/Text_Unbound/text_unbound.html.

35. By April, 2000 over 60 million people had downloaded ICQ, a phenomenal success story, with 700,000 or more logged onto it at any given moment. See http://www.icq.com. Other instant messaging programs were PowWow, Ding, and America Online's own Instant Messenger. ICQ was bought by America Online in June, 1998 and is so successful that by the time this book is published, some of the others may be out of business.

36. MUDs are text-based virtual realities, self-contained chat modes featuring role-play. I will explain about them shortly.

37. Although more sophisticated in other ways, these other chat modes did not necessarily enable one to see others' contributions while they were being typed. On IRC one saw other players' messages only after they hit "enter;" the message then appeared in its entirety on the screen.

38. This figure was provided to me by Alex Charalabidis, who maintained a Website of basic information on IRC worldwide (http://www.irchelp.org/irchelp/networks); personal email, July 15, 1998. As of July, 1998, "Saint's List" contained 114 servers; see http://www.geocities.com/~saintslist/. Alex Charalabidis estimated the number of networks at over 150.

39. The symbol # is used in activation of all commands relating to channels on IRC.

40. See "The MUD Connector," http://www.mudconnect.com/.

41. In practice, these three categories of MUDs and MOOs sometimes overlapped. Thus, a good deal of interaction on MediaMOO was quite playful. MediaMOO was based at Georgia Tech; see http://www.cc.gatech.edu/~asb/MediaMoo.

42. As of February 1996, there were 7,065 characters registered on LambdaMOO and 1015 on MediaMOO. See Danet (1998b) and the discussion of play with gender identity later in this chapter. This information was supplied to me by Lee-Ellen Marvin and Keith Wilson.

43. These issues are developed in further detail in Chapter 2.

44. See Werry (1996).

45. See http://www.kidlink.org/IRC/.

46. See, e.g., Abbott (1986); Inge (1990, Figure 1.6); Cooper (1984); Chalfant (1987).

47. Descriptions of action are represented in three different ways; see Figure 1.5, no. 7.

48. Collections of hundreds of other smileys circulated on the Net. See Chapter 5.

49. Thus, at the Hebrew University of Jerusalem, computers were called "pluto," "olive," and "spinach." There was actually a Website whose URL was http://www. atdot.com/atdot/net/slash/comdotnetslashdotdot.

50. Collections of screensavers were available at, e.g., Screensaver Heaven, http://www.galttech.com/ssheaven.stml; The Screen Savers Page, http://members.aol.com/Bellis4380/index.html; Screen Saver Bonanza, http://www.bonanzas.com/ssavers.

51. TUCOWs, a popular site offering a comprehensive, annotated catalogue of software for the Internet, created a separate site just for them. In the first three weeks up to 100,000 visitors a day accessed the site (Slatalla 1998). See http://www.freethemes.com/. Michelle Slatalla suggests that "The reason that themes are proving so popular is that people identify with their computers. Computers aren't just machines anymore. They have become little buddies. . ." (Slatalla 1998). See also Hutsko (1999)

52. See the Virtual Pet Website, http://www.virtualpet.com/vp/ for links relating to the physical objects. The company that developed this software is PF Magic, at http://www.pfmagic.com.

53. In fall 1999 this company marketed a similar "Babyz" program. See http://www.babyz.net.

54. See "Petz on the Web Ring," http://nav.webring.com/.

55. Bernard Chien's Home Page is at http://walt.cs.msstate.edu/~maynor. Natalie Maynor's Home Page is at http://www2.msstate.edu/~maynor/; Words-L is at http://www.words-l.org.

56. There are pet cemeteries on the Web, though this is not the pertinent point in this context, but rather, treating a dog as if it is a human.

57. By summer, 1998, this site had moved or disappeared. Unfortunately, I documented it via a temporary screen capture, rather than saving to a file, and thus have no record of the date I found it or the URL.

58. It is evident that these names for the bots are also forms of play with language and cultural content.

59. This site is no longer accessible.

60. The service was so successful that the Home Page no longer provided the information itself, directing the visitor to scores of affiliated sites around the world. The main URL is http://www.tucows.com.

61. Personal email from Scott Swedorski, March 22, 1997.

62. One apparent exception is the study of digital greetings in Chapter 4. While some of the sites offering digital greetings do so to promote commercial goods or services, in general this was not prominent on the sites studied, and the sites were created by design amateurs.

63. See, e.g., Bolter (1991); Landow (1992); Murray (1997).

64. On arcade video games and home video and computer games, see, e.g., Sudnow (1983); Loftus and Loftus (1983); Funk (1996); Griffiths (1997); Griffiths and Hunt (1998); Myers (1990). Murray's (1997) study of digital narrative also contains a great deal of material about computer games. To my knowledge no major study of online computer games – playing with partners who are remotely present – had been published when this book was completed. In any case, neither computer games nor hypertext fall within the domain of interpersonal communication, the mandate of this book.

65. See Csikszentmihalyi (1977; 1979 ; 1993) ; Csikszentmihalyi and Csikszentmihalyi (1988); Myers (1993).

66. So all-absorbing can chat modes be that many defined themselves as "addicted," sometimes ironically. In the course of writing this book, I encountered at least one person who spent all his waking hours online, to the detriment of his health and RL social life. While this book mainly celebrates the phenomena it documents, I do acknowledge the "dark" side to life in cyberspace. However, I believe that we should separate cultural analysis from clinical diagnosis, and that the activities I document have the potential to enrich participants' lives. There is an ongoing debate among psychologists and psychiatrists as to whether over-use of the Internet should be identified as a clinical addiction. See, e.g., Goldberg (1996); Suler (1999a); Young (1998); Bellock (1996). There is a Usenet newsgroup called *alt.irc.recovery*. On enthusiasm for digital fonts as a playful type of "addiction," see Chapter 7.

67. Green was in the midst of designing a logo for a friend. I am indebted to David Tuval for bringing this book to my attention.

68. In a fascinating form of self-ethnography, hacker culture is documented regularly by hackers themselves, in what is known online as "The Jargon File," updated every

six months. The printed version, *The New Hackers' Dictionary* (Raymond 1996) appeared in three editions. In late fall 1999, the Jargon File could be accessed at http://www.jargon.org/jargon.html; http://www.pvv.org/misc/jargon/html/index.html; http://www.memes.org/jargon/.

69. Members of the underground computer art scene followed these practices in the late 1990s; see Chapter 5.

70. The first example is mentioned by Meyer (1990), and the second by Quittner and Slatalla (1995). Other nicknames contain still other forms of wordplay, e.g., "Knight Lightning," also mentioned by Meyer and Thomas.

71. Unfortunately, I did not document the date and source of this example, but believe I found it on an IRC Website.

72. The underground computer art scene of the late 1990s continued to use this eccentric spelling and typography. For examples, see Lyons (1997). These groups are discussed in Chapter 5.

73. The HAKMEM document continues to be available at http://www.inwap.com/pdp10/hbaker/hakmem/hakmem.html.

74. As the last item in Figure 1.10 indicates, many hackers dissociate themselves from malicious or criminal activity.

75. I am grateful to Amos Cividalli for calling this phenomenon to my attention.

76. When activated, the Eudora Easter Egg reveals the names of the programmers; Netscape Communicator contains an animated aquarium; mIRC emits textual "sounds" as in cartoons. For links to many Easter Eggs, go to www.cnet.com/Content/Features/Howto/Eggs/. See also Nagy-Farkas (1997).

77. The image in Figure 1.15 is from "Chipworks-Silicon Art," http://www.chipworks.com/ home.html/. I learned of this phenomenon from a New York Times article by Bruce Headlam (1999). See Headlam's article and the "Silicon Zoo" at http://microscope.fsu.edu/creatures/.

78. See also Dave Healy (1997), "Cyberspace and Place: The Internet as Middle Landscape on the Electronic Frontier."

79. Still another term is "cybernaut," inviting the analogy with outer space in the Space Age.

80. Like the traditional stereotype of the cowboy, individuals are indeed solitary, in the sense that they are generally seated alone at their computers. However, communication in cyberspace was hardly "verbally terse." Trillions of words were exchanged daily among tens of millions of persons.

81. See McLaughlin et al. (1995); Reid (1996a); MacKinnon (1997); Smith and Kollock (1998).

82. See, e.g., Branscomb (1997a; 1997b).

83. And, indeed, as I revealed above, I was slow to realize that Bernard Chien Perro was a dog! The *New Yorker* cartoon may be viewed at http://www.cartoonbank.com/.

84. See Reid (1991); Bruckman (1992; 1993); Rheingold (1993), Chapter 5; Leslie (1993); Bechar-Israeli (1995); Turkle (1995), Danet (1998b); Kendall (1996; 1998).

85. Moreover, in some cases individuals log on from accounts or servers that are far from their actual geographical location, making it still more difficult to know who

they might be, or log off and log on again from a different account, with a different nickname. See Slater (1998; 2000).

86. Cf. Kalcik (1985) on the use of handles by women in CB radio.

87. See Curtis (1996); Bruckman (1996); Turkle (1995).

88. See also, e.g., Dickel (1995); Kendall (1996; 1998); Turkle (1995); Barnes (1998); McRae (1996; 1997); Rodino (1998); Suler (1996–97).

89. For a more extended discussion of these phenomena and their possible significance, see Danet (1998b).

90. The advisability of caution in this regard is also visible in the title of Rob Shields' (1996) collection, *Cultures of Internet: Virtual Spaces, Real Histories, Living Bodies*.

91. See, e.g., Cherny (1994); Dickel (1995); Bruckman (1992; 1996); Reid (1995; 1996b); Marvin (1995); Turkle (1995); Jacobson (1996); Beaubien (1996); Curtis (1996); Kendall (1996; 1998); Bromberg (1996); McRae (1996; 1997); Ito (1997); Stivale (1997); Danet (1998b). Coe (1998).

92. See Reid (1991; 1996a); Werry (1996); Shaw (1997); Rodino (1998); Powers (1997); Nir (1998), Paolillo (1999), and Slater (1998; 2000), as well as a study of nicknames on IRC by Haya Bechar-Israeli (1995), a past member of my research team.

93. See the studies by Reid, Werry, and Rodino cited in footnote 92.

94. The studies of gay channels by Shaw (1997) and Nir (1998) are both based primarily on interviews. Studies are also needed of IRC channels for groups whose language is not English, an issue this book does not address. A massive survey of Web servers established that over 80% of some 3,200 Home Pages representing Websites were in English. Data on 14 other languages were also supplied, in rank order. See http://www.isoc.org:8080/palmares.en.html. No such data existed at the time, however, for channels on IRC. Some evidence for the existence in French of phenomena like those discussed here for English was provided by Werry (1996). Two of my students analyzed similar phenomena in Russian and Italian IRC chat.

95. Chapter 3 integrates materials from an online monograph (Danet et al. 1995) with an unpublished paper (Danet and Wachenhauser 1997).

96. Cf., e.g., Ferrara, et al. (1991); Davis and Brewer (1997); Yates (1993); Collot and Belmore (1992; 1996); Yates and Orlikowski (1996). Additional references are provided in Chapter 2.

97. A somewhat similar approach appears in Judith Yaross Lee's (1996) study of the rhetoric of email. Unlike her paper, however, my chapter (Chapter 4), focuses on the analysis of specific corpora of letters. See also Moran and Hawisher (1998).

98. The associations of this name are explained in Chapter 3.

99. They are available on the companion Website to this book, URL in the Table of Contents.

100. Although I do discuss commercial digital greetings offered by Hallmark and American Greetings, the two giants of the greeting card business, this is not the main focus of the chapter.

101. Paint Shop Pro is a program for the creation and editing of images; Image AXS Pro is a database program that enables, e.g., slide shows.

102. "ASCII" means "American Standard Code for Information Interchange." This code established a set of 128 basic 7-bit codes that facilitate communication across operating systems. In effect, only 95 characters are available for ASCII art images. For further technical details, see Chapters 5 and 6.

103. ASCII artists displaying their work on the World Wide Web sometimes incorporated HTML-based color in images, or displayed it against a blue, rather than black background. However, ASCII art was not brilliantly colored to the same extent as the art observed on IRC. See, e.g., Joan Stark's ASCII Art Gallery, http://www.ascii-art.com/ . One exception to this generalization was a form of colored text-based art practiced by underground artists. See the discussion of the underground art scene in Chapter 5.

104. In another form of text-based digital art, underground artists had been using color at the DOS level since the 1980s, in images created for BBSs (Plate 5.2); as mentioned in footnote 103, some use of color also occurred on the World Wide Web, but colored art became widely accessible only with the advent of the Windows version of the IRC program. See Chapters 5 and 6.

105. The richness of effects is better discernible in color images. See, e.g., Plate 6.1.

106. This site had disappeared by the time this book was completed.

107. See http://www.fontsanon.com/.

108. See Chapter 7, Plate 7.13.

109. In the short run, a regularly updated companion Website to a book, such as that created for this book, can to some extent counteract the tendency toward obsolescence of a print text. However, there will come a time when such Websites will no longer be worth updating or when no one is alive who cares enough to continue the process.

110. See URL http:// mitsloan.mit.edu/.

2

"Feeling Spiffy:" The Changing Language of Public Email

This chapter is a study of public email in the mid-1990s. The language of email was in great flux at the time because of the relative newness of the medium to most users, and the absence of clear norms as to what was appropriate. While I will at times refer to personal, rather than official correspondence, the heart of the chapter is an analysis of two corpora of official or public letters between strangers. One is a set of responses to a Call for Papers that I distributed on the Internet in 1994–95. A Call for Papers is an invitation by the editor or guest editor of a journal or book to submit a proposal for a paper. The other corpus is my correspondence with a software developer in 1993–94 about the possibility of ordering the software. We will look at how he changed his style over time. I will also present some letters I received from students. The title of the chapter is a phrase in a letter I received from a student in the American Midwest. Surprisingly, at the beginning of the message he wrote that he was "feeling spiffy," hardly a conventional expression in a letter from a student to a professor. We will look at this remarkable letter in more detail, later in the chapter.

Email offers many advantages, notably, the speed and convenience of keeping in touch with family and friends, and the ease of initiating and maintaining communication with strangers. At the same time, it challenges deeply internalized, traditional norms about the language and form of letters, whether personal ones or official ones. How were people responding to this challenge in the mid-1990s? This is the subject of this chapter.

As I mentioned in the Introduction, the technology which made email possible already existed in the 1960s and 1970s, but only 20 or so years later did this new means of communication become truly widespread, a serious competitor of paper letters, faxes and the telephone. By the late 1990s, tens of millions of people were composing and sending email messages and even participating in chat on a daily basis. The expression "You've got mail!" no longer necessarily meant a paper letter waiting in a brightly painted mailbox.

So widespread was email by then that Hollywood film producers created a successful film of that title, starring Tom Hanks and Meg Ryan. They also created a Website where visitors could read fictional email letters ostensibly exchanged by "NY152" and "Shopgirl," the Hanks and Ryan characters.[1] However, these letters were too perfect. Shopgirl's sentences were all syntactically well-formed; there were no spelling mistakes, and her use of upper and lower case was perfectly conventional, e.g., all sentences started with a capital letter.

A New Kind of Letter-Writing

Email is not just a form of letter-writing in which printing is optional. Traditionally, Anglo-American culture recognized two main categories of letters, typically called the business[2] letter and the social or personal letter. The form and style of these two types of letters have been highly codified. We carry around in our heads a "template" – a pattern or model – for each type. Drawing on centuries of tradition, manuals for letter-writers have dictated how these two types of letters are to look.[3] Some modifications were called for, depending on the communicative function of the type of letter involved. In our own times, the most obvious distinction within the world of official communication was that between the inter-organizational letter and the intra-organizational one – the memorandum, popularly known as the memo.

We inherited the email format with its initial header from the intra-organizational memorandum. This template was originally invented for intra-organizational communication in the late 19th and early 20th centuries (Yates 1989: 95–98).

> Internal correspondence across distance had long been an accepted part of business, but in the late 19th- and early 20th centuries, considerable correspondence. . . emerged within facilities as a response to plant growth and systematization. The form and content of this style began to diverge from that of external letters, reflecting the preoccupation with efficiency and system that shaped downward and upward communication. While custom and courtesy restricted the form and style of external letters, internal correspondence evolved in ways intended to make it more functional to read and to handle. (Yates 1989: 95)

In several respects the memo format of email is disconcerting. First, it is anomalous to use it for communication between organizations. If it was all right to dispense with "custom and courtesy" in the name of efficiency in a paper letter within an organization, is it also all right to dispense with it in email to a person in another organization? Should we regard the header as part of the letter, or merely as a virtual "envelope," which happens to precede the text of the message? Do we need to add an opening and a closing to our message if some of the information customarily supplied this way in a traditional letter is perfectly obvious in the header? What difference does it make if the correspondents are acquainted or not? And if the name of the sender is in the header, why "sign" an email message?[4] Since the "signature" is intangible, it no longer serves as a physical "trace" of the hand of the sender or authenticates the document. In the past, this was important even in typewritten or word-processed letters, where the sender usually took pains to sign the letter personally.[5]

For those who grew up with the distinction between business and personal letter-writing, it is even stranger to use the memo format for purely personal written communication. It invites a "mock-serious," hence playful note to all personal communication by email. There is something incongruous, even slightly ridiculous about a memo whose subject line reads, say, "recipe for apple cake." Of course, many people become accustomed to this incongruity and hardly notice it any more, sometimes even playing intentionally with the subject line. Though novel, it is useful to tell our readers, even in a personal message, what its subject will be, especially if they have to cope with many messages per day.[6] Those growing up with email will not experience this incongruity.

By the mid-1990s, some manuals for letter-writers were beginning to take account of the emergence of fax and email correspondence, though typically, they paid only token attention to them, and did not confront the dilemmas faced by active users.[7] Similarly, arbiters of etiquette began to consider and even to prescribe which kinds of messages could appropriately be conveyed by email or fax, and which could not, and what form they should take. Miss Manners (Judith Martin), a widely syndicated columnist in American newspapers, devoted an entire book to this topic, *Miss Manners' Basic Training: Communication* (Martin 1997). In it she promised to explain "when to phone, when to fax, when a handwritten note is obligatory, a form letter forbidden and a chain letter out of the question."[8] Somewhat unsystematically, she referred to 10 different media, the handwritten note, the engraved missive, the fax, email, a computer-generated, presumably printed document, voice mail, a personal message in face-to-face interaction, a greeting card, a "live" phone message, and finally, a crayon! She forbade the use of email for love letters, divorce announcements, and telling one's spouse that one is pregnant or breaking bad (personal) news.[9] Thus, she approved of email for neutral or positive business communication, but not for bad news, or for very emotionally charged good news.[10]

More specialized manuals about email and Netiquette also began to appear. Shortly, I will examine five such publications. Three appeared in 1994, Donald Rose's *Minding Your Cyber-manners on the Internet*, Virginia Shea's *NETiquette*, and *The Elements of E-mail Style* by David Angell and Brent Heslop. *Rules of the Net: Online Operating Instructions for Human Beings*, by Thomas Mandel and Gerard Van der Leun, appeared in 1996, as did *Wired Style: Principles of English Usage in the Digital Age*, edited by Constance Hale of *Wired Magazine*. The first four were popular manuals, whereas *Wired Style* was primarily about language usage in print journalism about digital culture. However, it also dealt with some of the issues pertinent to this chapter.[11]

In what kinds of muddles did email writers find themselves? Two letters I received from a personal friend are illustrative. In September, 1994, on the occasion of the Jewish New Year, M.G., an old friend and colleague, wrote to wish me *Shana Tova*, "Happy New Year" in Hebrew. He had only been using email for a few months.[12] The letter began, "Dear Brenda," perfectly appropriate for a paper personal letter (Figure 2.1).

```
Date: Fri, 02 Sep 94 11:03:28 EDT

From: M.G. <XXXXX@xxxx.xxx.EDU>

Subject: Re: renovations, allergies

To: brenda danet <msdanet@pluto.mscc.huji.ac.il>


Dear Brenda,

The formal opening (inappropriate, I gather, for e-mail) is

meant to differentiate this message from all other messages:

Shana tova, a healthy happy and productive year, and best

wishes from all of us.

. . . . . . . . . . . . .

Again, best wishes for the new year and love from both of us.

M.
```

Figure 2.1. Letter with wishes for the Jewish New Year.

The body of the letter read,

```
The formal opening (inappropriate, I gather, for email) is
meant to differentiate this message from all other messages.
Shana tova, a healthy, happy and productive new year and best
wishes from all of us.
```

We can see that, despite the informal opening, M.G. felt a pull toward relatively formal language both because of the ritual nature of the message, and because he brought to the writing the general paper letter template. The comments in parentheses show that he was uncomfortable with his choice of opening. Such a self-conscious meta-comment about one's choices would not have occurred in a paper letter. The pre-closing was also very formal:

```
Again, best wishes for the new year and love from both of us.
```

In my view, M.G. was even hyper-formal, because of his uncertainty as to appropriate use.[13]

Seven months later, on the occasion of Passover, I received a second letter from M.G. conveying holiday wishes (Figure 2.2). It showed a process of adaptation over a short period of time. Although the function of the message was the same, many aspects of its form had changed.

All on one line, M. G. wrote:

```
Hello Brenda. Just a quick note to wish you Hag Same'ach[14]
etc.
```

He greeted me with the very informal, telephone-like "hello," and instead of arranging the opening on a separate line, as he had done in the first letter, here the text continued on the same line. The use of the abbreviation "etc." is a departure from formal ritual language. Another informal feature is ellipsis; the words "This is. . ." were omitted from the sentence. An interesting change is the use of all-caps for the word "LOSS" in the following passage:

```
I sent you an email last week but had no reply and wondered
whether you'd received it. There was nothing importanat there,
so if you did not get it, it's no great LOSS.
```

Thus, in the intervening seven months, M.G. had learned to use all-caps to heighten implied intonation patterns, bringing writing closer to speech. Notice also the uncorrected typo – "importanat" for "important," suggesting that he now felt less need to edit the message.

```
Date: Thu, 13 Apr 95 13:08:30 EDT
From: M. G. <XXXXX@xxxx.xxx.EDU>
Subject: Hag Sameach
To: brenda danet <msdanet@pluto.mscc.huji.ac.il>
```

```
Hello Brenda. Just a quick note to wish you Hag Same'ach etc.
I gather that you are going to a music festival this weekend,
and hope this reaches you before you leave.

I sent you an e-mail last week, but had no reply and wondered
whether you've received it. There was nothing especially
importanat there, so if you did not get it it's no great
LOSS. Amongst other things I asked whether you could let me
have Y.L.'s address. If you can do that, I'll be grateful.

Enjoy the music, and the holiday. Love from P. too. M.
```

Figure 2.2. A Passover greeting.

Our muddles were even greater in public than private email. Those of us who grew up in print culture bring implicit knowledge of many templates besides those of the personal and business letter to the experience of composing email messages. Other relevant templates are the telegram, the postcard, and the greeting card, as well as the oral, face-to-face conversation, the telephone conversation, and the intra-organizational memo. Rather than attempt to assess how each of these text-types[15] may impinge on email practice today – a task beyond the scope of this chapter – I shall ask: in specific situations where the traditional paper business letter could have been sent instead of an email message, what form did the email message take?

Anomalous Nature of the Medium

A Closer Look

In the Introduction I began to explicate the anomalous nature of the medium by arguing that digital communication is, paradoxically, both doubly attenuated and doubly enhanced. I noted that, considered as "writing," text-based digital communication has lost its physicality, but regained a sense of the presence of one's interlocutor. As "speech, " I argued, it lost the rich non-verbal cues of face-to-face interaction, but gained the possibility of re-examining what was "said," because this medium leaves visible traces on one's computer screen, and can even be printed if necessary.[16]

Email feels like talking because of the dynamic, interactive, ephemeral nature of the medium, especially when we draft our messages online, and even though they are asynchronous like paper letters. Thus, a woman in a *New Yorker* cartoon tells her interlocutor over the phone, "Richard, we need to talk. I'll e-mail you." The anomalous nature of the medium is also reflected in our occasional use of expressions like "Talk to you soon" or "nice 'talking' to you" in email.[17]

Letter-writing as Conversation

The perception of written interpersonal communication as "live" or as "conversation" is not really new. Bruce Redford (1986; 1993) calls to our attention the fact that 18th-century letter-writers, one of whose most famous practitioners was Samuel Johnson, saw themselves as engaging in a "converse of the pen." "One of the century's principal rhetoricians described epistolary correspondence as 'conversation carried on upon paper, between two friends at a distance'" (Redford 1993: 30).[18]

In the late 17th century, the penny post in London made it possible for individuals to exchange letters on the very same day (Staff 1992, Chapter 2). During the mid-Victorian and late-Victorian years, London had a postal delivery every hour, twelve hours of the day (Briggs 1988: 335). In the 20 or so months before their elopement, the poets Robert Browning and Elizabeth Barrett Browning exchanged hundreds of letters on a daily basis (Kintner 1969). Perhaps they could even smell the fresh ink as they opened a letter. To some extent, then, the new technology merely reinstated, rather than introduced, intensive, spontaneous written conversation, in an era in which conventional postal delivery was far less frequent than in the past.[19] Of course, the rapid exchange of messages is now global, and not just local, as it was back then.

"Oral," "Written" and Digital Features of Email Messages: a Brief Recapitulation

A growing number of studies has established that email messages are characterized by a distinctive combination of "oral," "written" and uniquely digital features.[20] Among the speech-like features are contractions and slang, as in "I'm gonna read the book", and colloquial expressions such as "How about?"

Messages also contain many first and second person pronouns,
with personal involvement.

Often, email messages also have many writing-specific characteristics,
including use of abbreviations, non-standard spellings, forms of shorthand or
speedwriting, as in "u" for "you" or "plz" for "please, ellipsis ("[I am] meeting
Mary tomorrow"), omission of definite and indefinite articles ("read [the] book
last night"), and use of all lower-case. Syntactically, sentences may be complex
rather than simple or compound, evidence of editing and planning, a feature
of many written texts generally. Other writing-linked features are the use of
lists, a high incidence of nominalizations (nouns instead of verbs, "make a
payment" instead of "pay") paragraphing – organizing material into chunks
separated by white space, and so on.

As we saw in the introduction, email messages also frequently contain
uniquely digital features, the best known being smiley icons to express emotion
or humor, and citation of all or part of a message when replying,[21] to provide
context for one's interlocutor.

The Business Letter Template

In the Anglo-American tradition, personal letters have always been more
conversational and informal than business or official ones. Thus, the transition
to a medium that fosters a partially speech-like mode should be less problematic
in the case of personal letters than in that of business or official ones, in which
the informal style facilitated by the new medium conflicts with traditional
norms.

The main features of the business letter template are no doubt familiar to
most readers. They are shown in Figure 2.3.[22] Most generally, the standard
paper business letter is supposed be cast in a formal style – to use language
appropriate to formal situations. It should contain a formal opening – a formal
salutation such as "Dear" + Title + Last Name (henceforth TLN), as in "Dear
Dr. Jones" – and a formal closing (a complimentary close such as "Sincerely,"
"Sincerely yours," or "Yours truly") followed by a signature, FN + LN,[23] on
a separate line. Formal letters also often include a pre-closing, such as "Thank
you very much" or "I look forward to hearing from you."

Sentences should conform to the rules of standard grammar. The writer
should use appropriately formal vocabulary, avoiding slang and colloquialisms
and abbreviations. Spelling, typography, and punctuation should all conform
with conventional written practice. Finally, the physical layout is also important. There should be white space between the opening, the body of the letter,
and the closing, as well as between paragraphs.[24]

Feature	Example
(1) Opening: salutation + formal address, TLN	"Dear Dr. Jones"
(2) Closing:	
optional pre-closing	"Thank you for your consideration of this matter."
complimentary close	"Yours truly,"
signature FN+LN	"John Doe"
(3) Standard syntax	
(4) Formal vocabulary	
(5) No abbreviations	
(6) Standard spelling, typography	
(7) Standard punctuation	
(8) Layout: white space between opening and body of letter, between body of letter and closing; between paragraphs	

Figure 2.3. Key elements of the business letter template.

What Did Manuals for Email Style Recommend?

What, specifically, did early manuals recommend, then, and were they consistent in their recommendations? I turn now to an overview of five manuals that appeared in the mid-1990s.[25] There is no necessary direct link between their recommendations and what the letter-writers studied here actually did. Rather, I seek to show that the manuals reflected uncertainty about what is appropriate, that they wrestled with the issues, and that they occasionally tried to differentiate between what might be appropriate in public versus private correspondence.

Openings and Closings

The popular manuals did not necessarily make a clear distinction between private email and group communication. In fact, their main emphasis tended to be on the novel situation of individual-to-group communication on Usenet and discussion lists, not private messages. Still, they did address many of the issues that are the subject of this chapter.

Only Angell and Heslop dealt with the problematics of openings and closings. They said that writers of personal email messages should "add a greeting for a friendly touch," but that such greetings are inappropriate in messages to a public forum (Angell and Heslop 1994: 21). They advised avoiding first names if one is not acquainted with the addressee, and recommended a simple closing such as "thanks" or "regards," advising against "carryovers from the old-fashioned business letter" such as "Sincerely yours" (Angell and Heslop 1994 30–31).[26] In other words, they suggested using a traditional pre-closing, but cast in informal language, as the email closing. As we shall see, this is in fact what was happening in business email.

Syntax

The manuals generally urged emailers to observe the rules of syntax. Angell and Heslop devoted an entire chapter to sentence structure, urging writers to make their subjects and verbs agree; avoid misplaced modifiers, sentence fragments and run-on sentences; use variety in sentence structures (simple, compound, complex); and manage sentence length for readability. However, the authors failed to see the potential contradiction between the great degree of planning and editing required to attend to these aspects of writing and their view that email "encourages an informal, conversational style of writing," that one should "err on the side of being too informal and conversational rather than too formal," and "use words and phrases that come naturally" (Angell and Heslop 1994: 56).

Abbreviations

Three manuals (Angell and Heslop, Rose, Shea) recommended abbreviations such as IMHO ("In my humble opinion") and BTW ("by the way"), mainly because they save time for readers and writers. All three gave lists of them for newbies on the Net.[27] Angell and Heslop supplied two lists, one of common business abbreviations before the Net (ASAP, FYI), the other of acronyms used on the Net (BRB, FTF). On the other hand, Mandel and Van der Leun (1996) condemned them as a "blight on the Net." Hale advised journalists that "acronyms are an essential part of wired culture" (Hale 1996: 125), though she conceded that they can be problematic: they "litter the digital landscape" (Hale 1996: 125), can be obtuse or imprecise, lack the richness of actual words, and should not be overused.

Spelling and Typography

All four popular manuals called for correct spelling, though they generally expressed understanding about the two main factors that lead to misspellings, the lack of an appropriate editor in email software and the speed with which messages are written and dispatched. They offered two main arguments for being careful about one's spelling: either misspelling makes a bad impression, or it hampers comprehensibility.

Virginia Shea commented, "You will. . . be judged by the quality of your writing. . . . So spelling and grammar do count," but then acknowledges in a footnote that preoccupation with them runs counter to spontaneity. Rose advised readers to fight the tendency to let spelling, grammar and punctuation go, and urged them to use a spell checker if available (Rose 1994: 33).

Angell and Heslop stressed both comprehensibility and impression management. They recommended a spell checker, reviewed many spelling rules, and even gave an extensive list of frequently misspelled words. Although Mandel and Van der Leun also came out strongly for correct spelling, they hinted at the possibility of increased tolerance for misspelling on the Net: "Shakespeare spelled his name three different ways in the same day, and he'd be great to have on the Net" (Mandel and Van der Leun 1996: 91). Predictably, *Wired Style* took the opposite position, reflecting its more general view of digital writing as spontaneous and close to everyday life.

The four popular manuals all urged that one should not write an entire message in all capital letters.[28] Yet, on closer inspection, they did not fully agree about application of the rule. Mandel and Van der Leun were the most adamant, yet they were also the only ones to say that if you really want to shout at someone, go ahead and use all caps, after all:

Shea said, "NEVER TYPE YOUR NOTES IN ALL CAPS, LIKE THIS. It's rude – like shouting constantly," and it is "hard on the eye," but added that all caps may be used in moderation for emphasis (Shea 1994: 61). The other two authors offered explanations for the rule. Rose (1994: 30) remarked that "Such text is hard for the eye and brain to assimilate because it exhibits no contrast." Angell and Heslop (1994: 11) concurred, and identified the latent motivation for using them as laziness – not having to use the shift key repeatedly.

May we use all lower case instead, since the faster we can type the better? Shea and Hale had nothing to say on the subject. Rose was generally permissive, but Angell and Heslop (1994: 12) came out strongly against this practice, claiming that it was also difficult to decipher. Mandel and Van der Leun (1996: 97) condemned all lower-case as, once again, a sign of laziness and even disrespect.

Smileys

The manuals also offered advice on the use of Net-specific features, including smileys, citation of the previous message, and signature files. The use of smileys was hotly debated on many discussion lists in the mid-1990s. Some people thought that they are too playful or juvenile, or that using them excessively is a tell-tale sign that one is a "newbie" in cyberspace. People identifying with traditional writing norms often said such things as "the words should convey all the meaning."[29] Others believed in the ability of smileys to disambiguate meaning. Their use was overtly discouraged on Usenet.[30]

Four manuals largely approved of smileys to express emotion or to mark an utterance as humorous or ironic, and gave lists of them, which go beyond the smile, wink and frown. Both Angell and Heslop (1994: 111–112) and Rose (1994: 12–14) said that they help the reader decipher the writer's original intent, but suggested that they should not be used in business messages. Both Shea (1994:58) and Hale endorsed them, though she also called them "treacly expressions of emotion" (Hale 1996: 69).

On the other hand, Mandel and Van der Leun detested smileys:

> In the dawn ages of the Net, someone decided to transmit emotions through the cunning use of typewriter symbols. These symbols were used to make the intent of the poster clear. The reason for this was that many people felt that they couldn't express themselves clearly using the twenty-six letters of the alphabet with which Shakespeare created Hamlet.
>
> The most primitive of these symbols was :-). . . . This symbol was amusing the first time it was used. . . . It is no longer amusing. . . . . Nothing. . . can substitute for a clear idea simply expressed. Avoid :-)'s and all associated emoticons. . . like the plague. (Mandel and Van der Leun 1996: 92).

There is an age-old tension between "showing" and "telling," between pictures and words. Literate culture has given precedence to words in contexts of letter-writing and expository prose, with important exceptions, such as scientific writing where illustrations may be needed. Antipathy by parents and teachers to comics is another expression of this view. Probably, this attitude also underlies strong opposition to smileys.

Signature Files

All four popular manuals approved of signature files but advised keeping them down to four to six lines. Of course, this entails a departure from previous letter-writing tradition. Shea urged, "Silly sigs are definitely not recommended for business correspondence" (Shea 1994: 62). On the other hand, Rose advised readers to choose a sig file "that illustrates your personality," adding that "when cleverly composed, they can show others your cyberstyle" (Rose 1994: 32). Departing for once from their generally conservative stance, and agreeing with Rose, Mandel and Van der Leun added, "Limit your sig files to useful information. . . and if you *must be colorful* (italics in the original), a two-line statement or quote that expresses something central about yourself" (Mandel and Van der Leun 1996: 90).

Summing Up

To sum up, the popular manuals all called for attention to correct spelling, and three explicitly called for attention to syntax. Mandel and Van der Leun were the most conservative and opinionated. All uniformly condemned the use of all caps, but disagreed about use of all lower case. They accepted the use of sig files, including those with a bit of expressivity, and apart from Mandel and Van der Leun, abbreviations and smileys too. Rose and Angell and Heslop advised against smileys in more formal email. By and large, then, with a few exceptions, they tended to advise conformity with old norms while adapting to a new medium.

Two Hypotheses about Public Email

In the remainder of this chapter I will make a preliminary case for two hypotheses about email practice: (1) public email practice in the mid-1990s was characterized by a state of extreme variability, reflecting a lack of consensus as to appropriate norms; (2) public email practice was drifting toward an emergent style at times more "oral," and even occasionally more playful than traditional official letter-writing style.

Although the literature on the language of email purports to generalize about email generally, in practice, the research has usually been carried out using a corpus from some context of individual-to-group communication, rather than private email. A rare exception is Alessandro Duranti's (1986) pioneering study of professor-student email in 1985. I concur with Naomi Baron (1998a) that important issues remain unexplored unless we also study email between individuals. While individual-to-group communication is itself certainly deserving of analysis, especially since it is a unique new mode in its own right and raises issues specific to it, it is, nevertheless, only part of the story of email as a new chapter in the history of letter-writing. Rather than analyzing a large corpus of messages for the statistical incidence of various features, as has usually been done in the past, I look holistically at a relatively small number of messages, carefully chosen for the context in which they were exchanged.[31]

It is not by chance that two-party email has not been studied previously. It is far easier both ethically and logistically to assemble a corpus of letters sent to listserv lists or Usenet newsgroups than to obtain one of two-party email.

Unlike letters sent to group fora, which are inherently public in nature, letters sent to individuals raise issues of privacy, even if their substance is not personal. My solution is to use portions of my own email correspondence, disguising identities of correspondents, and obtaining their permission to use their letters wherever possible.[32] The focus will be on letters sent to me by people who did not know me but knew my name and status.

Presentation of Self in First Email Letters

It is especially interesting to look at first letters sent by individuals to a stranger in some business or official capacity, about a matter of some importance to the writer. A first letter of any kind – on paper, a fax, or email, for that matter – is the written equivalent of a first encounter in person. In everyday interaction, we monitor our behavior in the presence of others. When the stakes are particularly high, we are especially careful to stage our behavior to conform to what we perceive to be recipients' expectations and standards (Goffman 1959; 1967).

There is evidence that our linguistic choices do make a difference. A large body of research has established that not only accent[33] and dialect variation of speakers affected evaluations of them,[34] but also aspects of syntax and vocabulary (Bradac 1982; 1990). Rudolf Kalin (Kalin and Rayko 1980; Kalin 1982) reviewed research on the social significance of speech in medical, legal and occupational settings. In one study (Fielding and Evered 1980), patients with lower-class accents were more likely to receive a physical diagnosis, while those with middle-class accents were more likely to have their problem labeled psychosomatic. Research led by William O'Barr (Lind and O'Barr 1979; O'Barr 1982) demonstrated experimentally that the speech style of courtroom witnesses influenced judgments of their credibility, even when they gave the same factual testimony. When testimony was worded in a "powerless" style, it received lower judgments of credibility than when speakers used a "powerful" style. The speech of job candidates has also been found to influence judgments of their suitability and competence (Kalin and Rayko 1980), as well as whether they are hired (Adelswärd 1988).

In contrast to the voluminous literature on social evaluation of speech, there is little research on the social evaluation of writing in everyday life. This is rather surprising, given the prominence of writing and written documents in modern societies. Researchers in technical and business communication study linguistic and structural features of letters, e.g., Yli-Jokipii (1996); Sims and Guice (1992), but not the social impact of letters.[35]

I know of no study of how letter-writing style influences judgments of writers by recipients or recipients' response to the letter.[36] Still, in order to make a favorable impression, a writer of a first letter is likely to take special care in its formulation. Traditional norms for letter form are likely to be salient, and writers are likely to be especially conscious of the impression their message may make on the recipient. In fact, monitoring of self-presentation might be even more careful in writing than in person, given the reduced number of aspects of communication available, even in a paper letter. Every aspect of a letter might "count," from the language to the quality of the paper to the amount of white space surrounding the text, whether it is typed or handwritten, the computer font used, etc. Since the email message is even more reduced than the paper letter, lacking the image-enhancing potential of quality stationery or a special typeface,[37] I would argue, the remaining features become still more critical.

Letters addressed to a person of higher status than that of the writer are especially likely to conform to traditional expectations. A large body of research in sociolinguistics has documented the influence of the relative status of addressor and addressee on linguistic choice: messages addressed upward tend to be more formal, more polite, and more conforming with conventional norms. Similarly, people are more formal and more polite in many matters of linguistic choice when addressing a stranger rather than a person with whom they are acquainted. These generalizations pertain both to norms of address and to many other aspects of linguistic communication.[38]

First Letters to a Professor

I first began to notice extreme variation in public email style when I received email letters from three students, all of whom wrote to request a copy of the same paper I had written. One studied at a community college in the American mid-West. The second was an undergraduate at a British university, and the third was a graduate student at an American university. The first letter was sent in 1994, and the other two in 1996.[39]

The letter in Figure 2.4 is a tour de force of playful performance, a far cry from the business letter template. Playfulness is evident in the userid TECHNO-SMURF in his email address, discernible in the header. Smurfs are blue cartoon characters that were a fad in the 1980s. While one's userid is fixed, and the writer might have forgotten that it would appear in this letter, he also includes it explicitly and intentionally, alongside his real name, at the bottom of the letter.

```
Date: Sat, 23 Apr 1994 19:27:04 -0400 (EDT)
From: TECHNOSMURF@xxxxxx.com
Subject: Help: need some articles for research paper
To: msdanet@pluto.mscc.huji.ac.il


*Hello*, Ms. Danet!

How are ya doin' today? I feel quite spiffy, too! My name is
T. L., and I'm doing a research paper on the social
implications of e-mail.

Jacques Leslie . . .referred me to you in acquiring your not-
quite-published-yet article. . . . It would help me very much
[and thoroughly suprise the socks off of my English II
teacher] if I could get a copy of this article. . . .
I greatly appreciate your help in this matter. Also, I'll be
sure to completely document my sources.

Thanks a bunch! [ . . . of grapes!] (:

T. L. <TECHNOSMURF@xxxxxx.COM>
```

Figure 2.4. A student letter to a professor.

This letter lurches between a wildly playful, informal style, out of place in conventional public correspondence, and a strictly formal, even hypercorrect style. Technosmurf began his letter with the conversational:

```
*Hello*, Ms. Danet!⁴⁰
```

He bracketed "hello" in asterisks, following the practice among initiated emailers of emphasizing certain words to enhance their speech-like quality. However, this is the only time in eight years of email correspondence that I ever encountered asterisks in an opening. Technosmurf addressed me formally by T+LN, but used an exclamation point, not customary in business communication at all, since it traditionally requires interlocutors to suppress emotion.

His opening remark was indicative of the wildly playful, oral style of much of his letter:

```
How are ya doin' today? I feel quite spiffy too!
```

Use of "ya" rather than "you", and dropping the "g" from "doing" are usually encountered only in colloquial speech, and are certainly not appropriate in a business letter. "How are ya doin' today?" could perhaps be Technosmurf's version of the purely ritualistic "How are you?" addressed to strangers in face-to-face encounters, but not appropriate in a first letter to a stranger.[41] The surprising, again strongly colloquial "I feel quite spiffy too!" violates the norm that in written initial interaction between strangers, one does not offer information about one's state of health. Notice also that in effect, Technosmurf supplied what counts as an answer to my implied but unasked question, "And how are you?" With these two utterances, he sought to establish an unusually dialogic, familiar mode of communication, as if he were acquainted with me personally, and we were chatting more or less as equals on the street. The expression "in acquiring your not-quite-published-yet article" is infelicitous, perhaps reflecting Technosmurf's less than full command of the English language, or difficulties expressing himself in writing. There is a second infelicitous expression: "referred to me in acquiring. . ."

The pattern of lurching between formal and informal styles reappears in

```
It would help me very much [and thoroughly suprise (sic) the
socks off my English II teacher] if I could get a copy of this
article.
```

The unbracketed part of the sentence is fully formed, conforms with spelling and syntactic requirements, and is entirely in the formal style. The bracketed material, on the other hand, introduces the grossly inappropriate colloquial idiom "surprise the socks off" someone, and contains a misspelling ("suprise") – perhaps just a typo, perhaps not. The brackets suggest that he knew that he was mixing styles.

The next two sentences,

```
I greatly appreciate your help in this matter. Also, I'll be
sure to completely document my sources.
```

conform in every way to the formal style. Finally, he lurched back to the wildly colloquial mode in playful fashion:

```
Thanks a bunch!
[ . . . of grapes!] (:
```

"Thanks a bunch" is much too colloquial for a business letter, perhaps even childish. Then he introduced a pun – "bunch" meaning "a whole lot" as well as "bunch" as in "bunch of grapes." Such wordplay is, of course, inappropriate in a traditional letter to a professor, in which the referential function of communication is supposedly dominant, and the language is expected to be transparent (Jakobson, 1960; Kirshenblatt-Gimblett, 1976). Punning foregrounds language, calling attention away from content to language itself. The effect is humorous, inappropriate in a formal letter. Two more exclamation points, plus a smiley icon, this time without the "nose," complete the text, ending in the same outrageously dialogic, playful mode that he began the letter. The smiley is also "backwards," perhaps reflecting the fact that Technosmurf is left-handed.[42]

Just what is going on here? Is this student knowingly playing with the conventions of letter-writing and with the emerging ones of communication in cyberspace? Is he showing off, mounting a virtuoso performance? Or is he perhaps a non-native speaker of English, or not well schooled in the norms of paper letter-writing, and struggling with writing difficulties?

While each of these factors may play a role, still another factor may also be involved. Technosmurf was writing to request a copy of an article about – the "orality" of email. He had read an article in *Wired Magazine* about this topic (Leslie 1994), in which a then-unpublished paper of mine on the hybrid nature of email was cited.[43] It was to receive a copy of this paper that he had written to me. Given the subject of both Leslie's article and my paper, Technosmurf may have felt that he had license to exaggerate the elements of street talk in his message. Perhaps he wanted to "show his stuff" specifically to me. Be that as it may, two other students who had also read Leslie's article and wrote to ask for the same article did not follow his route. Although to varying degrees, they too departed somewhat from the template, their letters were far more conventional, departing from the traditional business letter template only in quite minor ways.

Academics Adrift

Encouraged by the preliminary analysis just presented, I identified a more extensive corpus of first letters within the academic context. In 1994–95 I edited a special issue of the online *Journal of Computer-mediated Communication* on "Play and Performance in Computer-mediated Communication." All business in connection with this issue was conducted by email, resulting in a total of

```
==========================================================
          C A L L   F O R   P A P E R S
==========================================================
```

For a Special Issue of the New
Journal of Computer-Mediated Communication on

LANGUAGE, PLAY, AND PERFORMANCE

IN COMPUTER-MEDIATED COMMUNICATION

Brenda Danet, Guest Editor

There is a surprising return to playful, expressive "orality"
in digital writing, especially in synchronous modes like
Internet Relay Chat and Muds or MOOs, but even in ordinary
email, listserv discussion groups, Usenet newsgroups, etc.
People play with typography and orthography, with their
identities (nicknames, role-playing), with language, and with
cultural content, from real-world experience to fantasy,
folklore, the comics, and films. Aspects of "performance"
traditionally associated with genres of face-to-face
communication such as storytelling, joke-telling, verbal
dueling, etc., are flourishing on the Net. We find not only
unscripted improvisational performance, but even instances of
scripted performance.

This special issue of _JCMC_ will gather papers which engage
in ethnographic description and interpretive analysis of
playful phenomena. Appropriate topics may include (1) digital
playfulness as a postmodern phenomenon; (2) flaming as
"performance;" (3) nicknames on IRC, personas on MUDs and
MOOs; (4) improvisation in real-world theater vs. the Net;
(4) Net culture and the norms and practices of essayist
literacy. Papers may focus on a single mode of CMC, or
compare two or more.

JCMC is a multimedia electronic, peer-reviewed journal, and
is edited by Margaret McLaughlin, Annenberg School of
Communication, University of Southern California, and Sheizaf
Rafaeli, School of Business Administration, Hebrew University
of Jerusalem, and offers exciting new possibilities for
scholarly publication. Articles may include color graphics,
photographs, video, sound, etc.

Figure 2.5. Call for Papers for a special issue of a journal.

about 1,000 messages sent or received. I solicited papers for this issue by distributing a Call for Papers (CFP; Figure 2.5) to about a dozen online discussion lists.

The CFP is an accepted genre within the repertoire of academic communication, a text in carefully edited, formal academic style. To assemble a corpus of responses to this CFP, I screened out all letters that did not meet the criteria of a response from a stranger to its content. This yielded a set of 20 letters. Nine were from students, mainly graduate students, and eight from academic professionals (in three cases this status could not be determined). Twelve were from males and seven from females (the gender of one person could not be determined). Two wrote from England (one of whom was originally from Brazil, I learned from later correspondence), and one from Sweden; the rest were American.[44] I analyzed these letters using the criteria of the business letter template in Figure 2.3. All the letters either asked for more information or made an initial proposal for a topic and requested my response to it, or both. The range of variation in form of the letters turned out to be very great.

Extreme Variability: an Overview of 20 Letters

With respect to each feature of the template in Figure 2.3, I asked, did each letter conform to it, and if so, coded "yes," in Table 2.1. In the case of openings and closings, the letter was coded "yes" only if it contained both an appropriate opening and an appropriate closing, e.g., "Dear Prof. Danet" and "Sincerely." Informal openings like "Hi Brenda" and/or informal pre-closings such as "thanks" were coded "no."

As for abbreviations, letters were coded as "yes," conforming with the norm, if the writer wrote out, for example, the name of the journal, rather than using the abbreviation JCMC, or at least if the name was written out the first time, and then abbreviated.[45] If any of the expectations about spelling and typography were violated, for instance if the writer failed to capitalize the initial letter of a sentence, or used all lower case, or if the letter contained one or more typos, I coded "no" for "spelling/typography." As for punctuation, missing periods, use of exclamation points or the device of ellipsis, incidence of any of them was coded as not conforming with the template. The results are shown in Table 2.1.

Not a single letter conformed on all seven criteria, though one letter scored 6. One letter scored 0, two each scored 1 and 2; one letter scored 3, ten received a score of 4, three scored 5. It is evident that the numbers are skewed toward an attempt at conformity. This way of analyzing the letters is somewhat arbitrary, since it assigns equal weight to each of the criteria. Moreover, the results are somewhat influenced by decisions such as the one to unite judgments about openings and closings. Despite these limitations, this analysis allows us to compare letters fairly systematically.

Table 2.1. Conformity with the business letter template in 20 responses to a Call for Papers.

	Feature							Total
Letter no.	Op./Clos.	Syntax	Vocab.	Abbrevs.	Sp./Typog.	Punct.	Layout	"yes"
1	no	yes	yes	no	yes	no	yes	4
2	no	yes	yes	no	yes	no	yes	4
3	no	no	yes	yes	no	no	yes	3
4	no	no	yes	no	no	no	no	1
5	no	no	yes	no	no	no	no	1
6	no	yes	yes	yes	yes	yes	no	5
7	no	no	yes	yes	yes	no	yes	4
8	no	yes	no	yes	yes	no	yes	4
9	no	no	no	no	no	no	no	0
10	no	yes	no	no	no	no	yes	2
11	no	no	no	no	no	yes	yes	2
12	yes	yes	no	yes	no	no	yes	4
13	no	yes	no	yes	yes	no	yes	4
14	no	yes	no	yes	yes	yes	no	4
15	no	yes	yes	yes	yes	no	no	4
16	no	yes	yes	no	yes	no	yes	4
17	no	no	yes	yes	yes	yes	yes	5
18	yes	yes	yes	no	yes	yes	yes	6
19	no	yes	yes	no	yes	no	yes	4
20	no	yes	yes	yes	yes	no	yes	5
Total "yes"	2	13	13	10	13	5	14	

The vertical summaries in Table 2.1 enable us to ascertain which features were most likely to appear, and which were least likely to do so. We see that most letters conformed to expectations regarding syntax and vocabulary, as well as those for spelling, typography and layout. In contrast, almost none followed paper letter practice regarding openings and closings.

Let us look now at letters which least conformed to the template. Letter no. 9, shown in Figure 2.6, received a score of 0. It deviated in just about every possible way. Already in the header there is a typo and the writer didn't bother to correct it; instead he added the correction in parentheses.

The letter begins with the informal opening "Hi" (another typo) and has no closing other than the writer's name. It is full of ellipses, the first of which come right at the beginning:

From: S. C. <xxxxxxxx@xxxxxx.xxxxxx.com>
Subject: info on pares,etc(papers that is)
To: msdanet@pluto.mscc.huji.ac.il
Date: Mon, 5 Sep 94 12:37:18 EDT

¡Hi,

just got the email message from the IJVR (?) sorry, only
subscribed recently, and may have inverted letters) re: the
special edition, and the call for papers ...
am quite curious, and could greatly/would greatly appreciate
if you could forward further info....also, anything on some
research in the area - I am working on a new college course
with a colleague, on virtula reality, cyberspace, the virtual
world, and we are looking for data, evcerywhere. She did a
paper last year on the nuances and politicis and culture of
email. . . . its going into a cs journal, shortly; perhaps it
may be modifiable and adaptable to your issue? Also-I noticed
from your letter Prof. Rafaeli's connectionn with bus. admin-
I also treach management, and have been looking for some
extra info to help put together a course proposal forusing
internet to do business research....any suggestions? Ive
found a few syllabi online that are slightly in that area,
but not totally. . .
looking forward to hearing from you,
and best wishes in the new year to all. . .
S. C.
xxxxxxxx@xxxxxx.xxxxxx.com

Figure 2.6. Letter deviating most sharply from the template.

just got the email message from the IJVR (?) sorry, only
subscribed recently, and may have inverted letters) re: the
special edition, and the call for papers. . .

It is nearly one run-on stream of thought, with six instances of . . ., one double dash – , and only one period and one semi-colon in the entire body of the letter. The apostrophe in "it's" is omitted. "Re" is used incorrectly. He wrote "special edition," but he meant "special issue."

This letter mixes formal language appropriate to academic writing and to formal letter-writing generally ("would greatly appreciate if you could forward further"; "perhaps it may be modifiable and adaptable") with spoken collo-quialisms of academics ("did a paper"; "looking for data evcerywhere [sic]"; "put together"). There are no less than eight typos. The journal name (appa-rently, *Computer Science*) is abbreviated and in lower case. Other abbrevia-tions are "info" and "bus. admin." Punctuation is far from standard, mainly because of the profusion of ellipses. Layout is the only criterion on which the letter is fairly conventional; however, because there is no white space between the opening and closing and the body of the letter, I coded this letter "no" on layout too. Perhaps the writer reached the last word and then hit the "send" button. Note that although this letter resembles that of Technosmurf (Figure 2.4) in deviating so sharply from the business letter template, there is no playfulness here.[46]

When I presented this letter in class, one of my students commented that the extreme stream-of-consciousness style may reflect many hours in chat online. It is fairly common in chat for people to produce many typos. They may either not notice them or leave them, even if they do notice them, because of the need to move on. If this person was using a commercial service provider, and had to pay for every minute of use, he might have been constrained by time. Still, it is unlikely in my opinion that lack of an online editor alone could account for the many infelicities of this letter.

In one of the two letters scoring 1, the writer addressed me as FN + LN followed by two dashes, although we have never met and have not had any previous email correspondence. Feeling evidently that it would be presump-tuous to FN me, she chose the compromise sometimes encountered in paper letters too, "Brenda Danet." The closing was also deviant – there was no complimentary close such as "Sincerely." Ellipsis was present in her opening line ("Fascinating subject for a special issue"), and she employed a contraction, conventionally inappropriate in a formal letter ("what's happening"). There-fore she received a "no" on syntax. While there were no typos and she used a capital letter at the beginning of each sentence, she did not capitalize "net" and used this abbreviation instead of "Internet." She did not qualify on punctu-ation either since she used four periods at the end of the text. Neither were layout norms strictly observed. Her name was not on a separate line, though the rest of the material supplied with it was presented flush left, as in a paper

---

```
From: J. R. R. <xxxxx@xxxxxx.xxx.xxx.edu>
Subject: Call for papers for the JCMC
To: msdanet@pluto.mscc.huji.ac.il
Date: Mon, 12 Sep 94 20:58:31 EDT
```

Dear Ms. Danet,

My name is J. R., and I am a graduate student at _____ _____
University. My professor gave me a copy of the mail you sent
out calling for papers for the JCMC. I am currently working
on a paper for my sociolinguistics class that I would like to
submit when it is finished. Will you please send me some
information about the JCMC and the special article which you
are guest-editing.

Thank you very much.

Sincerely,

J. R. R. xxxxx@xxxxxx.xxx.xxx.edu

Figure 2.7. The most traditional response to the Call For Papers.

letter. And she did not leave white space between the body of the letter and her name and affiliation.[47]

Now let us turn to the letters which most conformed to the template. In Figure 2.7 we see the single most traditional response to the CFP in the corpus (score 6, Table 2.1). It contains a conventionally formal opening, pre-closing and closing. All sentences are syntactically well-formed; spelling and typography are standard; the writer has clearly attended to layout, spacing the various parts of the letter in a manner closing approximating a paper letter. The only deviation is the failure to spell out the full name of the journal at least the first time it was mentioned. This person is so careful to maintain a formal style that she uses the rare "Will you please send me some information . . ." instead of "Please send me," etc.

A letter scoring 5 is shown in Figure 2.8. Here, the language is formal, sentences are syntactically well formed, spelling and typography are conven-

```
Date: Wed, 7 Sep 1994 11:52:34 -0700 (PDT)
From: M, B. <xxxxxxx@x.xxxxxxxxxx.edu>
Subject:
To: msdanet@pluto.mscc.huji.ac.il


I am interested in more information concerning the electronic
journal on language and play. I am a doctoral student at the
University of _____ with a masters degree in Performance
Studies from _____ _____ University and have recently
placed a poetry/performance program on the Internet (under
construction until September 15) at
   http://xxxxxxxxxxxxxxxxxxxxxxxxxxxxxxx

Please write to me at your earliest convenience. M. L. B.
```

Figure 2.8. A letter scoring five points.

tional, and there is a traditionally formal pre-closing. This writer lost a point for not putting his name on a separate line, not a very serious departure from the template. This letter is one of the few containing a conventionally formal opening, pre-closing and closing. The second letter scoring five was also largely conventional.

One should not take the differences between letters scoring 4 and 5 too seriously. This becomes evident when we examine the letter in Figure 2.9, by a female graduate student, who scored 4. This letter was unusually long, and showed much evidence of careful planning. Deviations from the template include the lack of an opening, the contraction "I've been working", and run-on information about the writer's status on the signature line. However, sentences are well-formed, some of complex structure, carefully edited into paragraphs.

Lexical choice is quite formal, e.g., "delighted" rather than "happy" or "glad;" "incorporate" rather than "include." Spelling, typography and punctuation are standard. Instead of referring to the folklore list as FOLKLORE-l, she takes pains to call it the "Folklore List." Similarly, she writes out "American Folklore Society." Her use of MOO is acceptable since the full name is hardly ever used, even on the Net. The language is formal in other respects, e.g., the

From: xxxxxxx@xxx.xxxxx.edu (L.M.)
Subject: Language, Play and Performance
To: msdanet@pluto.mscc.huji.ac.il
Date: Mon, 5 Sep 1994 16:41:30 -0400 (EDT)

I was delighted to find your call for papers on the Folklore
List today. I've been working on a paper about language
within the MOO communities, and playfulness and performance
were themes I expect to incorporate as a matter of course in
this work. I have been observing and participating in the
MOOs in an effort to understand how language usage becomes a
mark of membership, and more specifically, the aesthetic and
ethic ideals of the community. I am considering these issues
against the Goffman and Bateson theories of framing and
conversational routines.

A version of this paper will be delivered at the American
Folklore Society's annual conference this October. After that
time, I would like to prepare it for a submission to your
project. I am wondering what other information you can give
me about making such a submission (it will be my first such)
and whether I should consider any particular themes other
than mentioned above.

When I began this research, I had heard that you were very
interested in this topic and made attempts to find you via e-
mail. At the time I was wondering if you had taught any
courses on electronic communication, or had a bibliography to
share. I'd still be very interested in such information if
you have the time to respond.

Sincerely, L. M., graduate student at Department of _____,
University of _____

xxxx@xxxxxxxx (xxxxxxxxxxxxxxxxx)

```
   L.M.              \Time exists so that everything doesn't happen
  xxxxx.edu          \all at once, while Space exists so that
folklorist-storyteller-\everything doesn't happen to you!
producer
```

Figure 2.9. A Letter Scoring Four Points.

passive in "A version of this paper will be delivered." There is even a conventional closing.

However, this letter includes a playful signature file ending with an exclamation point (hence it was coded "no" for punctuation). The sig file gives us information about the writer's occupation and interests, rather than supplying her institutional affiliation ("folklorist-storyteller-producer"). The right half of the sig file contains an evocative, playful saying. At the same time, perhaps we should not make too much of this (or any other) sig file, since it might have been appended automatically.

A second letter scoring five also mostly conformed to the template. The writer first gave the names of a journal and of a scholarly association in full, and only then abbreviated them. Especially notable was the presence of a systematic list in this letter. The only departure from the template was the unexpectedly very colloquial pre-pre-closing:

```
I've rattled on long enough. . . I hope to hear from you soon.
```

Openings and Closings

We have already seen from in Table 2.1 that the greatest departures from the template were in openings and closings. The complete set is presented in Figure 2.10. Thirteen persons felt the need for an opening, but they used no less than 11 different openings, which fall naturally into four categories:[48] (1) formal, traditional ones ("Dear Ms. Danet" or "Dear Professor Danet"); (2) forms which try to maintain etiquette while being a bit more informal ("Greetings"), or use my full name; (3) informal greetings ordinarily appropriate to face-to-face and telephone conversation, or personal letters ("hi" or "hello," with or without FN); (4) no opening. The letters were spread across all these options.[49] Note that no one combined "hi" or "hello" with "Ms. Danet" or "Professor Danet," (unlike Technosmurf or Alessandro Duranti's 1985 students).

Pre-closings and closings were extremely diverse too. As we saw in Table 2.1, few people used a closing. However, most used some type of pre-closing, ranging from the very formal "I hope to hear from you soon" or "I look forward to your reply" to the informal "Thanks!" or "Regards." We already learned in Table 2.1 that only two writers were consistent in choosing a formal opening and closing. Figure 2.10 adds that three letters were consistently informal. Another three consistently omitted both an opening and a closing. The rest were inconsistent. Clearly, this is a situation of great variability.[50]

Opening	Pre-Closing/Closing
(1) Dear Professor Danet,	I hope to hear from you soon. Sincerely,
(2) Dear Ms. Danet,	Thank you very much
(3) Ms. Danet –	I look forward to your reply
(4) Ms. Danet,	Thanks!
(5) Dear Brenda Danet,	Regards,
(6) Greetings;	Thank you,
(7) Brenda Danet –	_____
(8) _____	Please write to me at your earliest convenience.
(9) _____	Thank you for your work in this area.
(10) _____	Sincerely,
(11) _____	_____
(12) ¡Hi,	looking forward to hearing from you, and best wishes in the new year to all. . .
(13) Dear Brenda	Greetings
(14) Hi,	Thanks!
(15) _____	_____
(16) Hi Brenda,	Thanks,
(17) _____ .	Thanks,
(18) _____	_____
(19) Hello,	_____
(20) Brenda:	Thanks.

Figure 2.10. Openings and closings in 20 letters.

Signature Files

Six letters included a sig file. Two were totally serious and referential, resembling business cards. On the other hand, four were quite playful (Figure 2.11). In the first of these, an otherwise entirely serious, well-formed letter, the full name and email address were included on one line, followed by an enigmatically playful saying, "I offer you tea in perfect imperfection!" The second example is a complex typographic composition that not only cites the person's department and institutional affiliation, but presents him as "Guerilla Semiotician,"[51] and cites Johan Huizinga's (1955) *Homo Ludens*, with a corrupted version of its subtitle, "Culture as a form of Play." It also includes a Latin saying, *Cerebrum quaerit, caveat lector. Caveat lector* is evidently a play on *caveat emptor*, "Let the buyer beware." *Cerebrum* literally means "brain," but can also be read figuratively as "wisdom, understanding." The expression can be translated as "He seeks understanding, reader beware." However, a

```
M____ C_____, xxxxxxxx@xxxxxxx.xxx.se
I offer you tea in perfect imperfection!
```

```
|:   N____ p C____    :| // Dept. of Anthropology, _____ State Univ. |
<xxxxxxxx@xxxxxxx.xxx.edu>//      Cerebrum quaerit, caveat lector.     |
|  Guerilla Semiotician  |/----------------------=---------------------|
->pgp key by arrangement/|  Homo ludens:  Culture as a form of Play    !
```

```
xxxx@mediaMOO (purple-crayon.media.mit.edu 8888)
          L__ M____          \ Time exists so that everything doesn't happen
xxxxxxx@xxxx.xxx.xxxx.edu     \ all at once, while Space exists so that
folklorist-storyteller-producer  \ everything doesn't happen to you!
```

```
EMAIL: xxxxx@xxxxx.org (NeXTmail accepted) OR xxxxxxxxxxxx@xxxxxx.ac.uk
              WWW:   http://xxxxx.org/~xxxxx/
          . The Universe before the big bang (acutal size)


          S____ A. M____, B.A., Hons. (Exon)
              "Social Impact of Technology"
```

Figure 2.11. Playful signature files in responses to an online Call For Papers.

more feasible reading is, "He seeks (needs) a brain, reader beware."[52] There is also some play with typographic symbols, especially in the long line of dashes in the middle.

As for the third example in Figure 2.11, we have already encountered its evocative saying. There is a bit of play with typography here too – the back slashes marking off the saying from the rest of the file. The fourth example contains the amusing line

```
. The Universe before the big bang (acutal size)
```

This is a clever bit of play with the tiniest typographic symbol.[53]

It is noteworthy that at least three of these four sig files appeared in letters written by students, people whose professional identity was not formed.[54] In contrast, the examples containing only factual material occurred in letters from established academics. This hints that younger, less established academics may come to use a semi-playful sig file even in the most formal situations, reflecting a new norm that one can be serious and playful at the same time.[55]

Influence of the Topic?

It is possible that the topic of the CFP and personal dispositions of writers may have influenced them. Could it be that people who were attracted to the research topic of playful performance in digital communication were also likely to use an oral or playful style themselves? Might they have sensed that, given my interest in the topic, it could be acceptable to write in such a style? The fact that most people tried to conform to most of the template argues otherwise.

Mindful, nevertheless, of this possibility, I did consider comparing this corpus with another email corpus, but this did not prove feasible. In 1998 I wrote to all later guest editors of issues of the *Journal of Computer-mediated Communication*, in the hope of obtaining a comparable corpus on a more neutral topic. Unfortunately, either they had not saved the material, had changed institutions and had lost access to the account where the material had been stored, or they had mainly initiated contact with their authors.[56]

From Business Letter to Expressive Conversation

Research on the language of email to date has been synchronic. It has usually been based on analysis of letters from a given time period, and is therefore unable to inform us as to change over time among the same individuals. What happens over time to those who attempt initially to conform to the old norms? This question is especially important in a period of technological transition. Might experience with the medium, especially with others using a more informal style, "corrupt" writers, fostering a stylistic change in the direction of increased expressivity and informality? We had a hint of this possibility in the two letters conveying holiday wishes at the beginning of the chapter.

To address these issues in greater depth, I now analyze a prolonged exchange of messages I had with a software developer whom I have never met in person. Over a period of nine months, from November 1993 to August 1994, I exchanged about 25 messages with D.G., the developer of a program for bibliography database management.[57] In November 1993, I wrote to him to obtain information about the software.

Personal Style

In his first letter to me D.G. mostly maintained a formal style. It contained a salutation, the body of the letter, and his name and affiliation in place of a traditional signature. Syntax, spelling and typography were conventional. There was, however, no closing. His salutation consisted merely of my first name and two dashes, and he signed with his full name preceded by two dashes.[58] The layout of the letter strongly resembled that of a paper letter, with double spaces left between the salutation and the body of the letter, and with double spaces left between the salutation and the body of the letter, and between it and his name and organization. This practice was maintained in all his letters to me. White space was left between paragraphs, as well.

My response contained many compromises with traditional norms;[59] from the start, I adopted a more informal style than did D.G. The salutation, the body of my letter, and the pseudo-signature were all run-on as one single-spaced text, with no double spaces left to frame the body of the letter. I greeted him with an "oral" or telephonic "hello." Three times, I introduced the use of ellipses, a feature which we have seen is common in written representations of oral style.[60]

I also introduced the first exclamation point ("P____[61] sounds great!"), and the first use of asterisks for emphasis, thus enhancing the speech-like quality of the message. Also, I employed a colloquial expression common to Net culture ("snail mail" for regular paper mail), and introduced the first instances of ellipsis ("haven't been using it"; "Hope to hear from you soon"), writing-specific features which recur in email, as noted above.

Increased Expressivity over Time

D. G. was slow to "loosen up "but eventually did so. In a letter to me dated 9 February 1994 all was still conventional, except for his use of "nifty", a colloquial expression which he probably would not have used in a paper letter:

```
it [P____] even comes with a very nifty Windows icon of its
own.
```

My very next letter to him, written the same day, was particularly dialogic. Having decided to order the software, I opened with

```
OK: let's go for it!
```

as if we were chatting, face-to-face.

On 16 February 1994, D.G. wrote to say that the software was on its way to me. In this short letter he used exclamation points twice, heightening the emotional tone of his message for the very first time. I acknowledged receipt of this message with a short one of my own, and in it, I introduced the first smiley:

```
Hi D____: Glad to hear from you. . . And I look forward to learning
to use P_____. . . I'm sure we'll be in touch again.
Brenda :-)
```

Several weeks had passed, and I was feeling very guilty that I still had not sent payment for the software. Toward the end of a very long message, I wrote:

```
I will send the check this week. As you may remember, I have to
go to my bank to get a bank check made; if I had an American
checking account, I could just pop a check in the mail. . . but
life is harder in the Middle East. . .
```

This latter comment introduces material that is to some extent irrelevant to our transaction, though I am trying to explain how objective circumstances prevent me from doing the right thing.[62]

The next day, things changed dramatically. I had been working on the import of references from a database originally created using another program, and had encountered serious difficulties. I sent D.G. a very long letter of complaint. While this letter was mostly very proper in its communication strategies, I gave vent to my anger and disappointment in a mode straight from the comics:

```
Now those specifications will have to be typed all over again.
#%$*&#!!!!!
```

Never in my pre-digital letter-writing life would I have employed typographic symbols in a business letter in this way!

The most interesting development of all occurred in late March 1994. I had still not sent D.G. the check, and several times, in different letters, had mentioned the upcoming Passover holiday. On March 26 I wrote, saying that I had been sick with the flu, and that the holiday would prevent me from obtaining and sending the check and the diskettes containing my database, which he was supposed to reformat for importation into P____. Here is his brief reply:

```
Send the disks now, send the check whenever it's convenient.
Locusts, frogs, blood, bureaucrats. . . .
```

In several respects, this message is remarkable. Although D.G.'s last name had given away to me the fact that he is Jewish, he had never before openly acknowledged that we shared a common identity. After I had mentioned Passover several times, in a letter dated 26 March 1994, he had written, "I hope your Passover is going well." However, this could be construed as merely sending good wishes for my holiday, not ours.

Now, two days later, D.G. finally explicitly acknowledged our common heritage, in surprisingly poeticized fashion. At the substantive level, he tells me to send the disks right away so he can continue with the job, and that I don't have to worry about payment; the check can be sent later. This message contains multiple parallelism – "the foregrounding of certain aspects of text or discourse by the introduction of extra regularities, not called for by the basic rules of language" (Leech 1969: 64). D.G.'s message contains both "horizontal" and "vertical" forms of parallelism. The two halves of the first line contrast "disks" and "check, "now" and the implied "later." It is serendipitous that "disks" and "check" are one-syllable words each containing /k/. The second line can also be divided into two halves, each of which contain two elements – "locusts, frogs" vs. "blood, bureaucrats." The dry referentiality of the first line contrasts sharply with the surprising, poetic/expressive second line. This is vertical parallelism.

Most interesting of all, in the second line, perhaps puzzling for some readers, D.G. conflates material from the Haggadah, the text that is read aloud at the traditional Passover Seder, with information about my current situation. Probably the most famous portion of the Seder is the recitation of the Ten Plagues, the ten afflictions that God brought down on the Egyptians for their treatment of the Jews, before the Jews' departure for the Promised Land. Only a "member of the tribe" would have this in-group knowledge. Locusts, frogs and blood are three of the ten plagues mentioned in the original text, but they do not appear in the standard order in D.G.'s letter. The order in the original is: "Blood, frogs, lice, swarms of wild beasts, pestilence, boils, hail, locusts, darkness, death of the first born." Traditionally, in a high point of the Seder ceremony, each item in the list is pronounced by all at the table, slowly and dramatically. As each item is recited, all dip their little finger into their wine and then create a drop of wine on their plates, to accompany the utterance.

Obviously, bureaucrats are not in the original list of plagues – though they are a plague of modern life! D.G. intuitively changed the order of the three plagues mentioned in his letter for poetic purposes. Notice also that "blood" and "bureaucrats" both begin with /b/, thus introducing alliteration to the expression.

The addition of "bureaucrats" preserves the list-like structure of the original text and recalls the mode of its performance. Both lines also show evidence of what is known as the "principle of end-weight:" the latter half of a two-part parallel structure contains more phonetic material than the former, thereby contributing to a sense of weight or closure (Danet 1984; Herrnstein-Smith 1968).

In a follow-up letter, I continued the language game:

```
>Locusts, frogs, blood, bureaucrats, . . .
Well, locusts and frogs, blood, etc. are behind us ;-) -but
bureaucrats are not.
```

Soon after that, D.G. was relaxed enough to begin the body of a message with "ok" and to mention that he is "too exhausted to type it all into this message tonight" – thus revealing information about his bodily state at a late hour.

```
Okay, the same format works for the _____ files and for _____.
I'm too exhausted to type it all into this message tonight, but
tomorrow I'll start my day by preparing and mailing your disks,
and providing a detailed e-mail message with full instructions.
```

Finally, in the last letter, he wrote to notify me that he had completed the technical job for me. This message contained an entirely expressive subject line: "Ta-Da!" something like a ceremonial drum-roll or trumpet fanfare.

There is no way of knowing to what extent my own style actually influenced D.G., though at least some of the changes I have noted do seem to suggest this. It is possible that experience with many email correspondents and not just myself was beginning to have an impact. One thing is certain, however: D.G. had come a long way from the quite formal business letter I first received from him. More important, the poeticized line, "Locusts, frogs, blood, bureaucrats" was not directly inspired by anything in my informal style. Unexpectedly, he later wrote to me on 12 October 1998, after having discovered an earlier online version of this chapter, including my analysis of his treatment of the Ten Plagues. I learned only then that he had received a prize for poetry in college. Perhaps not everyone has the potential for this creativity. This case study suggests not that every emailer can become a poet, but that, at least for those that have the talent, the new medium fosters forms of creativity which had been suppressed in the letter-writing tradition of scribal and print culture.

Comparison with *84, Charing Cross Road*

Even in paper letters, extended communication between strangers can, of course, become more informal over time, as the parties feel that they are getting to know each other. I am thinking of *84, Charing Cross Road* (Hanff 1990), the famous correspondence between Helene Hanff, an American writer, and an English bookseller called Frank Doel, over a period of 20 years. Hanff developed a close personal relationship with Doel without ever meeting him in person. A play and film were created from the book. Anne Bancroft played Helene Hanff in the film, and Anthony Hopkins was Doel.

Hanff's very first letter to the London bookstore (dated 5 October 1949) was entirely conventional, but she soon adopted a much more informal, style, unusually expressive and occasionally even outrageous. For instance, after receiving an edition of the Bible which did not please her, and skipping all preliminaries, she wrote:

WHAT KIND OF A BLACK PROTESTANT BIBLE IS THIS?

Kindly inform the Church of England they have loused up the most beautiful prose ever written, whoever told them to tinker with the Vulgate Latin? They'll burn for it, you mark my words. (Hanff, 1970: 5)

With typical British reserve, Doel regularly signed his letters "FPD, For MARKS & Co." Only when Hanff provoked him to identify himself by writing "FPD, whoever you are" (Hanff 1990: 7), did he begin signing his full name, in December 1949. After two-and-a-half years of correspondence, he finally addressed her by her first name. Only a full eight years after the correspondence had begun did he sign his first name alone.

The eccentric Ms. Hanff, unusually expressive and informal even for an American, often wrote letters which sounded like spoken monologues. Consider the one abridged in Figure 2.12. Sharing her annoyance at a friend who had given her an edition of works of John Donne and William Blake which does not please her, she opens her letter

Both the unconventional way of noting the date and the dialogic opening make this letter sound like the middle of a face-to-face conversation. Other devices are the use of capital letters ("You've GOT to help me"), colloquialisms ("boys" for "men," "authors", "writers"), and her typographically eccentric signature ("yrs, h. hffffffffffffffff").

In the case of email, not only personality and culture, but also the novel medium influences our choices. Because it fosters informality, it can facilitate changes of style and substance in a matter of days or weeks which would have taken years, if at all, in the case of paper letters.

Implications

Culture vs. Technology

Although I have argued that the new medium invites informality even in business or official contexts, it would be a great mistake to attribute too much to the effect of technology per se. Rather, I believe that the new technology is strengthening, or converging with, a general cultural trend, which was already in place.

To begin with, Douglas Biber and Edward Finegan documented "historical drift" in a number of genres of English, including personal and professional

Sunday night and a hell of a way to start 1960

I don't know, frankie –

Somebody gave me this book for Christmas. It's a Giant Modern Library book.
Did you ever see one of those? It's less attractively bound than the Proceedings of
the New York State Assembly and it weighs more. It was given to me by a gent who
knows I'm fond of John Donne. The title of this book is:

The Complete Poetry
        &
Selected Prose
        of
JOHN DONNE
        &
The Complete Poetry
        of
WILLIAM BLAKE?

The question mark is mine. Will you please tell me what those two boys have in
common?. . .

. . . I don't like Blake anyway, he swoons too much, it's Donne I'm writing about, I am
being driven clear up the wall, Frankie, you have GOT to help me.

. . . So break it to me gently: how hard is it going to be to find me John Donne's
Complete Sermons and how much is it going to cost?
I am going to bed. I will have hideous nightmares involving huge monsters in
academic robes carrying long bloody butcher knives labelled Excerpt, Selection,
Passage and Abridged.

            yrs,
           h. hffffffffffffff

Figure 2.12. Letter from Helene Hanff to Frank Doel, New Year's Eve, 1960.

letters. Analyzing samples of texts on six dimensions of linguistic variation, they found that over the last three centuries these genres have been moving in an "oral" direction (Biber and Finegan 1988; 1989). With respect to letters, their research radically under-estimates the changes. Letters representing the "modern" period in their research were written between 1865 and 1950 (!), and included exemplars from well-known professional authors – a fact which may have biased the results toward a more literary style than was typical of the general public.

In a 1982 paper written largely before the advent of computers, Robin Lakoff developed the thesis that

> in the past couple of millennia. . . at least in written media. . . the assumption has been made that the written form of communication is basic, is more valid than the oral, and that even originally oral discourse must be represented in terms of the rules of written communication to be valid and intelligible. But in the last generation or so, there is much to suggest that this position is being reversed; that the oral medium is considered more valid and intelligible. . . than the written, and that even written documents are now tending to be couched in forms imitative of the oral mode. (Lakoff 1982: 240)

To illustrate her point, Lakoff cited, for instance, the speech-like literary style of authors such as Tom Wolfe,[63] and the decline in prestige of the perfectly composed, non-spontaneous political speech. Seventeen years later, Deborah Tannen confirmed this view, in comments on Al Gore's rhetorical style during his campaign for the Democratic nomination for President:

> Being a great communicator in the age of television does not mean being an orator . . . Oratory in our age is conversational . . . President Clinton thrives in televised town hall meetings because he can talk to hundreds of people and sound like a friend who just pulled out a chair at your kitchen table to have a chat. (Tannen 1999).

Another development not mentioned by Lakoff was the Plain Language movement, which flourished in the United States and Britain in the late 1970s. This movement called for the reform of legal and bureaucratic language to make it more comprehensible to laypersons. Although language reformers did not expressly set out to make documents more like speech, this was, in fact, the effect of the changes they introduced. In revisions of bureaucratic and legal forms, they preferred active to passive verbs, and verbs with first and second person pronouns instead of nominalizations. For instance, in the reform of a bank loan form the expression, "If you don't pay" was substituted for "In the event of default in the payment of this or any other obligation" (cf. Danet, 1980).[64]

Lakoff also suggested that the electronic media are having an impact. Long years of exposure to films and television have partially reinstated the prominence of speech that characterized oral cultures. A similar point was made by Walter Ong, with his concept of "secondary orality" (Ong 1982: 136–138.[65]

The increased salience of speech lurking "behind" writing is also discernible in the print media. During 1996–97 I followed the style of op-ed articles by Thomas L. Friedman in the New York Times. Excerpts from five of his articles appear in Figure 2.13. These articles are peppered with "oralisms" and related devices which deviate from the model of purely serious, transparent prose. He uses repetition ("nothing – nothing"), capital letters ("VERY, VERY IMPORTANT"), the colloquial "sure," wordplay ("throwing out the bathwater with the Bibi"),[66] eccentric, speech-like spelling ("baaaaaaack"), "well" as the very first word of an article, and the colloquial "So I was thinking. . ." to begin another, as if picking up the strands of an ongoing dialogue.

The titles of several of the articles are very playful too. "Eyeless in Hebron" is a play on "eyeless in Gaza," an expression in the poem "Samson Agonistes" by the 17th-century poet John Milton. Contemporary Gaza and Hebron have been (along with Jerusalem) "the eye of the storm," both major centers of the Arab–Israeli conflict. "Pulp Fiction" is a recycling of the title of a contemporary film and points to the mock memo to Friedman's literary agent proposing a novel about Saddam Hussein. The colloquial expression "Have I Got a Deal for You" is unusual in writing and in such a context. While Friedman's style certainly does not characterize the New York Times as a whole, the fact that he repeatedly used such a style with tacit support from the Times contributes toward its legitimation.[67]

A *New York Times* advertisement for theater and dance events at New York's City Center, which also appeared during the period studied, contained a striking oralism too. In bold letters, the advertisement shouted: "Fuhggeddaboutit! There's no way you'll find a more exciting fall than City Center's."

Analyses by Naomi Baron (1998a; 1998b; 2000) of the role of ideology versus technology in shaping writing in the age of email come to similar conclusions, via a different route. In a review of the history of the teaching of writing in American education, she shows that there have been ideological transformations regarding appropriate subjects for student compositions, the importance of grammatical correctness, and thinking about the extent to which writing is monologue or dialogue. Curriculum reform at Harvard University had great influence around the United States:

> Instead of learning a rhetorically based imitation of classical style whose goal was to expound on abstract themes, college students were asked to formulate their own observations of individual daily experiences. While the required medium was writing,

"Eyeless in Hebron" (30 October 1996)

. . . There is nothing – *nothing* – that Mr. Netanyahu could tell the Israeli religious right, which helped him get elected, that would make this proposed Israeli withdrawal from Hebron acceptable to them. . .

. . . The fact that Mr. Netanyahu is ready to go ahead with it anyway, if he can get the security terms he is seeking, is *VERY, VERY IMPORTANT* [capitals, italics in original].

"The Arab Burden" (20 November 1996)

. . . But Egypt has to help. *Sure*, it's easy now for Arab leaders to generate support at home by pummeling Mr. Netanyahu. Because of the high-handed way he tends to deal with Arabs, he really agitates them, right down to the man in the street. He's now a popular target. Egypt's very able Foreign Minister, Amr Moussa, is the most popular diplomat in the Arab world today, precisely because of the way that he has been bashing Mr. Netanyahu – without ever saying a good word for the rest of Israel, or encouraging the peace coalition that still exists there. This has got to stop. It's cheap. It's counter-productive and *it's throwing out the bathwater with the Bibi* [italics added].

"Pulp Fiction" (4 September 1997)

MEMO TO: My Literary Agent

Dear agent:

You recall last summer I sent you a proposal for a novel about how Saddam Hussein was deftly using his relationship with the U.N. to influence oil prices . . .

Well, he's baaaaaaack [italics added].

"Cover Story" (16 October 1997)

Well, Prime Minister Benjamin Netanyahu had good news and bad news this week . . . " [italics added]

"Have I Got a Deal for You" (20 October 1997)

So I was thinking about buying an office building in Shanghai. You know, something with lots of glass and steel to impress my friends. To do it right, I thumbed through the latest Jones Lang Wootton research on the state of the Asian-Pacific real estate market. I was surprised. There was a lot to *choose from*. The vacancy rate for Shanghai office buildings was 32 percent, and many more new buildings were coming up. I checked out Beijing; the vacancy rate there was 33 percent. *So I checked out bangkok, Thailand. Same story as China* [italics added].

Figure 2.13. "Oralisms" and other devices in op-ed articles by Thomas I. Friedman in the *New York Times*, 1996–97.

the redefined theme opened the door to what would become in the decades that followed the expression of a personal voice. And over time, the expression of that voice, although in writing, came to sound more and more like speech. (Baron 1998b: 42)

A complementary development within academia in the 1980s and 1990s was the trend to move away from the "scientific," ostensibly objective prose of positivist social science, toward a postmodern style which acknowledged the personal voice of the author and the role of social processes in the construction of "facts."[68]

A More Personal Business Style

In the light of these trends, it is not surprising to discover that some authors of recent manuals for writers of business letters – paper letters – encouraged their readers to write in a somewhat more informal style. Thus, the opening paragraph of one such manual for business people begins:

> Second to grammatical correctness, achieving an appropriate business style may be the biggest problem for the writer of business letters. A sure sign of an inexperienced writer. . . is the obvious attempt to sound too "business- like."
>
> As per your request, please find enclosed herewith a check in the amount of $16.49.
>
> Such expressions as "herewith" and "as per" contribute nothing to the message while making the letter sound stilted and stiff.
>
> The first step, then, to writing successful business correspondence is to relax. While business letters will vary in tone from familiar to formal, they should all sound natural. Within the limits of standard English. . . you should try to say things in a "regular" way:
>
> As you requested, I am enclosing a check for $16.49.
>
> (Geffner,1995: 1)

Like the bureaucratic and legal documents whose language was simplified by Plain Language Reformers, this author's revision changes a nominalization to an active verb ("your request" vs. "you requested") and a passive construction to an active one ("please find enclosed" vs. "I am enclosing"). To refer to "you" and "I" is, once again, to bring the formulation closer to speech.[69]

Email and Changes in the Academic and Business Registers

Consider the unique sig file of a professor at a southern American university, who flaunts her rebellion against the requirements of conventional typography and spelling:

I DO NOT CORRECT EMAIL TPYOS [sic]. THAT WOULD DEFEAT THE PURPOSE OF EMAIL.[70]

Although I personally sympathize with this person's willingness to "go" with the new medium, ultimately, we cannot expect normative expectations regarding these matters to disappear altogether. To understand why, we need to attend to the concept of register.

Sociolinguists and ethnographers of communication use the concept of register to point to language variation by context of situation. Two recent definitions of register are "a language variety viewed with respect to its context of use" (Biber and Finegan 1994, Introduction: 4), and "a variety of language defined according to its use in social situations" (Crystal 1991); cited in (Biber and Finegan 1994, Introduction: 4). Charles Ferguson (1994) identified the basic working assumption implicit in the study of register variation:

> A communication situation that recurs regularly in a society (in terms of participants, setting, communicative functions, and so forth) will tend over time to develop identifying markers of language structure and language use, different from the language of other communication situations. (Ferguson 1994: 20)

One may speak not only of a formal versus an informal register, but of registers associated with different occupations and spheres, e.g., the legal and the medical registers.[71] Compared to these registers, however, the academic register has been much less studied. Research on academic discourse has mainly paid attention to written text types, rather than to spoken ones. In particular the features of "scientific" discourse, e.g., in journal articles, have been extensively studied.[72] Other registers are notable for being forms of simplified language, e.g., baby talk (Ferguson 1964; 1977), sports talk (Ferguson 1983; Romaine 1994), and ham radio talk (Gibbon 1981; 1985). It is evident that within many registers there are usually both spoken and written text-types. Now, with the advent of email and other forms of digital communication, we need to make room for digital text-types too, e.g., within the two spheres discussed here, the academic and business ones.

Until now, researchers have tended to speak of "the language of email" or "the language of computer-mediated communication" in monolithic fashion. An influential paper by Kathleen Ferrara and her associates (Ferrara et al. 1991), cited earlier, coined the term "interactive written discourse" for what they saw as an emergent register of the English language. They pointed to similarities between this language and simplified registers like the ones mentioned above – baby talk and sports announcer talk. However, the notion of register is typically applied to substantive domains of human communication and action – not to all communication in a medium per se, as Ferrara, et al. do.

It is useful to think in terms of spectral models of communication, to use Naomi Baron's (1998a; 2000) term, rather than dichotomous models which too sharply contrast speech and writing. In such an approach, there is room for speech-like digital text-types as well as writing-like ones.[73] My focus on first letters in the academic context is thus an attempt to make room for private, relatively formal email text-types, some of which will not resemble Baron's profile:

> Email is informal.
> Email helps develop a level conversational playing field.
> Email encourages personal disclosure.
> Email can become emotional ("flaming"). (Baron 1998a: 147)

There will be text-types in which writers allow themselves to relax spelling and typographic requirements, but others where they will be suppressed, and writing will mostly conform to older models. The various text-types will not form a unilinear continuum between the "writing"-like ones and the "speech"-like ones.

Consider a message I sent to a member of my research group the night before a conference that I had organized about the Internet (Figure 2.15). Written at 1:30 AM when I was exhausted, this message is not at all "oral" except for the informal, dialogic opening, "hi. yes, it's already Sunday." But neither does it closely conform to the template of the standard official letter. It is written in all lower case, contains many instances of ellipsis, an abbreviation ("pls"), and, surprisingly, given how tired I was, just one typo. Written under duress to a person I know well, it most resembles a telegram. The emergent repertoire of academic text-types will make room for this type of message too.

"Leakage" in Email Style

One way to interpret the material presented in this chapter is via the concept of "style leakage."[74] Letter writers in both corpora no doubt bring their primary experiences to the task of composition. Thus, younger people, especially students, having grown up in a relatively informal cultural climate in which informal speech patterns had been influencing uses of writing even before computers, and who have had relatively little experience with writing generally, might therefore use a speech-like style. Older academics, on the other hand, with much experience with the business letter template and style, no doubt brought this experience to their letters. Thus, previous experience with the template might take precedence over exposure to an increasingly informal cultural climate. The notion of style leakage suggests that Technosmurf mixed street style, his dominant mode of communication, with a sprinkling of features

---

```
Date: Jun 11 01:37:06 1995
To: _____
From: msdanet@pluto.mscc.huji.ac.il (brenda danet)
Subject: Sunday


hi. . yes it's already Sunday…exhausted, really pushing hard.

have to be at univ for computer check probably early

afternoon, reception at 7. will want to be home by 5 latest

to get ready. plan to come, I guess, at 4:30 or I may not be

here (phone first if earlier??)

pls bring 1-2 printed copies of the virtual virtuoso paper; I

guess y already wrote to ask this; it's for the report due

Thursday. thanks, b.
```

Figure 2.15. A letter written under duress.

only poorly internalized from written letter-writing tradition. Whatever the explanation in his particular case, these thoughts reinforce my argument that the language of email was in a state of transition as we approached the millennium.

Some Predictions

I have generally avoided predictions in this book. The one topic for which I think it is safe to do so is the language of email. The material presented in this chapter suggests the following predictions:

1. Informal, partially speech-like email style will increasingly characterize public as well as personal two-person communication. Differences between official and personal letters will become less sharp than they have been in the past. In particular, openings and closings are likely to be less formal than in the past.
2. Normative expectations will change to provide increased legitimation for this style.
3. At the same time, there will be greater variation within public-official email in the future than was tolerated in the past in paper letters. While much communication will be far more informal than in the past, in certain

situations adherence to practices associated with paper letter-writing will persist, notably in first letters, to persons of higher status than oneself, to strangers, and where the stakes are high for the writer.

4. As email matures as a medium, different text-types will come to have differing degrees of normatively approved formality. Some text-types will be normatively informal, at least in certain respects, and others will be formal, continuing to resemble parallel formal text-types on paper.

5. Younger people, who have not deeply internalized the norms of traditional letter-writing, and who have had little practice applying them, will more quickly adopt the new style than older persons, even when writing to strangers, to persons of higher status than themselves, and even in first letters. They will do so with little ambivalence or uncertainty, and will feel comfortable introducing playful material, e.g., a signature file, even when the rest of the letter is in a serious frame.

Playful performance has been only a secondary theme in this chapter. I turn now to a full-fledged study of playful performance in online parodies of Shakespeare's *Hamlet* and *Macbeth* on IRC.

Notes

1. See http://www.youvegotmail.com/.

2. The term "business" letter has been used in the past both to refer generically to public, official or non-personal letters, e.g., between a municipal agency and a citizen, and more narrowly, to correspondence in the private, profit-making sector. For the most part, I will use "business" to refer to official or public letters. The second corpus, of correspondence with a software developer, belongs to the business domain in the narrower sense, since I was a potential customer of this man. I am grateful to Naomi Baron for calling to my attention the need to clarify this point.

3. Letter-writing manuals have existed in the West since the Middle Ages. The first treatise on epistolary rhetoric was written at the end of the 11th century by the Benedictine monk Alberic of Monte Cassino. Within 20 years, religious letter-writing rhetoric became secularized and was introduced into Bolognese polite society. By the mid-12th century it spread to Orleans, and from these two centers to the rest of Europe (Boureau 1997: 36–38). See also Murphy (1974: 194–268) and Constable (1976), both cited by Boureau. Manuals continued to flourish into the 19th century and our own times (Chartier et al. 1997).

4. I refer not to signature files, which are discussed below, but to typing one's name. Of course, to some extent, adding one's name may be a habit from pre-email correspondence.

5. For a discussion of some interesting exceptions to the rule, see Danet (1997b). I note, for instance, that when signing letters on their bosses' behalf, secretaries typically

added their initials to signal that this is not the actual handwriting of the sender, but done at his/her instructions.

6. In a very early study of email, Alessandro Duranti (1986) offered the insight that the subject line runs counter to the spontaneity of personal messages. Delineating one's topic requires more planning than is typical of informal messages, at least in the past.

7. See, e.g., Myers (1993); De Vries (1994); Geffner (1995) for American examples, and Elliot (1990) for a British one.

8. This formulation appears on the jacket of the book.

9. By decrying even commercial greeting cards in the case of condolence, she implicitly ruled out email in this case too. And she ignored the possibility of email invitations or announcing the birth of a new baby by email.

10. The issue of what media can be used appropriately for ritual communication is a central theme of Chapter 4.

11. Like authors of all such manuals, the source of the authority of these writers is evidently their own personal opinions.

12. Like many email correspondents, both experienced and not so experienced, M.G. had not bothered to change the subject line from previous correspondence in the first letter. This was because instead of initiating a new letter, he took the path of locating one from me and hitting the "reply" button.

13. M.G.'s comment that the formal opening is "meant to differentiate this message from all other messages" has two resonances. It acknowledges that ritual language is usually supposed to be different from ordinary language, more formal; second, this is a veiled reference to a line in the *Haggadah*, the text performed orally at the Passover Seder, when the youngest male present at the table asks the traditional Four Questions, beginning, "Why is this night different from all other nights?"

14. *Hag Sameach* means "happy holiday" in Hebrew.

15. On the notion of text types, see Biber (1989).

16. See the introduction for a fuller explication of this argument.

17. There were other signs of uncertain adaptation to a new medium, e.g., inconsistent patterns of reference to the message – a "letter," an "e-message," or an "email."

18. This does not mean, however, that a speech-like writing style was valued. On the contrary, polished, planned, eloquent writing was highly valued. See, e.g., comments by Robin Lakoff about Boswell's representation of the speech of Samuel Johnson, in Lakoff (1982: 243–244).

19. Michael Hancher brought to my attention the frequency of mid-19th century mail delivery in London and the Browning correspondence.

20. I make no attempt to include every finding but merely to summarize the highlights of this research. See, e.g., Eklundh (1986); Eklundh and Macdonald (1994); Duranti (1986); Schaefermeyer and Sewell (1988); Ferrara, et al. (1991); Murray (1991); Wilkins (1991); Sims and Guice (1991); Yates and Orlikowski (1993); Porter (1993); Lindeborg (1993); Spinuzzi (1994); Uhlirova (1994); Maynor (1994); Horowitz and Barchilon (1994); Baldwin (1996); Collot and Belmore (1992; 1996); Yates (1996); Lee (1996); Spooner and Yancey (1996); Davis and Brewer (1997); Rice

(1997); Moran and Hawisher (1998); Cho (in press); Georgakopoulou (in press). For an extended summary of the features of email, that is complementary to this chapter in many ways, see Baron (1998a; 2000). The papers by Cho and Georgakopoulou, in a volume edited by Susan Herring (in press), were not available to me when this manuscript was completed.

21. Email software typically marks citations with right-pointing angle brackets appearing at the left of the quoted material. In some software citation is automatic.

22. The list of features in Figure 2.3 does not include other basic elements, such as the date and address of the recipient; these are of no research interest in this chapter since variation in their presentation is not significant.

23. These abbreviations mean First Name + Last Name.

24. There are, in fact, many more specifications in the business letter template, such as the "inside address," the full address of the addressee, which conventionally precedes the opening, the dateline, the signer's identification, material supplied below the signature to identify the sender, etc. For an explication of the full template, see, e.g., Geffner (1995), Chapter 2. For present purposes, the elements in Figure 2.3 suffice.

25. I learned from 1999 sales data on these books at Amazon.com that Hale and especially the Angell and Heslop volume had sold quite well. *Wired Style* was still in print, and a second edition was in press. Of course, the majority of new emailers did not rush out to buy these books, and sales figures cannot tell us whether these books influenced people in any way.

26. They caution that a more formal closing may be called for in international email, i.e., if the addressee is a member of a traditionally more formal culture.

27. Actually, Rose contradicted himself, advising readers on the very same page both to abbreviate when possible, and, half a page later, to avoid abbreviations when possible (Rose 1994: 28).

28. See Shea (1994: 61); Rose (1994: 30); Mandel and Van der Leun (1996: 97); Angell and Heslop (1994: 11–12).

29. As one person put it in a debate about smileys and email as written speech on COLLAB-L, a list for people interested in theater and performance, " I've always thought of smilies as a crutch to people who can't write effectively" (posting to COLLAB-L, 1 March 1995).

30. Personal communication from Lucia Ruedenberg-Wright.

31. Duranti's (1986) study, which I obtained only after completing a first draft of this chapter, followed the same strategy.

32. In some cases I was able to obtain permission to use and cite letters; in others, I was unable to reach people. See later footnotes for details on each set of letters analyzed.

33. Accent is, of course, not usually a matter of choice, though non-native or non-prestige speakers can to some extent make their speech conform to prestige patterns.

34. See, e.g., Giles and Powesland (1975); Ryan and Giles (1982); Bradac (1990).

35. Among other topics, they study cross-cultural differences in letter style and substance, a topic of increasing importance in an era of globalization.

36. In an earlier incarnation as a researcher on bureaucrat-client communication, I analyzed letters of petition to the Israel customs authorities. The focus of the analysis

was on the persuasive appeals that clients used, and aspects of their identity that they made salient (Danet 1971; Danet and Gurevitch 1972). Some attention was also paid to whether the identity of the writer or the content of the letter influenced customs officials' decisions (Danet 1973). However, I did not investigate the influence of the form of letters.

37. In email of the 1990s one generally had to use, or at least tended to use, a standard fixed-width font such as Courier New for the PC or Monaco for the Macintosh, thus enabling communication across all operating systems. By the late 1990s this began to change; see Chapter 7. For an explanation of fixed-width vs. proportional fonts, see Chapter 5.

38. The classic research on the influence of status and solidarity on address is by Roger Brown and his colleagues. See Brown (1960); Brown and Ford (1964). For a fairly recent overview of the large literature on this topic, see Philipsen and Huspek (1991). Choice of request strategies is also very sensitive to the influence of status and solidarity. See Blum-Kulka, et al. (1985; 1989).

39. Unfortunately, I was not able to locate any of these individuals several years later to obtain permission to present their letters in this chapter. In the natural course of things, students move on; the volatility of the Internet is another factor. Still, I have taken the liberty of presenting the full text of the most surprising of these three letters (Figure 2.4), since the potential for violating the writer's privacy was extremely low. These are one-time impersonal queries, not personal letters containing sensitive private content. In all cases in this chapter I have disguised identities thoroughly. In the case of the letter in Figure 2.4, many aspects suggest that the writer is showing off, eager to be thought an entertaining performer. Making the letter public is likely to please him.

40. This choice resembles openings used in student first letters to Alessandro Duranti. He cites three examples: "PROFESSOR DURANTI, HI!;" "HELLO MR. DURANTI;" and "HI, PROFESSOR DURANTI!" However, these were all students who knew him in class. The use of all caps was no doubt due to the limitations of email at the time. See Duranti (1986).

41. On the phatic function of ritualized greetings in face-to-face communication see, e.g., Malinowski (1972); J. Laver (1974); R. Laver (1981); Coupland, et al. (1992).

42. I received a second letter from Technosmurf. By and large, it had the same characteristics. Unfortunately, I did not save a copy of my response to his first letter, and thus have no indication of whether it rewarded his playfulness in any way.

43. The paper was an earlier, online version of Danet (1997b).

44. With some effort, I was able to locate 11 of the 20 writers; all gave permission to use their letters. Some asked first to see a copy of what they had written. Given that all contacted agreed, and that the content is not personal, I have once again taken the liberty of presenting one letter from a person I was unable to reach. All others are cited with permission.

45. Use of acronyms such as "MOO" and "IRC" was deemed acceptable, since these are known entities on the Internet whose full names are rarely spelled out. Strictly speaking, "Internet Relay Chat" could be spelled out in a letter (and indeed, at least one letter did so), though the full name for MOOs, "Multi-User Dungeons,

Object-oriented," is so unwieldy that it is unreasonable to expect use of the full expression.

46. I never had to make a judgment as to the competence of this person, since he never submitted a paper. The literature reviewed earlier suggests that there is some chance I might have been influenced by it. Only one of the 20 persons initially contacting me eventually became an author.

47. The only criterion met by the other letter scoring 1 was that of vocabulary.

48. We cannot know, of course, whether the others used no opening because they thought it was unnecessary, or because they were uncertain as to which opening might be appropriate.

49. Similarly, in a study of salutations in 75 paper letters of application for an academic position (Nilsen 1984), the majority of writers avoided a masculine greeting. Masculine-marked salutations were distributed across only four categories (e.g., "Dear Sirs"), whereas there were 19 different gender-neutral strategies (e.g., "To Whom It May Concern," "Personnel Committee Members"). Nilsen concluded that extreme variability was a sign of experimentation in an era moving toward gender-free communication.

50. A July 1999 article in the New York Times (Kelley 1999) reported extreme variability in "ways to say goodbye" in official as well as personal email. The article also documents many examples of playful inventiveness in this respect.

51. This may be an in-group reference to Umberto Eco's (1986) essay "Towards a Semiological Guerrilla Warfare."

52. Walter Cahn helped with this translation.

53. One can only wonder at the typo "acutal" in this sig file. These files are usually carefully composed.

54. All may have a single sig file which is automatically inserted, a possibility I mentioned earlier. Since in some cases the file is not visible to the writer but is inserted only when the letter is sent, writers may forget that a playful sig file will be attached.

55. If my corpus had been larger, it would have been interesting to analyze the letters by gender and status. One could ask, for instance, were women and students more conforming with the template than men and professors? Here, the numbers are too small to allow such an analysis.

56. Another possibility would have been to compare my corpus with a set of paper letter responses to a paper CFP, in roughly the same time period. However, I do not believe that we need empirical research to show that paper letters were different.

57. I analyze this corpus with D.G.'s permission.

58. Evidently, this is not an idiosyncratic device. Angell and Heslop (1994: 31) recommended setting off one's name at the end of a message in this manner.

59. Unfortunately, neither D.G. nor I saved the text of my initial letter to him. I have reconstructed the corpus of our correspondence as best I could by combining our two files. Only a few letters are missing, as far as we know.

60. I am making a brief exception here to my general principle of focusing on how people write to me, to ask, among other things, whether my informal style influenced him. But as we shall see shortly, the main shift in his style did not have anything directly to do with my style.

61. This letter is not shown here. The name of the software is deleted.

62. The main source of my difficulty was that, at the time, Israeli citizens could not hold foreign currency accounts, and therefore I could not write a check in dollars. I had to order the check specially at my bank, and come back three days later to pick it up.

63. E.g., Wolfe's book *The Right Stuff* (1979).

64. For reviews of the activities and accomplishments of the Plain Language movement and research on its effectiveness, see Danet (1980; 1985; 1990).

65. We should be careful here, however. Ong is primarily concerned with the effects of types of media on thought processes, not with patterns of language use per se.

66. To decode this, one needs to know that Netanyahu's nickname is "Bibi."

67. Friedman may not have created the titles himself.

68. See, e.g., Gusfield (1976); Gilbert and Mulkay (1984); Latour and Woolgar (1986); Simons (1988); Clifford and Marcus (1986).

69. The trend toward greater informality in business communication is echoed by developments in norms for dress in the corporate world. In the late 1990s it became acceptable in the United States for employees to come to work on Fridays in casual clothes.

70. Guy Haskell told me about this sig file, documented in June 1997.

71. I reviewed research on the legal register in Danet (1980; 1985; 1990). For an extensive review of empirical research on register, including the legal and medical ones, see Atkinson and Biber (1994).

72. See the references in Atkinson and Biber (1994: 354–355).

73. A large body of literature on the linguistic features of speech and writing has documented that some forms of speech are writing-like, and some forms of writing are speech-like. See, e.g., Tannen (1982); Chafe and Danielewicz (1987); Biber (1988).

74. I am indebted to Naomi Baron for calling this concept to my attention.

3

Typed "Jazz": Writing, Play and Performance on Internet Relay Chat

In Chapter 1 I suggested that interactive digital writing frequently becomes a form of artful, stylized performance, partially resembling both oral performance and improvisational jazz. In Chapter 2 we saw that even in primarily serious business email, evidence of playful, artful performance occasionally "bubbles up."[1] However, it is in synchronous modes that playful performance particularly flourishes – in purely spontaneous, online social chat as well as in scripted events that invite improvisation. This is the subject of this chapter.

I document and explicate this phenomenon in two studies of playful interaction on IRC. The first study is an analysis of a sequence of interaction that took place in December, 1991, in which the players simulated smoking marihuana by typing.[2] The second study is of a group called the Hamnet Players, who experimented with the idea of virtual theater in 1993–94, in partially scripted, partially improvised performances of parodies of Shakespeare's *Hamlet* and *Macbeth*. My analysis will show that Hamnet performances were Bakhtinian carnivals of textual and typographic play.

I argued in the Introduction to this book that the digital medium is inherently playful and dramatic because of its interactivity and immersive quality, the release from physicality, and the rich array of easy-to-use possibilities at the user's disposal. Two features of IRC enhance its dramatic potential: its inherent script-like quality and the fact that it employs direct speech as its main mode of communication. In ordinary chat, participants' contributions are listed on screen in sequence, as registered by the IRC servers.[3] With players' nicknames shown at the left of their contributions, their words look like lines in the script of a play. Unlike MOOs, which render most contributions in the third person, thus resembling fiction more than drama, typed "talk" on IRC is rendered in the first and second person.[4] In addition, the software guarantees orderly turns at talking. Unlike RL conversations, where obtaining the floor is a potential issue and people often talk at once, there is no struggle to be "heard" in IRC chat, no overlap in the contributions of various players. Each individual's contributions automatically appear on screen exactly in the order received by the server. It becomes possible, then, to perform a prepared script: Performers can produce their "lines" in the required sequence, as in RL performances.

This chapter asks: what forms does playful performance take when the performance is typed, not spoken? What is the basis for my suggestion that there are similarities between typed online interaction and jazz? What accounts for the fact that artful, stylized communication – occasionally, even brilliant improvisation – can flourish in a context in which the participants have never met, cannot see one another, and can only participate by typing?

"Hmmm. . . Where's That Smoke Coming From?" Typed Simulation of Smoking Marihuana

In late 1991, my then-collaborator, Lucia Ruedenberg-Wright, had arranged to meet an IRC acquaintance online, a Columbia University student nicknamed <Thunder>.[5] <Thunder> knew in advance that she was interested in "perform-ance," but chose his own channel name and topic. Once the two were in the channel, other participants gradually joined them, evidently by chance, except, perhaps, for one fellow student at Columbia University, who may have known about <Thunder>'s plans. The ensuing improvisation was much like a jazz jam session in which some of the players happen to appear and spontaneously begin playing with the others, without necessarily having played with them before.

What followed was a kind of typed pantomime or game of textual charades. In pantomime, one person mimics physical/social activity, and the audience must decode it. Charades is a group game in which individuals sequentially use their bodies and gestures to act out, non-verbally, some verbal content or idea, and each time the others must guess what is intended. In the present case, then, typed words and sequences of typographic symbols chosen for their graphic shapes "acted out" the activity, not the bodies of the players.

Five Frames and the Relations among Them

The simulation took place in a complex symbolic environment of five different frames of interaction, nested within one another: (1) REAL LIFE; (2) the IRC GAME; (3) PARTY; (4) PRETEND; and (5) PERFORMANCE (Figure 3.1).[6]

By dint of being alive and functioning, the IRC players were already in the REAL LIFE mode, which in Western culture is dominated by the expectation of "serious" activity in the workaday world (Goffman 1974; Schechner 1988). The meta-message (Bateson 1972; Handelman 1976) of this frame was, "Everything inside this frame is everyday life, grounded in physical space and time; actors are accountable for their physical and verbal actions, for the well-being of their bodies, and for their social commitments." This frame was relegated to the background when participants logged onto IRC, thereby activating frame #2, the basic IRC GAME, though participants occasionally talked about things that were happening or that they had to do in REAL LIFE. For instance, at the beginning of the log, <Thunder> sent <Lucia> a private message, using the /msg command:[7]

```
Line 9 *Thunder* I am gonna shower soon
```

Any interaction made possible by the constitutive rules, the commands of IRC, would occur by definition within the frame of the IRC game.

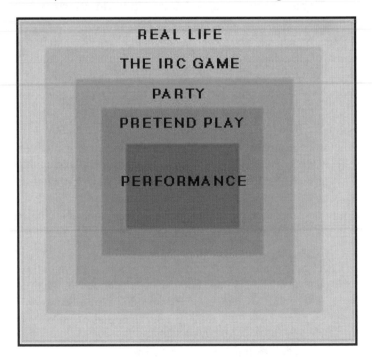

Figure 3.1. Five nested frames of interaction at a virtual party on IRC. Reprinted with permission from Danet, et al. (1998), Fig. 1. Copyright © 1998 American Association for Artificial Intelligence.

The third frame in the sequence was PARTY: its meta-message was, "Let's have a party; let's have fun; participants enjoy reduced accountability; action and utterances are primarily in a playful mode."[8] This was the first of three frames for genres of culturally constituted, playful activity, the others being PRETEND-PLAY and PERFORMANCE. The players got acquainted, chatted, fooled around, "drank" various substances, both intoxicating and non-intoxicating, and "flirted" with <Lucia>, the only apparently female-presenting player present.

The party started when <Thunder> created the channel. At first he used numbers playfully to suggest possible names for the channel (Figure 3.2). Then he switched to typographic symbols (lines 62–63, 65–66, Figure 3.2), playing with the word "bagelnosh,"[9] reversing the two components of the word, and then typing it backward (line 71). A brief proposal for "kinky sex with riding crops and handcuffs" (line 74) offered the possibility that the party could turn into seduction and "dark play" (Schechner 1988). Finally, <Thunder> settled on the channel name +weed, issuing the invitation five times – repetition being in itself playful. Finally, he sets the topic as:

```
Line 90 ssssssssssssss hmmm wheres all that smoke from?
```

At first Ruedenberg thought "weed" referred to "garden." <Thunder> had to make his intentions explicit:

```
Line 103 <Thunder> I was thinking more of grass, herb, pot,
marijuana :-)
```

In a study of the nature of improvisation in jazz, the ethnomusicologist Paul Berliner wrote:

> Composed pieces or tunes, consisting of a melody and an accompanying harmonic progression, have provided the structure for improvisations throughout most of the history of jazz . . . Performers commonly refer to the melody or theme as the head, and to the progression as chord changes or simply changes. It has become the convention for musicians to perform the melody and its accompaniment at the opening and closing of a piece's performance. In between, they take turns improvising solos within the piece's cyclical rhythmic form. (Berliner 1994: 63)

Thus, like the first jazz player to arrive at a session, <Thunder> had "idled" for a while, "warming up" while waiting for others to arrive, finally setting out a theme for improvisation. As others arrived, they quickly decoded what "weed" was supposed to be about,[10] and the group began developing the theme, eventually taking it to new heights. Both verbally and pictorially, they

```
Line    *** Thunder invites you to channel *private*
        *** Thunder invites you to channel 1
        *** Thunder invites you to channel 2
55      *** Thunder invites you to channel 3
        *** Thunder invites you to channel 4
        *** Thunder invites you to channel 5
        *** Thunder invites you to channel 6
        *** Thunder invites you to channel 0
60      *** Thunder invites you to channel hmmm this is
        confusing
        /msg thunder hmmmm so much to choose from! hehe
        *** Thunder invites you to channel -)
        *** Thunder invites you to channel \
        /msg thunder hahahaha
65      *** Thunder invites you to channel -)
        *** Thunder invites you to channel \
        /msg thunder no way!
        /msg thunder no way!
        *** Thunder invites you to channel ok..I will stop now
70      *** Thunder invites you to channel +bagelnosh
        *** Thunder invites you to channel +noshbagel
        /msg thunder oh yeah?
        *** Thunder invites you to channel +hsonlegab
        *** Thunder invites you to channel +kinky sex with
        riding crops and handcuffs
75      /msg thunder I'll think about it.
        *** Thunder invites you to channel +weed
        *** Thunder invites you to channel +weed
        *** Thunder invites you to channel +weed
        *** Thunder invites you to channel +weed

                    ——

86      *** Thunder invites you to channel +weed
```

Figure 3.2. "Warming up" for the improvisation: naming the channel.

portrayed the sequence of holding a joint, taking it into one's mouth, inhaling, exhaling and experiencing pleasure (Figure 3.3, below).

The PRETEND Frame

The simulation of smoking marihuana took place within a fourth frame, "LET'S PRETEND" (cf. Figure 3.1). All symbolic activity in this frame contained the meta-message "Let us make-believe; let us suspend belief" (Handelman 1976). Thus, in the first example in Figure 3.3, <Thunder> "inhales" and "exhales" via a long sequence of the letter "s." This is both the first letter of the word "smoke" and a graphic simulation of the undulating smoke, as well as, very likely, a rendering of the sound of exhaling the smoke between one's teeth. The strategy of writing out sequences of letters to convey sounds, as in "grrrr," "oof," "bam!," is a well known convention in comic art (Abbott 1986: 156; Inge 1990, Chapter 2). <Thunder> then passes the joint to a player nicknamed <Kang>, who simulates smoking the joint with the words *puff*, *hold*, and *exhale,* third-person descriptions of his own actions marked with asterisks, thus following another convention known from the comics.[11] <Kang>'s improvisations are deeply "in synch" with <Thunder>'s own moves. They are beginning to "strike a groove," to borrow an expression from the world of jazz (Berliner 1994: 349).

In the second example the dissipating smoke is rendered by a sequence of decreasing rows of the letter 's'. The high point of this sequence comes in line 430 of the third example. Here, <Thunder> mimes the entire sequence of taking the joint in one's mouth (represented by the smiley :-Q[12]), inhaling, releasing the smoke and experiencing pleasure.

The PERFORMANCE Frame

The fourth frame activated during this sequence is the PERFORMANCE frame. Its meta-message is "Let's show each other what we can do with the keyboard." Richard Bauman's[13] formulation of the nature of oral performance fits online interactive writing strikingly well too:

> In this sense of performance, the act of communication is put on display, objectified, lifted out to a degree from its contextual surroundings, and opened up to scrutiny by an audience. Performance thus calls forth special attention to and heightened awareness of the act of communication and gives license to the audience to regard it and the performer with special intensity. Performance makes one communicatively accountable; it assigns to an audience the responsibility of evaluating the relative skill and effectiveness of the performer's accomplishment. (Bauman 1992: 44)

The players showed keen interest in showing off, and expressed admiration for their own and each others' skills. Thus, in the first example in Figure 3.3, <Lucia> and <Kang> reacted to <Thunder>'s improvisation with a smile and a wink, respectively. In the second example, <Kang> and <Thunder> both expressed enthusiasm for their own performances, typing "yea" in the one case, and "wow" in the other. And in the third example, Thunder complimented

Example #1:
  Line 126 <Thunder>sssssssssssssss *passes joint to kang*
            . . . .
         <Kang> thanx dude *puff* *hold*
            . . . .
         >:-)
            . . . .
      138 <Thunder> kang exhale.. you will die :-)
           <Kang> *exhale*
           <Kang> ;)

Example #2:
  Line 340 <BlueAdept> <gives first bong rip to
            Thunder. . .
                  . . . .
      365   <Thunder> *gurble gurble gurble*
      366   sssssssssssssssssssssss
            <Kang> yea!
                  . . . .
            <Thunder> sssssssssssssssssss
      370   <Thunder> sssssssssssssssssss
            <Thunder> ssss
            <Thunder> ss
            <Thunder> s
            <Thunder>
      375   <Thunder> wow

Example #3:
  Line 419 <Kang< :|
            <Kang> :|
            <Kang> :\
            <Thunder> heheheh
            <Thunder> heheheheheh
            <Thunder> that was great
      425   <Kang> :/
            <Kang> :)
            <Thunder> hehehehehhe
            <Kang> *exhale*
            <Kang> :0
      430   <Thunder> :| :| :\sssss :)
            <Kang> hheeeheee
            <Thunder> :-Q :| :| :\sssss :)
            <Thunder> heheheh
      435   . . . .
         >:-) cute

Figure 3.3. A textual and typographic simulation of smoking marihuana.

<Kang> with "heheheh/that was great," and <Lucia> praised <Thunder> by typing "cute."

Just as in a jazz session unexpected things may happen musically, a typo by <Thunder> spurred a clever pun during this simulation. One of the other players, nicknamed <BlueAdept>, had "thrown" some new dope, red sense, on the "end table," leading <Thunder> to contribute:

```
Line 397 <Thunder> need to pack a new bowel heheheheh
                   hehehehehe. . .
```

Instead of "bowl" he had typed "bowel." "What a typo!" he chortled, in line 400. <Kang> hastened to type:

```
Line 401 <Kang> not bowel!!!! bowel?
```

<Thunder> corrected himself, laughing at his mistake:

```
Line 403 <Thunder> need to pack a new bowl hehhehehehe
```

Kang "packs" the bowl for him. Then Thunder offers:

```
Line 408 <Thunder> that is shitty pot I would say if it was
                   packing a bowel
```

Just as some jazz is mostly spontaneous and improvised, other forms are more extensively precomposed. There is a continuum from the most spontaneous to the most pre-structured forms. Berliner (1994: 63) notes that "composed pieces. . . have provided the structure for improvisations throughout the history of jazz." In the remainder of this chapter, I will contrast the largely improvised sequence just discussed with the much more extensively scripted performances of the Hamnet Players.

Shakespeare "Live" Online: the Hamnet Players

Who Were the Hamnet Players?

The Hamnet Players were founded in 1993 by Stuart Harris, an Englishman living in San Diego, California, a former actor, a computer professional and author of computer manuals, including one on IRC (Harris 1995a). Harris brought to the Hamnet Players five years' experience in theater in England, three as a semi-professional actor on the festival circuit, and two more as a professional in London and in provincial repertory theater. In addition, he had further experience as a director in television. His unique background and combination of talents led him to recognize the dramatic potential of IRC.

> . . .since all participants in an irc conversation may choose whatever nickname they wish to be known by. . . and since an irc channel may contain many people who contribute nothing, but merely watch, the elements of theater are there: a cast of characters with names like Hamlet, Ophelia, Polonius etc. can be convened and an audience invited to watch. (Harris 1995b: 500).

Harris's irreverent spirit and love of wordplay strongly influenced all Hamnet activities. Consider his email address and his regular nick on IRC:

```
sirrah@cg57.esnet.com (The_Tijuana_Piss_Artist)
```

The userid "sirrah" is a sly anagram: "Harris" spelled backwards! According to the Oxford English Dictionary, "sirrah" is an archaic term of address to an inferior, "expressing contempt, reprimand, or the assumption of authority on the part of the speaker." It was used in Shakespeare's time and even by Shakespeare himself, as in *Macbeth* IV.ii.30. Exploiting the opportunity to add a bit of text alongside his email address, Harris sometimes called himself The_Tijuana_Piss_Artist," a reference to the fact that he lives near the Mexican border, and often goes to bars in Tijuana, where people call him "El Ingles" ("the Englishman"). Sometimes, another expression appeared alongside his email address:

```
sirrah@cg57.esnet.com (irco_ergo_sum).
```

This is a playful reworking of *cogito ergo sum*. Instead of Descartes' famous "I think, therefore I am," he wrote, "I IRC, therefore I am."

The name "Hamnet Players" is rich in cultural resonances. A "ham" is "an ineffective or overemphatic actor, one who rants or overacts" (Oxford English Dictionary). Thus, besides being an obvious pun on "Hamlet," the expression invites association to "hamming it up on the Net." Another association is to amateur ham radio. Ham radio culture shares with hacker culture, as well as with Net culture more generally, something of its subversive, "alternative" nature. It also so happens that Shakespeare actually had a son called "Hamnet," one of a pair of twins, who died at the age of 11 on August 11, 1596 (Muir 1971).

The Case for Virtual Theater

An ostensible oxymoron, a contradiction in terms, the expression "virtual theater" is actually quite on the mark. Until recently, many people believed that what makes theater unique is "the fact that it's live and unmediated, that it can put us in the presence of other living, breathing human beings" (Copeland 1990: 30). In conventional thinking about the performing arts, "these arts require the physical presence of trained or skilled human beings whose demonstration of their skills is the performance" (Carlson 1996: 3). In Jerzy Grotowski's hard-line stand against technological mediation, he argued that we could do without makeup, costume, scenography, the stage, lighting and sound effects, but we could not do without "the actor-spectator relationship of perceptual, direct, live, communion" (Grotowski 1968: 19; cited in Copeland 1990: 32).

Hamnet performances were a form of virtual theater, first of all, because they were focused gatherings, just like face-to-face encounters (Goffman 1963). Although participants could not see one another, and their bodies were not co-present to one another, they cooperated to sustain a single focus of attention, taking turns at talking (Goffman 1963: 24).

Discussions of "live" vs. mediated performance generally assume that the latter is "taped," "canned," broadcast or experienced at a later time than that of the original performance, or, at best, that a live event happening "somewhere else" is being relayed in real time, e.g., by satellite. These assumptions strongly colored an online debate about theater and performance in an era of mediatization which took place on the PERFORM-L discussion list in May-June, 1995.[14] In one posting, Richard Schechner, a prominent practitioner as well as theoretician in the field of theater,[15] listed a number of reasons why live performance is prized in areas where media are also widely available. Of these, four are pertinent to the idea of virtual theater: (1) contingency, accident, unexpectability; (2) direct competition among known individuals; (3) interaction and participation by the audience; (4) a sense of control, in the here-and-now, not present when performance is not "live".[16]

Hamnet activities are of theoretical importance because this group was one of the first to challenge the conventional dichotomy between the "live" and the "mediated." Hamnet performances shared most of the characteristics Schechner ascribes to "live," unmediated performance, as is attested by this public relations statement prepared by Stuart Harris:

> True to the concept of theater, the production is presented in real time with live performers and audience, with all the opportunities for spontaneous genius and imminent disaster that entails. The debut performance of "Hamnet" was interrupted by a thunderstorm which cut the producers' online access; the play had to be restarted after the producers logged back on via Taiwan. The second performance

was enlivened by a "bot"[17] which accidentally killed Hamlet halfway through the production.[18]

As is evident from Harris's comments, Hamnet performances were characterized by contingency and suspense. The challenge to maintain the focus online may be greater than in a conventional theater space, but perhaps not more so than in outdoor theater. Two main factors foster this sense of contingency, the vulnerability of the technology to breakdown, evident in Harris's comments, and the distraction of other conversations – of people "coming and going."

One type of technical problem that plagued communication on IRC in the 1990s was "netsplits," the sudden loss of a link to a server, and the consequent "dumping" from the channel and from IRC of all logged on via that server. Netsplits interrupted Hamnet performances constantly, causing key performers, including Harris himself on at least one occasion, to disappear from the screen. During the second performance of "PCbeth" in July 1994, netsplits were so frequent that it was remarkable that the players managed to get most of the script on screen.

A second technical problem was "lag," a gap in time between the moment of hitting the "enter" key after typing one's contribution and when it appears on the screens of others logged onto the channel. On IRC generally, lag was much like the weather; there was not much one could do except complain about it.[19]

IRC could be quite chaotic, with scores of people potentially "dropping in" and then disappearing from any given channel. Dozens of conversations might compete for attention on screen; snippets of different conversations may be interwoven in surreal fashion. The challenge, then, was not to be "heard" – barring technical difficulties, the words will appear on screen – but to get others to pay attention to what one is saying. Moreover, individuals might be simultaneously logged onto several channels and therefore not concentrating on what is occurring in a given channel. But I should not exaggerate. The challenge was perhaps no greater than in street theater, where performers can and do compete with traffic and noise for their audience's attention.

Artful Performance and Competition among Individuals

Hamnet activities were performances in two distinct but complementary senses. First, as we have seen, they were scheduled, programmed events, whose centerpiece was the theater-like performance of a script. There were roles, cues, "sets," a plot to be realized from beginning to end, and a producer, director and stage manager to keep things in hand, all components we associate with conventional theater. Strictly speaking, players did not so much "act" as collectively put the pieces of a textual puzzle together on screen.

This collective enterprise was embedded in a wider performance frame, both a social performance in Erving Goffman's sense – "all the activity of an individual which occurs during a period marked by his continuous presence before a particular set of observers and which has some influence on the observers" (Goffman 1959: 22) – and, of course, an artful one.[20]

The complex symbolic environment of Hamnet performances can be rendered graphically by making a small change in Figure 3.1, yielding the revised diagram in Figure 3.4.[21] Once again REAL LIFE is the outer-most frame; when online, all are in the frame of the IRC GAME. Now THEATER is the answer to the question "What is going on?" – not PARTY. Within that frame are concerns for casting and logistics, distributing parts, explaining how to perform one's role, etc. PRETEND-PLAY is the frame within which the "actors" play their roles, pretending to be <Hamlet>, <Ophelia>, etc. The innermost frame is PERFORMANCE, in which the actors perform their lines, improvise on them, and compete for recognition. Additionally, improvisation by members of the audience is part of PERFORMANCE in the broader sense too.

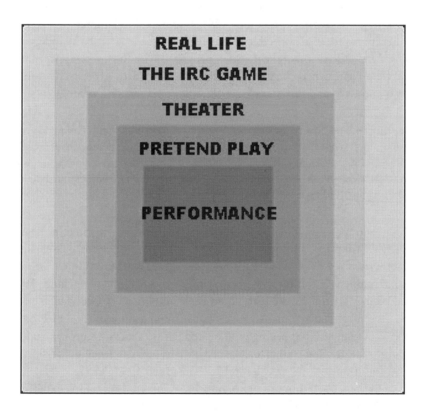

Figure 3.4. Five nested frames of interaction during Hamnet performances.

Many kinds of zany improvisation enlivened the time before and after performances of the script, as well as realization of the script itself. "Audience" was scripted as a role to be played during performances. At least one person had to change his/her nick to <audience> and to type "Clap clap clap." But the dozens of people who attended needed no prodding to simulate audience behavior spontaneously. Some of the best improvisation was by people in the audience. A fourth feature of performance mentioned by Schechner is the sense of control that derives from being present in the "here-and-now." This is, of course, closely related to contingency. The here-and-now performance is the sum total of a host of individual choices made in sequence by all participants who are coordinating their joint activities.

Taken together, these four features created a strong sense of "presence."[22] Roger Copeland has noted that technological components of theater events may not merely mediate or complicate living presence but, rather, even intensify it, and even produce sensory overload, the result sometimes being a heightened, rather than diminished sense of presentness (Copeland 1990: 32). A key word here is "immersion," a term we encountered in Chapter 1, in my discussion of the defining features of the medium. "When [players] feel immersive presence they are involved. . . absorbed. . . engaged, engrossed" (Lombard and Ditton 1997).[23] In a discussion of theatrical improvisation on the Internet, Antoinette LaFarge, a writer, director, and performance artist with experience on both MOOs and IRC, and founder of the "Plaintext Players,"[24] wrote:

> Players in online theater consistently report a unique sense of total immersion and exaltation. It is not the things imagined that create this sense, not the act of imagination per se; it is the experience of imagination. What happens in online theater is the immediate embodiment of the imagination; what you think comes immediately to light and life. (LaFarge 1995: 421).

What is important, then, is simultaneity with respect to time, not being literally in the same physical space. The critical component is a sense of "reciprocity, a sense that what transpires onstage. . . is affected almost as much by what happens in the audience as the other way around " (Copeland, 1990: 34). Hamnet participants coordinated their activities via Greenwich Mean Time. Lively audience improvisations constituted as important a part of the action as in many RL happenings and related performances. Copeland's notion of reciprocity is close to that of interactivity in social science discussions of digital communication (e.g., Laurel 1991; Rafaeli 1988; 1998).

Even in their "bare-bones," textual form, many kinds of online experience are emotionally gripping, visceral, sometimes even traumatic. An extreme example is the case of "textual rape" on LambdaMOO (Dibbell 1996). Not only were the women "victims" traumatized by "mere words," these events caused a major crisis in the life of this virtual community. Emotions of course have their basis in the body.[25] Therefore, if people are reacting with their bodies, the body is implicated in online performance, even if invisible to the other bodies involved.

Because they took place over a period of months, and required a good deal of behind-the-scenes coordinated activity, Hamnet productions also engendered a strong sense of community, even if fairly short-lived. An exuberant sense of "collaborative expectancy" (Bauman 1977: 16) and a festive "sense of occasion," shared by audience and performers, permeated all performances. Thus, at the first performance of "Hamnet," one person declared, "We are making cyber-history," and a young participant gushed, "I want my MOM to see me!!!" Many participants were eager to receive logs of performances or to make one themselves.

In the belief that he was making history, Harris also prepared mock souvenir "programs" which people could receive by email. A portion of the program for "PCbeth" is shown in Figure 3.5. During the premiere April 1994 performance of "PCbeth," Harris and his companion Gayle Kidder, a professional writer who authored the "PCbeth" script and created graphic images to illustrate it (Plate 3.1), wore Elizabethan costumes (Figure 3.6). The premiere was timed to coincide with Shakespeare's 430th birthday.[26] The group exchanged effusive compliments after the performance, and celebrated afterwards by "drinking" virtual champagne and other intoxicating substances.[27]

Involvement of Professionals and Semi-Professionals

Quite a few professional and semi-professional theater people became involved, not only as members of the audience, but as "actors" or behind-the-scenes personnel. A member of the Royal Shakespeare Company played <Hamlet> in one performance. A Hollywood actor with major film credits played <Ross> in the second production of "PCbeth." Antoinette LaFarge, the performance artist mentioned earlier, played Blanche in one of the "#Desire" performances. An English actor with many theater credits as well as appearances in BBC and Thames television films played <Mac> (Macduff) in one of the "PCbeth" performances. A buddy of Harris's, a critic with 35 years' experience in all areas of theater, followed Hamnet productions closely. Although he did not play an active role during the proceedings, he prepared a mock review of the premiere of "Hamnet" (Figure 3. 7). One of Harris's closest pals, a semi-professional actor in Bath, England who has played Macbeth in an RL production, appeared as <R_krantz> (Rosenkrantz) in "Hamnet," <PCbeth> in the first performance of "PCbeth," and <Stanley> in "#Desire." The stage manager

```
\/\/\/\/\/\/\/\/\/\/\/\/\/\/\/\/\/\/\/\/\/\/\/\/\/\/\/\/\/
                  OFFICIAL SOUVENIR PROGRAM
/\/\/\/\/\/\/\/\/\/\/\/\/\/\/\/\/\/\/\/\/\/\/\/\/\/\/\/\/\
~~~~~~~~~~~~~~~~~~~~~~~~~~~~~~~~~~~~~~~~~~~~~~~~~~~~~~~~~~~~
```

The World Premiere of the irc-play "Pcbeth"
An IBM clone of Shakespeare's Scottish play

irc-play by Gayle Kidder "minou"

Saturday, 23rd April 1994 [the Bard's 430th birthday]
17:00 GMT in the #hamnet auditorium

***************** STARRING *************************

"Gazza" as Pcbeth — from Bath, UK
"Fem" as LadyM — from Fairbanks, Alaska

****

PRODUCTION/CAST LIST

	Who	Where
PRODUCTION	El_Ingles	SAN DIEGO
STAGE MANAGER	aurra	MICHIGAN
TECH MANAGER	rokinduck	NEWARK
ASM	zarquon	LONDON
SET DESIGN	zendar	SAN DIEGO
Pcbeth	gazza	BATH
Banquo	foosh	
1witch	jewelie	LANCASTER
2witch	kashka	TEL AVIV
Lady_M	**fem	FAIRBANKS
King	**infonut	GAUTIER, MS
Porter	rokinduck	NEWARK
Mac Macduff)	snug	LONDON
Malcolm	valerie	?
Donalbain merp		LANCASTER
Ross	erdor	VANCOUVER,CA
Lady_R	hidi	PITTSBURGH
Doctor	Dudester	ROCHESTER, NY
SCENE	Bopeep	VIRGINIA
_Enter	clive	LONDON
_Exit	othernick	S. AFRICA

Figure 3.5. Mock souvenir "program" for performances of "PCbeth."

Figure 3.6. Stuart Harris and Gayle Kidder in Elizabethan costume.

SHAKESPEARE QUARTO UNEARTHED IN BINARY FORM*

Internet Production of "Hamnet - Prince of the Danes" debuts to delight[ed] international audience.

Royal Shakespeare Company rumored to be acquiring PC clones.

by

The Critic
OldBear@world.std.com

Cyberspace - Feb 5. Much to the delight of a small audience of devoted internet relay chat afficionados and wannabee theatre goers, the world premier of Hamnet opened to audience acclaim at 20:25 hrs universal time on channel #hamnet this afternoon.

The delayed curtain was a result of a number of opening night snafus including a leading lady who had not retreived [sic] her script from email, a rowdy bunch of understudies, and a last minute debate over the merits (or folly) of having the entire cast on the same irc server.

The script, an abridgement of the original shakespearian quarto, was rumored to have been recently unearthed on a mass storage device located somewhere on the internet. Thankfully, it was brought to the attention of producer sirrah@cg57.esnet.com (El_Ingles) prior to its being authenticated and submitted for auction at Christie's....

All and all, I found the production refreshing and surprisingly complelling [sic] inspite [sic] of occasional lapses in the actors' delivery of their lines in Elizabethan ASCII. The identities of many of the players appeared to change frequently during the performance, giving an other-worldly quality to this theatrical classic.

In an off-the-record statement, one member of the company suggested that the cast may reconvene for a production of something by Samuel Beckett or Sam Shepard. Given complimentary tickets, I can assure you that this reviewer would make a reasonable effort to attend.

(c) 1994 by OldBear@world.std.com. May be freely distributed in its entirety for non-commercial purposes only or reasonably quoted in part with attribution for either commecial [sic] and non-commercial purposes. Any resemblance between irc users, living or dead, without satirical purpose is purely coincidental and should not be taken personally. Besides, if you're that sensitive, you shouldn't be on the internet anyway.

*Abridged.

Figure 3.7. Mock review of the Premiere of "Hamnet."

for the first performance of "PCbeth" was active in student and summer stock theater in the United States.

Hamnet Productions and the Problem of Genre

On various occasions Harris called his group "Internet Theater," a "participatory performance art forum," "an emerging art form," "a "romp," an "extravaganza," "an obscene pastiche," "virtual theater," and even "virtual reality drama" . Other possibilities are "travesty," "spoof," "burlesque", and "take-off." Whatever term we choose, Hamnet scripts and productions were quintessentially postmodern in their irreverent, pastiche-like hijinks. Yet, behind the playfulness were serious aspirations to use the technology of IRC in a new and creative way.

Like classic farces (Davis 1978), Hamnet scripts did away with psychological depth of characterization; plots and characterization were butchered, so that a mere shell of the original survives. The verbal frolics in Hamnet scripts and productions were the textual equivalent of wild physical slapstick or Punch-and-Judy puppet shows.[28] The typed, online medium greatly constrained the representation of action, just as glove puppets severely limit physical movement in RL puppet theater. Harris "grew up on" the Goon Show, the popular English radio comedy program of the 1950s which later inspired Monty Python antics. He also acknowledged the influence of the Reduced Shakespeare Company, famous for its outrageous 97-minute performance of all 37 Shakespeare plays.[29]

Despite affinities with various forms of farce, Hamnet scripts and performances were not simply classical farces; they are better designated as parodies or satires or both. The parodic elements would be obvious to most people who have been exposed to Shakespeare. The butchering of these tragedies into laughable comedies of course suggests that this is a form of parody. Nash (1985), among others, distinguishes between two forms of parody, rewriting a traditional work in modern terms, and the use of formal means from one period or text to produce another work or text of entirely different content. Hamnet scripts clearly fall into the former category. "Pastiche" is an apt term too – a number of different styles pieced together to form a medley. As Maurice Charney (1978: 15) puts it, "this is parody of the most virtuoso sort."

To appreciate Hamnet scripts and performances, one must both know Shakespeare well and have a good knowledge of Internet and IRC culture. The texts of *Hamlet* and *Macbeth* were parodized by being rewritten in "IRC-ese," while retaining the bare bones of the original. Linda Hutcheon's (1985) definition of parody as "repetition with critical difference" is pertinent. Postmodern parody, she argues, is often devoid of ridicule. The new text does not necessarily ridicule the old, as has often been the case in the past. It may pay homage to canonical artistic creation of the past, yet at the same time, serve as a means to innovate, ironicize, and invite critical thinking. We are not required to give priority to one of the two texts. "It is the fact that they differ that parody emphasizes, and, indeed, dramatizes" (Hutcheon 1985: 31).

Hamnet scripts can also be seen as a form of satirical commentary on IRC. Satire has traditionally been thought of as judgmental – having victims and specific objects of attack – not literary texts but social institutions and practices, individuals or social groups. It can be savage or it can be gentle, but it is always aggressive (Hutcheon 1985; Test 1991). The satirical style in the Hamnet scripts was of a more contemporary variety, a heightening of the agonistic style of communication prevalent on IRC. The parodic and satirical aspects of Hamnet productions were a matter of figure and ground. If the focus is primarily on treatment of the Shakespearean sources, we are in the realm of parody; if it is primarily on the many references to IRC and computer culture, we are in the realm of satire.

Hamnet Scripts: a Closer Look

Although we are primarily interested in actual performance online in this chapter, there are several reasons why we need also to look fairly carefully at Hamnet scripts. First of all, just as a jazz scholar needs to understand composed aspects of jazz,[30] the better to elucidate what happens during performance, so we need to know just what provided the basis for improvisational performance of Hamnet parodies. Second, the scripts themselves are a form of play with digital writing – the unique form of writing that is IRC style, as well as with language more generally, and with the commands of the IRC software and Shakespearean texts.

As we have begun to see, the scripts of "Hamnet" and "PCbeth" outrageously and incongruously[31] juxtaposed Shakespeare's canonical plot and archaic literary register with contemporary low register, outright slang, and even the slurred speech of drunks, as well as with content taken from contemporary popular and computer culture.

The complete script of "Hamnet," authored by Harris himself and including a miniature ASCII set of Elsinore Castle, is shown in Figure 3.8. Scene 2 of "PCbeth," written by Harris's companion Gayle Kidder, appears in Figure 3.9.[32] In the preface to his book on the language of humor, Walter Nash (1985) listed a remarkable grab bag of phenomena that fall under the rubric of verbal humor:

Here we find wit and word-play and banter and bumfun; slogans and captions and catchwords; allusion and parody; ironies; satires; here are graffiti and limericks; here is the pert rhyme, and here the twisted pun; here are scrambled spellings and skewed pronunciations; here is filth for the filthy. . ., and here are delicacies for the delicate. (Nash 1985: 1)

Nash's list reads like an inventory of Hamnet textual pyrotechnics.

```
"HAMNET" ==== Shakespeare's play adapted for irc
First performed 12 December 1993 20:00 GMT on #Hamnet
copyright 1993 The Hamnet Players, San Diego, CA
all enquiries to: sirrah@cg57.esnet.com
/\/\/\/\/\/\/\/\/\/\/\/\/\/\/\/\/\/\/\/\/\/\/\/\/\/\/\/\/\
THE COMPLETE SCRIPT........OFFICIAL SOUVENIR EDITION
/\/\/\/\/\/\/\/\/\/\/\/\/\/\/\/\/\/\/\/\/\/\/\/\/\/\/\/\/\
<audience> rhubarb. . .
**<< Action >>** : _The CURTAIN RISES to reveal the stage set...
<_Set> :     *            *          *            *
<_Set> <   |        <   |         |   >       |   >
<_Set> <___|        <___|         |___>       |___>
<_Set>       |                 |             |             |
<_Set>       ^^^^^^^^^         ^^^^^^^^^    ^^^^^^^^^    ^^^^^^^^^
<_Set>     |  +  |         |  +  |         |  +  |       |  +  |
<_Set>     |  +  |_____|   +  |_____|   +  |_____|   +  |
<_Set>     |                                                  |
<_Set>     |  +      +        +      +        +      +      +  |
<_Set>     |__                                              __|
<_Set>        |      +        +      +        +      +        |
<_Set>        |                                              |
<_Set>        |      +        +              +      +        |
<_Set>        |                    |########|                |
<_Set>     /  |      +        +    |########|   +      +     |\.
<_Set>    /   |                    |        |                | \.
<_Set>   /    |_____    | ||||||  |_____| . \.
<_Set>  /.        .          .      ||||||       .          .    \.
<_Set> _____||||||_____
<_Set>
<_Set>
<_Set> W E L C O M E   T O   E L S I N O R E!!!
<_Set> ~~~~~~~~~~~~~~~~~~~~~~~~~~~~~~~~~~~~~~~~~
<_Set> [0]
```

<audience> Clap,clap,clap.... etc.... [1]

   =====PROLOGUE /TOPIC World_Premiere _irc_Hamlet_in_Progress [2]

*** PROLOGUE has changed the topic on channel #Hamnet to "World_Premiere _irc_Hamlet_in_Progress"<PROLOGUE> All the world's a Unix term.... [3]

<PROLOGUE> . . .and all the men & women merely irc addicts. . . . [4]

<PROLOGUE> This show is Copyright 1993 The Hamnet Players [5]

<PROLOGUE> Enjoy our show + no heckling plz [6]

<PROLOGUE> Script should not be re-staged w/out permish [7]

<< Action >> : SCENE 1: THE BATTLEMENTS [8]

<< Action >> : _Enter Hamlet [9]

<< Action >> : _Enter Ghost [10]

<Hamlet> re, Ghost. Zup? [11]

<Ghost> Yr uncle's fucking yr mum. I'm counting on u to /KICK the bastard. [12]

   ======== GHOST /MODE * +o Hamlet [13]

*** Mode change "+o Hamlet" on channel #Hamnet by Ghost

<Hamlet> Holy shit!!!! Don't op me, man!!!! I've gotta think abt this, + I've got chem lab in 1/2 hr. :-(((([14]

<< Action >> : _Exit Hamlet [15]

<< Action >> : SCENE 2: AFTER HAMLET'S CHEM LAB [16]

<Hamlet> 2b or not 2b. . . [17]

<Hamlet> Hmmmmmm. . . [18]

<Hamlet> :-(Bummer. . . [19]

<Hamlet> Ooops, here comes Ophelia [20]

<< Action >> : _Enter Ophelia [21]

<Ophelia> Here's yr stuff back [22]

<Hamlet> Not mine, love. Hehehehehe ;-D [23]

<Ophelia> O heavenly powers: restore him! [24]

<< Action >> Ophelia thinks Hamlet's nuts [25]

<Hamlet> Make that "sanity-deprived", pls. . . . [26]

<Hamlet> Oph: suggest u /JOIN #nunnery [27]

<Ophelia> :-([28]

*** Signoff: Ophelia (drowning) [29]

<< Action >> : SCENE 3: INTERIOR [30]

<< Action >> : _Enter R_krantz [31]

<< Action >> : _Enter G_stern [32]

<R_krantz> re [33]

<G_stern> re [34]

<Hamlet> re, guys... :-\ [35]

<R_krantz> zup? [36]

<Hamlet> Fucked if i know. brb. . . [37]

<< Action >> : _Exit Hamlet in a sulk. [38]

<G_stern> fuckza matter w/him? [39]

<R_krantz> Guess he must be lagged. Let's lurk [40]

<< Action >> : R_krantz lurks [41]

<< Action >> : G_stern lurks [42]

<< Action >> : SCENE 4: THE QUEEN'S CLOSET [43]

<Hamlet> Ma: what the fuck's going on? [44]

<Queen> Don't flame me, i'm yr Ma! [45]

<Queen> Er. . . . [46]

<Prompter> Psst! Thou hast thy father much offended.. [47]

<Queen> Oh, right. . . . Yr dad's pissed at u [48]

<< Action >> : Hamlet slashes at the arras [49]

<Polonius> Arrrghhhh!!! [50]

   ========= HAMLET /KICK * Polonius [51]

*** Polonius has been kicked off channel #Hamnet by Hamlet

<Queen> Now look what u've done u little nerd. :-([52]

<Hamlet> Wrong man...... Bummer... [53]

<< Action >> : SCENE 5: GRUESOME FINALE [54]

   ========= QUEEN /TOPIC DEATH [55]

*** Queen has changed the topic on channel #Hamnet to "DEATH"

<< Action >> : _Enter Hamlet, Queen, King, Laertes, R_krantz, G_stern [56]

<< Action >> : Queen takes a drink [57]

<< Action >> : King gives Ham & Laer swords [58]

<King> Go for it, lads! [59]

<< Action >> : Laertes stabs Hamlet [60]

<< Action >> : Hamlet stabs Laertes [61]

<< Action >> : Hamlet stabs King [62]

<Queen> Holy shit this Danish vodka is like poison :-@ [63]

<Hamlet> and u always thought i was just wasting my time in chem lab, hehehe [64]

<< Action >> : Queen dies in agony [65]

<King> Aaaaarrgghhh! [66]

<< Action >> : King dies [67]

<Laertes> AAaaaarrrrrhhhhh!!!! [68]

<< Action >> : Laertes dies [69]

<Hamlet> AAAAaaaaaarrrrrhhhhhhhh!!!!!!!!!!!!!!!!!!!!!!!!!!!!!!!! !!!!!!!! [70]

<< Action >> : Hamlet dies [71]

<< Action >> : R_krantz + G_stern GULP!!!!!! [72]

```
**<< Action >>** : _Enter Fortinbras + drum + colours + attendants
[73]
<Fort_bras> EEEEEEEuuuuuucchhhhhh!!!!!! What's been hpng here?
[74]
<Drum> Like, rat-a-tat, man [75]
<Colours> Hmmmmmmm...... [76]
<Attndts> Holy sheeeeet!!!!! [77]
     =========== FORT_BRAS /NICK _King [78]
** Fort_bras is now knwn as _King
**<< Action >>** : _The CURTAIN SLOWLY FALLS. {{{{{{{—THE END—
}}}}}}} [79]
<audience> hmmmmmmmmm..... [80]
```

Figure 3.8. "Hamnet," the script, by Stuart Harris.

```
* SCENE 2: Pcbeth's castle. [18]
* Lady_M swishes about in front of mirror, trying on royal costumes.
[19]
<Lady_M> Me, a queen! I always knew I'd be a star. But that wimp
Pcbeth —
he doesn't have the balls to do what he has to.[20]
* Enter Pcbeth. [21]
<Lady_M> re sugar buns, how was yr day? [22]
<Pcbeth> Bloody awful. Did u hear? We're having the king for
dinner. [23]
<Lady_M> You bet we are, darling. Just leave it to me. [24]
* Enter King. [25]
<King> What a great pad you have here. [26]
<Lady_M> So glad you like it. I decorated it myself. [27]
<King> Marvelous view. Is that Birnam Wood? [28]
<Pcbeth> (aside) I can't do it. [29]
<Lady_M> Just listen to me, marshmallow. I'll get the guards
smashed, then
you take care of the King. Screw up yr courage. [30]
<Pcbeth> (aside) That lady's got balls. [31]
```

Figure 3.9. "PCbeth," Scene 2, by Gayle Kidder.

Play with Shakespeare

Harris and Kidder made "mincemeat" of the characters, plots and texts of the originals. Reduced size is often a key to the presence of playfulness (Sutton-Smith and Kelly-Byrne 1984). Think of toys such as dolls and doll houses, tin soldiers, toy cars. A manual for collectors of doll houses comments, "Our sense of fun and fantasy [is] stimulated by miniatures" (Consumer Guide, 1979: 4).[33]

As Susan Stewart (1978: 101) notes, "The miniature always tends to exaggeration." Particularly in "Hamnet," gross reduction of the length of the text and caricaturization of plot and action, along with transformation of Renaissance poetry into late 20th century colloquial prose and even lowly slang turn the play into a kind of typed Punch and Judy show. The number of named characters in *Hamlet* is slashed from 17 to 9. A five-act script that ordinarily takes hours to perform is impertinently reduced to a mere 80 lines.[34] Some characters barely have one or two lines. The part of Polonius, poor man, is reduced to his one-line death cry:

```
<Polonius> Arrrghhhhh! [50]
```

Play with the Conventions of Script-writing

The "Hamnet" script contained parts not only for Ophelia, Hamlet, the King and Queen, etc. but also for "Enter," "Exit," "Prologue," "Scene," and even inanimate objects like "Drums" and "Colors. "Among these "textual" roles, that of "Prologue," at least, was not entirely Harris's invention. One of the characters in the play-within-the-play in the original *Hamlet* is also called "Prologue." At the opening of the play-within-the-play, he steps forward to declare:

> Prologue. For us, and for our tragedy, Here stooping to your clemency, We beg your hearing patiently.
>
> (*Hamlet*, Act III, Scene 2: 159–161)

Inanimate objects also have to be realized textually, as in

```
<Drum> Like, rat-a-tat, man [75]
```

The scripts included these "roles" because the players actually perform not the play but the text. When all actors perform their lines, they recreate the text online. But they also improvise on it, as will be shown below.

Play with Language

The most obvious contrast in the "Hamnet" scripts was between the now-archaic literary language of the Renaissance English original and the colloquial, often slang, register of contemporary Anglo-American English. Only two of the 80 lines of "Hamnet" cited Shakespeare's own words, intact; the rest was in "IRC-ese." Thus, in Scene 2, when Hamlet and Ophelia meet, the original line "O heavenly powers: restore him!" (Act III, Scene 1: 147) is embedded in an otherwise late 20th-century rendering of their encounter, part colloquial ("stuff"; "nuts"), part digital chat style ("yr" for "your"; the comics-like "hehehehehe," the "smiley" ;-D):

    <Ophelia> Here's yr stuff back [22]
    <Hamlet> Not mine, love. Hehehehehe ;-D [23]
    <Ophelia> O heavenly powers: restore him! [24]
    <<Action>> Ophelia thinks Hamlet's nuts [25]
    <Hamlet> Make that "sanity-deprived", pls. . . . [26]

Note also the politically correct "sanity-deprived."

The script of "PCbeth" was mainly rewritten in IRC-ese and contemporary colloquial English. Only rarely did Kidder contrast the original with contemporary language, as in:

```
Is this a dagger I see before me? Crikes this castle's spooky
at night! [34]
```

Scene 4 of "PCbeth" was an amusing version of Act II, Scene 3 of the original, and contained amusing wordplay and a parody of children's "knock, knock" jokes:[35] Macduff and Lenox are knocking at the gate. <Mac> (Macduff) and the porter play the "knock knock" game:

```
<Mac> Knock knock. [46]
<Porter> Who's there? [47]
<Mac>irc. [48]
<Porter>irc who? [49]
<Mac>: irc u in my dreams, sweet'eart [50]
```

Obscenity was rampant in "Hamnet" and "PCbeth." As Harris put it, "This is not your father's Shakespeare" (Harris, 1995 #2283: 501).[36] The profusion of profane language mocked the canonical status afforded to Shakespeare's works and language in the 20th century. At the same time, the obscenity should not be taken as standing in too strong a contrast. Even in Shakespeare's

language – though not necessarily in Hamlet specifically – the
wide range of registers and styles, and, indeed, much has been w
colloquial and even bawdy language in his plays.[37] In general, IRCers took
particular delight in writing what ordinarily might only be spoken, or at best
scrawled behind the closed door of a public toilet wall. In the pre-digital era,
socialization to the norms of literate culture worked to suppress the use of foul
language in writing.[38]

Play with IRC and Email Conventions and Practices

Both parodies relentlessly spoofed IRC, email and other Internet conventions
and practices. A striking example in "Hamnet" was the line

```
<Hamlet> Oph: suggest u /JOIN #nunnery [27]
```

Instead of "get thee to a nunnery," Hamlet is made to tell Ophelia to join an
IRC channel named *#nunnery*. The script cites the IRC command /join. Ordinarily, the slash is necessary to activate the command online; here, of course
its only function is to make us laugh.[39]

In Scene 1 of "PCbeth." PCbeth and Banquo enter, "armoured for KICK/
BAN/DE-OP wars." Their wars are to be fought with three IRC commands: /
kick removes a person temporarily from a channel, */ban* prevents him or her
from returning; *de-op* is a variant of the notion of chanop, for "channel
operator," a person enjoying certain privileges in managing a channel. To
de-op someone is to deprive him or her of these privileges.

In a second round of the "knock, knock" game, it is the porter's turn:

```
<Porter> Knock, knock. [51]
<Mac> Who's there [52]
```

Mac types */who* to find out. In a clever bit of inter-textuality, eight famous
characters from other Shakespearean plays are revealed to be "lurking" –
King Henry IV, Caesar, Romeo, Othello, Kate (from *Taming of the Shrew*),
Rosenkrantz and Hamlet from *Hamlet*, and Titania from *Midsummer Night's
Dream*! Their identities were rendered as email addresses, ending in appro-
priate domains, "gov," "mil," "edu," etc. (Figure 3.10).[40]

Harris also played with the IRC */nick* command. The software allows
for no more than nine typographic symbols with no empty spaces between them.
"Rosencrantz," "Guildenstern " and "Fortinbras" are cropped to <R_krantz>,
<G_stern>, and <Fort_bras>, with whimsical effect.[41]

```
<Mac> /who                    [54]
<Porter> Channel Nickname     S     User@host (name)
<Porter> #hamnet Hal          H*    henryIV@england.gov
<Porter> #hamnet Romeo        H     rmontague@cs.verona.ac.it
<Porter> #hamnet Caesar       H*    julius@senate.rome.gov
<Porter> #hamnet Othello      A*    moor@doge.venice.mil
<Porter> #hamnet shrew        H@    kate@padua.edu
<Porter> #hamnet rkrantz      H     buddy@cam.ac.uk
<Porter> #hamnet Hamlet       A     prince@castle.elsinore.dk
<Porter> #hamnet Titania      H@    queen@fairies.org
<Porter> hehehe.              [55]
```

Figure 3.10. Characters from other Shakespearean plays "lurking" in "PCbeth."

In Scene 7 of "PCbeth," in which PCbeth consults the witches, the famous line from Act IV, Scene 1 of the original,

Eye of newt and toe of frog,
Wool of bat and tongue of dog

is cited verbatim, but then the witches react in contemporary Net terms:

```
<2witch> Yech! Where'd you get this recipe? [111]
<1witch>: Off the net. I ftp'd it from
mthvax.cs.miami edu of course. [112]
```

The "Hamnet" script also imitated the IRC practice of abbreviating others' nicks. Motivated online by considerations of efficiency, the use of chopped-up nicks here has a comic effect, as in Hamlet's line,

```
<Hamlet> Oph: suggest u /JOIN #nunnery [27]
```

"Oph" is of course "Ophelia."[42]

Textual Freezing of Online Style

The very idea of freezing ephemeral IRC chat style in a solo-authored, quasi-literary text is amusing. The script nicely captured the mix of speech-like, writing-like and digital features that characterized online writing in the 1990s, as one can see even in just these three short lines from "Hamnet:"

```
<Hamlet> 2b or not 2b. . . [17]
<Hamlet> Hmmmmm. [18]
<Hamlet> :-( Bummer. . . [19]
```

These lines contain the speech-like "Hmmm" and "bummer,"[43] speedwriting ("2b or not 2b"), and a frowning smiley, a uniquely digital phenomenon.[44] When one character after another dies, Harris has a field day with multiple exclamation points and the comics-like representation of sounds, so common in ordinary IRC chat:[45]

```
<Polonius> Arrrghhh!!! [50]
<King> Aaaaarrgghhh! [66]
**<<Action>>** : King dies [67]
<Laertes> AAaaaaarrrrrrhhhh!!!! [68]
**<<Action>>**: Laertes dies [69]
<Hamlet> AAAAaaaaaarrrrrrhhhhhhh !!!!!!!!!!!!!!!!!!!!!!!!
  !!!!! [70]
**<< Action >>** : Hamlet dies [71]
```

Logistics of Hamnet Productions

How were Hamnet performances actually produced? Harris worked out most of the details himself. We have already seen that performances were coordinated via Greenwich Mean Time. He used two different strategies to cast the various roles. For the performances of "Hamnet," Harris tried to do all casting more or less at the last minute, inviting all, ahead of time, to convene in the *#hamnet* channel several hours before performance time. During preparations online, he loaded what he called his "*/pora*" file, as in the following example from the December 1993 performance:

```
Line 252   /1 pora
           Please enter P if you wish to be a performer
           Please enter A if you would prefer to lurk in
             the audience
           <NickD> a
```

Here, a person nicknamed <NickD> chose to be a member of the audience by typing "a". Harris then displayed a list of roles to be cast and general instructions for how to perform them.

This system proved too slow and cumbersome, and with the performances of "PCbeth," Harris switched to pre-casting at least the major roles a few days

```
Harris:

Enter the speech, I pray you, as I /QUERY'd it to you,
trippingly on the kybd but if you screw it up, as many of our
Unix users do, I had as lief the town-crier took my /LOADs.
Nor do not flame the chan too much with your attributes,
thus, but use all gently for in the very torrent, tempest,
and, as I may say, whirlwind of your passion, you must
acquire and beget a temperance that
may give irc smoothness.
```

Hamlet:

Speak the speech, I pray you, as I pronounced it to you, trippingly on the tongue: but if you mouth it, as many of your players do, I had as lief the town-crier spoke my lines. Nor do not saw the air too much with your hand, thus but use all gently; for in the very torrent, tempest, and, as I may say, the whirlwind of passion, you must acquire and beget a temperance that may give it smoothness.

(*Hamlet*, Act II, Scene 2: 1–9)

Figure 3.11. Hamlet's advice to the actors and Harris's advice to the "actors".

ahead. To maintain as much spontaneity as possible, he generally sent people only their own lines by email, not the entire script. His file of advice to "actors" parodied Hamlet's famous speech to the actors in the play within the play (Figure 3.11).

To get into "costume," all the players had to do was to change their nicks. Thus, in the February 1994 performance of "Hamnet," in his guise as <Producer> Harris typed:

```
<Producer> OK, ALL PRE-CAST ACTORS CHANGE YR NICKS PLZ
```

The IRC software acknowledged the changes, as in:

```
***Dudester is now known as _Enter
***LoverMan is now known as Colours
***Nibbles is now known as Ghost
***SysBotMgr is now known as Kingg
***PROLOGUE is now known as Prologue
```

The number assigned to each line produced on screen served as a cue for the next person to deliver his or her lines, either by typing them, or by loading prepared miniature files of them.[46]

As noted earlier, performances of "Hamnet" included the display of an ASCII "set," the castle (Figure 3.8). In performances of "PCbeth" two ASCII sets were displayed, as well as some sophisticated color graphics. The ASCII images were of the heath and the banquet table for the famous scene when Banquo's ghost returns (Figure 3.12). In what was evidently the first ever attempt to introduce visual images during an online performance, Kidder also created three striking graphic images to be deployed during performances of "PCbeth" (Plate 3.1). The first image displays a replica of a male Renaissance statue, posed with a computer monitor attached to his head and a computer keyboard in his hands. The same principle of incongruous juxtaposition that characterized the verbal text is evident here too.[47] An idealized male body, the very symbol of yesterday's humanism, is contrasted with today's machines and culture in which the body is seemingly made to disappear and yet is developing an increasingly symbiotic relationship with technology. The second image is a close-up of the hand of the murderer, dipped in bright red paint to symbolize the blood on Macbeth/PCbeth's hands. Finally, in the last one, the statue has been broken, and is scattered on the ground. A reproduction of Edvard Munch's famous "The Scream" has been pasted to the monitor.

Integration of the graphic images into performances was pioneering but primitive, to say the least. They were not displayed collectively online. Individuals could request them and then receive them via the IRC command for immediate transfer of files. Depending on the technology available to them, they could either view them immediately online in a separate window, or, in other cases, could only examine them offline, after the performance.[48]

Hamnet Performances: Some Highlights

Performers did not simply recreate the text on screen, although it is true that they performed the text, not the play. Indeed, if they had only performed the text, word for word, I would not be able to speak of artful performance. Harris was all for improvisation. He told me, "If irc actors ever got so skilled, and the irc audience so tame, that the entire script came out exactly as written, the performance would be a failure by definition."[49]

Improvisations included: (1) play with Shakespeare's text and with the Hamnet Players' scripted version of it, as well as with other Shakespearean plays; (2) play with the theater game – with the roles of actors and audience, etc.; (3) play with frames of interaction; (4) play with the IRC software; (5)

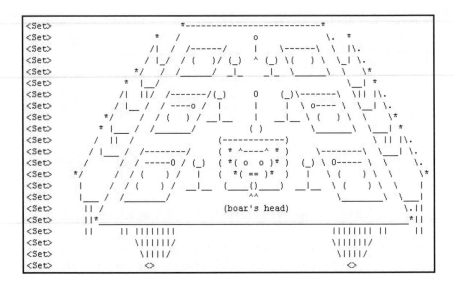

```
<Set>            \\\\\\\\          !           ~  ~
<Set>                                           \        ~~~
<Set>                                  ```\      ----- \|''
<Set>                                   - - -           \
<Set>                                               ~`        /
<Set>                                         ~                /
<Set>                                   ~                     \
<Set>                               ~------    ~               |
<Set>                         ~             0       \
<Set>                                           \  .   \
<Set>      tree bent over by the merciless wind--> \ o   \
<Set>                                             \    . o
<Set>  ---------------------------------------------\ .. \--------------------
<Set>      .                                      \   . 0
<Set>      .            (blasted heath)     .         .  \ .             .
<Set>                      .            .          .   \ 0   \
<Set>      .                  .                        \     \               .
<Set>                           .             .           \    \
<Set>                                                      \.    \       .
<Set>                (cute, huh??)                .         \    . \
<Set>      .              .
<Set> [4]
```

a. The heath.

```
<Set>                     *---------------------------*
<Set>               *    /              o              \.  *
<Set>             /| / /------/      |   \------\  \  |\.
<Set>            / |_/ / (   )/ (_)  ^  (_) \( )  \  \_| \.
<Set>          */  /  /_____/  _|_    _|_  \_____\  \  \*
<Set>         *  |_/                               \__| *
<Set>         /| ||/ /-------/(_)   0   (_)\-------\  \|| |\.
<Set>        / |__ / / ----o /  |       |  \ o---- \  \_| |\.
<Set>      */    /  / ( ) / _|_    |   _|_ \ ( ) \  \    \*
<Set>      * |__ / /_____/       ( )       \_____\ \ \__| *
<Set>     /  || /            (------------)           \ || |\.
<Set>    / |__ / /--------/   ( * ^----^ * )   \--------\  \_| |\.
<Set>   /      / / -----0 / (_) ( *( o  o )* } (_) \ 0----- \ \      \.
<Set>  */     / / (   ) /  |   ( *( == )* }  |   \ ( ) \ \        \*
<Set>  |    / / ( ) /  _|_    (___()___)  _|_   \ ( ) \ \      |
<Set>  |__ / /_____/           ^^            \_____\ \__|
<Set>  || /              (boar's head)                 \.||
<Set>  ||*_____*||
<Set>  ||     || ||||||||                   |||||||| ||    ||
<Set>         \|||||||/                      \|||||||/
<Set>          \|||||/                        \|||||/
<Set>            <>                             <>
```

b. The banquet table

Figure 3.12. ASCII "sets" for "PCbeth."

play with language; (6) play with norms of decorum. Some forms of improvisation were individual, others collective. Individuals who had received their lines beforehand sometimes modified their lines before a performance. But many hijinks were completely spontaneous. Here are some highlights.

Play with Shakespeare

The players often cited snippets from plays other than the one being performed. Thus, in the first performance of "Hamnet," <gazza>, a buddy of Harris, located in Bath, England, popped in during the preparations, and announced that he would have to sign off, drive home from the university, and then log on again. His execution of the /signoff command in IRC appeared on screen as follows:

```
***Signoff:  Gazza (A horse, a horse, my kingdom for a
horse. . . .)
                    ("Hamnet" performance, December 1993)
```

Citing the most famous line in *Richard III* was a humorous way of commenting on his need to go home.

Similarly, during preparations for the second performance of "Hamnet," someone pretending to be <Hamlet> typed

```
<Hamlet> Oh titus come hither. . .
                Oops wrong play

                    ("Hamnet" performance, February 1994)
```

This person had cited a line from *Titus Andronicus*. Another variation is to pretend to be a character from another Shakespearean play. For instance, during December preparations for "Hamnet," someone suddenly changed his/her nick from <Spectator> to <MacBeth>. The move did not go unnoticed:

```
<Recorder> Wrong play Spectator. ;-)
```

One of the best extended examples of an individual playing with Shakespearean texts occurred in the waning moments of an ill-fated November 1993 first attempt to perform "Hamnet". The performance was already in shambles, as a result of an electricity outage in California. Harris himself was about to log off when someone from Israel's Technion began to spout clever parodies of *Hamlet* and *Macbeth* (Figure 3.13). Changing his[50] nick to <Hamlet>, he produced a brilliant improvisation on the famous "To be or not to be" soliloquy." "To be or not to be" was rendered in even more condensed form than in Harris's

HAMLET, Act III, Scene 1.

Line 56   To be, or not to be, that is the question:
           Whether 'tis nobler in the mind to suffer
           The **slings and arrows** of outrageous fortune
           Or to take arms against a sea of troubles
     60   And by opposing end them. **To die: to sleep.**
           No more; and by a sleep to say we end
           The heart-ache and the thousand natural shocks
           That flesh is heir to; 'tis a consummation
           Devoutly to be wish'd. To die: to sleep.

The Improvisation

Line 1   *** RosenKRNZ is now known as Hamlet
           <Producer> . . . . but u'd hv been great
           <Hamlet> **2B | !2B.** . . the question
           <Producer> Welcome lobber. . . the perf is
               cancelled
     5   <Hamlet> Whether tis nobler to the mind
           <tyree> So pls keep me posted on retry huh
               Producerf?
               <Hamlet> To suffer the *splits and lags*
               <Hamlet> That *net is hair* to
               <Producer> tyree:u bet
    10 <Hamlet> Tis a **logoffing** devoutly to be
               wished
           <lobber> was wondering where everybody
               was
           <Producer> Hamlet:u hv definitely got the
               idea
           <Hamlet> **To lag, to split** no more
           /whois Hamlet
    15 *** Hamlet is
           s2887087@techst02.technion.ac.il (The Quantum Cat)
           *** on channels: #hamnet on irc via server irc.technion.
           ac.il
           ([132.68.1.9] Technion, Haifa +Israel)
           <Hamlet> Why don't we do MacBeth
    20 . . .
           <tyree> Fraility, thy nick=woman
           <Hamlet> and tomorrow Tomorrow and
               tomorrow
           <Hamlet> Creeps this pitty *Boudrate d*
           <Hamlet> From **channel to channel**

```
25  <Hamlet> Til the last bit of logged in
            time
    <Hamlet> And all out /whowases out merely
            carriers. . .
    <Hamlet> Lighting the \path or blinded
            fools
    <Hamlet> Is this a channel I see before
            me?
    <Hamlet> Hail McBOT that shall be Choped!
    <Hamlet> Double double noise and
            troublelag +troub
```

Figure 3.13. Parody of Hamlet's soliloquy, aborted performance of "Hamnet," November 1993.

script: "2B | !2B" is mathematicians' formal way of expressing "is/is not." He substituted "splits" and "lags" for "slings and arrows," an appropriate choice both semantically and phonetically: all are single-syllable words and the first word in both expressions begins with /s/ and contains /l/ as well. Moreover, fortuitously, "splits" and "slings" even contain the same vowel sound.

Note especially the transformation of "the heart-ache and the thousand natural shocks/ That flesh is heir to" into "the splits and lags/ That net is hair to." Not only does he substitute one pair of troubles for another, he substitutes the near-homophone "hair" for "heir", because of his association to "net" as in "hair net" (in "hair" the "h" is aspirated; in "heir" it is not).[51]

He substitutes "logoffing" for "consummation," implying that to log off is a kind of "Net-death." "To lag, to split/ No more" is a clever adaptation of "To die, to sleep no more." All are one-syllable words. Both expressions conform to the poetic "principle of end-weight"[52] – in both instances, the member of the pair with the larger amount of phonetic material falls into the second slot, e.g., it takes longer to pronounce "split" than "lag." Third, "sleep" and "split" contain the same three consonants!

Was this parody entirely improvised online or was it prepared ahead of time? We should also ask: was English this person's native language?[53] After all, Hebrew is the mother tongue of native Israelis. It is unlikely that a person whose first language is Hebrew would have such an impressive command of Shakespeare in English. Perhaps this person was an immigrant, or the child of English-speaking immigrants. In any event, it was serendipitous that the electricity outage jibed with his reference to netsplits.

The players frequently changed lines in the scripts, either beforehand or online. For example, in the second full performance of "Hamnet," <Ophelia> modified her original line

```
<Ophelia> Here's yr stuff back [22]
```

to

```
<Ophelia>:   Here's yr crap back, babe: your Mac, your WP 51.a,
             and your dirty mags [22]
```

("Hamnet" performance, February 1994)

This Hamlet uses Word Perfect and reads pornographic magazines. The presence of the line number suggests that this person had changed the line beforehand.

Play with the Theater Game

The players devised verbal equivalents of actors' onstage and backstage behavior. They textually tried their costumes on, and took them off:

```
* G_Stern tries his costume on

* Ophelia slips out of her costume and tosses it aside. "I hate
  stage clothes!"
```

("Hamnet" performance, December, 1993)

The actors peeked out at the audience, sent virtual roses, and took bows:

```
* The_King looks out between the curatins [sic] - whoah-big corwd
  [sic]

* laertes orders roses for ophelia. hopes they will be delivered
  after +performance

* exKing finishes strongly, then takes a *bow* to rapturous
  applause
```

("Hamnet" performance, December 1993)

Still another game was to invent lines having to do with one's "occupation" as a professional actor, as in

```
<GeekChrus> is thre [sic] a rep of actor's guild in the house. . .

*The_King thinks this wait wasn't in his contract.
```

("Hamnet" performance, December, 1993)

The audience did what is expected after the performance, and the person pretending to be a critic did too:

```
<tardy> Bravo! Bravo!Pass the popcorn. . .
<Doctor-> Cheers!
* Vermont claps!
<Doctor-> What a great play! :-)
* SHNELLS gives a standing ovation
<Hacky> bravo !
<GhostBan> hazah! hazah!
<Hacky> bravo !. . .
<TheCritic> CLAP CLAP scribble scribble CLAP scribble CLAP
CLAP
```

("PCbeth" performance, April 1994)

The actors had fun elaborating their roles. In the first performance of "PCbeth," before the actual performance of the script began, the two witches "put on black costumes," gave each other compliments, and improvised some grins and cackles. (Figure 3.14). Then, <witch_1> parodied the famous line "eye of newt, toe of frog," etc., substituting the nicks of known players on IRC for the animals mentioned.

```
*Witch_1 boils up a bit more broth; leg of merp,
  eye of kashka, hair of hidi, tongue of neilm
```

<merp>, <kashka> and <hidi> were all "actors" in the performance itself. <neilm> was a prominent member of a crowd which spent time on the channel *#gb* (one of Harris's online haunts),[54] though he didn't participate in this performance.

Individuals playing inanimate objects used textual means to flesh out their roles.

```
<Drum> Boom Boom Boom Boom BoomBooom. . .
. . .

<GHOST> BOOooooooooo HHHOOOOOOooooooooooo How's that for
        haunting?. . .
<GHOST> I left my sheet a [sic] home. . . .
<GHOST> Better clean up this ghost of an act.[55]
```

("Hamnet" performance, December 1993)

```
*** kashka is now known as Witch_2
<Witch> Am I supposed to be knows [sic] as this.
*** Witch is now known as Witch_1
<Witch_1> that makes sense.
<Witch_2> hello fellow witch :)
        ...
<Witch_1> Witch_2: [grin]
        ...
<Witch_1> Witch_2: Rather suitable for me, don't you
think. ;)
        ...
<Witch_2> W1: oh yes :) you make a wonderful witch :)
<Witch_2> W1: what about me? they say black is my
colour :)
        ...
<Witch_1> W2: Same here really.
        ...
<Witch_1> W2: Well its either a witch or an ugly
sister.
<Witch_2> black is a lovely colour :)
        ...
<Witch_1> w2: ain't it just. 8)
        ...
*Witch_2 cackles
* Witch_1 boils up a bit more broth; leg of merp, eye
of kashka, hair of hidi, tongue of neilm
```

Figure 3.14. Improvisation by the witches, April 1994 performance of "PCbeth."

As I mentioned earlier, after performances, the players had virtual cast parties. Simulated drinks and drugs were handed around, the actors behaved exuberantly, exchanged evaluations of the performance, and so on:

```
SNELLS whips out a few kegs...
* zarquon: attacks the stolichnya...
<zarquon> jeesus more stolichniya...
* kashka looks around for the champagne...
* valeriE is hungover like all hell.
```

("Hamnet" performance, December 1993)

Some of the players gushed about the performance. After the February 1994 performance of "Hamnet," <Hamlet> was especially effusive:

```
Darlings you were wonderful!!!!
```

Play with Frames of Interaction

From within any of the four inner frames of interaction (Figure 3.4), participants could step "out of frame," and into REAL LIFE momentarily, while still logged on and interacting with the others. This happened frequently during Hamnet performances. A cute example was the sudden mention by a member of the audience that his mother was calling him to dinner!

There was also playful blurring of frames. A fine example was the flirtation between <Laertes> and <Ophelia> during the preparations for the December performance of "Hamnet."

```
*laertes eyes ophelia longingly. . .
*ophelia winks at laertes. . .
*laertes slyly moves towards ophelia. . .
*ophelia giggles. . .
*laertes wonders what ophelia is doing after the show. . .
*laertes is feeling realy [sic] excited. . .
*ophelia Kisses laertes and thinks he is such a midevil STUD. . .
```

("Hamnet" performance, December 1993)

This continued, off and on, during the performance:

```
*laertes is falling for ophelia he thinks. . .
*ophelia gives laertes a SMOOCH (you big stud you)
```

In the play, Laertes and Ophelia are, of course, brother and sister, whereas the individuals playing them are not. Thus, these players are blurring the theater frame, within which they are actors playing parts, and the pretend frame within which the performance is taking place.

Play with the IRC Software

Participants played with the IRC software in a host of ways. Occasionally there were spontaneous, non-performative references to IRC commands. Thus, in a one-liner during the December "Hamnet" performance, <G_stern> typed:

```
<G_stern> /set lag off
```

This seemingly innocuous line looks just like many IRC commands. However, there is no such command! Lag is not subject to IRC commands at all. The players could only complain about it. No one but <Recorder> noticed this little move; he typed "Haha" in the next line.

Whereas <G_Stern> only pretended to use an IRC command, <Ophelia> really activated one – the */topic* command – for a playful purpose: to comment on how long it was taking to get organized:

```
*** ophelia has changed the topic on channel #Hamnet to SOMEDAY
    THIS WILL START
```

("Hamnet" performance, December, 1993)

Play with Language

We have already seen many instances of play with language, notably by the person calling himself <Hamlet> in the abortive November 1993 performance. There was not only play with phonetic material, the most prominent feature in the November sequence. Puns were quite common too.[56] Sometimes they were spontaneous one-liners; in other cases they were interactively produced. The most impressive, most extended sequence of punning occurred during the first performance of "Hamnet," as part of ongoing flirtation between the <King> and <Queen>. The transcript in Figure 3.15 has been edited heavily – not to censor it, but, rather, to eliminate material which distracts from the clever wordplay.

In this striking instance of "ping-pong punning" (Chiaro 1992: 114), participants exploited the ambiguity of words used, and tried to outdo each other. This type of punning is generally quite conscious; people hear (in this case, read) each others' contributions and try to keep up the flow of puns. In contrast, other types of punning, in speech at least, may be unconscious or unintentional (Sherzer 1978).

Wordplay hinged on the sexual connotations of "thing", "part", "member", "log", and "enter." */PART* had no less than three meanings in this context. Initially, with the slash in place, it was both a reference to the IRC command by which one leaves the channel (to */part* is to leave), as well as "part" in the sense of role in the play. "Log" first appeared innocuously, when <Scene> asked, ""Is this going to be logged?" and <Recorder> replied, "I am logging it." The <Queen> fell victim to the pun when she typed,

```
* ThE_QuEeN would like a log file sent to her...
```

This extended punning sequence was the high point of the entire session.

* King wonders if queen wishes to produce Any litle heirs?. . .
<King> Queen?
* QuEeN re evaluates the King//. . .says..'with that
little *thig*' [sic] ???
<King> Melady?. . .
<King> Queen - but, you ain't got me excited yet!. . .
<QuEeN> King...what..so then I won't need the
tweezers???. . .
<King> Queen - no . . . calipers, maybe. . .
<DRUM> PLease keep it in the royal Chamber, you too [sic].
<QuEeN> Microinches??. . .
* ophelia thinks that the king and queen should be
BANISHED. . . (or at least thrown in the dungeon *evil
laugh*). . .
* King sits on his thone, unabashed. . .
* King unfolds his full manhood . . . better?
* ophelia chucks the king twards [sic] and [sic] audience **member**
eheheh. . .
<G_Stern> give king his */PART*
<King> heh heh
* King has a HUGE **part**. . .
* QuEeN chuckles . . . at her witless mate. . .
<King> Queen - no wits maybe, but a very nice ****. . .
* *King enters Queen*
* *TheGhost exits right. . .*
<SCENE> Is this going to be *logged*?. . .
<Recorder> SCENE: I am *logging* it. . . .
<DRUM> I am *logging*
* Recorder is *logging* this session. . . .
* ThE_QuEeN would like a *log* file sent to her. . .
* The_King gives the Queen his *log*. . .
* ThE_QuEeN examines said *log*. . . . and puts it toflame
[sic]. . .
* KaiKul warms his hands on the burning *Log*

Figure 3.15. "Ping-pong" punning during the December 1993 performance of
"Hamnet."

Another aspect of the humor in this long sequence depends on still other kinds of play with language. Look again at

```
* King enters Queen
* TheGhost exits right. . .
```

The two sentences appear to be syntactically and semantically analogous. However, "Queen" is a noun, while "right" is an adverb. Here, the humor derives from play with syntax (Chiaro 1992: 40–43). The underlying meanings of "exit right" and "enters Queen" are, of course, entirely different!! Antoinette LaFarge (1995: 418) gives a similar example as characteristic of vaudeville humor:

First Man: "Would you hit a woman with a child?
Second Man: "No, I'd hit her with a brick!"

Play with Norms of Decorum

Finally, there was play with the norms of decorum. The players simulated all kinds of inappropriate behavior on stage and in public, gleefully doing things textually which they would never have done in public (at least not intentionally) in real life. Thus, when the audience in the first "Hamnet" performance got restless, waiting for the show to begin, it began to "throw popcorn and fruit" around:

```
<jeffrey68> I think the audience is hgtting [sic] restless. . .
<jeffrey68> theater owner should have passed out free
            drinks. . . .
<fan> more popcorn please. and could someone tell that lady in
            the third row to take hat off. . .
<AUDIENCE>  throws fruit at javalima. . .
*KaiKul has eaten all his popcorn and started on the box. . .
<AUDIENCE>  mild clapping and shouts of "this better be good!
            we have fruit!"
```
                                  ("Hamnet" performance, December 1993)

There are examples of "urinating" and "passing wind" in public in both the December and the February performances of "Hamnet":

```
*The_King wonders [sic] off for a leak. . .
<The_King> *piddle*. . .
<The_King> *washes hands*
```
                                  ("Hamnet" performance, December 1993)

The choice of "piddle" is apt: it is a word of Elizabethan origin, and one we use nowadays mainly in connection with children and pets. In the February performance one of those present "passed wind:"

*Dudester pases the wind *blat*
Dudester excuses himself. . .
* _Producer freshes [sic] the chan. . .
<_Producer> with a cyber-aerosol

None of the participants even "blinked," textually. <_Producer> quickly "freshened the "air" in the channel with a "cyber-aerosol" spray, and the preparations for the performance continued. In both examples there was also a comics-like element of onomatopoeia: "piddle" and "blat" imitate the sounds of the action.

In the preparatory stages of the first performance of "PCbeth" there was quite a disgusting preoccupation with the contents of noses, spearheaded by <SHNELLS> (Figure 3.16). He textually examined the contents of the noses of <lsb> and <kwis>, and <witch2> suggested putting "nose goblins" in the broth "so we can all have some."

Discussion

A Bakhtinian Carnival of Wordplay

Unlike real-world carnivals, there was no smell of roasting meat, no rollicking music, no jostling crowd of people bumping into one another, no wild dancing in the streets, no dazzling play of color in celebrants' costumes at Hamnet performances. Except for relatively minor additions of graphics and sound, all that occurred was just a lot of typing. Nevertheless, I suggest, Hamnet performances had much in common with RL carnivals.

In Roger Caillois's (1961) terms, both PAIDIA, spontaneous manifestations of the play instinct, and LUDUS, a taste for gratuitous difficulty, were present in Hamnet productions. The theater aspects fell at the Ludus end of the continuum, and the spontaneous, carnivalesque, improvisational aspects, at the Paidia end. Despite the lack of visible bodily presence, the template of Bakhtinian carnival[57] (Figure 3.17) fits these materials remarkably well.

To begin with, the valorization of Eros, or the life force, was unmistakably present in the exuberant spirit of these performances. Second was the Punch-and-Judy-like killing off of characters. Third, as in carnivals, people wore masks – textual ones, their nicks – that transformed their identities and gave them license to be and do what they wanted. There was, in effect, double masking;

```
* SHNELLS:#HAMNET checks lsb's nostrils to pass the
  time. . .
<lsb:#HAMNET> *sneeze*
<Witch_2:#HAMNET> lsb: hahahaha. . .
* SHNELLS:#HAMNET gets a new sample of snot for hre
  [sic] collection. . .
<mAlcOlM:#HAMNET> snot?
<Witch_2:#HAMNET> W1: put some in the broth so we can
  all have some. . .
<lsb:#HAMNET> nose goblins!
<SHNELLS:#HAMNET> boogers :)
* lsb:#HAMNET lurves nose goblins. . .
* mAlcOlM:#HAMNET gives shnells a Kleenex(tm)
<SHNELLS:#HAMNET> boogers dammit
* SHNELLS:#HAMNET thanks malcolm. . .
<SHNELLS:#HAMNET> what a lovely gentleman. . . he gave me a
  kleenex. . .
<Witch_2:#HAMNET> enter: lsb :) he coughs and he farts
* and he crunches. . .
<SHNELLS:#HAMNET> and he loves nose goblins. . .
* SHNELLS checks kwis's nostrils. . .
* Witch_2 burps. . .
* SHNELLS starts to yawn loudly
```

Figure 3.16. Violation of decorum during the first performance of "PCbeth."

the players exchanged their regular nicks for the special ones required by the performance. Fourth, there was much preoccupation with the body, though of course in a simulated manner. Recall the virtual representations of urinating, passing wind, and picking other people's noses.

As for subversion of established power, the parodization of canonical Shakespeare was paramount. Making fun of the rules and practices of IRC seemingly subverts them; I would argue that it also contributes to their validation. The gleeful intermingling of theater professionals with rank amateurs was also potentially subversive of the theater establishment.

Perhaps the prime characteristic of carnivals is the sense of *communitas*, (no. 6, Figure 3.17), the temporary suspension of hierarchical difference while participants are in a liminal state, and the resultant feelings of solidarity among equals. We have seen that team spirit and an awareness of making history characterized both performers and audience members. This spirit also led to celebration at "cast parties." In RL carnivals, there is a temporary leveling

Feature	How Expressed
1. Valorization of Eros, life force	exuberance of Hamnet activities
2. Concatenation of life and death	slapdash, Punch-and-Judy-like treatment of death
3. Transformations of identity	masking of identity through nicks; license to be and do what you want; textual costumes" for roles; gender-bending; age irrelevant
4. Preoccupation with the body	virtual representation of bodily functions: "picking noses," "farting," "cutting toenails"; aggressive, even cannibalistic sexuality – "peach buns"
5. Subversion of established power	parody of Shakespeare; validation of rules, practices of IRC through mockery; theater professionals mixing with amateurs
6. *Communitas*	team spirit; awareness of mutual undertaking; making history together; celebration; champagne
7. Valorization of "low" language	obscenity; slang; colloquialisms
8. Rejection of decorum	breaches of theater, IRC etiquette: "Hamnet": flirting among "actors;" noisy audience; throwing fruit; stealing nicks " Pcbeth": flirting among "actors"
9. Anticlassical aesthetic	multiplicity of improvisational styles and voices: juxtaposition of oral/written; old/new; high/low
10. Carnival as participatory spectacle	textual spectacle; beginning & end; blurring of performer-audience boundaries; sense of occasion; desire for logs
11. Sense of abandon	the ilinx of wordplay

Figure 3.17. Elements of carnival in Hamnet performances.

:rsal of full RL status hierarchies. The poor people have their
liberties not allowed in ordinary everyday life, and so on. In
carnivals discussed in this chapter were elite events in which,
y well-educated, relatively sophisticated middle-class, computer-
literate persons with access to advanced technology could participate.[58]

Valorization of "low" language is a seventh feature of carnivals. We saw
that there was abundant obscenity in "Hamnet" performances – well beyond
that already in the script. Also present was rejection of behavioral decorum,
(no. 8, Figure 3.17), exploring other people's noses, "throwing" popcorn and
fruit, being noisy and interrupting the proceedings, flirting, and so on.

Yet another feature of carnivals stressed by Bakhtin, the presence of an
anticlassical aesthetic – the mixing of styles and voices – was prominent. The
players elaborated constantly on the mix of contemporary low language and
Shakespearean materials in the script, adding snippets from other Shakespearean
plays, mocking Shakespearean style, and so on.

Like RL carnivals, Hamnet performances were participatory spectacles: the
boundaries between performers and spectators became blurred, as spectators
joined in the festivities, and all became part of the same milling crowd. As in
carnivals, the primary sense involved was that of sight, since everything took
place on the computer screen. Audience members were very active, inventing
all kinds of virtual bits of behavior, verbal and non-verbal – passing popcorn,
hissing and booing, expressing impatience, "clapping," "cheering," "throwing
flowers," yelling "bravo," and so on.

Finally, we come to another important component, the sense of abandon.
In Stam's synthesis of Bakhtin's model of carnivals, he emphasizes uncontrollable, wild laughter:

> The culture of real laughter (as opposed to canned or forced laughter) is absolutely
> central to Bakhtin's conception of carnival: enormous, creative, derisive, renewing
> laughter that grasps phenomena in the process of change and transition . . . Carnival-
> esque laughter can be raucous, subversive, even angry. . . laughter is profound,
> communitarian, erotic, a current passing from self to self in a free and familiar
> atmosphere. (Stam 1989: 120)

In a situation of typed communication among persons only remotely present
to one another, what evidence can we provide for the sense of abandon that
accompanies uncontrollable laughter?

There are some instances of written-out laughter in the logs, usually written
as "hehehehe." However, they are rare. At the same time, judging by the
reactions of my research group to Hamnet scripts and performances, I am sure
that both players and audience were not just having a wonderful time, but

had many a belly laugh. Moreover, there is evidence in the logs themselves that justifies this claim.

In RL carnivals uncontrollable laughter is one expression of ilinx. In Caillois's (1961) classification of games, those characterized by ilinx incorporate features which "attempt to momentarily destroy the stability of perception. . . (and) reality with sovereign brusqueness" (Caillois 1961: 23). I agree with Test (1991) that

> no linguistic phenomenon can compete with physical activity in inducing this condition. . . . But language can shock, inflict pain, induce instability, and otherwise disorient perceptions and feelings in such a way that is as real as dizziness or the feeling of falling (Test 1991: 133).

In any instance where the formal aspects of language are foregrounded, where the free play of signifiers predominates, there is potential distraction from taking in referential meaning (Kirshenblatt-Gimblett 1976, Introduction; Palmer 1994: 140–141), but the distraction is usually relatively limited. When wordplay is as rich and prominent as it is in Hamnet materials, and experienced in a rowdy crowd atmosphere, even if virtual, participants share a sense of heightened excitement. I suggest that even a one-line pun is a "tiny ilinx", which can induce an explosion of laughter. Moreover, there is a cumulative effect of being present at, and participating in extended sequences of wordplay in "Hamnet" performances.

The Flowering of Verbal Art Online

A vast research literature in folklore and the ethnography of communication has long documented playfulness and stylization in many oral genres of communication, in societies without writing and in certain sub-cultures within literate societies, e.g., Afro-American culture.[59] This chapter broke new ground by documenting the flowering of artful uses of language and typography in interactive writing – a new phenomenon in the history of human communication. The analysis adds strength to the argument earlier in the chapter that online group communication can afford a sense of presence not so very different from that in face-to-face encounters. We saw that, contrary to common sense expectations, hearing the sounds of words is not essential for extensive interactive punning to take place. The punning and other forms of wordplay in Hamnet productions were very much in the spirit of Shakespeare himself. His works are full of puns (Hussey 1992: 142–145), even in contexts where, to many modern eyes and ears, puns seem perhaps inappropriate, as in Mercutio's line in *Romeo and Juliet* (III.1), "Ask for me tomorrow and you shall find me a grave man" (Culler 1988: 3).

We can see that digitization invites us once again, as in oral cultures, to pay attention to the form of messages. The bias of print culture has been to suppress stylization in the name of transparency of meaning (Palmer 1994, chap. 11). As august a literary figure as the 18th-century Samuel Johnson nastily condemned the puns in Shakespeare as being against "reason, propriety and truth" (Attridge 1988: 140; Palmer 1994: 141). Test (1991: 156) suggests that puns have had a particularly bad press in relation to the English language. Maurice Charney noted, in reference to the rise of literature and the status of the comic in literature, that

> Writing, and especially printing . . . tends to fix and stabilize meanings . . . In an oral culture, the sounds are literally the basic units of meaning, with almost unlimited possibilities for punning. The awareness of spelling tends to restrict the free play of the comic imagination. (Charney 1978: 19)

During online typing we are released from the need to pay attention to spelling.

Bolter made a similar point when discussing the nature of the new electronic medium. He wrote: "there is a solemnity at the center of printed literature – even comedy, romance, and satire – because of the immutability of the printed page" (Bolter 1991: 130). As Nash puts it, "We take punning for a tawdry and facetious thing, one of the less profound forms of humor, but that is the prejudice of our time" (Nash 1985: 138). Even in contemporary conversation they are often looked down upon, or seen as a distraction (Sherzer 1978; Stewart 1978; Test 1991). But the most prejudiced attitudes clearly pertain to writing, and especially to print. There has been discomfort with figures of speech that pluralize meaning; this is reinforced by a positivistic desire to set boundaries, to establish structure and unity.

> We take monist reasoning for granted. Truthfulness [has been] equated with simplicity, not complexity. . . Figures of speech such as metaphor or irony confuse binary thought because they add the complexities of 'both/and' to "either/or", thereby blurring the lines we like to draw between truth and falsehood, fact and non-fact . . . punning is not respectable . . . Most Europeans. . . are trained to admire irony but to disapprove of puns. The socially expected response to a pun is a ritual protest: a groan. (Ahl 1988: 21)

From the vantagepoint of her experience in online theater in MOOs, Antoinette La Farge of the Plaintext Players argued that MOO language has a special beauty – because it is condensed, allusive, and rhythmic. It is condensed because the speed of online writing requires a short typed utterance.

If you take the time to construct a whole paragraph, you'll be left behind in the flow. So you quickly develop a sense that you are contributing lines to a larger whole, rather than fashioning fully formed thoughts. A single text of many voices sounds very different from what we normally expect of writing; closer to cantata than to prose.[60]

It is allusive because of constant topic shifts and because simultaneous voices appear on the screen out of order; unexpected conjunctions "create the poetry of metaphor." Finally, says LaFarge, "MOOspeak's rhythms tend to be staccato because of the quick, shifting lines of thought," and to be "oral", creating a kind of "vocal counterpoint." Earlier, I spoke of the jazz-like quality of playful verbal performance on IRC. Note the recurrence of musical metaphors in LaFarge's description too-"cantata," "staccato," "vocal counterpoint."

Why Shakespeare?

It is not by chance that Shakespeare was the butt of Hamnet parodies. Many people have commented on the fact that we tend generally to parodize what is very familiar. Again and again, in different times and places, we turn to Shakespeare, especially when consensus wavers, or in times of change. When Thomas Edison toured cities promoting and demonstrating his new invention, the telephone, about 100 years ago, he drew on Hamlet's "To be or not to be" soliloquy (Aronson 1971).

Lawrence Levine (1988) analyzed vagaries in the popularity of Shakespeare in American culture from colonial times to our own times. Shakespeare was extremely popular in 19th-century America, so much so that performances of his plays and derivatives of them, including parodies as outrageous as those discussed here, were a major form of popular culture. By mid-19th-century, his plays had become "a staple of theaters in the Far West" (Levine 1988: 19). Levine comments, "Shakespeare's popularity in frontier communities. . . [fits] our knowledge of human beings and their need for the comfort of familiar things under the pressure of new circumstances and surroundings" (Levine 1988: 20).

For all the attractions of the strange new world that is the Internet, we too hanker after the familiar. No doubt, Stuart Harris chose plays by Shakespeare intentionally, in order to reach as wide an audience as possible. The choice was also a natural one for him, given his background as an Englishman with experience in theater now living in the United States.

There is clear independent evidence of the continuing centrality of Shakespeare in contemporary English-speaking culture. In this postmodern era when the very notion of canon is being undermined, there are those who are working desperately to save it. Harold Bloom's (1994) "heroically brave" (Fruman 1994:

9) attempt to restore or salvage the canon in the humanities placed Shakespeare among the four masters of Western drama. In a survey carried out for the *New York Times* at the beginning of 1995, respondents were asked which is the most important drama in current Western culture.[61] Remarkably, seven out of the dramas in the top ten were plays by Shakespeare, and *Hamlet* won first place. These results suggest that not just technological change, but disquiet in times of major cultural change, pushes us toward the familiar. Thus, Shakespeare remains an important cultural anchor as we enter the 21st century and the enormous technological changes that it will bring.

Globalization, Democratization and The Hamnet Players

There has been, and no doubt will continue to be, a good deal of overly optimistic talk about the potential of the Internet to foster globalization and democratization of culture. Although there were many channels on IRC for non-English-speaking groups in the mid-1990s, most were English-speaking/writing. Hamnet scripts were written in English, and performances were also in English. Did the group mainly attract people from English-speaking countries, thereby fostering in its small way the continuing domination of English language and culture on the Net? Did these activities mainly attract members of an elite, or was their appeal broader than that?

Examining logs for the addresses[62] of participants in all six Hamnet performances – not only the two of "Hamnet", but also those of "PCbeth" and "An IRC Channel Named #Desire," I found that at the beginning, people from American universities stood out both as participants and as audience (addresses ending in "edu" dominated). However, over time the British element became more prominent, and people from a wider range of countries joined in. Among the countries represented, in addition to the United States and England, were Slovenia, Switzerland, Israel, Finland, Ireland, Slovakia, Austria, Canada, Taiwan, New Zealand, South Africa, Norway, the Netherlands, and Sweden. People from Asian countries were notably absent. To some extent this reflected the slowness of some of these countries (especially China) to discover and join the Internet. Another difficulty was that some public servers, e.g., that in Taiwan, were frequently used by people in the West to gain access to IRC, so an address including any of these servers did not always indicate a participant logged on from that country.

Nevertheless, the international element steadily grew over time, and the dominance of Americans and of people belonging to academic institutions declined. In part this reflected more general changes in the Internet itself, as wider sectors of society joined it. Among Americans, a higher proportion of persons whose addresses end with "com " (commercial sector) participated in the later performances.

The record for women in Hamnet activities was encouraging, a modest reflection of the increased entry of women in cyberspace in the latter half of the decade. While there were relatively few women among the performers in "Hamnet", by the time of "An IRC Channel Named #Desire", roughly half the performers were women.

At the same time, let us not romanticize these developments. As long as the English language continues to dominate virtual theater, and indeed, many other activities on the Net, the ability of persons whose native language is not English to participate will remain problematic – unless, of course, they are fairly competent bilinguals.[63]

Virtual Theater after the Hamnet Players

Stuart Harris and Gayle Kidder ceased Hamnet activities as of 1995, primarily because of the technical problems of netspits and lag, and perhaps also because, despite Harris's professional and semi-professional theater experience and interests, he was, after all, primarily a computer professional, and had to get back to making a living.[64] This had been entirely a volunteer effort, done "for love." I know of no other attempt to create virtual theater on IRC, up until the time this book was completed, whereas experimentation with MOOs for this purpose began to flourish in the years that followed.

In the late 1990s the term "virtual theater" came to include a wide variety of experimental modes both text-based and spoken, including performances combining real and virtual actors, events involving virtual actors only, use of avatars to represent actors graphically, online performance among actors all in one place but broadcast on the Internet, etc. This is not the place to review these developments in any detail, except to comment that they were part of the enormous ferment with respect to technology and the arts as the millennium approached.

What is pertinent to the chapter, however, was continued interest in the use of text in performance online. Some half dozen or more individuals and groups continued to experiment specifically with this mode, after the Hamnet Players ceased their activities. In Figure 3.18 I have listed five of the most prominent individuals and groups.

The most extensive accomplishments were those of Antoinette LaFarge and the "Plaintext Players." Unlike Hamnet performances, her group did not use scripts; rather, LaFarge usually created detailed scenarios for actors, which they then realized in improvisation under her direction. She called performances "directed textual improvisations" (LaFarge 1996). With experience both in IRC and MOOs, LaFarge continues to believe in the dramatic potential of this seemingly limited medium. She sees it as a hybrid form, drawing

(1) "The Plaintext Players," Antoinette LaFarge, founder, director, performer, University of California, Irvine
http://yin.arts.uci.edu/~players/
Home Page: http://yin.arts.uci.edu/~forger

Performances: "The Candide Campaign;" "Gutter City;" "Little Hamlet;"
ID MOO, PMCMOO.

(2) Steve Schrum, script-writer, director, University of Charleston, West Virginia
http://socks.ntu.ac.uk/archive/net/netseduction.html
Home Page: http://www.uchaswv.edu/theatre/SSchrum.html

Performances: "NetSeduction," ATHEMOO

(3) Rick Sacks. Toronto
http://www.vex.net/~rixax/Kafka.html

Performances: "MetaMOOphosis," ATHEMOO

(4) Twyla Mitchell-Shiner, script-writer, director, Santa Barbara, California
"A Place for Souls,"
http://www.geocities.com/Wellesley/2190/souls/aplaceforsouls.html.

Performances: "A Place for Souls," March, 1998, ATHEMOO

(5) The Oudeis Project, Monika Wunderer, Vienna
Oudeis Project Website: http: www.oudeis.org/
Home Page: http://st1hobel/phl.univie.ac.at/~wunderer/

Figure 3.18. Individuals and groups involved in text-based online theater In MOOs, 1993–1999.

as heavily on the performative tradition as it does on the written. Among its theatrical antecedents I count such forms as vaudeville and commedia dell'arte . . .

. . . Like vaudeville, online theater lends itself to the extravagant, the absurd, and especially the comic.

. . . One must look all the way back to W.C. Fields and the Marx Brothers – who. . . also came out of the vaudeville tradition – for predecessors who would have appreciated the physical and verbal elaborations of online theater. (LaFarge 1995: 417–418)

In more recent writing she added:

> Online theater. . . is marked by loose (often episodic) structure, tangled narrative, chaotic rhythm, uncontrolled utterance, superfluous detail, and refusal to end. Seen through the critical lens by which we usually examine theater, it often looks crude, sloppy, and buffoonish, a caricature of theater as it could be, or as our egos think it should be. Seen as what it is, a true collective form, a networked art through which the id comes into its own, it shines with the beauty of the complex, the uncertain, and the unknown. (LaFarge 1997)

The Website of the Plaintext Players listed performances of four different groups of works, in venues that made a claim for legitimation in the performing arts. Their 1997 production "Orpheus" was shown at "Documenta X," the prestigious avant-garde art venue in Kassel, Germany. "The White Whale" was inaugurated for the Venice Biennale, also in 1997. "Still Lies Quiet Truth" was performed at the 1998 New York International Fringe Festival. Several of the group's productions were screened "live" in New York art galleries, while being performed online.

Stephen Schrum, the second person listed in Figure 3.18, is a theater director and academic, convenor of the COLLAB-L list[65] for persons interested in theater and performance, and editor of a collection of papers on theater in cyberspace (Schrum 1998).[66] Schrum created a work called "NetSeduction." He described it as set in an Internet chat room and meeting place, with a bar, dance floor, and people to meet. Visitors to ATHEMOO,[67] a theater-oriented MOO run by Juli Burk, head of Theater and Dance at the University of Hawaii, where it was performed, were invited to "take costumes" and participate. There were three categories of participants, lurkers, players, and "supers," audience members who interact with players.

"MetaMOOphosis," a project inspired by Kafka's short story "Metamorphosis," was created by Rick Sacks, who described himself on his Website as "a percussionist/composer/multimedia artist." He created "MetaMOOphosis" as a "permanent installation of interactive theater" at ATHEMOO. Twyla Mitchell-Shiner developed a project, "A Place for Souls," in connection with an M.A. thesis on Internet theater. A Ph.D. student at the University of Hawaii, Manoa, she wrote the script of "A Place for Souls" with her husband. It was performed three times in ATHEMOO.

Finally, I have listed Monika Wunderer's ambitious project, "Oudeis – a World Wide Odyssey." This group aspired to tell the story of Homer's Odyssey via the Internet with actors from eight countries interacting simultaneously but remotely, each in his or her own language. On the opening page of its Website (viewed in August 1999), Wunderer, a Viennese playwright, described it as "a work in progess on hold."[68] Because of difficulties raising money and coordinating a complex international project, there had been no full-scale performance as this chapter was completed, though a partial performance did take place in September 1997, in a workshop in Vienna and at Ars Electronica in Linz, Austria. It combined elements of the Oudeis concept, including both action on a live stage and textual material on a MOO.[69]

It is evident that these people all treated the topic of online text-based theater with great seriousness. Nearly all them had formal academic training and/or experience in theater, and some of them had academic affiliations. From browsing at the various Websites, I also learned that several had been in close touch, and had participated in each others' events.

Why was activity since the Hamnet performances concentrated in MOOs and not IRC? I addressed this question to these others experimenting with virtual theater. Stephen Schrum, Antoinette LaFarge and Monika Wunderer all mentioned the open-ended, programmable nature of the MOO environment, in which one can construct (textually) sets and other objects that persist over time.[70] LaFarge added two other factors: the dependable anonymity of the medium,[71] and the ability to "spoof" others – to contribute text attributed to others rather than oneself.[72] She argued that "True pseudonymity allows for much more adventurous performance and a psychologically richer experience."[73]

Apart from the Plaintext Players, the accomplishments of these groups and individuals seemed fairly limited at the time this chapter was completed in the fall of 1999, despite, or perhaps because of their ambitions.[74] It is likely that the "bare bones" nature of communication on IRC and the simplicity of Harris's solutions to production problems were the secret of his group's success. At the same time, it was perhaps inevitable that the limitations of IRC would lead others to look elsewhere for progress in the development of virtual theater. In a very few years all these experiments will seem archaic. Whatever direction future developments in virtual theater take, I have no doubt that the Hamnet Players will retain a place in the history of Internet performance in the late 20th and early 21st centuries.

Notes

1. See my discussion of a letter I received from a student nicknamed "Technosmurf" and my correspondence with D.G., a software developer, both in Chapter 2.

2. For a more complete presentation of this sequence and its analysis than I can include here, see Danet, et al. (1998) or Ruedenberg, et al. (1995). An abridged version of the 1998 paper is available online (Danet et al. 1997).

3. In some chat programs, dialog is also sometimes displayed with each person's contributions in a separate window. ICQ, for instance, offers the option of either IRC-style or the separate-window mode, as was customary in UNIX @talk mode.

4. Despite this difference, MOOs have also been featured in online performance. See Figure 3.18 and the discussion of text-based performance on MOOs at the end of the chapter.

5. I follow the IRC convention of brackets around nicknames, or "nicks," as they are called.

6. The idea of frames nested within one another draws on a paper by Victor Turner (1986c). This diagram was created by Fay Sudweeks for online and print publication of the paper from which this summary is excerpted (Danet et al. 1997; 1998).

7. The asterisks around <Thunder>'s nick are an indication from the IRC software that this was sent as a private message.

8. Cf. Handelman (1976); Honigmann (1977); Turner (1986).

9. *Bagelnosh* was a channel that Ruedenberg and Madeline Slovenz-Low, another graduate student at New York University at the time, had often created on IRC. It had become a "hang-out" where regulars chatted daily.

10. They were much quicker than Ruedenberg-Wright to figure out what was happening, no doubt a function of their younger age and life experience.

11. *Puff* and *hold* may be either nominalizations or infinitives, the names of the actions, or even first-person verbs with the pronoun "I" deleted. I cannot determine whether <Kang> was directly influenced by knowledge of comics conventions, but it seems reasonable that players reinvented such conventions in response to needs experienced online.

12. In collections of smileys this combination of symbols appears as a representation of a person smoking. See, e.g., Godin (1993: 13).

13. See Bauman (1975; 1977; 1992).

14. The address of this list is PERFORM-L@lists.nyu.edu. This is a forum for discussion of all aspects of theater and performance.

15. See. e.g., Schechner (1985; 1993).

16. These categories appeared in a posting by Schechner to PERFORM-L on 3 June 1995.

17. A bot is a small program; bots on IRC are additions to the basic program which perform specific functions. The term "robot" contains the word "bot."

18. This statement was written just after the first performance of "PCbeth." I received a copy on 1 May 1994.

19. An example of humor about lag on IRC appears in Plate 6.14, though not very clearly, because the image clashes with two others played at the same time. The one about lag is the narrowest of the three.

20. See the passage from Bauman (1992) cited above.

21. Tsameret Wachenhauser revised the original diagram by Fay Sudweeks.

22. For a review of conceptualizations of "presence" in a number of academic fields, see Lombard and Ditton (1997).

23. See also discussions of immersiveness in Laurel (1991) and Murray (1997), Chapter 4.

24. The Plaintext Players use MOOs to perform textually online; the URL of this group is http://yin.arts.uci.edu/~players/. See also Figure 3.18 and the discussion of virtual theater at the end of the chapter.

25. Academic psychology even tends to define them as a physical phenomenon: "Affects are sets of muscular and glandular responses located in the face and also widely distributed throughout the body, which generate sensory feedback, that is either inherently acceptable or unacceptable" (Tomkins 1980: 142).

26. A *Los Angeles Times* journalist was present, at Harris's invitation. Harris and Kidder had their pictures taken in costume. The individuals listed in Figure 3.5 as playing <Lady_M> and <King> did not show up for the performance; others took their place.

27. Harris succeeded in attracting a good deal of attention for Hamnet productions in the media, including the *Los Angeles Times*, the *San Diego Union-Tribune*, *U.S. News and World Report*, the *Guardian*, the *London Sunday Times*, and *Internet World*. I published a short article on them in *Wired Magazine* (Danet 1994), and Harris himself authored one for *Online Access* (Harris 1994). In addition, he was interviewed on national and local radio.

28. See Stewart (1978); Spaeight (1990).

29. Personal email from Stuart Harris, 20 September 1994. This show is enormously popular. It opened in London in March, 1996, and as of summer, 1999, was the longest-running play in the West End, and was booked well into 2000.

30. See Berliner (1994).

31. On incongruity in humor, see, e.g., Charney (1978); Hutcheon (1985); Test (1991); Oring (1992); Palmer (1994).

32. Original materials relating to the Hamnet Players are available on the companion Website to this book, URL in the Table of Contents.

33. See also my examples of one-line ASCII art, Figure 5.25.

34. "PCbeth" is not quite so extreme in this respect – it contains 163 lines.

35. The phrase "Knock, knock. Who's there" actually occurs in the Porter's original speech, and is not simply imported from the children's game. Perhaps Shakespeare took it from the children's game too.

36. See, e.g., lines 12, 14, 37, 39, 44, 48, and 63 in "Hamnet," Figure 3.8.

37. See Partridge (1968); Hussey (1992); Hughes (1991), chap. 5.

38. See, e.g., Allan and Burridge (1991). Even long after the revolutionary trial of the 1960s which allowed D.H. Lawrence's *Lady Chatterley's Lover* to be published at last, four-letter words relating to bodily excretions or sexuality continue to shock many people when written or in print. There were other kinds of play with language during performances, e.g., word games and spelling games. See Danet et al. (1995).

39. Harris and Kidder incorporate IRC commands in their scripts in two very different ways. Sometimes, the command is merely mentioned in a witty manner, without any intention of its being activated when the script is actually performed online, as in

```
<2witch> Hail PC, Thane_of_Cawdor! soon 2b /nick King /mode
+0 [10]
```

PCbeth will really only become King, as it were, the day he types */nick King*. In other instances the script is designed so that typing the command online will actually bring about a change via the IRC software.

40. Earlier in "PCbeth" there is another playful email address. The previous Thane of Cawdor is rendered as

```
traitor@saint.colmes.inch.uk.
```

The real Thane of Cawdor had betrayed the English at St. Colmes, Inch. "Uk" is the standard abbreviation for "United Kingdom" in email addresses.

41. This was not just playing with the convention in the script. Nicks really had to conform to this requirement in order to function during performances.

42. The similarity to the sounds "Ooof" or "Oops," as in comics, may also be a source of humor.

43. The slang term "bummer" is "an unpleasant or depressing experience, especially one induced by a hallucinogenic drug; a disappointment, a failure" (Aytot and Simpson 1992).

44. For other examples of smileys in the "Hamnet" script, see lines 14, 23, and 63, Figure 3.8.

45. See Werry (1996).

46. See the "Hamnet" script, Figure 3.8.

47. The idea of a computer monitor as the "head" on a human body was not unique to Harris and Kidder. In the November 18, 1998 edition of *Ha'aretz*, a Hebrew daily newspaper in Israel, there was an advertisement for Unisys Corporation with the same idea.

48. For additional details on logistics, see Danet, et al. (1995).

49. Personal email, July 27, 1995.

50. I say "he" only because more males than females study technical subjects.

51. It is possible that "hair" was a serendipitous misspelling of "heir," done on the fly.

52. See, e.g., Malkiel (1959); Gustafsson (1974; 1975; 1976); Danet (1984).

53. I was unable to ascertain this person's email address and therefore could not ask him these questions.

54. "gb" stands for Great Britain, a channel for English people.

55. Note the playful merging of "ghost of a chance" with "clean up one's act."

56. I did note the possible pun "heir" vs." "hair" in the November sequence, but play with phonetic aspects was predominant in that sequence.

57. See Bakhtin (1968); Turner (1969; 1986a; 1986b); Stam (1989).

58. I should not exaggerate this point since I have no information on the education, occupation or social class of most participants, but the claim is reasonable, given the time at which these performances took place. The social profile of players in the text-based art channels discussed in Chapter 6 is quite different. There, I document the later entrance of lower middle-class and lower-class groups into the new digital culture.

59. See, e.g., Hymes (1964); Kirshenblatt-Gimblett (1976); Edwards and Sienkewicz (1990); Bauman (1977). I do not mean to suggest that stylization and playfulness necessarily go together. Indeed, in many settings they do not.

60. Personal email from Antoinette LaFarge, 19 August 1999.

61. This appeared in a 1995 *New York Times* article, and was cited in the Hebrew newspaper *Ha'aretz*.

62. These are the addresses of the host computers via which people logged on, not their personal email addresses.

63. There are countries where bilingualism and even multilingualism are routine, e.g., the Netherlands, where people speak German, English and French as well as Dutch. Perhaps full bilingualism must be a goal of many countries in the future.

64. See the Website of Harris and Kidder's partnership in producing computer manuals, among other things: http://www.beachmedia.com/.

65. The address of the list is COLLAB-L@lists.psu.edu.

66. In the late 1990s he moved from Pennsylvania State University to the University of West Virginia. Schrum reports that several chapters in his book relate to MOOs. Unfortunately, I was not able to examine them as this chapter was completed.

67. ATHEMOO was the site of much discussion and experimentation regarding online theater in the latter half of the decade. See http://moo.hawaii.edu/athemoo/.

68. The site was created in 1996 or 1997, but had not been updated since March, 1999.

69. Telephone interview with Monika Wunderer, August 29, 1999.

70. Personal email from Stephen Schrum, August 17, 1999, from Antoinette LaFarge, August 16, 1999; telephone interview with Monika Wunderer, August 24, 1999.

71. She claims that, with a little effort, it is often possible to discover people's email addresses on IRC.

72. She also mentions the continuity of MOOs as persistent worlds, though this appears to be a restatement of the first point.

73. Personal email from Antoinette LaFarge, 16 August 1999.

74. Schrum, for instance, admitted to being on a "hiatus," while he waited for a richer, multimedia environment, which could offer more interactivity and the ability to combine text with graphics. Personal email, 17 August 1999.

4

"Don't Just Send a Card, Send a Cyber Greeting!" Digital Greetings on the World Wide Web

In this chapter, we move from textual to visual and multimedia phenomena. I offer a cultural critique of a fledgling phenomenon on the World Wide Web in the mid- to late 1990s: multimedia greetings as an alternative to traditional paper postcards and greeting cards. A site called "The Animated Musical Greeting Card Store" was typical (Plate 4.1). The virtual equivalent of a greeting card rack in a physical store, the site offered greetings with music and animation in a number of categories, including Birthday, Love & Romance, Congratulations, Get Well, Anniversary, Thank you, Friendship, and Invitation. Like many such sites, this one radiated playfulness: the use of many colors and particularly the prominence of red, the expression "WOW!" displayed at an angle in a handwriting-like font and with a breathless exclamation point, the dancing musical note, and the little party hat all signaled "This is fun!" However, life is not all fun. Death and many other kinds of troubles are part of life too. Note that whereas paper cards conventionally include a category for condolence or sympathy greetings, they were strikingly absent from this site. Nor were there categories for apologies or encouragement in time of difficulties.

Introductory examples of digital greetings are shown in Plates 4.2 and 4.3. The birthday greeting (Plate 4.2) was for sale in the fall of 1997 on a Website called "Cyber Greetings," and cost $1.25. The title of this chapter comes from the slogan of this Website: "Don't just send a card, send a cyber greeting!"[1] The enthusiasm of the slogan is enhanced once again by an exclamation point. Unlike many others, however, greetings offered on this Website are by named professional artists.[2] The Christmas greeting in Plate 4.3 was documented in December 1997, and contained a light touch of animation. The halos on the angels "glowed," off and on, and their mouths opened and closed. A MIDI snippet of "Jingle Bells" played while one viewed it. Unlike the birthday greeting, those on this site were free.[3]

I report here on the first of two case studies of digital greetings. The present chapter stands on its own, but also provides important background for the study in Chapters 5 and 6 on ASCII art. As explained in the Introduction, ASCII art is a form of making pictures with typographic symbols. While people have mainly made and collected such pictures just for fun, ASCII art images have also circulated by email as birthday and holiday greetings. Communicative functions of these images takes center stage in Chapter 6, where I focus on interactive text-based greetings exchanged in real time on IRC. But first, we need to consider the history of paper greetings – postcards and greeting cards – and their migration to the World Wide Web, the subject of this chapter.

My main source of information for this chapter was Internet Card Central, an index created and maintained by Margaret Collins, a professional librarian who manages it as a hobby and contribution to emergent Web culture.[4] Collins started the index in March 1996, with fewer than 30 sites. By the end of September 1997, when most of the research for this chapter was conducted, her site contained 650 entries, and was not exhaustive since she omits those that charge sizable amounts of money. However, commercial sites that charge modest sums but offer free demos are included. By August 1999 the number of listings had nearly doubled.[5]

Greetings were sent in either of two ways. Either they were stored on a Website for a limited period of time, and a message was sent to the recipient inviting him or her to view the greeting on the Website, or, less commonly, the greeting was sent directly to the recipient as an email attachment. Recipients viewing a greeting on a Website could capture a screen shot of it or print it, but it was meant primarily to be viewed online and then to disappear.

This chapter asks: what types of greetings were offered on the Web in the mid- to late 1990s? How were life's troubles presented, if at all? Was there evidence for incongruity and even inappropriateness in the handling of these issues? In contrast to other chapters in this book, which by and large celebrate the forms of playfulness investigated, this chapter will argue that in their incipient state, digital greetings were too playful, or merely playful, and that incorporation of sympathy or condolence greetings was particularly problematic. I explore some of the reasons why this was so. I also ask: what did formal aspects of greeting sites communicate? Here, I will look carefully at the use of animation, color, graphics, fonts, music and even punctuation (as I have already begun to do). I ask, what is the significance of the transition not just to a digital medium but to a multimedia one?

To put the discussion into historical context, I offer a capsule history of paper postcards and greeting cards. I review how the two genres came about, and ask: what have been their communicative functions? In what ways have they appealed to the senses in the past? What major categories crystallized, not only to celebrate life-cycle events such as birthdays, weddings and graduations, but also in response to life's troubles?

The chapter is based primarily on analysis of a database of images of over 100 digital greeting sites listed at Internet Card Central in the fall of 1997, their welcoming screens, and exemplars of greetings offered.[6] Images were captured, saved and lightly edited using Paint Shop Pro,[7] and were stored in a database created with Image AXS Pro, a program for the management of multimedia images.

I focus on what was offered to users, not on use of digital greeting sites by visitors to them.[8] Most sites were created by people who had not been involved in the past with the design or distribution of cards. The story of Jenny Brahney, a Canadian woman who created the site "Tip of the Day" greetings[9] is fairly typical. When she lost her income as a fabric designer, she took up computer graphics:

> I could not think of anything else but making greeting cards, although I tried a few other ideas (I wrote and illustrated three children's books, painted furniture, murals, even delivered newspaper[s]. My cards were free for a while, but the visitors grew so quickly that my service provider asked me to move or close the cardshop . . . The categories. . . grew as I continued with my life and realized all the reasons I went into a cardshop to buy paper greeting cards.[10]

Traditional Postcards and Greeting Cards

Paper postcards and greeting cards are both similar and different. The *Random House Unabridged Dictionary* defines a postcard as "a small, commercially printed card, usually having a picture on one side and space for a short message on the other." And a greeting card is "a piece of paper on thin cardboard, usually folded, printed with a message of holiday greeting, congratulations, or other sentiment, often with an illustration or decorations, for mailing to a person on an appropriate occasion."[11] Typically, in both a prominent visual image is combined with a very short textual message on rather heavy cardboard or paper, as these definitions indicate. In both, there is usually more picture than text, and, one could also say, more object than text. Greeting cards conventionally contain a prefabricated text, whereas postcards customarily call for a short text inscribed by the sender. There are also some differences in their material manifestations as well as their functions.

A quick tour of a greeting card store[12] confirmed that American greeting cards appeal richly to the senses. Most commercial greeting cards are printed on rather thick, often textured paper or cardboard, sometimes with a rough deckle edge, and conventionally come with envelopes, whereas postcards do not. Postcards are generally unadorned, whereas greeting cards are often enhanced with decorative elements such as ribbons, bits of shiny satin, sparkles, and lace, or may be padded or embossed, or even pop up when opened, creating a three-dimensional effect, thus appealing richly and directly to the senses. Three-dimensional cards have been around since the 19th century. The handsome antique Valentine in Plate 4.4 is three-dimensional. The one shown in Plate 4.5 incorporates delicate lace, images of angels, etc. Full-fledged pop-up cards continue to be available today, both as reproductions of Victorian ones, and in modern form.

Postcards and greeting cards conventionally differ in shape and size.[13] Today's postcards are rectangles of a fairly standard size which varies little from one country to another (there are also oversize ones). Greeting cards are not at all standard in size or shape. They may be square, rectangular, or even irregularly shaped, and are generally folded, with space for a message inside. The manner of folding may differ; there may be a single fold, or more, or even none at all. Another difference is that greeting cards are sometimes sent on their own but may also accompany a gift, whereas postcards have no connection with gifts. This difference also has to do with the differing communicative functions of the two genres, discussed below.

Many types of early paper greetings invited recipients to interact with them, rather than merely hold and look at them passively, or appealed richly to the senses. Thus, the idea of the "interactive" greeting is not new, even if the term is recent. There were "trick cards," which invite a person to manipulate a rotating wheel. In one such card, one could produce over 4,000 different faces by turning each of four superimposed wheels, thus changing, e.g., the haircut, the eyes, the moustache, etc. So-called "puzzle purse" Valentines invited the recipient to unfold them, figure out the order of the different parts of the verbal message, then refold them.[14] Other cards had silk fringe and cords with tassels, inviting the recipient to touch and feel the soft silk. Among early American get well cards were small boxes filled with "Comfort Powders" or "capsules," verbal messages to be opened on different days (Chase 1971 [1926]: 157).

There have also been early attempts to combine greetings with music, e.g., the Singing Telegram, in which a person comes to one's door and sings "Happy Birthday," and the less known gramophone card, which combined a visual image with a musical recording. Chase (1971 [1926]) reports a "talking machine record" greeting which came in a decorated box, around the time of World War I, but which failed because of people's need to economize at the time.

A Capsule History of Postcards and Greeting Cards

Both postcards and greeting cards have their immediate roots in 19th-century urbanization, industrialization and developments in printing technology, and, I would add, at least in the case of postcards, the spread of literacy to large segments of the population. Greeting cards have a much older history than postcards.

Postcards

Precursors of the postcard include scrimshaw carvings by whalers for their wives and mistresses, playing cards (sometimes used as visiting cards), commercial trade cards, and pictorial visiting cards, used in the late 18th and 19th centuries (Banfield 1989; Staff 1966). Carline (1959) traces postcards back to 17th-century popular prints. In 1865 a North German postal official named Dr. Heinrich von Stephan proposed the idea of the postcard at an Austro-German postal conference in Karlsruhe:

> The present form of the letter does not. . . allow of sufficient simplicity and brevity for a large class of communications. It is not simple enough, because note-paper has to be selected and folded, envelopes obtained and closed, and stamps affixed. It is not brief enough, because, if a letter be written, convention necessitates something more than bare communication . . . Let there be sold at all post offices . . . forms for open communications. Let such a "post-sheet" (Postblatt) have the dimensions of ordinary envelopes of the larger size, and consist of stiff paper . . . on the face of the card there might appear at the top the name of the district . . . On the left hand a space could be left for the date stamp of the receiving office, on the right the postage stamp already impressed upon the form. (Staff 1966: 44–45)

Dr. von Stephan's idea did not catch on at once. It was revived a few years later by Dr. Emanuel Hermann, a professor at a military academy, and this time it took off.[15] The first Austrian postcards appeared in 1869 (Staff 1966; Willoughby 1994). A half million sold within two months of issue (Carline 1959). Issued by government post offices, they were without pictures, and were of a sober-looking pale beige color. The message was to be written on the back.

The idea quickly spread to other European countries, and was facilitated by the creation of an international postal organization in 1874, and its agreement to adopt a standard size of 5½ by 3½ inches. By the end of that year, countries issuing cards included France, Romania, Russia, most of Scandinavia, Spain, Japan, Italy, Chile, and the United States (Willoughby 1994: 31). All members agreed that postcards could be sent for half the rate of letters

(Staff 1966). For a while postcards were only issued by governmental agencies and remained plain. The idea was a huge success. Millions were sent, all over the world.

But postcards also had their detractors. Some of the objections raised to them echo current attitudes toward email.

> at least in England the main objections came from members of the upper classes who felt threatened by this new, more democratic epistolary device; it is easy to forget that until the mid-nineteenth century letter writing was a privilege of the mighty and the propertied:
>
>> They imagined that it would become all too easy for people to read other people's messages and private concerns, and that it would become easy for people to indulge in public libel and defamation of character as a means of venting spite or malice. There were others, too, who considered the use of a halfpenny postcard to be an insult, believing that if a penny was not paid for a message, then it was hardly worth sending at all; for many years the use of postcards was frowned upon by a certain class of person. (Schor 1992: 210–211; cited passage from Staff 1966: 47)

There was similar hostility to postcards in the United States (Ryan 1982).

The popularity of pictorial envelopes and stationery, commercial trade cards, and decorated visiting cards all contributed to the rise of the picture postcard in the second half of the 19th century. Shortly after the official postcard was introduced, many European government authorities decided to allow private manufacture of postcards. Picture postcards containing views of towns, resorts, and castles proliferated, and cards were now sent more for their pictures than for the message (Willoughby 1994: 39).

World's Fairs fostered interest in travel and helped disseminate the idea of the picture postcard. At the Great Exhibition of 1851 at the Crystal Palace in England pictorial envelopes had been sold as souvenirs. Postcards were offered at exhibitions elsewhere in Europe in the 1880s and 1890s (Willoughby 1994: 39). Visitors to the brand-new Eiffel Tower at the Paris Exposition of 1889 could buy a picture postcard of it and go up the tower to mail it (Carline 1959; Willoughby 1994). Cards commemorating great occasions such as the death of Queen Victoria also became popular. In the United States, souvenir picture postcards were sold at the World Columbian exposition in Chicago in 1893. These were the first commercially produced pictorial postcards in the United States (Willoughby 1994: 43).

Plain postcards were already being sold by government in the United States 20 years earlier, but it was these commercially produced cards which spurred interest in the genre (Carline 1959; Ryan 1982). By the turn of the century a craze for sending and collecting postcards with pictorial views had begun, and many homes proudly displayed postcard albums (Schor 1992; Staff 1966). Although most postcards have always been made of cardboard, at one time there was a rage for postcards made of silk.[16]

Greeting Cards

The roots of greeting cards are apparently in ancient practices involving the magical manipulation of objects on ritual occasions.[17] According to Hillier (1982: 8), ancient Egyptians gave others small blue-glazed flasks with an inscription on the occasion of the new year. The Romans exchanged greetings via presents such as oil lamps, containing inscriptions such as *Anno novo faustum felix tibi sit* ("May the New Year be happy and lucky for you!"). Jack Santino adds, "In the Rome of Julius Caesar, people gave each other tokens and coins expressing good wishes for the coming year" (Santino 1996: 87). The tradition continued in European courts and aristocratic culture. Nobles, courtiers and monarchs exchanged elaborate gifts, and a parallel pattern of exchange of modest gifts was a feature of popular culture (Schmidt 1995: 111).[18]

The history of printed greetings begins in the period 1490-1500, shortly after the invention of print in the West by Gutenberg and others. A study of folk art of nuns in a late medieval convent by Jeffrey Hamburger (1997) includes photographs of two New Year's greetings. In one of these two woodcuts the Christ Child is holding a bird, and at his feet are a box of sweets and the slogan *Ein gut iar* ("A good year"). Hamburger writes:

> Cloistered women traditionally distributed loose-leaf images as gifts, some as amulets, others as keepsakes or tokens of affection . . . Other images . . . were given as tokens of gratitude for donations. New Year's was a favorite time for the distribution of these visual momentos. (Hamburger 1997: 197–198).[19]

Despite these earlier roots, the modern phenomenon of greeting cards really began in the 1900s:

> Between 1910 and 1920, cards for a variety of occasions. . . appeared. Underlying the economic take-off of the industry was the introduction of the penny post, the fascination with photography and new printing processes, the increasing transience brought about by urbanization and industrialization, and the changing American family structure . . . greeting card production went from personal messages to standardized verse, from artisan to mechanized production, from recognized authorship to anonymity, and from printshop to corporation. (Papson 1986: 100)

Valentine Cards

Valentines are often mistakenly traced back to the Roman festival of the Lupercalia which took place on 15 February, in which names of eligible young women were drawn from an urn by young men (Schmidt 1995: 40–41; Staff 1969: 12). St. Valentine was a Roman priest who was martyred in Rome, but there is nothing in his story to explain how the name came to become associated with love (Staff 1969: 10).[20] In the late 14th and early 15th centuries, the image of St. Valentine was transformed from a Christian martyr to a patron of love. "This transformed imagery is first discernible in the poetry of Chaucer, his contemporaries, and his heirs" (Schmidt 1995: 41). In Chaucer's "Parliament of Fowls" an assembly of birds are portrayed as choosing their mates on St. Valentine's Day.[21]

By the 15th century St. Valentine's Day was considered an appropriate day to become engaged, as is evidenced by one of the Paston letters, the medieval family correspondence studied by many scholars (Staff 1969). For many centuries, it was a custom to draw one's Valentine by lot, and this person became one's Valentine for the year (Staff 1969: 18). It was also the custom to give a gift on Valentine's Day, mainly by the man, in many instances a gift of gloves. In some cases the Valentine was a paper cut-out in the shape of a glove with a heart on it.[22]

The earliest recorded handmade paper Valentine was noted in Samuel Pepys' diary:

> 14th February, 1667. This morning come up to my wife's bedside – I being up and dressing myself – little Will Mercer to be her Valentine; and I brought her name writ upon blue paper in gold letters, done by himself, very pretty, and we were both well pleased with it. But I am also my wife's Valentine, and it will cost me £5. (Staff 1969: 21)

The physicality of Valentines was given a boost when it became the custom to give a love-token or leave it at the beloved's door. In Scotland and Wales it sometimes took the form of a carved wooden spoon, from which comes the term "spooning." Another form of Valentine was the puzzle-purse, mentioned briefly above. Other types of handmade Valentines were images of "love knots" and paper cut-outs. A "bundle" Valentine was a 30-inch square printed on silk, which could be used to carry items or as a scarf. In one type of comic Valentine, pulling a tag caused a head to wag or a tongue to come out (Staff 1969: 67). Some Valentines contained puns such as "You are a good old Sole – as ever trod" or "Can you cypher, dear? Yes, dear – I sigh for you."[23]

Between the 1840s and 1860s commercially printed Valentines became a craze; handmade ones continued to flourish too, but were overtaken by commercial ones (Schmidt 1995, Chapter 2). Fancy printed or engraved Valentines became popular. Paper lace making, either by pin pricking, or later by embossing, was the rage both in Europe and in the United States (Staff 1969: 41–42).[24] In the handmade Valentine in Plate 4.5 two delicately colored chromolithograph "scraps" – angels – surround a scene viewed through pale pink gauze; the border is paper "lace." At each corner is a colored nosegay of flowers.[25]

In the 19th century Valentine Writers, little books with suggestions for messages, were popular items in England and America (Schmidt 1995: 56–62; Staff 1969: 47). In the 1860s perfumed sachets – cotton wool scented with perfume – in heavily decorated and embossed envelopes became a popular form of Valentine, thus appealing not only to the eye and the sense of touch, but also to the sense of smell.[26]

Christmas Cards[27]

Christmas cards flourished in Victorian England. The first Christmas card was designed in 1843, at the suggestion of Sir Henry Cole, the man who was later to found the Victoria and Albert Museum. The rapid spread of printed cards was spurred by developments in color printing and changes in postal policy. The introduction of the Penny Post in 1840 made it possible for the first time to send cards very cheaply anywhere in Great Britain for a penny; it was now the sender of a letter, not the recipient who paid. Valentine's cards had already undergone commercialization and it was a short step to manufacture Christmas cards as well (Hillier 1982: 8).

According to Bevis Hillier (1982: 11), the first American Christmas card was issued some time between 1850 and 1852. At first, cards resembled Valentines, because they were made by the same manufacturers (Hillier 1982: 20). The most popular type of card was a chromolithograph with a paper "lace" border. Throughout the remainder of the 19th century, commercial Christmas cards flourished, until about 1900, went they they went into decline, and postcards became the favorite vehicle for holiday greetings.

Get Well and Sympathy Cards

As stated earlier, the main focus of this chapter is greetings relating to life's troubles: get well greetings, wishes extending support or encouragement in time of difficulties, apologies, and condolence for the loss of a loved one. These are the four prominent types of "trouble" greetings in late 20th-century American paper greeting cards. Both get well cards and sympathy cards were tremendously popular in the 1990s. Among non-holiday categories, they ranked

Reasons/Categories

1. Birthday
2. Friendship
3. Anniversary
4. Get well
5. Sympathy
6. Wedding
7. Baby congratulation
8. Thank you

*Source: American Greetings Research, cited on the American Greetings Corporation Website, URL http://www.greetingcard.com/corporate/html/fast_facts.html.

Figure 4.1. The eight top non-holiday reasons Americans send or buy paper cards.

fourth and fifth in total sales in the United States, respectively (Figure 4.1).[28] Thus, in both these instances, we can infer that it was conventionally appropriate in the United States to send such cards. (The other two trouble categories did not appear in these figures, so we cannot make a parallel claim for them though such cards were widely marketed.)

According to Chase (1971 [1926]), the first get well cards in the United States were created by a "Sunshine Society " in Western Massachusetts in 1911. Condolence was apparently not a popular theme in the early history of postcards. Ryan (1982: 245) documented a rare exemplar in a book on American postcards in the period 1893–1918. Normally mailed today rather than presented in person, sympathy or condolence cards evidently emerged from visiting cards presented during face-to-face condolence visits. By the beginning of the 19th century, visits by women were a serious social obligation in England (Banfield 1989).

The circumstances under which people presented or left a card at a home were highly prescribed. A Mrs. Beeton, author of *The Book of Household Management*, distinguished among three categories of visits: ceremony, friendship, and congratulation or condolence (Banfield 1989). Like any visiting card, a condolence card was required for presentation when visiting a bereaved person, and was to be left if the person was not at home (Banfield 1989). Banfield's book contains an illustration of an 8 x 5 cm. rectangular, black-edged visiting card for visits of condolence; only the name of the visitor is engraved on it.[29]

Chase (1971 [1926]) claims that condolence cards were among the first greeting cards to be published, once the custom of sending cards rather than presenting them personally became established at the beginning of the 20th century. The earliest example he documents is dated 1911. This card and others he discusses, from the 1920s, contained a limited range of colors, white, black, lavender, silver, gold and gray-green. Some contain poems, others merely the words "In sympathy."

Conventional condolence cards have not changed much in form or content since then. In one fairly contemporary study of 110 cards, muted, soothing colors predominated – white, beige, gray or light pastel backgrounds (McGee 1980–81). Flowers were the most common motif, followed by candles, and most verbal messages were rhymed. A study of 70 cards by Woods and Delisle (1978) found that decorative covers or images of nature predominated. Death was handled euphemistically – the words "death" or "deceased" themselves rarely appear; expressions like "loss" or "time of sorrow" are preferred.

The Communicative Functions of Postcards and Greeting Cards

As the preceding discussion implies, the functions of postcards and greeting cards are mostly quite different. A postcard is not usually linked to an occasion in the life of the recipient; on the contrary, it has more to do with the life of the sender. In contrast, non-holiday greeting cards are sent on the occasion of some important event in the life of the recipient, whether a celebratory one such as a birthday or wedding, or a sad one such as the loss of a spouse, or they may accompany the presentation of a gift. A greeting card may be sent from anywhere, whereas a postcard is usually sent from far away.

Postcards are the universal, ubiquitous souvenir, bought in all places by most everyone, even by those who otherwise never indulge the souvenir instinct. They are the largest seller, by far, of any souvenir, and are found in spots that carry no other souvenir items (Gordon 1986). On the face of it, they are trivial – a few fairly predictable words, scribbled onto the back of a view of a sunset or a famous landscape. Examined more closely, postcards, like letters, are embodiments of the sender's experience, and sometimes of the recipient's experience too. They are "messengers of the extraordinary" (Gordon 1986; Stewart 1984) – testimony to the non-everyday experience of the sender.

When saved by recipients, postcards can become repositories of memories for them too. Traces of the sender's existence, personality and taste, embodied both in the words and in the image chosen, become central, and after the sender's death, these objects, like letters from him or her, take on added poignancy. Having lost two dear friends to cancer and racked with grief, Kenneth Brecher would take out his postcard collection, which contained postcards both received and bought as souvenirs. Looking through it helped lessen his grief (Brecher 1988: 2).

Greeting cards are the material manifestation of private performative acts, such as thanking, congratulating (birthdays, weddings, anniversaries, graduations), expressing condolence, apologizing, and inviting to a formal event such as a wedding.[30] In all these cases, "saying is doing." Speech act theorists, sociolinguists and discourse analysts have focused on the linguistic realization of only one of these ceremonial acts, that of apology.[31] Material expression of this act, or any of the others just mentioned, via cards, has not been much investigated.[32] Except for apologies, these are not customarily oral speech acts-ordinarily, we perform the act in question by dispatching or transferring a written message to a recipient, physically embodied in an object one can hold in the hand. Signing a birthday card, putting it in an envelope and mailing it transform a prefabricated utterance into a "natural" one (Herrnstein-Smith 1978).

Greeting cards have to do with ceremonial acts that are integral to the maintenance of a social self:

> It is . . . important to see that the self is in part a ceremonial thing, a sacred object which must be treated with proper ritual care and in turn must be presented in a proper light to others. As a means through which this self is established, the individual acts with proper demeanor while in contact with others and is treated by others with deference (Goffman 1967: 91).

While Erving Goffman had in mind the niceties of face-to-face interaction, this passage is just as pertinent to those aspects of social life which are conducted in writing and/or via the manipulation of objects – gifts and greeting cards.

Valentines appear to be a unique case. Intriguingly, they are never spoken (Davies, 1988) and could not be performed orally. As the brief overview of their history suggests, they have always been an inscribed, materially embodied, performative genre.[33] There is no spoken equivalent of a Valentine message because, as we have seen, Valentines emerged from a long history of objects proffered to or exchanged by lovers.[34]

The Greeting Card Industry

Greeting Cards are Big Business

Paper greeting cards were very big business in the second half of the 20th century. Two corporations dominated the world market, the Hallmark Corporation and American Greetings, Inc. The Hallmark empire alone did $3.6 billion worth of business in the 1997 fiscal year, with cards sold in over 20 languages in 100 countries (Hallmark Corporation 1997).[35] It ranked 35th in Forbes Magazine's list of the largest private U.S. corporations (Hallmark Corporation 1997). Its main competitor, American Greetings, Inc., took in $2.16 billion worth of revenues in the 1997 fiscal year, and sells cards in over 75 nations. The Greeting Card Association, which includes all the major American card manufacturers, estimated that in 1997 over 7 billion greeting cards were purchased by Americans, and reported that that the average American receives 30 cards per year, eight of which are birthday cards.[36]

Why are Greeting Cards Such Big Business?

How greeting cards came to be such big business has hardly been investigated. One exception is Leigh Eric Schmidt's (1995) analysis of the interrelations between consumerism and ritual in the emergence of American holidays. He shows how the career of Joyce Hall, the founder of Hallmark Cards, illustrates the entrepreneurial and cultural forces that turned holiday greetings into a huge business in the late 19th and early 20th centuries.

A few social science studies have focused on social aspects of Christmas cards, the most popular type of card of all time.[37] Status considerations and mobility aspirations have been shown to affect who sends cards to whom. Micaela di Leonardo (1987) observed that women's sending of holiday cards is part of the "work of kinship." The greeting card industry confirmed that women buy 85–90 percent of all greeting cards, and that the average purchaser was a middle-aged woman.[38]

The official rationale for greeting cards, as propagated by the big players themselves, is that people need help in expressing their emotions. Thus, the Hallmark Website declared,

> At Hallmark, we create products that help people capture their emotions and share them with one another. After nearly a century, this is what we do best; and we are still dedicated to creating the very best. We strive to offer people a rich array of vivid and memorable ways to express their feelings, and their countless relationships, all over the world. Yet within this diversity, we seek, always, to honor and serve what is universal to the human heart: the need to love and be loved, to be understood and

to understand, to sustain hope, to celebrate, to laugh, to heal. We are in a rare business: we help to bring people together, make them happy, and give them ways to show how much they care.[39]

Similarly, American Greetings urged that "Greeting cards. . . express love, spread good will and connect people. They make our lives more pleasant, joyous and meaningful."[40]

Although commercialization and clever marketing no doubt played an important role in encouraging the market for cards, it must also be that they met deep social and personal needs, despite the hostility of arbiters of etiquette to them. Thus, Miss Manners (Judith Martin) rejected greeting cards, declaring that "Such mechanical wonders as typewriters, telephones, greeting cards, and computers have not eliminated the need for writing by hand" (Martin 1982: 501). She was right that choosing a preprinted card can involve more time and expense than writing and mailing a short, handwritten note (Martin 1997: 182), adding:

> no stranger, however professionally talented, can be expected to understand the particular conditions that may arise in the lives of one's intimates and thus tell them what they want to hear, in the way someone who actually cares about these people could do. (Martin 1997: 162)

Miss Manners' admonishments aside, millions bought commercial cards.

Getting on the Bandwagon: Computerization

Hallmark, American Greetings, and a consortium called Greet Street were all quick to get on the digital bandwagon in the 1990s. In some stores where Hallmark and American Greetings cards are sold, computer kiosks were installed for a time, enabling customers to personalize greeting cards and have them printed out. However, this venture did not prove economically viable, and was eventually phased out (Canedy 1997). Second, both Hallmark and American Greetings developed software for do-it-yourself creation of cards to be printed at home, and market special paper and envelopes for this purpose.[41] More important, these and other commercial organizations began to market digital greetings alongside paper ones online.[42]

Digital Greetings

"Postcards" Versus "Greeting Cards" Online

Some Websites offered more or less the digital equivalent of real-world postcards. These digital greetings were not generally linked to occasions in the lives of recipients. The sender just chose an image and composed a message to go with it. This is the format pioneered by Judith Donath in the "Electronic Postcard Store at MIT," and copied by many others (Figure 4 .2).[43] At a site called "Just So Postcards" visitors were invited to choose from famous book illustrations and photographs. Occasionally, virtual postcard sites also offered options for the composition of the image. Some sites were hybrids, combining elements of postcards and greeting cards as we have known them. However, once the link to materiality is abandoned, the distinction often becomes obsolete.

Multimedia Greetings

Many digital greetings were miniature multimedia performances, with animation, spoken words, beeps and other sounds, and music. A site called "Animated Greetings," a Website developed by American Greetings, Inc., invited visitors to order "personalized greetings costing about $2.00 that move, talk and sing!" "Digital Internet Postcard" was especially rich in possibilities. Although animation was not offered, senders could choose from 12 languages, 200 images, eight different songs or instrumentals, 15 text colors and four backgrounds. Moreover, they could use their own image and background instead, if they wished.[44]

Digital Greetings and Life's Troubles

Early digital greetings and their Websites were often delightful – humorous, cute, charming, clever, or downright silly. A person depressed by illness could indeed be cheered up, e.g., by the animated get well greeting in Figure 4.3. As this book attests or implies, playfulness can be life-enhancing, healthy and pleasurable. Still, sometimes these sites are too playful, or inappropriately so.

Digital greeting sites were so saturated with playfulness that they rarely took account of the troubles of everyday life. As of fall 1997, all or most of the four trouble categories I have been discussing were missing in most digital greeting sites. Moreover, a ludic frame dominated the presentation of digital greetings, regardless of content.

The ludic frame was discernible, first of all, in the appeals that most site developers used to motivate visitors to use their services. The most common

The Electric Postcard

To **send** a postcard go to the <u>Postcard Rack.</u>

To **pick up** a postcard go to the <u>Pick-up Window.</u>

The <u>**Postcard Rack**</u> has a wide variety of postcards for you to choose from. You pick the card you like, write your message, and send it off. The recipient will be notified by email that a card has been sent and to claim it at the <u>**Pick-up Window**</u>.

Cards are held at the <u>**Pick-up Window**</u> for two weeks after they are sent. In addition, they are held for two weeks after they are claimed (if they are viewed additional times, they are held longer).

It's free! There is no charge to send or receive these cards.

<u>The Mad Teaparty</u> **(courtesy of** <u>The WebMuseum</u>**)**
Sir John Tenniel

To whom should this postcard be sent (email address, please)?

The subject?

Figure 4.2. The Electric Postcard, M.I.T. http://persona.www.media.mit.edu/ Postcards/.

appeal was one variant or another of the slogan, "It's fun, fast, and free!" Some sites appealed seriously to the altruism of potential users, urging them to "save a tree," but even in them the "fun" motif was also usually present. Other sites appealed to the desire to be "with it," and in them the motif of "fun" was usually present too.

Figure 4.3. Two frames from an animated get well greeting. "Tip of the Day Greeting Cards: Animated E-mail Greeting Cards," http://jenny.org/cards.html.

Rarity of Trouble Categories in Digital Greetings

Internet Card Central lists the number of sites offering cards in specific, occasion-related categories. Table 4.1 presents this distribution as of September 1997, rank ordered from most to least frequent, with parallel figures for August 1999 and October 2000. Ideally, one should have a time span longer than about three years for analysis. Still, a general trend is discernible. As mentioned earlier, this index contained 660 entries in September 1997; thus, it had doubled in about two years. However, most sites did not contain any of these categories; they were general postcard sites only. Thus, even in late 2000, most sites were still not attempting to meet ritual needs.

The figures in Table 4.1 are intriguing but equivocal. In all three time periods, birthday greetings were offered by the largest number of sites, with love/Valentines in second place. While the number of sites offering birthday greetings doubled between 1997 and 2000, the number offering love-related messages and Valentines just about tripled.

Of my so-called "trouble" categories, "get well" was fourth in 1997 and 1999, but traded places with "thank you" in 2000, even though the number of sites offering get well greetings doubled over the two-year period, while sites

Table 4.1. Non-holiday greeting categories on the World Wide Web, 1997, 1999, and 2000

Category*	1997	1999	2000
Birthday	117	192	233
Love, valentines	79	185	231
Thank you	52	76	85
Get well	42	71	88
Congratulations	38	64	75
Wedding	32	51	64
Baby	32	68	85
Anniversary	31	56	62
Graduation	23	31	35
Sympathy	11	26	33
Sorry	10	32	54
Total sites	660	1202	1263

*Source: Internet Card Central, http://www.cardcentral.net, September 23, 1997, August 14, 1999, and October 23, 2000.

offering "thank yous" grew at a slower rate. Most notably, "sympathy" and "sorry" were initially extremely rare, and remained so over the entire period. In 1997 only 10 sites offered greetings for apologies, and only 11 offered condolence.[45] By October 2000 only 33 sites offered condolence greetings. Even though in absolute terms the number had tripled, it remained the rarest of all, relatively speaking. And although apologies increased at a far greater rate than any other category, they also remained quite rare.[46]

Although a comparison of these data with the figures in Figure 4.1 is not strictly valid – the one is a compilation of numbers of paper cards actually bought, the other of numbers of Websites offering these categories – it is certainly interesting that birthday greetings appeared in first place in both cases, and that get well was in fourth place on both, whereas sympathy was much farther down the list in Table 4.1. Thus, death continued to be absent from nearly all the sites even in October 2000.

In the fall of 1997 there was only one non-commercial, non-professional site that included all four trouble categories, "Tip of the Day Greeting Cards," the source of the animated get well greeting shown in Figure 4.3.[47] Few non-commercial sites offered even three categories. Another site, Blue Mountain Arts,[48] also offered greetings in all four trouble categories. However, this very popular site was run by a small but well established paper greeting card company, and thus was professionally attuned to traditional ceremonial needs. Surprisingly, this company did not have a parallel site for its paper cards, nor did they market paper cards on this site.[49]

To probe actual use of various greeting categories including condolence, I wrote to managers of the 16 sites that offered condolence greetings in 1997. Unfortunately most Webmasters did not keep such statistics. One person replying had started her site in September 1996. At first it had contained only celebratory categories. Significantly, "Sympathy/ sorry", combining sympathy and apology, was added in February 1997, at the request of visitors to the site.[50]

Same Company, Different Greeting Categories

We have seen that most sites were created by individuals and organizations without previous occupational involvement in the world of greeting cards. Their offerings were mostly free, or in some cases cost only a moderate amount of money. Many created these sites as a hobby, to show off their Web design skills, or as a way to entice visitors to buy other goods or services.[51] Thus, they probably did not invest much serious thought in their development.

It is interesting, therefore, to examine sites managed by major commercial players in the paper greeting card business, who have the motivation, the familiarity with the subject matter, and the financial resources to invest in these sites, e.g., to hire professional planners and Website designers. I begin with American Greetings.

The only trouble category on the American Greetings Website for digital greetings was get well. This stands in contrast with their offerings for their paper cards, even online, which included all four trouble categories. As for the Hallmark Corporation, it did offer digital greetings in all four trouble categories, but, significantly, none of the condolence cards contained animation, whereas greetings in the other trouble categories did contain it. I will have more to say about animation later on. Next, I looked at the digital greetings site of the Greet Street consortium. While all four trouble categories appeared on their paper cards Website, among their digital greetings only get well was included.[52] Thus, even the major professionals in the greeting card business did not treat life's troubles in the same way in digital greetings. Evidently, they too felt uncomfortable introducing them into digital greetings, or intuited that there was some problem in doing so.

Multimedia Packaging

Design Aspects of Digital Greeting Sites

I turn now to the design of these sites – how their offerings are packaged. In the 1990s the World Wide Web was still very new. There were no recipes for how to organize a Website for digital greetings, or what use of which media would be considered appropriate, either for the welcoming screen or for specific categories of greetings. The World Wide Web only came into being, after all, in 1992, and as I have said, many of the people who created these sites were hobbyists or lacked expertise in the greeting card business. Nevertheless, I believe that we should look critically at the design of these sites.

Congruous versus Incongruous Websites

Two sites which were consistently playful – congruous in form and content – whose initial screens communicated a playful frame, and which stayed away from trouble categories, were "Send@Card" and the "Digital Dream Post Office" (Plates 4.6, 4.7). In both cases a cute, cartoon-like initial screen, brilliantly colored and graphically rich, invited visitors to play, to send celebratory or other general messages; neither included even one trouble category. The name "Send@Card" was in a multicolored font that appeared to bounce up and down, rather than sitting on a line. At the "Digital Dream" site, a "sad-sack" cartoon character with wings peered out at us through a life raft, perhaps saving him from falling from heaven to earth. The slogan "Welcome to Digital Dream Post Office!" ended with an exclamation point, as did the labels for each greeting category (not shown in Plate 4.7).

At a site called "Gestures" a multicolored font signaled playfulness and the multicolored streamers of parties or carnivals, as was consistent with its substantive and alliterative message, "fun, fast, free." In the style of children's books it also contained the slogan, "L'il pockets of love across cyberspace and more. . ." A rare site which offered three of the four trouble categories, and which also presented itself in a sober, quite neutral manner was "PC Greetings".[53] This site offered greetings in the categories of cheer, get well, sympathy, and retirement.

A good example of incongruity is the site shown in Plate 4.8, which contained three trouble categories. The icons for these categories, and these only, were variants of the "smiley" face. The face for get well was a wry variant of the basic smiling face with a bandage, not inappropriate if a humorous approach is desirable, but jarring if the patient is terminally ill. The adaptations of the frown for apologies and sympathy were even more questionable, especially the latter.[54] An engagement ring is less suitable than a wedding ring as an icon for anniversaries, and a cupcake looks meager to represent birthdays. Also, the rectangles in which the icons were displayed were irregular and askew, approximating the effect of animation – as if these little boxes were jumping around. The combination of these quasi-animated boxes with brilliant rainbow colors communicated "Come have fun!"[55]

Paper Versus Digital Greetings on Commercial Sites

We might have expected a more serious presentation on the commercial sites, given their long experience with greeting cards, and the involvement of professional designers in these sites, but in fact, once again a playful mode prevailed. For instance, in a site called "Animated Greetings," the icon for each category was a little envelope turned into a cute smiling face, with an additional icon, in a paler shade, just "behind" it. The use of brilliant colors, a different shade for each category, also contributed to the party mood. Also, the little envelopes were tilted at an angle, as if they were dancing or bouncing around, thus resembling the bouncing "boxes" in Plate 4.8.

The Hallmark digital greeting site was also quite playful. It contained prominent cartoon-like icons leading to both free, non-animated greetings and to animated ones available for a fee. The icon for animated greetings contained two colored, animated hands moving to look like animal heads. Several exclamation points were also in evidence. This screen contrasted considerably with the more neutral opening screen of the general Hallmark Website, which contained no cartoon-like images, and was full of matter-of-fact links to all kinds of information.[56]

The design of Greet Street's paper and digital sites also contrasted sharply. That for paper cards contained almost no graphics, and its colors were very subdued. In contrast, the digital site contained brilliant, even lurid colors. Of the nine rectangles dividing up this screen, seven contained animation and changed constantly at differing rates. The site for paper cards did not contain a single exclamation point; on the Pix screen there were two.

In short, not only amateurs but even the three major commercial sites treated matters of both substance and design differently in sites for digital greetings. Perhaps different Web designers created the paper and digital greeting sites for each of these companies, and therefore they had different styles. However, this does not, in my opinion, explain why the treatment of digital greetings was consistently more playful in all three. I will come back to this issue, later on.

Further Evidence for Incongruity of Form and Content

Even when initial screens on digital card sites appeared to take account of life's troubles, later screens deeper in the Website often treated them inappro-

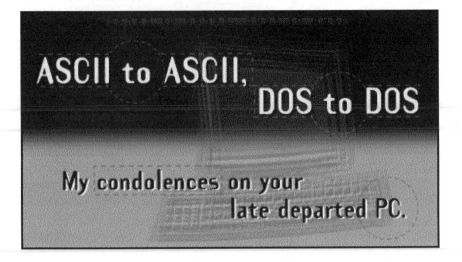

Figure 4.4. Inappropriateness in the treatment of condolence.

priately or incongruously. Two of the four sympathy greetings on a site called "Byte Size" greetings turned out to be jokes; one of them is shown in Figure 4.4.[57]

Figure 4.5 is one of three sympathy greetings I found on a Website created by second-year students in the Mass Communication Department of the Ngee Ann Polytechnic in Singapore. All three incorporated three-dimensional effects, like images in computer games. In one, the cross had sprouted wings; the second contained a cartoon image of a ghost, and in the third (Figure 4.5), the size of the coffin has been distorted unrealistically. These images looked fine for computer games, but were not appropriate for condolence.

Yet another instance of solely playful use of this medium is "Mark's Apology Note Generator" (Figure 4.6), a site offering options for composing an apology. The creature "in the dog house" and the "scrawled" font tell us that all is done tongue-in-cheek. Sometimes humorous apologies are fine, but then again, sometimes they are not.

Inappropriate Music in Greetings

We have already seen that some sites offered music with their greetings. On many, the welcoming screen itself was accompanied by music. In some instances, like the animated greetings sold by American Greetings, Inc., a musical accompaniment was chosen by them for a particular greeting, and the customer had no choice in the matter. In other instances, the sender could customize the music.

Figure 4.5. A digital condolence greeting.

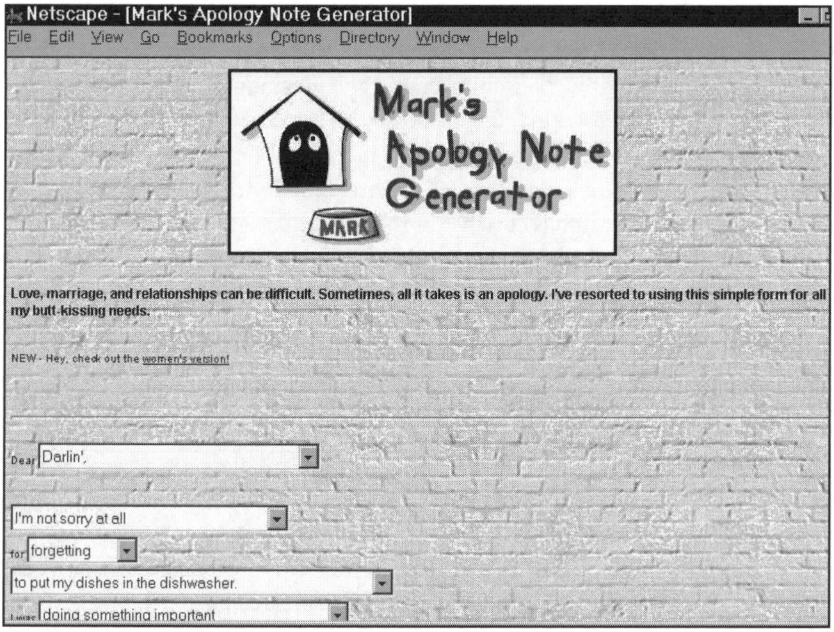

Figure 4.6. "Mark's Apology Note Generator," http://www.karmafarm.com/
formletter.html.

A site particularly rich in its musical offerings was "The Musical Cardshop at the Muse's Music Hall." With its heavy dose of alliteration and excessive length, the title of this site was perhaps a hint that the dominant communicative frame was not serious – even if sympathy greetings were offered. In the music menu for condolence messages at this site in 1997, one could choose from no less than 52 different songs. There was not only popular music but classical as well. However, most of the titles were inappropriate, even grossly inappropriate: love songs with titles like "Gimme! Gimme! Gimme!" or "Kisses of Fire," and even "Staying Alive" (!).[58] Readers might think that the same menu had simply been appended to every greeting category; however, this was not so. The menu was different in each instance. I am happy to report that by August 1999, Webmasters had replaced this offensive musical menu with a more appropriate one offering many hymns.[59]

Why Were Greetings Websites So Playful?

Why were digital greetings seemingly "stuck" in a playful mode? Why did these sites ignore life's troubles or treat them in an inappropriate manner? In Chapter 1 I reviewed five factors that promote playfulness in digital communication: qualities of the medium itself (ephemerality, interactivity, invitation to immersion), the release from physicality, the frontier-like nature of cyberspace, the influence of hacker culture, and the masking of identity. With the exception of the ephemerality/ physicality issue and the frontier-like nature of cyberspace and its liminal character, these factors do not seem relevant in the present context. In particular, there is no direct link with hacker culture, and anonymity of the medium is clearly not relevant, since greetings are sent from one known individual to another, and anonymity of site developers is not relevant. Perhaps other factors are at work.

One possibility, of course, is that this situation was temporary and transitional. Perhaps this was simply an unformed, very new and experimental phenomenon on the digital frontier. I have hinted that another possible explanation is that site developers assumed or intuited that this new medium is incompatible in some ways with perceptions and beliefs about real-world troubles, especially in relation to death and the powerful emotions in connection with it. They may have sensed that a real-world tangible object is essential for serious and ritual purposes, and that, particularly in the case of death and condolence, a greeting without physicality is unacceptable. Literature on the anthropology of ritual has often pointed to the importance of the direct involvement of the senses in such experiences.[60] Perhaps the card as tangible object is needed to counteract the ephemerality of life, to stave away the implications of "dust to dust, ashes to ashes," even if in a very trivial way, and despite the fact that paper itself is ephemeral too.[61]

There is yet another possibility regarding condolence. The speed of interaction with computers conflicts with conventional expectations regarding the handling of death and funerals. Think of a funeral procession. The normal pace of everyday life is deliberately slowed to a snail's pace. Bells may toll slowly. The idea of animation thus appears particularly incongruous in the context of death. To animate is literally "to bring to life!" Today, many people associate animation only with Saturday-morning children's cartoons, despite a long tradition of high-quality art animation.

Yet another explanation might be that it was mainly young people who were creating and applying these new technologies. Young people are slow to come to terms with their own mortality, and have had less need to cope with the deaths of others than older persons. Perhaps even other categories of personal troubles were not salient to them, since their life was "all before them." No information is available on the age of developers of digital greeting sites; we can assume that most were relatively young. But there is no reason to assume that developers of commercial paper card sites were any older than those creating parallel sites for digital greetings. Moreover, in any case, we saw that commercial digital greetings were also primarily playful or at the least, were treated differently from paper cards too.

As for users, data available at Internet Card Central strongly suggest that that it was mainly middle-aged women who were exploring and using them, the same group that cultivates social ties via paper cards (Greeting Card Association 1997; Di Leonardo 1987). Internet Card Central invites visitors to take advantage of "Netminder," a service that notifies them when the site has changed. Those signing up for this service are asked to fill out a short questionnaire. From the resulting data, Netminder provided the breakdown by age and sex shown in Table 4.2. Nearly 4,000 people had filled out the questionnaire by the fall of 1997, though far fewer had disclosed information on their age and gender. Nevertheless, we can see that of about 1300 individuals who had done so, 29 percent were male and a high 71 percent were female. The data for age[62] certainly do not support the idea that it was mainly young people who were using these services. Less than a fifth were 25 or less, and nearly half were over 40.

Although this is by no means a random sample of visitors to the index site, of those subscribing to Netminder, or of actual users of any of the greetings sites, signing up for Netminder is itself a strong indication of personal investment in the new greetings, making these data quite valuable, in my opinion. If middle-aged women were indeed already the main senders of digital greetings in the late 1990s, they might very well be open to sending greetings relating

Table 4.2. Distribution of subscribers to the Netminder service on Internet Card Central, by age and gender, 1997.

Gender	
Male	29%
Female	71
	———
	100%
Age	
15 or less	2%
15–20	7
20–25	8
25–30	12
30–35	12
35–40	13
40–45	18
45–50	13
50–55	8
55–60	3
60–65	2
over 65	2
	———
	100%
	(1311)

*Source: Internet Card Central, URL http://www.cardcentral.net, October 1997.

to life's troubles too. Thus, problematic as they are, these data point in the direction of eventual normalization.

Like online greetings, software programs for do-it-yourself, offline creation of paper greetings were also remarkably playful, sometimes incongruously so. CreataCard, the American Greetings program, offered options in only one of the four trouble categories, get well, even though it marketed ready-made cards in all four, in stores and online. The party atmosphere of this digital environment is instantly evident in the brilliant colors on its digital card rack.

The Hallmark Connections CD-ROM offered sympathy as well as get well/ I care cards. The latter category included support or encouragement. Thus, only apology was absent. But many aspects of the interface of this program were also playful and even juvenile. Clicking the different options in the colorful main menu causes musical "pings" of different pitches to be heard. A cute animated dog with wagging tail accompanied our every move even as we customized a sympathy card.[63]

Playfulness was also present in the packaging of @*loha*, a program for the creation of animated email attachments with musical accompaniment. @ was playfully substituted for the initial "a" in the name, and in version 1.0, a birthday cake, an airplane, and a snowman whooshed out of a mailbox. Four breathless slogans with exclamation points surrounded this graphic image: "For all E-mail programs! Tiny files, fast downloads! Easy, Creative and Fun! Add animation & sound to e-mail!" In the Website logo, the "o" in @*loha* was a ball bouncing up and down.[64] The menu of this program offered design elements only for celebratory and holiday greetings; trouble categories were once again completely absent.

The fact that these programs stressed playfulness, and that the big-time manufacturers of paper cards treated even do-it-yourself creation of paper cards as a form of play strongly suggest that something fundamental about how computers and the Internet were perceived is at work here. Perhaps software developers thought that people are phobic about computers and have to be treated like children in order to get them to use programs at all, and that playfulness promotes the perception of programs as user-friendly. One could argue that this need was temporary, for generations who did not grow up with computers, and that computer-savvy children will not need such coddling when they grow up.[65] However, this factor is less relevant in relation to online greetings, since people accessing these sites were already quite computer-literate and open to new ideas, regardless of their age.

A Look to the Future

This chapter has shown that digital greetings in the late 1990s were a form of playful experimentation with a very new medium and new varieties of older communicative genres. Perhaps some of the grosser incongruities noted in this chapter can therefore be overlooked.

Changing Attitudes toward Text, Graphics and Multimedia

Much larger issues than those pertaining to greetings alone were at stake as we adapted to new possibilities made available by computers, the Internet, and particularly the Web. The entire process of "going digital" (loss of the tangible object) and of "going multimedia" (enhancement of text with pictures, the switch to color, inclusion of music and animation) challenges deeply rooted attitudes. Everywhere in contemporary culture we see aspects of the struggle to adapt to this trend toward expanded appeal to the senses, and a new mix of the senses, so it is no surprise that these issues are problematic in this context too. It remains to be seen in which social circumstances an ephemeral greeting will become an acceptable equivalent of a material one. A *New Yorker* cartoon brought this point home nicely: a receptionist sitting at her desk and glancing toward her computer screen commented, "How thoughtful. Mr. Kessler sent a dozen roses." The roses were, of course, virtual.

While I was working on this chapter in the fall of 1997, the *New York Times* introduced color into its hallowed black and white pages. The main use of color is in photographs, though it is also introduced in some advertising. On the day it did so, 15 September 1997, it published a cartoon by Jules Feiffer on the Op-Ed page. In shock Feiffer's reader cries,

> NO! Not the New York Times in color! No! The color of the Times is gray! . . . Not the stressful, distressing news of the day dressed up in reds and yellow and pinks and oranges – "The Good Gray New York Times."[66] That's tradition, that's history, that's the way the world works when the world is working . . . I think, a touch of Prussian Blue here would heighten the graphics perceptibly.[67]

Right before our eyes, Feiffer's reader changed his attitude toward color. Because tabloid papers introduced color long before the serious ones, color has traditionally been associated with less serious journalism. A cynical explanation for the trend to adopt color is that the *New York Times* and other quality papers had to do it in order to compete economically with the more popular press. While this may be true to some extent, I believe that changing cultural attitudes toward the appeal to the senses in different communication contexts were at issue too.

Related developments were discernible in the world of classical music:

> Classical musicians and the impresarios who sponsor their concerts have been thinking a lot lately about how performances look, and what can be done to drag classical concerts toward the 21st century . . . why not engage the eye as well as the ear? . . . For some, even the mention of visual enhancement is proof that the barbarians are at the gates . . . With classical music fighting for attention in a world that prizes visual qualities of color, texture, movement and variety, it is suicidal to disdain on principle a potential audience that grew up in the age of film and television and that can find visual stimulation in virtually every other form of arts and entertainment. (Kozinn 1997)

Thus, the Kronos Quartet, who perform contemporary chamber music, dress much like rock stars, and employ a lighting designer to create dramatic visual effects projected behind them. Unlike ordinary concerts of chamber music, the lights are dimmed and the players are spotlighted.

Another case in point is *Wired Magazine*, which flaunts psychedelic-colored, complex, computer-generated graphics intertwined with chunks of text in many different fonts and going off in many directions. Some people hate the magazine and the reduced transparency of its verbal texts, and even say they can't read it; others take to it without difficulty. Once again, this may be in part a generational matter, with younger people exposed to computer games, the Internet, and television, especially MTV, taking to the magazine with enthusiasm.

Television had a great deal to do with the shift in the relation between the visual and the verbal in the late 20th century. Think, for instance, of televised versions of literary classics; in the late 1990s people first saw the show, then read the book. Experience with multitasking in the world of computers also had its effect. What was too much stimulation only yesterday was just enough today or tomorrow. A new aesthetic heavily based on simulation was emerging, whose contours could only be dimly grasped as this book was completed.

The Integration of Death and Mortality in Digital Culture

Although life's troubles and the need to deal with mortality were slow to penetrate digital greetings, death was by no means absent from the Internet in the late 1990s. First of all, on discussion lists many people shared eulogies for recently deceased individuals. There was also a trend to create virtual memorial Websites.

At a free site called "Virtual Memorials" (Plate 4.9), memorials could contain photos, videos and testimonies. Begun in 1996, this site contained over 300 memorials as of early October 1997.[68] At "World Gardens" people could commission a memorial page for someone who has died. When the contract for the page expires and the page is removed, a digital "plaque" is created in the site's "Mausoleum." Started at the beginning of February 1996, the site contained only about 50 memorials as of early October 1997.[69]

"World Wide Cemetery" was unusually explicit in its view of the Internet as a suitable context for memorials:

> The Internet . . . is an ideal place to announce the loss of someone we cherish and to erect a permanent monument to their memory. Such virtual monuments, unlike real ones, will not weather with the passage of time and can be visited easily by people from around the world.[70]

Paradoxically, then, the Internet is ephemeral[71] and yet, in some contexts was perceived as more long-lasting than stone.

Consider also the dramatic collective response on the Internet to the deaths of Yitzhak Rabin in 1994, and of Princess Diana and Mother Teresa in 1997. It strongly suggests that given very powerful motivation, ordinary users do perceive the World Wide Web as a suitable and convenient medium for the most solemn purposes. Within hours and days of their deaths, dozens, and in the latter two cases, hundreds of Websites sprung up, often inviting visitors to sign virtual condolence books. In the cases of Princess Diana and Mother Teresa, these sites were quickly linked in "Webrings" – each site providing links to the next ones, thus providing a sense of global community.[72]

These sites incorporated imagery from real-world ritual practice, especially relating to flowers and candles. Thus, at one site created shortly after Rabin's death, people could "light a candle" by clicking on an image of one; whole screens of these virtual candles were still visible at a commemorative site in September 1997. Many sites honoring Prince Diana and Mother Teresa also incorporated animated virtual candles.[73] Some may feel that simulating the lighting of a candle in this way is ridiculous. But many forms of real-world ritual have also involved simulation. Think of the wafer and wine in Catholic communion, or the eating of matzoth at the Passover Seder, when Jews recite, "This is the bread of affliction, that our forefathers ate. . ." Admittedly these are instances of substitution of one tangible substance for another. In the present case there is an additional leap to be made from the tangible to the intangible.

A handful of greeting sites also quickly put up memorials to Princess Diana on their initial pages. Significantly, all but two, as far I could determine, had already included sympathy/condolence on their site. Many sites included the text and instrumental version of "Candle in the Wind," the song Elton John sang at Diana's funeral.

The Future of Digital Greetings

To sum up, there seem to have been five related changes which affected our openness to digital greetings in the mid- to late 1990s: increased predominance of the visual over the verbal and textual; the move from black and white to color; the increased integration and acceptance of simulated, intangible experience into everyday life; the shift from pure text to multimedia – animation, music, video; and an overall increase in amount of stimulation cognitively processable and considered suitable in a given context.

In light of all these changes, it is likely that multimedia-enhanced greetings will become increasingly acceptable and legitimate in the 21st century. One very strong indication of growing public interest in digital greetings just before the millennium was the fact that Blue Mountain Arts had become one of the most popular sites on the entire Web. "According to MediaMatrix, an Internet audience measurement firm, it. . . ranked 14th among sites on the Web" in the fall of 1999 (Kaufman 1999). By the millennium, America Online, ICQ, and Yahoo-together serving a huge public – all offered a large range of free greetings, including some for apology and condolence.

The major players in the commercial market for paper cards claimed not to be worried by digitization. In a telephone interview with Marianne McDermott, the Executive Vice President of the American Greeting Card Association, in September 1997, I asked if the industry sees digital greetings as potentially undermining the market for paper ones. She replied that greetings executives were at all not worried about this, that on the contrary, they viewed digital greetings as merely another "niche" in the market. At the same time, an extensive *New York Times* report on the industry only two months later revealed that paper card "sales volume has been flat or down for several years . . . And more people communicate by E-mail, have little time to shop or are bored with outdated greetings" (Canedy 1997: 1). The article didn't even mention digital greetings, and claimed that the industry was adapting by creating new types of less conventional paper cards, including some to deal with life's troubles in new ways, and by diversifying the locations where cards were marketed. However, these changes perhaps also indicated that digital greetings were already beginning to compete.[74] I doubt that the competition was merely between something that is free and paper cards that cost money.

As the year 2000 approached, the huge volume of business for paper cards suggested that they would not soon be replaced. The more solemn and formal the occasion, the less likely that individuals will choose a digital message if a tangible one is feasible. At the same time, recall the strong hint that middle-aged women were apparently already showing keen interest in digital greetings (as evidenced by the data from Internet Card Central). As digitally sophisticated children and teenagers, for whom being online is part of everyday life, grow up, they will use these greetings as a matter of course, except when a card is needed to accompany a tangible gift, and perhaps even to express condolence.

In the course of my research, I observed experiments with condolence which might point toward future developments. In one, lightly animated condolence greeting, a poem, consisting of six stanzas, the decorated background remained the same, while the stanzas changed. Another example, perhaps, of things to come was a condolence greeting I observed at Blue Mountain Arts. In this greeting the text was displayed in a black font on a background in two shades of yellow, and was accompanied by music of a more or less appropriate variety (though once again only MIDI). In a very light touch of animation, a pair of blackbirds slowly flitted across the screen. Perhaps this greeting seemed potentially quite appropriate because it was designed by greetings professionals.[75]

These attempts suggest that the day may come, perhaps even very soon, when standardized digital condolence greetings will be widely available. Perhaps significant numbers of individuals will even design their own, using do-it-yourself software. People could combine an image of their choice, even including a touch of animation, with a hymn, a prayer, or a passage from, say, the elegiac second movement of Mozart's *Sinfonia Concertante for Violin and Viola* or the ethereal slow movement of Beethoven's *Ninth Symphony*. The latter suggestions may be too elitist and out of step with cultural changes in the music world for the majority of people. But good-quality sound combined with music considered appropriate by future generations is bound to come. Despite the obstacles discussed here and the expected opposition of arbiters of etiquette, digital greetings will increasingly be accepted. Future research must turn to the study of the users of greetings Websites, who they are, for what communicative purposes they use them, and when and why they continue to prefer paper cards.

Notes

1. This site is at http://www.teleport.com/~ronjbeav/cybercard.shtml.

2. This birthday greeting was designed by Heidi Anderson.

3. The pink frame around the greeting is, no doubt, incongruous to Western eyes, which associate it with Valentine's Day rather than Christmas. This greeting comes from a non-Western source, a site run by a group in Hong Kong. Despite the incongruity, I chose this example because its interface was typical of many digital greeting sites. This site is no longer available.

Some aspects of appropriateness of graphic aspects of greetings will be discussed in this chapter.

4. Eventually, Collins changed the name. See http://www.cardcentral.net or the even newer http://www.cardlady.com.

5. As with any Web index, how complete this one is, is a function of the time and energy put into it. Even if there is lag in updating such a site, it does document tremendous growth in a short time. Collins reported in 1999 that the site received 7,000–15,000 visitors per day, and more at holiday times. By October 2000 she claimed that 10,000–30,000 persons accessed the site on the average, and that over 3 million persons had visited the site since its inception (this figure no doubt includes repeat visitors).

6. The index at Internet Card Central saved me many hours of tedious work. I was selective in my choices, including only sites that offered substantial variety in categories. To this basic database I added images of sites maintained by commercial companies, the Hallmark Corporation, American Greetings, Inc., Greet Street, a consortium of smaller companies.

7. By "editing," I do not mean that images were changed in substantive ways, but rather, e.g., that I created borders for them, cropped screen captures, etc..

8. This chapter has also benefitted from an examination of collections in the Archives Center of the National Museum of American History at the Smithsonian Institution. The Center houses the Norcross Greeting Card Collection, which contains greeting cards from 1800 through 1981; Norcross was a major rival of the Hallmark Corporation until it went out of business in 1981. Other valuable collections are the Victor A. Blenkle Postcard Collection and the Olive Leavister 19th Century Antique Valentine Collection.

9. See http://jenny.org/cards.html. I will refer again to this site, later in the chapter.

10. Personal email from Jenny Brahney, 15 August 1999.

11. These definitions came from an online version of the Random House Unabridged Dictionary, which is no longer available.

12. I made observations on the physical features and display of paper greeting cards in a series of visits to a typical Hallmark greeting card store at 955 L'Enfant Plaza, Washington D.C., the building where the Center for Folklife Programs and Cultural Heritage at the Smithsonian, my base during my sabbatical in the United States, is located. I also observed card racks in supermarkets, pharmacies and specialty card and stationery shops, as well as other Hallmark card stores.

13. These generalizations also hold for Israel, the other country I know best, and probably for Western Europe as well.

14. On puzzle purse Valentines, see, e.g., Staff (1969); Victorian Rituals Valentine, http://home.kendra.com/victorianrituals/Victor/val.htm; the Hallmark history of Valentines, available at the Hallmark site, http://www.hallmark.com/ during the Valentines Day season.

15. See Carline (1959); Staff (1966); Willoughby (1994).

16. For some examples, see Willoughby (1994: 118–119).

17. See Buday (1954); Staff (1969); Hillier (1982); Papson (1986); Santino (1994; 1996).

18. This European tradition of exchanging objects which are more like tokens than cards may still flourish today. Several years ago I received in the mail a New Year's greeting from a friend at the University of Vienna. It consisted of a round, coaster-like object of thick beige cardboard, with a multicolored "Happy New Year!" on one side, and four pre-printed lines for the message on the other. The general look of it resembled commercial, disposable coasters, e.g., for beer.

19. Walter Cahn called these greetings to my attention. For another example, see Santino (1994: 79).

20. Schmidt (1995: 40–41) reports that actually, there were two St. Valentines, whose stories were conflated into one, and which had nothing to do with love and courtship until the late 14th century.

21. See also Oruch (1981) and Kelly (1986), cited by Schmidt (1995), Chapter 2, footnote 4.

22. See Staff (1969), Figure 24, p. 30, for some examples. At least two interpretations of the glove are possible, one that it hints at the desire to put a wedding ring on the beloved's finger, the other a more directly sexual one.

23. We will encounter puns in greetings again in Chapter 6.

24. In this brief summary I am only including material on Britain and the United States. Staff's (1969) history also contains some material on continental Europe.

25. Strictly speaking, this Valentine is only partially handmade; the chromolithographs are, of course, printed mechanically, then glued in place by hand. In the 19th century there was also a tradition of comic Valentines; they were satirical, transgressive, lewd, and even downright insulting; see Schmidt (1995: 77–85).

26. This information comes from the seasonal presentation on Valentines at the Hallmark Website, February, 1997, URL in footnote 14.

27. For contemporary social science research on Christmas cards, see, e.g., Johnson (1971); Kunz and Woolcott (1976); Searle-Chatterjee (1993).

28. Although paper greeting cards are available in Israel, there is no tradition of sending commercially produced sympathy cards in Jewish tradition. Cards are called *brakhot* – from the verb *l'varekh*, "to bless" or "to greet," and are almost exclusively congratulatory. Personal condolence calls during a seven-day mourning period are de rigueur to this day.

29. See Banfield (1989), Figure 1.5, p. 5. That specific categories of greeting cards have roots in the practice of visiting cards is also documented by the fact that the Olive Leavister 19th Century Antique Valentine Collection at the Smithsonian Institution contains some two dozen visiting-card-size Valentines.

30. See Goffman (1967); Austin (1970a; 1970b); Searle (1979).

31. Basic references on apologies begin with Austin (1970a; 1970b), and Searle (1979). Empirical studies of the language of apologies include Holmes (1989; 1990; 1993); Keenan (1993); House and Vollmer (1988); Blum-Kulka, et al. (1989). Cupach, et al. (1986); Suszczynska (1994); Clyne, et al. (1991); Meier (1996); Davies (1987); Hale (1987); Garcia (1989).

32. On birthday cards, see Cacioppo and Andersen (1981); Mooney and Brabant (1988; 1987); Brabant and Mooney (1989); Dillon and Jones (1981); Demos and Jache (1981). For a study of humor in get well cards, see Bologh (1979).

33. Davies' own study examined Valentine messages published in a newspaper, a different sub-genre from the anonymous ones that have a long tradition in English culture. See Davies (1988).

34. When saved, greeting cards can serve, like postcards, as repositories of memory. Schmidt (1995: 90) refers to 19th-century albums or scrapbooks of them. This custom has continued in the 20th century.

35. This information was obtained from the Hallmark Website, http://www. hallmark.com.

36. This information comes from the 1997 GCA Industry Fact Sheet, www.greeting card.org/gca/facts.htm. Fact sheet data available in 1999 reported that the average number of cards received had dropped to 24. According to data cited in Canedy (1997), Hallmark captured 42 percent of the U.S. market in 1996, and American Greetings, 35 percent. The rest of the market belongs to a large number of smaller players.

37. See Hill (1969); Johnson (1971); Kunz and Woolcott (1976); Meer (1986); Searle-Chatterjee (1993).

38. This information comes from the Greeting Card Association Website, http://www.greetingcard.org/.

39. This passage comes from the Hallmark Website, section on corporate information, URL in footnote 35.

40. This citation is from the American Greetings Website, http://www.american greetings.com, section on corporate information.

41. American Greetings' product, CreataCard Plus!, was produced together with Micrografx, Inc. The Hallmark "Connections" Greetings Workshop was created in collaboration with Microsoft. There are quite a few other software packages for the creation of cards at home, too numerous to mention here.

42. Hallmark's "Connections" Website for digital greetings was at http://www. hallmark.com/. American Greetings' Animated Greetings line was at http://www. animatedgreetings.com/. Greet Street, the consortium of smaller greeting card makers which markets both paper and digital cards online also had a separate Website for digital greetings, called Pix Digital Postcards." This group changed its name to Egreetings.com, at http://www.egreetings.com/.

43. Other sites using Donath's interface sometimes acknowledge their debt to her, sometimes not.

44. This site was at http://www.all-yours.net/. In practice, the two types of Websites often overlap. Even paper cards ostensibly of one type also sometimes resembled the other, as we saw in the capsule history of paper postcards and greeting cards presented above.

45. "Support/encouragement" is absent in Table 4.1 because Margaret Collins did not tabulate it.

46. It is puzzling that total sites appear to have increased by only 61 between 1999 and 2000. I was unable to ascertain why this might be so. Note: totals include categories other than those appearing in Table 4.1.

47. This is the site run by Jenny Brahney, the woman I cited earlier.

48. This site was at http://www.bluemountain.com/. In late 1999 the company was sold to Excite@ Home. In 1997 there was no overt evidence on this site of the commercial nature of the company, e.g., no links to marketing of their paper products. I learned of the RL company only from New York Times articles (Napoli 1998; Kelley 1998; Kaufman 1999). Unfortunately, Blue Mountain arts repeatedly ignored my requests to reproduce images from their site.

49. I observed paper cards by Blue Mountain Arts for the first time in the Yale Bookstore in New Haven, CT, well after this chapter was drafted.

50. I am grateful to Anna Goodwin for this information. The manager of "Debbie's Greetings From the Heart" (available now at http://www.chawni.com/~funtime.html) told me that although she couldn't provide any data, sympathy cards were the least used on her site.

51. Sites requiring recipients to come to the site to see their greeting thus double the number of visitors exposed to their products and services.

52. This site was also unique in offering a category for divorce.

53. By fall 2000 this site had disappeared.

54. In one of the general indexes of digital greetings the category "Sorry/Sympathy" conflated the "sorry" of condolence with the "sorry" of apologies. It too used the frowning smiley as the motif for this category. This Website was no longer available in August 1999.

55. Goldie Rivkin commented that this shape looks like wash buckets!

56. Hallmark refused permission to include a screen capture of this site.

57. This saying has been around for some time; it appeared in several collections of computer humor on the World Wide Web. Tsameret Wachenhauser located these collections. See, e.g., http://www.jr.co.il/humor/signatur.txt; http://www.rose-hulman. edu/~hansencp/compendium.html; http://www.photobooks.com/~grimm/text/com phum.txt.

58. Goldie Rivkin informs me that "Staying Alive!" has a strong beat and is used in aerobic exercise classes, making it grossly inappropriate here. This musical menu was captured in September 1997.

59. In my opinion, MIDI music sounds especially "tinny" and unaesthetic in the context of condolence. In the future high quality audio with full orchestral or instrumental sound will become available.

60. See, e.g., Moore and Myerhoff (1977); Hibbitts (1992; 1995); Danet (1997b).

61. It is ironic in the present context that paper collectibles are actually called ephemera.

62. Strictly speaking, age categories should have been mutually exclusive, e.g., a 20-year-old should not appear in both those aged 15–20 or 20–25. Unfortunately, cross-tabulation by both age and sex is not available. Nevertheless, these data offer a rough indication of who is using these services.

63. A third package for the creation of paper cards is Greeting Card Maker, which did contain all four trouble categories, but most of the images offered were of playful cartoon characters. It did not suggest cartoons as images for sympathy cards, however.

64. The site for @loha is no longer available. The product evidently underwent major transformation.

65. See Don Tapscott's (1997) *Growing Up Digitally: the Rise of the Net Generation*.

66. Goldie Rivkin commented that the epithet "Gray Lady" for the *New York Times* is very old, and probably refers to its unvarying typeface and format patterns.

67. This cartoon appeared in the New York Times on 15 September 1997.

68. Virtual Memorials are at http://virtual-memorials.com.

69. See http://www.worldgardens.com.

70. This site was at http://www.interlog.com/~cemetery.

71. The Web is ephemeral in two senses, both its non-tangibility, and the volatility of Websites, appearing and disappearing daily.

72. Most Websites for Yitzhak Rabin were eventually taken down. A Princess Diana Memorial Webring was at http://www.geocities.com/RainForest/Vines/1009/diring.htm. A Mother Teresa Memorial Ring was still available in 2001 at http://nav.webring. yahoo.com/.

73. There were, e.g., pages commemorating Princess Diana at http://www.angel-stardust.com/cybercards/login.html.

74. Canedy did not mention the possibility of multimedia attachments to email, but instead seemed to imply that plain email may be superceding paper cards. In 2000 the Greeting Card Association invited Barry Wellman, a University of Toronto sociologist studying networking and community in the era of the Internet, to speak at its annual convention on how the Internet was changing social life. This suggests that the paper greeting card industry did start to worry about its future. Wellman revealed this fact in a keynote address at the first conference of Internet researchers, held at the University of Kansas, 14–17 September 2000.

75. I regret being unable to show readers this greeting; as noted in footnote 48, Blue Mountain Arts ignored my request for permission to reproduce it, as well as the image of their initial screen.

5

ASCII Art and Its Antecedents

This chapter is the first of a pair on text-based art – pictures or visual images created with letters, numbers, and other typographic symbols on the computer keyboard. This is one of the best known forms of play with computers, dating back to the early days in the development of computer technology in the 1960s and 1970s. Some older readers of this book will recall having seen early printouts of ASCII images on large teleprinter paper, hung on office walls. It is almost impossible now to find such images on paper, though many Websites store hundreds of them in digital form. ASCII art gained new prominence in 1999 in connection with the Hollywood film *You've Got Mail!* The Website for this film included an ASCII art gallery, containing images, e.g., of Tom Hanks, one of its stars. Visitors to the site were invited to submit images too.[1]

ASCII art is text art – that is, art made from the elements of text. Note the etymological relationship between "text," "texture," and "textiles." All share the Latin root *textus*, "woven." The link between ASCII art and textiles is not merely metaphorical. Just as the strands in cloth are interwoven row by row in a geometric Grid, so ASCII art is "woven" line by line, from the upper left, in the "slots" where letters and other symbols normally fall in word-processed text.[2] This underlying similarity is latent in the pictorial ASCII art featured in this chapter, but will become much more evident in Chapter 6, where we will see striking resemblances between newer, abstract forms of text-based art displayed on IRC and quilting, needlepoint, and other textile arts.

In this chapter I survey the history and development of ASCII art from approximately 1960 to 1995. This was the era of experimentation with early computers. In the 1970s, in bedrooms, basements and garages, hobbyists, mainly male technophiles, experimented with computers such as the Commodore and the Amiga (Campbell-Kelly and Aspray, 1996, Chapter 10; Cringely, 1996). Tinkering with the new technologies, they pushed them beyond their instrumental capacities for expressive purposes, including making pictures with keyboard symbols (Bell 1998; Raymond 1996). Others, computer professionals and statisticians, working with then-huge mainframe computers in offices, also found odd moments to produce images on teleprinters. In the 1980s and into the early 1990s, ASCII art blossomed on thousands of BBSs, electronic bulletin boards, run on early personal computers by hobbyists from homes and linked by the telephone system.

BBSs began to die out with the advent of the Internet and the World Wide Web. However, well into the late 1990s, ASCII art flourished in Usenet newsgroups and in the ASCIIART listserv discussion list. [3] Moreover, as we shall see, the World Wide Web brought about dramatic changes in the prominence and accessibility of ASCII art, and enriched the ability of ASCII artists to communicate with one another. This chapter will focus on the period up until 1995. Chapter 6 will continue with a discussion of developments after 1995, when a Windows version of the IRC chat software called "mIRC" became available, and a distinctive new form of text-based art developed. Suddenly, chat could incorporate not only typed text but also visual images and even sound files.

Inevitably, the overview in this chapter is somewhat sketchy. No full-fledged, systematic history of the phenomenon exists in print.[4] Many pieces of the story are missing, and because of the ephemeral nature of this art, only a few firmly dated early examples survive. In particular, the highly elaborated underground computer art scene that was flourishing as this book was completed, reviewed briefly below, requires a separate research project in the future.[5]

In this chapter I attempt to answer the following questions. Just how is ASCII art created? What are the main types of this art? In what ways is it new and unique, and in what ways is it related to certain earlier forms of artistic expression? Which aspects of computers and the Internet most fostered its development? How did it change over time? Who were the practitioners of this art and how did this change in the 1990s?

Technical Aspects

In the Introduction to this book I explained that "ASCII" refers to the set of standard computer keyboard characters which are used to communicate plain text across all systems and software on the Internet.[6] Let us take a closer look at these characters now.

Printable Characters and Their Profiles

Although the basic ASCII set is often said to contain 128 characters, in fact not all are usable. In a FAQ (Frequently Asked Questions) file for newcomers to Usenet newsgroups dealing with ASCII art, Matthew Thomas explains:

> The ASCII character set is a set of 128 characters, numbered from 0 to 127,which are standard on almost all types of computer. The first 32 characters (0 to 31) are various control codes for signalling things like an end of transmission, a beep, escape, backspace, and so on. The last ASCII character, 127, is another control code representing the Delete key. (Thomas 1997)

Since digital information is encoded only as a series of 0s or 1s, each of the characters has a different profile of seven 0s and 1s. Thus, the code for A is 1000001, for B it is 1000010, for C 1000011, and so on.[7] Figure 5.1 shows that there are 95 printable characters with which to "draw" and create images.

032	[space]	048	0	064	@	080	P	096	`	112	p
033	!	049	1	065	A	081	Q	097	a	113	q
034	"	050	2	066	B	082	R	098	b	114	r
035	#	051	3	067	C	083	S	099	c	115	s
036	$	052	4	068	D	084	T	100	d	116	t
037	%	053	5	069	E	085	U	101	e	117	u
038	&	054	6	070	F	086	V	102	f	118	v
039	'	055	7	071	G	087	W	103	g	119	w
040	(	056	8	072	H	088	X	104	h	120	x
041	)	057	9	073	I	089	Y	105	i	121	y
042	*	058	:	074	J	090	Z	106	j	122	z
043	+	059	;	075	K	091	[	107	k	123	{
044	,	060	<	076	L	092	\	108	l	124	|
045	-	061	=	077	M	093	]	109	m	125	}
046	.	062	>	078	N	094	^	110	n	126	~
047	/	063	?	079	O	095	_	111	o		

Figure 5.1. The basic ASCII characters. Matthew Thomas, "Welcome to ASCII Art FAQ (1998). Accessible via http://www.ascii-art.com.

Fonts

ASCII art is created and viewed in fixed-width or monospaced fonts, digital typefaces that display the same number of characters per inch, no matter what the width of the individual characters. The best known fixed-width fonts are FixedSys and Courier New for the PC and Monaco for the Macintosh (Allison, 1996).[8] In fonts which do not meet this criterion, the image will not look right when displayed. Compare the following:

iiiiiiiiiiiiiii   i i i i i i i i i i i i i i i

mmmmmmmmmmmmmmm   m m m m m m m m m m m m m m m

On the left, 15 instances each of the letter "i" and of the letter "m" are shown in a proportional font called Arial. On the right they are displayed in Courier New, a fixed-width font. Only in the latter case do the two sets of characters take up the same amount of space. Even among fixed-width fonts, a somewhat different effect is created, depending on the font chosen, though I will not pay attention to this secondary issue.[9]

Antecedents of ASCII Art

ASCII art is a contemporary expression of a very old phenomenon. People have been making pictures by putting small bits of various materials together for thousands of years. Mosaics are among the earliest antecedents:

> A decorative covering for walls, vaults, floors and panels made up of small colored fragments or tesserae set in cement to form patterns or pictures. Tesserae can be made of natural colored stone, of pottery, and of colored glass. (Myers and Copplestone 1981: 312)

This art dates back at least to 4th century A.D. Rome. The first mosaics were made of pebbles (Hawley 1997: x). Among the most famous mosaics in the world are the 6th-century portraits of Justinian and his followers in Ravenna. Mosaics can be geometric, abstract or figurative, or a combination of both. Tiles and tile patterns are a related precursor, small ceramic units of regular shape combined (usually) in rows and columns to make designs on walls and floors.[10] Like mosaics, tile designs may be entirely or primarily figurative or geometric. Whether figurative or abstract, a pattern is created by systematic repetition of the motif.

More relevant to our topic, and to this book as a whole, are techniques that create images from writing – from letters and typography. A commonly used, general term is "pattern poetry." The phrase refers to poems that are both visual and literary works (Higgins 1987: 3). Explicitly visual poetic works appear in the fourth and third centuries B.C. Greek manuscripts with memorial texts in the shape of urns or other more fanciful forms established a tradition of pattern poetry which continues to the present day (Drucker 1996).[11] The practice was introduced into Christian Europe in the 6th century (Gaur 1994: 147), and apparently flourished in medieval and Renaissance times. One of the earliest examples is an ancient Greek poem called "Wings of Eros" by

Theocritus, in which the text of the poem was arranged vertically to create the effect of two "wings."[12] A well-known 19th-century example is the "Mouse's Tale" in Lewis Carroll's (1960 [1965]: 51) *Alice's Adventures in Wonderland*. The text of the poem is arranged in a vertical tail-like shape. The lines get shorter and shorter, and the words are set in smaller and smaller type.

There have been many 20th-century experiments with the visual aspects of poetry, and with the inter-relations between the visual arts and language. Various avant-garde literary and artistic movements, notably Futurism and Dada in the 1920s, and the "concrete poetry" movement in the 1960s and 1970s, engaged in these experiments (Riddell 1975).[13] Guillaume Apollinaire (1918) is famous for his "calligrammes," poems which play with typography. The best known example is "Il Pleut" ("It Is Raining"), in which the words are arranged in vertical streams down the page, imitating falling rain. Another example is "La Petit Auto" ("The Little Car;'" Figure 5.2). A particularly striking, more contemporary example of a "concrete" poem is "Forsythia" by Mary Ellen Solt (Plate 5.1), in which the brilliant yellow background and arrangement of the letters of the word "forsythia" dramatically express the idea of a blooming forsythia bush in spring.[14]

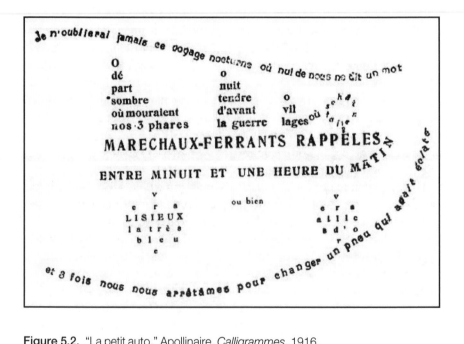

Figure 5.2. "La petit auto," Apollinaire, *Calligrammes*, 1916.

The advent of digitization, hypertext and the Web opened up exciting new possibilities for play with typography in poetry. One of the most prominent pioneers is Eduardo Kac. Both he and others represented in an anthology he edited (Kac 1996) experimented with the possibilities of digital interactivity, hyperlinks, animation, multiple simultaneities, and so on.[15]

An example of the new possibilities is "Sunrise and Sunset" by Komninos Zervos, a performance poet and Ph.D. student in English at the University of Queensland, Australia. In this animated work (Figure 5.3), the word "SUNRISE" is shown in a monumental-looking font. It "peeks" over the horizon, slowly rises, reaches its zenith, changes to "SUNSET," and then slowly "sets," finally disappearing.

Figure 5.3. "Sunrise/Sunset," an animated cyberpoem by Komninos Zervos, http://experimedia.vic.gov.au/~komninos/animgif.html.

This example hints that digitization is taking poetry far away from the familiar fixed, printed black and white text.

At first glance concrete or visual poetry seems similar to what is called typewriter art, but theorists have attempted to distinguish the two. Serious visual artists of the 1920s became interested in the expressive potential of the typewriter to create visual art without semantic content. Students of Josef Albers, a member of the Bauhaus movement,[16] produced works, some of which were later exhibited at a Bauhaus exhibit at the Royal Academy in London in 1968 (Riddell 1975: 11–12). Some artists exploited the possibility of manipulating the paper in the typewriter carriage to produce various effects.

Sometimes it was hard to distinguish poems with visual enhancements from "art" which incorporated words or typographic symbols. At one extreme were

Figure 5.4. "SPOOL," typewriter art by Andrew Belsey.

"poems" in which the visual helped communicate a primarily verbal message; and at the other were primarily visual statements in which graphic arrangements of typographic symbols were part of the composition but did not necessarily convey a clearly identifiable verbal message. Figure 5.4, a contemporary work by Andrew Belsey, illustrates some of the latter art.

The earliest surviving example of naive typewriter art (without avant-garde aspirations) is an 1898 large image of a butterfly by a woman named Flora F. F. Stacey. It was created by moving the paper in the carriage many, many times.[17] From online correspondence with typewriter collectors and typing teachers I learned of another form of typewriter art, a sort of "puzzle" that was used to help teach typing. Instructions told typists what to type, and only when the image was finished or nearly so would they discover the image.

I encountered three instances in which artists recalled having created typewriter art as young people. John Barger, a Chicago software designer and author of one of the main ASCII art FAQS (Barger 1993), cited below, reported that "In high school back in the 1960s I took a photo of myself and painstakingly converted it to typewriter grayscale, which did impress people."[18] Similarly, Joan Stark informed visitors to her digital gallery that

> I remember as a kid, my father would take me to work with him on an occasional Saturday. While there, I would play on the secretary's typewriter and make pictures on a sheet of paper using commas and lines – my "first" ASCII drawings! . . . I had a lot of fun those weekend mornings . . . I guess you could say that I've been making text art – even before computers! :)[19]

A player on one of the art channels on IRC that I investigated (Chapter 6), wrote to me that he created pictures on a typewriter when he was young. The idea of the shaped text is not limited to poems. One example is a 1997 advertisement for the Weizmann Institute of Science in Rehovot, Israel in the New York Times, in which the text was arranged in the shape of a test tube.

One of the most spectacular instances of pictures from writing is the practice of Islamic calligraphers from medieval times of creating striking visual images from stylized writing.[20] This was a way to get around the proscription against the visual representation of living forms in Islam (Gaur 1994: 147; Grabar 1992). Figure 5.5 is a face made up of the names of Allah, Muhammad and three Imams.

Figure 5.5. A human face made up of the names of Allah, Muhammad and three Imams. Reprinted with permission from Gaur (1994), Fig. 100, p. 148. © 1994 Copyright The British Library.

Still another famous type of pictures from writing is micrography, "minute script written into abstract patterns or formed into the shape of objects, animals, or human figures" (Avrin 1984: 87). This phenomenon is known in the Far East, Southeast Asia, India and Western Europe (Gaur 1994: 150), but is especially associated with Jewish tradition (Avrin 1984; 1991; Ferber 1977; Cohen 1988). Filled shapes are less common than use of minute text to outline a figure, as in the charming example from a 13th-century Catalonian Hebrew prayer book in Figure 5.6 (Avrin 1984: 87).

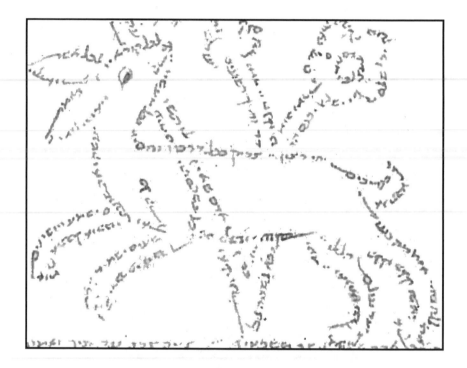

Figure 5.6. Micrography in a Hebrew prayer book, Catalonia, c. 1280, detail. Jewish National Library 8° 6527. Reprinted with permission.

In 20th century advertising and graphic design letters and symbols often became mere graphic shapes-to-design-with. In other cases, play with graphic form was mobilized to enhance meaning. One striking phenomenon is creating "faces" from typography. So common was this practice that Gerry Rosentswieg (1995) assembled nearly 600 examples by 33 different designers in a book with the punning title, *Type Faces*.[21]

From Teletype Art to ASCII Art

Teletype Art

The most immediate predecessor of ASCII art is teletype art, better known among the initiated as RTTY art. This art was created and circulated on *Radio TeleTYpewriters* in the 1950s and 1960s, and even well into the 1980s. Sometimes this art is confused with ASCII art because much of it looks very similar. Like both ASCII art and works done on a typewriter, it is displayed in a fixed-width typeface and is created line by line on a machine from letters, numbers and other typographic symbols.[22] Unlike typewriter art but like ASCII art, it encodes information in digital "bits." In regular typewriter art no coding is involved; the art is local, not intended to be transmitted to another location.

RTTY art was created in a 5-bit code, sometimes called the Baudot code, rather than the later, 7-bit ASCII code.[23] Thus, for the letter "A" one typed "00011," for "B" "11001," and so on.[24] Because of the limitation of only five digits, only capital letters could be used. "Almost all the classic pictures were punched out on 5-level tape (Baudot) . . . We stored all of our pictures on punched paper tape."[25] One could print an image locally where it was created, or one could transmit it to others elsewhere. One of the first images created in this manner was a Madonna and Child made at Christmastime, 1947.[26] A quite spectacular RTTY image is "Winter Wonderland" (Figure 5.7). With careful use of characters of differing thickness or blackness, and some overstrikes as well, it has a feeling of texture which is rare in both RTTY art and ASCII art. Figure 5.8 is an RTTY portrait of John F. Kennedy by Ralph Larsson.[27] It is constructed of the letters "M," "X," and "W," along with some colons, commas, apostrophes, periods, etc.[28]

Images were circulated at first by telegraph and then by radio:

> . . .it all started out on the landline telegraph circuits around the country which had advanced to the stage of using Teletype machines in place of Morse keys and sounders. These pictures were originated by the "telegraph" operators during the holiday season . . . The swing over to the use of radio took place by radio amateurs in the 1950s when we were first allowed to transmit the Baudot code via amateur radio. This provided a great medium to "play" with picture transmission.[29]

These comments by John Sheetz indicate that teletype art in fact predated amateur radio, though most art was created and circulated by ham radio operators. Annual contests were held for the best art.[30]

Not only amateur radio operators were involved. Jack Lally, a newcomer to ASCII art, recalled his earlier experiences with RTTY art:

Figure 5.7. Winter wonderland, an RTTY Image.

Figure 5.8. An RTTY portrait of John F. Kennedy by Ralph Larsson.

I am a retired Merchant Marine Radio Officer and in later years at sea we did a great deal of communicating by Radio Teletype. I believe it was there that I first saw "Stick Men" as my kids used to call them in an art form. Some of the Coast Station operators would while away the lonely Midnight watch hours by creating these drawings and then sending them to the ships at sea.[31]

A very long 1969 United States Marine Corps greeting preserved by Charles Struble – too large to reproduce in this book – belongs to the same era.[32] Stationed in Okinawa at the time, he and his colleagues sent out this greeting to military installations all over the globe. Rick Hoover wrote to Joan Stark, the ASCII artist whose work will feature prominently in this chapter:

My first exposure to ASCII/typeface art was as a radio deejay around Christmas and New Year's Eve of 1968. The AP newswire service would send out "pictures" of Santa landing on a houseroof, or Christmas trees, or such on their news wire printers.[33]

Themes in Teletype Art

In the summer of 1999 a gallery of RTTY art was created on the Web. As part of a collective effort to reconstruct the history of RTTY activities, 62 images were put on display. While these images became accessible to a wide audience for the first time on the Web,[34] they were too few to examine for research purposes. John Sheetz, a ham radio operator and collector of RTTY art, kindly shared with me his classification of 1094 images collected as of May 1981 (Table 5.1).[35] I might have classified some of the images somewhat differently. For instance "famous paintings" like the Mona Lisa are included with "art, mythology and literary characters", not "portraits, famous people." ASCII versions of famous paintings later became quite common. Still, the material is very useful.

The single most common theme in this collection was cartoon characters. In second and third places, respectively, were Christmas imagery and greetings and "pinups" or centerfolds – images of beautiful, scantily clad or nude women. Animals and portraits of people followed; all the other categories were

Table 5.1. Themes in RTTY art.*

Theme	Number
1 Cartoon characters	249
2 Christmas imagery, greetings	134
3 Pinups, centerfolds	124
4 Animals	113
5 Portraits, famous people	107
6 People	67
7 Vehicles	49
8 Symbols and flags	48
9 Holidays other than Christmas	43
10 Objects	36
11 Science Fiction	30
12 Scenery, buildings	28
13 Art, mythology, literary characters	26
14 Jokes, cartoons, humor	17
15 Messages	17
16 Religious	6
Total	1094

*Data supplied by John Sheetz from his personal collection.

Plate 3.1. Color graphics for "PCbeth" by Gayle Kidder.

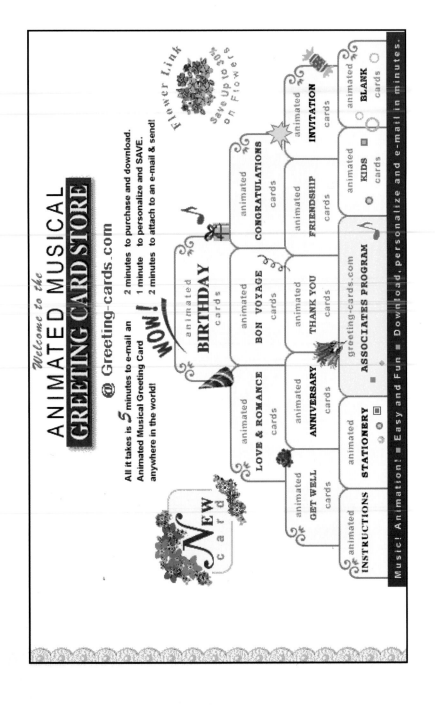

Plate 4.1. "The Animated Musical Greeting Card Store," http://greeting-cards.com/.

Plate 6.3. Images containing the word "hug".

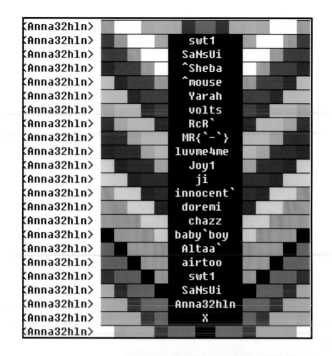

Plate 6.2. "Multiples:" group greetings, designed by <sher> and <icy2>.

Plate 6.1. A series of "hellos" on *#mirc_rainbow*.

Plate 5.4. Four ANSI art images of the late 1990s, "Acheron.org," http://www.acheron.org.

Plate 5.5. An ANSI image by Sandy Chidester, "Outworld Arts," 1997, www.outworldarts.com/ansi.html

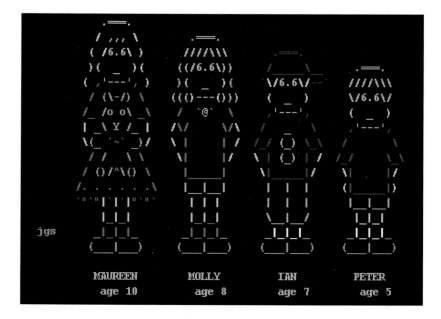

Plate 5.3. Colored ASCII art by Joan Stark, Joan Stark's ASCII Art Gallery, http://www.ascii-art.com/.

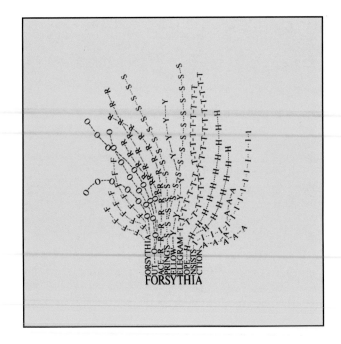

Plate 5.1. "Forsythia" by Mary Ellen Solt. Reprinted with permission.

Plate 5.2. An ANSI BBS screen by Dave Hartmann, http://inlink.com/~dhartman/ansi.html.

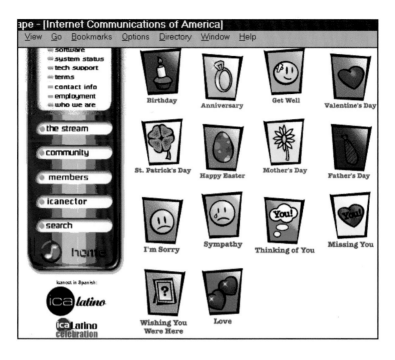

Plate 4.8. Incongruity in a greetings site.

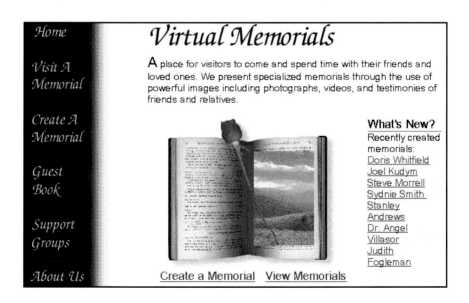

Plate 4.9. "Virtual Memorials," http://www.virtual-memorials.com/.

Plate 4.6. "Send@Card," http://www.heaven.com.my/channelx/ecard/.

Plate 4.7. "Digital Dream Post Office," http://www.digitaldream.com/.

Plate 4.4. An Early Pop-Up Valentine. Norcross Greeting Card Collection, Archive Center, National Museum of American History. Smithsonian Institution, (negative #77-14866). Reproduced with permission.

Plate 4.5. An Antique Handmade Valentine. Olive Leavister Collection of Antique Handmade Valentines, Archive Center National Museum of American History, Smithsonian Institution (negative #94-3777). Reproduced with permission.

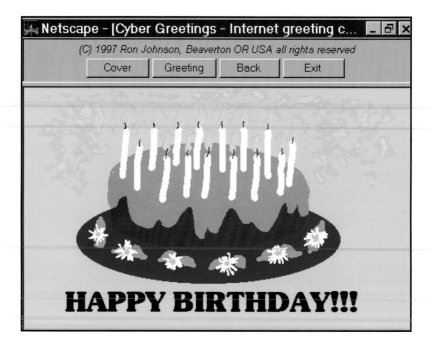

Plate 4.2. A digital birthday greeting, by Heidi Anderson. "Cyber Greetings," http:www.teleport.com/~ronjbeav/cybercard.shtml.

Plate 4.3. A digital Christmas greeting from Hong Kong.

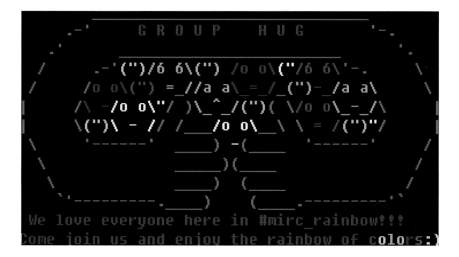

Plate 6.4. The "group hug" motif on the *#mirc_rainbow* Website, by <diedra>, adapted from art by Joan Stark.

Plate 6.5. Entrance: to the *#mirc_colors* Website, a castle by <elusive>.

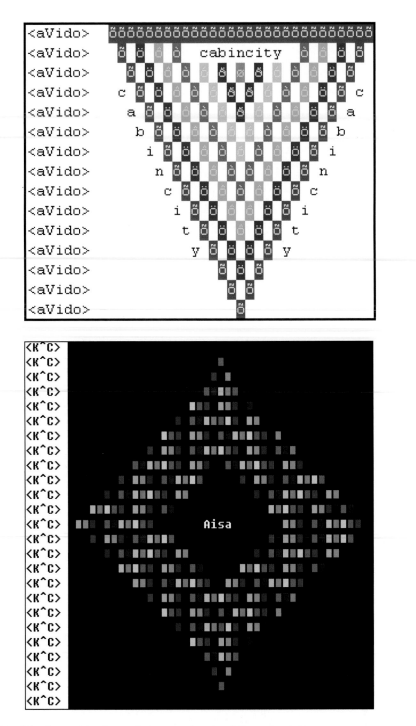

Plate 6.6. Geometric shapes in images, by <twotall> and <nightrose>.

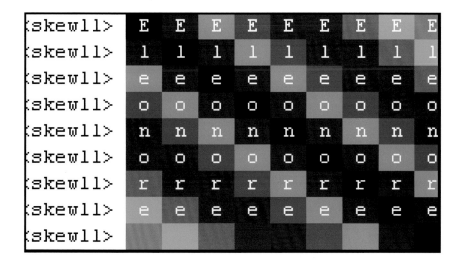

Plate 6.7. An image with a diagonal effect.

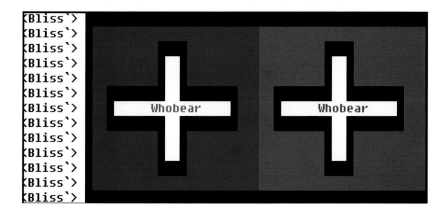

Plate 6.8. Play with color and summetry, by <twotall>.

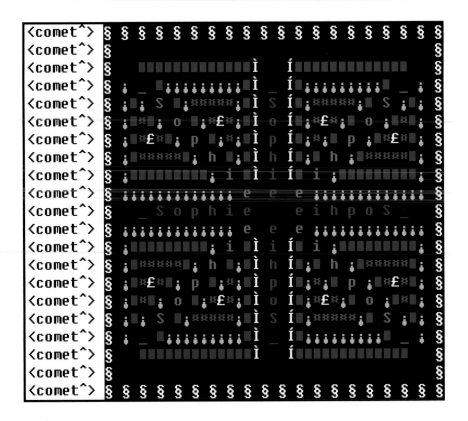

Plate 6.9. An abstract design with extended ASCII characters, by <[blue]>.

Plate 6.10. Repetition in images.

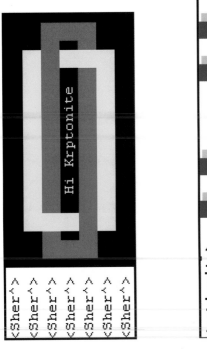
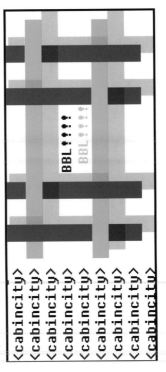

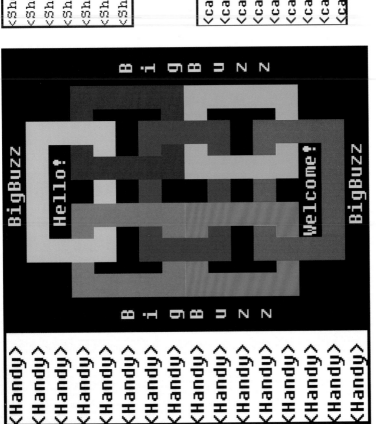

Plate 6.11. Interlace and "woven" patterns, by <sher> and <joesin>.

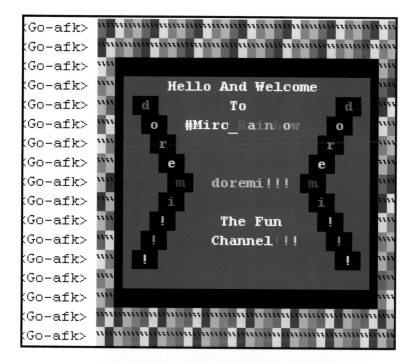

Plate 6.12. Images with extended ASCII borders.

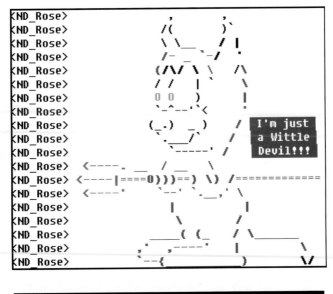

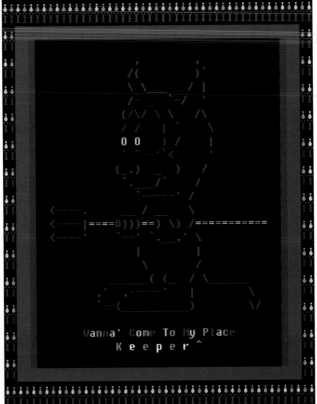

Plate 6.13. An image with an empty and a filled background.

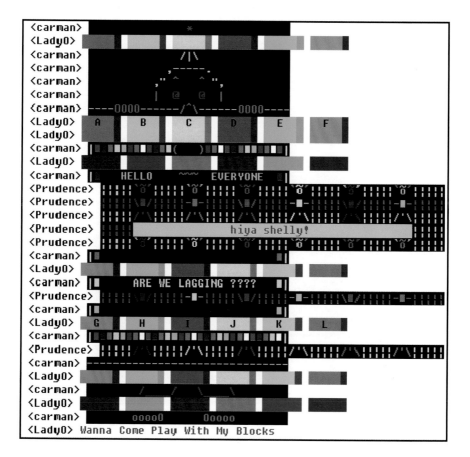

Plate 6.14. A "picture collision" on **#mirc_rainbow**.

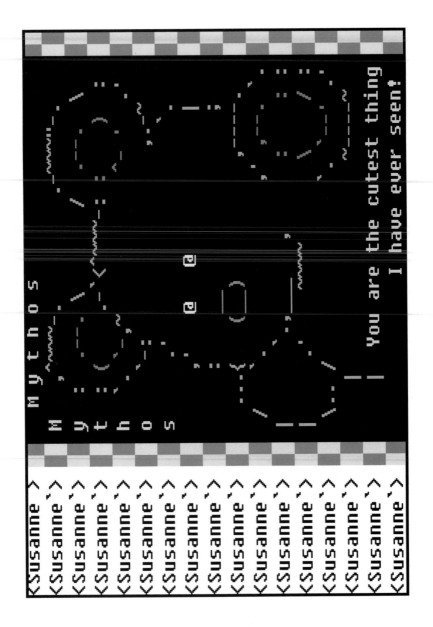

Plate 6.15. A cute teddy bear, original by Robin Chokie, adapted for IRC by <bamacutie>.

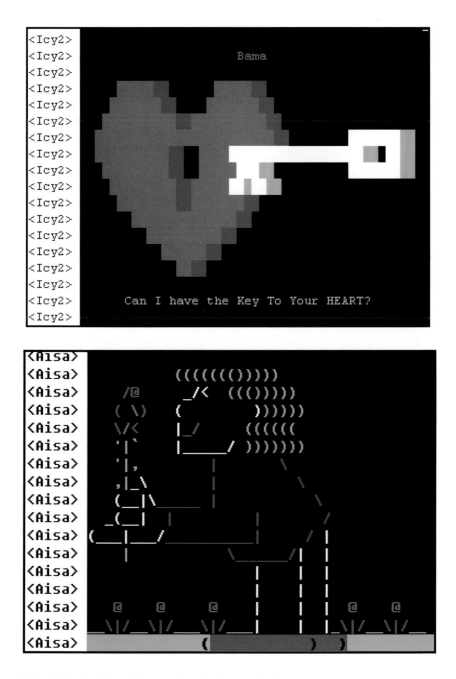

Plate 6.16. Hearts and flowers, by <joesin> and <aisa>.

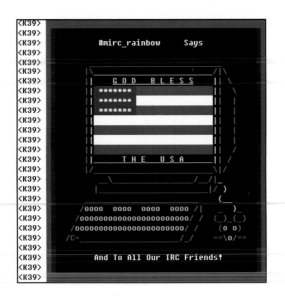

Plate 6.17. A Fourth of July image incorporating components from IRC culture.

```
Galaphile>
Galaphile>      _  ***                                 .---- *** ----.
Galaphile>    ( `\( ) *      Beauty      My        || ( `\( )/`)  ||
Galaphile>    `> /^\_I   COMPUTER ANGEL:            || > /^\ <    ||
Galaphile>    (_/ /\/                               || (// \\)    ||
Galaphile>      \ \                                 ||__`\ | |`__||
Galaphile>      / /       I met an angel            `-)--|_|--(-'
Galaphile>      \/        while on IRC              [=== -- o ]--.
Galaphile>      `        Whose sweet love            `_____'__ \
Galaphile>               is heavenly!               [::::::::::: :::] )
Galaphile>                                          `.........'........'/T\
Galaphile>    You are a special person                               /T\
Galaphile>          Beauty                                           \/
Galaphile>
```

Plate 6.18. "My computer angel," adapted by <elusive> from a design by Joan Stark.

```
<Aisa>
<Aisa>
<Aisa>
<Aisa>                           Whobear
<Aisa>
<Aisa>                           You're
<Aisa>                           such a
<Aisa>                           barrel
<Aisa>                           of fun.
<Aisa>
<Aisa>
<Aisa>
<Aisa>
```

```
<Nuffers>
<Nuffers>    {@}{@}{@}{@}{@}{@}{@}{@}{@}{@}{@}{@}{@}
<Nuffers>    {@}    Well, since you asked    {@}
<Nuffers>    {@}         karol^               {@}
<Nuffers>    {@}                              {@}
<Nuffers>    {@}      ()())))))))             {@}
<Nuffers>    {@}     (((())))))))))           {@}
<Nuffers>    {@}      (())        (())        {@}
<Nuffers>    {@}      (())   (@ \  (())        {@}
<Nuffers>    {@}      (())    < |  (())        {@}
<Nuffers>    {@}      (())   (@ /  (())        {@}
<Nuffers>    {@}      ())()       (())        {@}
<Nuffers>    {@}     ((()))-  -()))))))       {@}
<Nuffers>    {@}      (())))   (())))))       {@}
<Nuffers>    {@}      ((((()   ())))))       {@}
<Nuffers>    {@}      /   |    |  \          {@}
<Nuffers>    {@}      |   |    |   |         {@}
<Nuffers>    {@}      |  |/:\___/:\|  |      {@}
<Nuffers>    {@}      |  |::::::::::|  |      {@}
<Nuffers>    {@}    The doctor said it's from  {@}
<Nuffers>    {@}   looking at mIRC smiley faces. {@}
<Nuffers>    {@}{@}{@}{@}{@}{@}{@}{@}{@}{@}{@}{@}{@}
<Nuffers>
<Nuffers>
```

Plate 6.19. Humor in images.

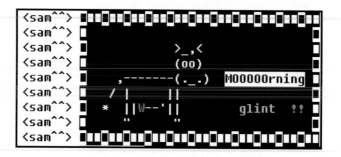

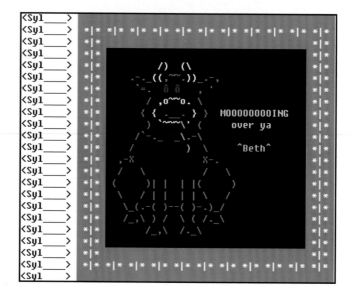

Plate 6.20. A "run" of cows.

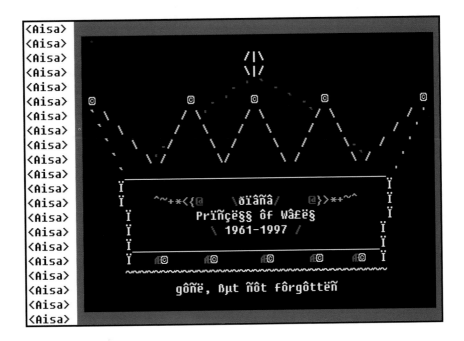

Plate 6.21. Commemorating Diana, Princess of Wales.

Plate 6.22. A tribute to <nuffers> on the **#mirc_rainbow** Website, adapted by <aisa>.

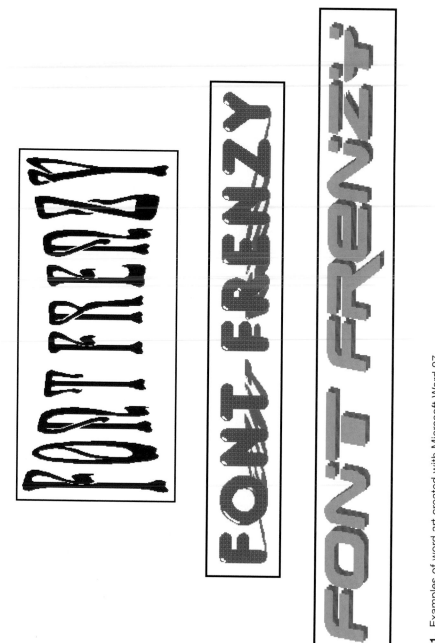

Plate 7.1. Examples of word art created with Microsoft Word 97.

Plate 7.2. Alliterative logos of font Websites.

Welcome to Fontazm! Browse around. If you find something you like, download it! If you don't find what you're looking for, see the Links page.

Plate 7.3. Wordplay in logos of font Websites.

Plate 7.4. A selection of free fonts at "Acid Fonts," http://www.acidfonts.com/.

Plate 7.5. Katgyrl's "Fontain of Youth", http://www.katgyrl.com/.

much less frequent. The first five categories accounted for 66 percent of the total.

There is a great deal of overlap between these categories and themes in ASCII art. This is not by chance. Given that nearly all ham radio operators were men, and there was little pressure to be politically correct in those days, it is not surprising nudes and "pinups" were quite common (over one out of every 10 images); other categories overlap too. I learned from the RTTY.COM Website that large pinups were often created for RTTY calendars, and were named, e.g., "Miss March," "Miss September," and so on. Sheetz's collection also included an unusually large Christmas banner, for which I was able to obtain a computerized version. When printed in tiny 9-point Courier New, it spreads across seven 8 1/2 x 11" pages.

A special type of RTTY art is "overstrike art." On a teletype machine it was possible to return to the beginning of a line and to insert additional characters, overstriking previous ones, thus producing darker effects and creating contrast, just as one could do on a regular typewriter. It was possible to go over a line as many as four times.[36] In the close-up of Albert Einstein's eye (Figure 5.9), we can see the overstrikes creating different degrees of blackness in greater detail.[37]

Figure 5.9. Overstrike art: an image of Albert Einstein and his eye.

The Earliest ASCII Art

Despite the visual and encoding similarities between the two, RTTY art and ASCII art involve completely different technologies of transmission. No one knows when the first ASCII art picture was made or what it looked like, because there is little systematic record of this phenomenon in the early years. Since any 5-bit RTTY image can easily be transferred to a computer, 100s of them migrated to ASCII art collections.[38] If an image contains only capital letters there is a good possibility that it was originally an RTTY image. Hackers, programmers and other computer professionals experimented with ASCII images too. Many of the images stored in Web collections in the late 1990s were probably created in the early years, but it is rarely possible to date them.

The 1990s: BBSs, Usenet Newsgroups and the World Wide Web

Fidonet, Usenet Newsgroups

Even for the late 1980s and early 1990s the story of ASCII art is rather sketchy. A letter to Joan Stark from Ian Wallis helps fill in some of the blanks:

> ASCII Art probably reached it's [sic] zenith from about 1987 to 1994/5 on the Bulletin Board Systems that were prevalent before the opening of the Internet to the general public. At one point there was [sic] well over 150,000 active BBSs around the world and the largest collection were linked together via the email network "FidoNet"[39] which had some 35,000 BBSs linked worldwide. FidoNet had several highly active ASCII art email groups that were prolific in the quantity of material generated.

It should also be noted that virtually all system operators (SysOps) of BBSs generated or at least borrowed ASCII Art for use on their welcome screens.[40] Thus, in this period ASCII art flourished primarily on BBSs, run on Amigas, Commodores, IBMs, and other early computers, and circulated by email. System operators decorated their screens with ASCII art to liven it up.

In 1979, the American National Standards institute issued a new format for digital communication, called "ANSI" for short. ANSI means "A textmode medium which consists of the standard IBM PC 245-character set, enhanced by sixteen foreground colors, eight background colors, and the ability to control and move the cursor."[41] The new format doubled the number of characters one could use and, much more important for the art of that time, allowed artists to use bold color at the DOS level for the first time. To use the new features one had to install a special driver (ANSI.SYS) in the DOS operating system on one's computer and then reconfigure the functions of certain keys. One has to have fairly advanced computer skills to create colored art in this manner; few people knew about it. In practice, the excitement was mainly over color, not the addition of exotic typographic characters, something that was to come only with IRC art (Chapter 6). Working with "blocks"[42] of color, artists created graphics with a minimal amount of (or no) text, and created oversize "fonts" from blocks of color.

From the mid- to late 1980s and even into the early 1990s, this format was widely used to create initial multicolored screens for BBSs. Images filled exactly one screen. The Website of Dave Hartmann archived a selection of screens he created for his own "Tin Roof" BBS in St. Louis, Missouri in the late 1980s and early 1990s, and some he created for other BBSs too (Plate 5.1). Shapes look jagged precisely because the images are constructed in blocks.[43] Although thousands of people may have created or been exposed to ANSI art, in the late 1980s into the 1990s "plain vanilla" ASCII art was far more common and much more likely to be seen by the general public.

Black and white[44] ASCII art gained new momentum in the 1990s, when two newsgroups devoted to it were formed on Usenet: *alt.ascii-art* and *rec.ascii. art*. *Alt.ascii-art* celebrated its fifth anniversary in September 1998. Other groups were *alt.ascii-art.animation* and *alt.binaries.pictures.ascii*. In *alt.ascii-art*, an unmoderated group, people posted original images, or improved versions or variations of other people's work; others wrote asking for an image they needed, such as a birthday cake for a birthday greeting. *Rec.arts.ascii* was similar except that it was moderated (Thomas 1997: 1998).[45]

The World Wide Web

The other important development which greatly spurred interest in ASCII art in the 1990s was the rise of the World Wide Web in 1992. The Web made it possible for the first time to store images in a manner accessible to millions. Previously, images had been stored at FTP or gopher sites, and only people with in-group technical knowledge knew how to access them. The latter sites were visually uninteresting, and it was impossible to browse images. One had to download individual images or whole sets of them, sight unseen, and then view them offline. FTP and gopher sites were convenient ways for practitioners involved in newsgroups and the listserv list to store their work for themselves and enthusiasts, not to make the work available to the general public online. In the late 1990s, in contrast, tens of thousands of images were displayed attractively, or at least accessibly on dozens of Websites, and visitors could browse at leisure. Many artists created their own digital galleries. Others were collectors and curators. In addition to maintaining her own gallery, Joan Stark maintained a set of links to the work of about 150 artists.[46]

Another result of migration to the Web was that technical information on how to create ASCII art became more accessible. Like the art itself, FAQ files had previously been available only at FTP and gopher sites; now they were easily downloaded from the Web. As a result of these developments it became very difficult to estimate how many people were involved as the year 2000 approached. Tens of millions might incorporate an ASCII image in their sig file, or send an occasional ASCII image as an email attachment or celebratory greeting. However, the number of collectors maintaining substantial Web displays was in the dozens, and the number of prolific ASCII artists was perhaps even smaller.

Styles and Genres of ASCII Art

There was an amazing variety of ASCII art, given the limited range of possibilities of this graphic palette and the strictly linear medium. Indeed, the desire to stretch this ostensibly "primitive," limited medium to its limits and beyond was just what kept many ASCII artists busy.

As I began to suggest earlier, this is a geometric medium. Every image is a grid, constructed line by line, with each "slot" or space in a line either filled by a symbol or left empty, just as when one is creating a verbal text. One could not do many things graphic designers routinely do, such as mixing fonts, turning letters upside down, or blowing up selected ones to over-size.[47] Nevertheless, the range of visual effects was often astonishing.

In Figure 5.10 I have compiled a fairly exhaustive list of all the recognized types of ASCII art by style and/or genre.[48] Some may be quite familiar to people who have been using email for a few years and have sent or received them in email attachments, or who have browsed ASCII art Websites. Others are less known. The list was partially compiled from FAQ files for initiates to ASCII art and the Usenet newsgroups,[49] but also incorporates other categories that I identified. Some art is made completely "by hand," symbol by symbol. Other images are generated via programs that convert graphic images to ASCII. In still other cases, the initial image is created via a conversion program, and is then refined by hand. Many people expressed a preference for "handmade" images.

Some varieties have been in existence since the 1960s; others are much newer. Practitioners or collectors of ASCII art do not generally make my distinction between representational and abstract images, basic in art history

---

(1) **Representational images**
  - line style
  - solid style
  - mixed style
  - reverse
  - gray-scale
  - miniatures
  - three-dimensional

(2) **Shaped texts**

(3) **Calendars**

(4) **"Fonts:" stylized lettering**

(5) **Holiday and birthday greetings**

(6) **Humor**

(7) **Smiley icons**

(8) **Signature files**

(9) **"Calligraphy"**

(10) **Scroll animation**

(11) **Color images and animations**

(12) **Abstract patterns**

*Partially compiled from Allison (1994, 1996); Thomas (1997, 1998); Atkins (1998).

Figure 5.10. Genres and styles of ASCII art.

and the study of folk art and the anthropology of art.[50] In any case, most images are representational, as was true for teletype art. They are typically "drawings" of people or objects. Scores of sites classified images by subject matter – the type of object or creature depicted. I have tried to develop a more analytical classification, albeit not a totally systematic one. The bias toward representational images in artists' and collectors' classifications is also evident in the fact that ASCII art is often described as "pictures from typographic symbols." In the IRC variety featured in Chapter 6, in contrast, abstract patterns resembling quilt or rug designs are very prominent, making such a definition too narrow today.[51]

I list twelve categories. The first four pertain to matters of form, whereas categories six–eight pertain primarily to aspects of communicative function.

The last three are novel. Scroll animation and DOS or UNIX color images and animations require special skills and facilities to view them online, and are therefore less common. As I will show later on, the Web now makes it possible to view some of these innovations without having to know esoteric commands to execute them.

Note that the categories are not entirely mutually exclusive. Thus, a holiday greeting may contain an ASCII "drawing" as well as oversize lettering created with ASCII "fonts," and a signature file may contain one-line ASCII art and a border creating an abstract pattern. These distinctions between the formal-aesthetic and social-communicative aspects of text-based art will become very important in Chapter 6.

Representational Images versus Abstract Patterns

As I have noted, the vast majority of ASCII art images are representational "drawings" or "pictures" of objects in the physical world. Their content comes primarily from everyday life and popular culture. There are images, e.g., of famous people; famous paintings, notably the Mona Lisa (Figure 5.11), machines (cars, computers, airplanes, spaceships); buildings (castles are a favorite; Figure 5.12); animals (teddy bears, dragons, cats), science fiction characters such as Picard from Startrek; cartoon characters (Mickey Mouse, the Simpsons, Garfield, etc.); and creatures in children's books ("Winnie the Pooh"); angels, witches, knights in armor, mermaids, etc.[52]

Notably absent from the art on the Web, on the other hand, are abstract patterns, though minimal concern for pattern was discernible in the creation of decorative borders in signature files. A rare black and white example of a full-fledged pattern, by Normand Veilleux, is displayed in Figure 5.13.

The three main styles of "drawing" or "painting" figurative images are "line-style," "solid-style," and gray-scale. Figure 5.14 shows an image of a horse in both line-style and solid-style by Normand Veilleux;[53] skillful use of characters helps execute curved lines in this linear medium. Line-style comes closest to drawing as we normally understand it. In practice, many images are a mixture of line-style and solid-style, as is the lion by Joan Stark in Figure 5.15. Most of the shape of the animal is "drawn" in outline form, but the mane is done in solid-style.[54] As for "gray-scale," using characters of differing degrees of thickness enables one to create effects of modeling, as in the image of the Mona Lisa (Figure 5.11).

The characters that are used in solid style influences the effect created. The flower by Susie Oviatt in Figure 5.16 seems light and airy because of the use of "light" characters of few pixels each like semi-colons, apostrophes, and commas. The effect is very different from that in images full of "heavy" 8s like that in Figure 5.17.[55]

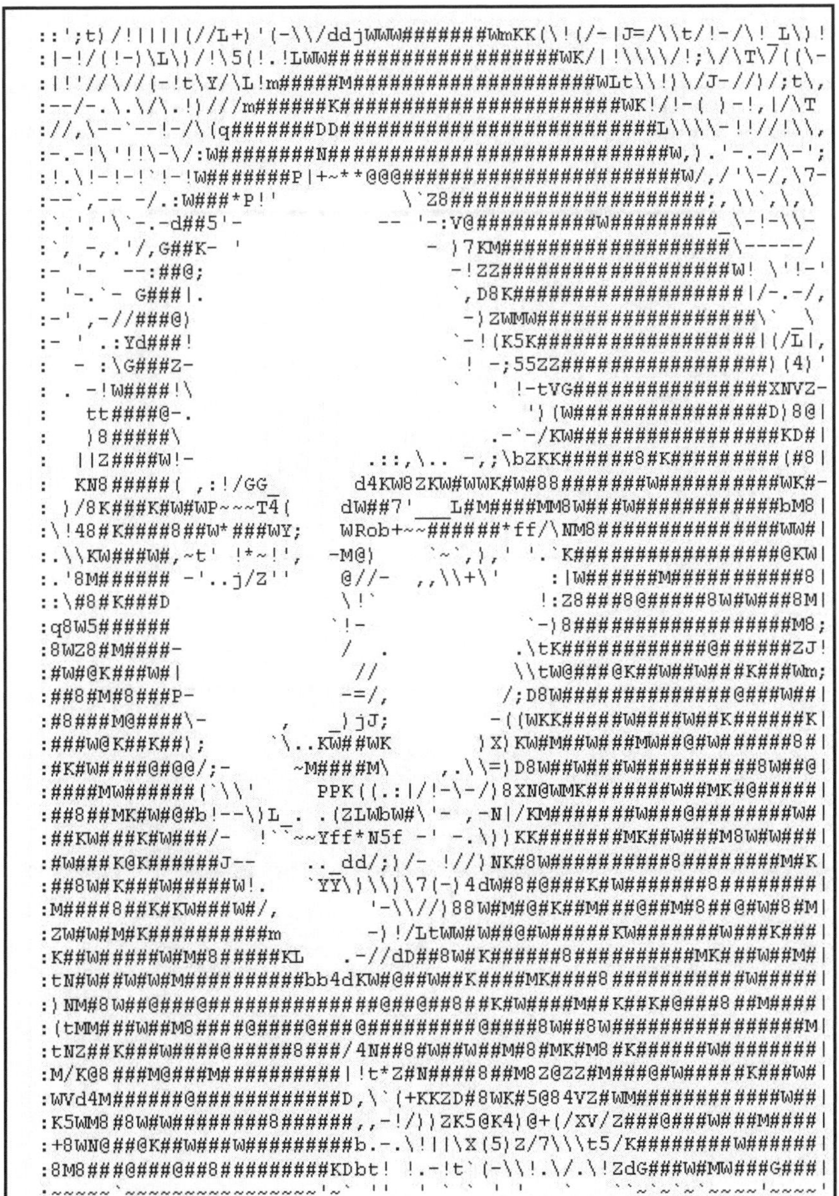

Figure 5.11. The Mona Lisa "painted" with ASCII characters.

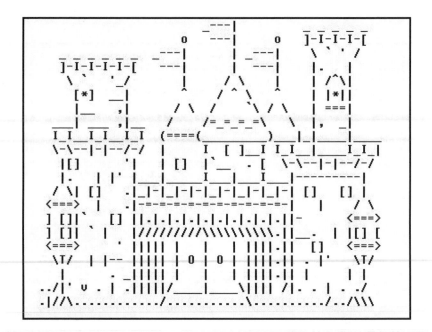

Figure 5.12. An ASCII castle.

Figure 5.13. A pattern by Normand Veilleux.

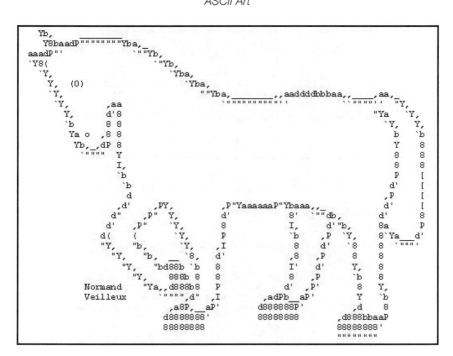

Figure 5.14. Line-style and solid style horses, by Normand Veilleux.

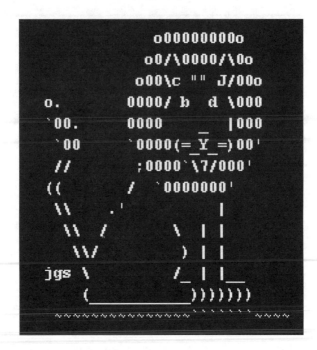

Figure 5.15. A lion in mixed style by Joan Stark.

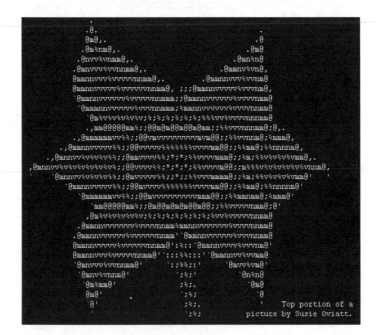

Figure 5.16. A flower by Susie Oviatt (detail).

Figure 5.17. Logo of the World Wildlife Fund, by Normand Veilleux.

The introduction of "soft" or "feminine" themes such as flowers reflects the arrival of increased numbers of women on the ASCII art scene. Formerly dominated by males, the art had featured stereotypically male imagery, such as transportation vehicles, spaceships, the weapons of war – tanks, guns, etc., and skull and bones motifs.

Miniatures

A distinctive type of art is what practitioners call "small pictures" or "small pix," miniatures created with just a few symbols in a small number of rows (Figure 5.18). With minimal means, clever representations of action – bike-riding and rowing – are rendered. And the variations on the theme of a penguin are reminiscent of certain genres of ASCII humor, like the "cows" and "smiley' icons to be displayed shortly (Figures 5.26 and 5.27 below). One senses that the individuals who created these miniatures took great pleasure in accomplishing so much with so little. ASCII artist Dave Bird told *Hotwired*:

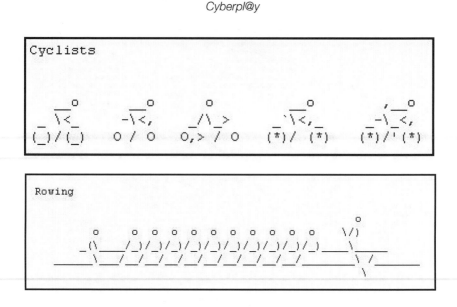

Figure 5.18. ASCII miniatures.

The real essence of "character art" is simply to take the fixed and arbitrary shape of written characters, and make that into a drawing. The highest form of it is not block or shade but "line," as small as you can possibly get a meaningful drawing from. (cited in Frauenfelder 1997).

Perhaps the greatest challenge of all is to create art in just one line (Figure 5.19). Like many other images and motifs in pre-IRC ASCII art, the minnows at the bottom of Figure 5.19 resurfaced in the IRC channels I discuss in Chapter 6, in colored form. In the amusing set of one-liners in Figure 5.20 a "keyboard" menu includes items such as "shrimp," "popcorn," "fig newtons," and "Chinese take out."

A novel type of ASCII art is three-dimensional images. The image becomes three-dimensional, for people with similar vision in both eyes, if one stares as if looking at the back of the monitor, or if one puts one's nose up close against the monitor (Allison 1996).[56]

Shaped Texts

While most ASCII art images have no verbal "meaning," and keyboard symbols are merely graphic shapes to "paint" or "draw" with, one genre does contain minimal verbal content which is subordinated to a graphic shape. In these shaped visual images, the text may merely consist of the same words repeated over and over, or generated in "reverse" fashion, as the white space between

```
          ]==[iiii]>-----  syringe

<>*<>*<>*<>*<>*<>*<>*<>*<>*<>*<>*<>-   necklace or bracelet

    oxx(----------       small foil for fencing

      <')))))><    <`))))))><    minnows
```

Figure 5.19. One-line ASCII art.

```
\&&&&&&/   Pretzels!

\66666666/   Shrimp!

\********/   Popcorn!

^<**>^  ^<**>^  Hot steamed Maryland blue crabs : )

\_><{{{{">_/   Whole Fish Soup!!

[::] [::] [::] [::]   Fig Newtons

(#) (#) (#)   Warm Peanut butter cookies

\--------/   Chicken soup for all your sick friends

(@)  (@)  (@)  Fresh Cinnamon Rolls!

OooOooOooO   Onion  rings

[:::] [:::] [:::] French toast sticks with powdered sugar

======#   Celery

\_/   \_/   Chinese Take Out

\ ) ) ) ) ) /    (~~~~~)  Chips and Dip

@@@@ (_) (_) (_)   Chocolate Chip cookies and Moo juice ;)

(|===|)(|===|)   Hot dogs

(m) (m) (_)   (_)  M&M's and Kool-Aid

* o  o  o  o   Single AND O O O O O Double Stuff Oreos!

<) <) <) <) <)    Pizza!
```

Figure 5.20. The keyboard restaurant menu. Posted to the ***#mirc_colors*** ops list
by Stephanie/<Star Ann>, January 17, 1998.

```
                    +
                   "X"
                  "XXX"
                 "XXXXX"
                "GOD JUL"
               "BUON ANNO"
              "FELIZ NATAL"
              "JOYEUX NOEL"
             "VESELE VANOCE"
            "MELE KALIKIMAKA"
          "NODLAG SONA DHUIT"
        "BLWYDDYN NEWYDD DDA"
       """""""BOAS FESTAS"""""""
            "FELIZ NAVIDAD"
           "MERRY CHRISTMAS"
         "KALA CHRISTOUGENA"
         "VROLIJK KERSTFEEST"
       "FROHLICHE WEIHNACHTEN"
       "BUON NATALE-GODT NYTAR"
      "HUAN YING SHENG TAN CHIEH"
     "WESOLYCH SWIAT-SRETAN BOZIC"
    "MOADIM LESIMHA-LINKSMU KALEDU"
   "HAUSKAA JOULUA-AID SAID MOUBARK"
      """""""'N PRETTIG KERSTMIS"""""""
        "ONNZLLISTA UUTTA VUOTTA"
        "Z ROZHDESTYOM KHRYSTOVYM"
       "NADOLIG LLAWEN-GOTT NYTTSAR"
      "FELIC NADAL-GOJAN KRISTNASKON"
      "S NOVYM GODOM-FELIZ ANO NUEVO"
     "GLEDILEG JOL-NOELINIZ KUTLU OLSUM"
    "EEN GELUKKIG NIEUWJAAR-SRETAN BOSIC"
  "KRIHSTLINDJA GEZUAR-KALA CHRISTOUGENA"
  "SELAMAT HARI NATAL - LAHNINGU NAJU METU"
 """""""SARBATORI FERICITE-BUON ANNO"""""""
     "ZORIONEKO GABON-HRISTOS SE RODI"
    "BOLDOG KARACSONNY-VESELE VIANOCE "
   "MERRY CHRISTMAS AND HAPPY NEW YEAR"
  "ROOMSAID JOULU PUHI -KUNG HO SHENG TEN"
 "FELICES PASUAS - EIN GLUCKICHES NEUJAHR"
"PRIECIGUS ZIEMAN SVETKUS SARBATORI VESLLE"
"BONNE ANNE BLWYDDYN NEWYDD DDADRFELIZ NATAL"
"""""""""""""""""""""""""""""""""""""""""""""""""""
                 XXXXX
                 XXXXX
                 XXXXX
             XXXXXXXXXXXX
```

Figure 5.21. An ASCII Christmas tree.

typographic symbols. A variation on this theme is Figure 5.21, a Christmas "tree" composed of the expression "Merry Christmas" in many languages.

"Fonts": Stylized Lettering

Still another recognized form of ASCII art, mentioned briefly earlier, is stylized "lettering." Letters can be made "by hand"[57] or one can download and use collections of "fonts" from the World Wide Web (Figure 5.22). These are fancy "lettering" styles for sparing use, for instance, in banners or signature files. With a program called "Figlet," one can convert text to one of these fonts automatically. While one can download the program, there are many Websites where one can do this instantly, online.

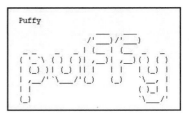

Figure 5.22. ASCII "Fonts."

Holiday and Other Celebratory Greetings

People circulated ASCII holiday greetings by email for several decades, and continued to do so even after Web-based greetings became available. A former assistant of mine sent an ASCII notice of the birth of his daughter (Figure 5.23) to many of us in 1998. There are entire collections of ASCII birthday greetings on the Net, such as the one in Figure 5.24. Valentines were also popular. A former student and her husband incorporated the one shown in Figure 5.25 in their unconventional paper wedding invitation in Jerusalem in August 1995.

Humor

ASCII versions of well-known comics and cartoon characters were very popular.[58] One of the best known forms of humorous art is collections like the

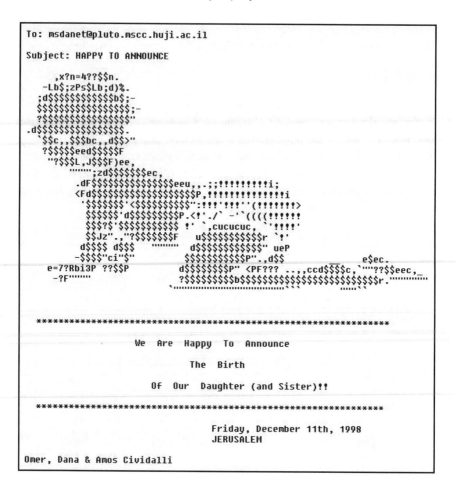

Figure 5.23. Arrival of a new baby.

popular ASCII "cows," a portion of which is shown in Figure 5.26. These are done simply, in line style. As we shall see in Chapter 6, images from these collections recurred on IRC. These cows could also have been classified under miniatures.

Smiley Icons

In the Introduction I discussed smiley icons, clusters of typographic symbols that are used to convey emotion or qualify an utterance, as part of a general overview of common features of digital writing. Apart from the three, which are quite commonly used, especially the basic smiley :-), there were hundreds

Figure 5.24. An ASCII birthday greeting.

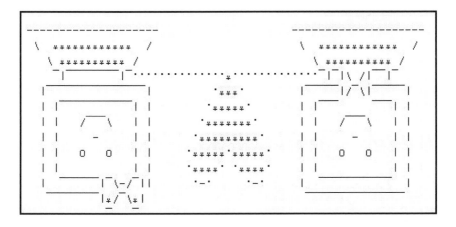

Figure 5.25. A "computer" Valentine.

of other icons that were rarely used, if ever, in actual messages, but circulated widely on the Internet in collections. Many are amusing or clever mini-drawings or cartoons. Figure 5.27 is a small selection of some of the less common ones.

Signature Files

Sometimes ASCII logos are incorporated in signature files, along with a humorous or pithy saying (Figure 5.28).[59] Some incorporate text in Figlet "fonts" (Figure 5.29).

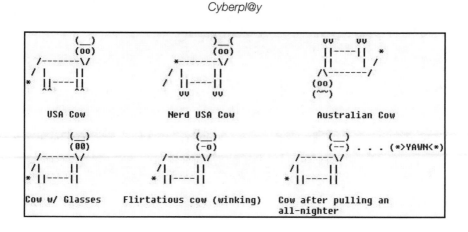

Figure 5.26. A sampling of ASCII cows.

```
(1) Represent the speaker's facial expression, emotional
    state

    :-D     laughter
    :,-)    crying
    :-/     skepticism
    :-||    anger

(2) Describe the  physical appearance of the speaker

    8-)     smile of a person who wears glasses
    :-{)    smile of a person with a  moustache
    :-)=    smile of a person with a beard
    [:-)    smile of a person wearing a Walkman
    8:-)    a little girl
    :-)-8   a big girl

(3) Describe the physical state of the speaker

    %-)     speaker is sleepy, drunk, dazed after staring
            at computer screen for many hours
    |-I     person is asleep
    |-O     person is yawning/snoring
    :-~)    person who has a cold

(4) Represent  physical actions of  the speaker

    :-Q     person smoking a cigarette
    :-?     speaker smokes a pipe
    :*)     a kiss
    [ ]     a hug
```

Figure 5.27. A selection of uncommon smiley icons.

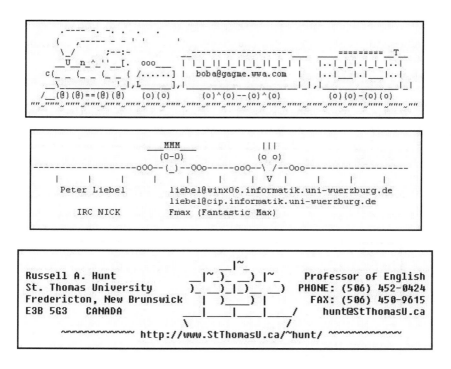

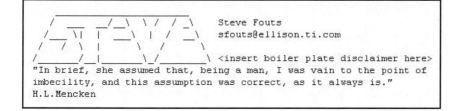

Figure 5.28. Signature files incorporating ASCII art.

```
  /       _ __/_\  \ / / /_\       Steve Fouts
 /__  \I  |  __\  |  / / _\        sfouts@ellison.ti.com
 /  / \  |  _\   \ /     \
/_____/_|_____/_____\       <insert boiler plate disclaimer here>
"In brief, she assumed that, being a man, I was vain to the point of
imbecility, and this assumption was correct, as it always is."
H.L.Mencken
```

Figure 5.29. A signature file containing a Figlet "font."

ASCII "Calligraphy"

Next is ASCII "calligraphy," the creation of messages in calligraphic style, but using only typographic characters. Quite a few examples of Chinese greetings for holidays and birthdays are stored on ASCII art Websites.[60] In all the great non-Western traditions of calligraphy, Islamic, Chinese and Japanese, our conventional Western distinction between "art" and "writing" is blurred, and the visual shape of the features of this writing is as important as the content, if not more so. It is, of course, a gross contradiction in terms to produce calligraphy with ASCII characters. In calligraphy what is cherished is the material/aesthetic evidence of the unique skill and hand-made artistry of the calligrapher. As one student of Chinese calligraphy has written,

> Westerners . . . approaching Chinese writing. . . content themselves with jotting down the characters, without taking the time to look at them and get the feel of them . . . what is required is a fresh bestirring of oneself, . . . it takes a certain liking for play and gesture to get the knack of it. . . (Billeter 1990: 86).

An example of ASCII "calligraphy," a New Year's greeting, is shown in Figure 5.30.

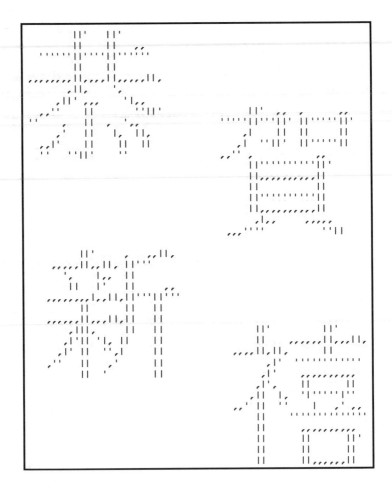

Figure 5.30. A Chinese ASCII New Year greeting.

Scroll "Animation"

Scroll "animation" is an unusual form of ASCII art.[61] One scrolls rapidly down the text, using the "page down" or arrow keys. Usually the same words or phrase, repeated over and over, seem to slide back and forth across the page. The effect is something like the little flip-books we knew as children, and is thus a kind of pseudo-animation. Unfortunately, in the print medium it is impossible to illustrate this effect properly.

Two Contemporary ASCII Artists

We have seen that is difficult to draw a sharp distinction between ASCII art before the Web and after its arrival, because both pre-Web and post-Web art can be viewed there, often undated and mixed up together. There are important technical developments that help to identify some of the newer art, however. With HTML codes, this art could be created and displayed on the Web in color, if the artist so wished. Moreover, unlike art on Usenet newsgroups or the ASCIIART listserv list, which could only be displayed in black on white, images could once again be displayed as "white" or light symbols on a dark background, usually black or dark blue, thus resembling the original mode of display in DOS on black monitors.[62]

I have noted that probably the biggest change was accessibility of images. Another change was that, with the advent of the Usenet newsgroups, the ASCIIART listserv list, and the arrival of a much wider range of social groups on the Internet, people of all walks of life joined the ranks and some even became quite famous.

In this section of the chapter I compare and contrast the work of Joan Stark and Allen Mullen, both active in the late 1990s, and both of whom broke stereotypes about ASCII artists. Each maintained an elaborate, personal online gallery containing many works, as well as offering a great deal of useful information about technical matters, and links to others' ASCII art sites. The two took a leadership role in curating a collection of links to the work of many others, though eventually Mullen dropped out of this project.[63]

Both created works to be displayed on the Web against a glowing dark background. Both worked in black and white as well as in color. Both were much admired, yet their styles and mode of working were completely different. Stark's work in particular was often borrowed by others, with or without acknowledgment.[64]

Mullen's images were unusually large, some of them so wide that they could not be viewed on an 80-character-wide normal screen, nor printed in their entirety unless one went to very elaborate lengths, or didn't mind that the printed version would extend over several pages or be cut up into separate screen captures. More often than not, the viewer had to scroll down many times in order to take in the entire image. The large size of his images, as well as the fact that most were ASCII versions of copyrighted material, made it very difficult for me to show readers examples of his art. I have had to make do with just one, a detail from his version of Picasso's *Guernica* (Figure 5.33, below). A contrast between the two artists is interesting in its own right, but is also a valuable means to bring into the discussion controversies about methods (freehand "drawing" versus use of a conversion program).

Joan Stark: Queen of ASCII Art

Joan Stark is a Cleveland, Ohio housewife with four young children and a master swimmer (Figure 5.31). She acquired a personal computer in 1995, and soon after that began experimenting with making ASCII pictures. I mentioned earlier that as a child she had made typewriter pictures in her father's office. She was active both on the ASCIIART listserv list and on the Usenet newsgroup *alt.ascii-art*. Others found her work so impressive that on *alt. ascii.art* she was dubbed "Queen of ASCII Art." Each month she added many images to her Website, well organized by subject. Mostly she works in white on black, but colors a fair amount of her creations too. A white-on-black work, an image of a fairy, is shown in Figure 5.32, and two colored works in Plate 5.3.

Figure 5.31. Joan Stark, queen of ASCII art.

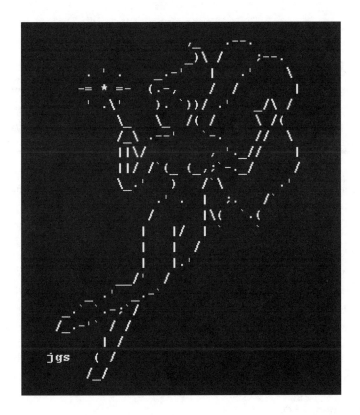

Figure 5.32. A fairy, white on black ASCII art by Joan Stark.

The colored works resemble free-hand embroidery.[65] These non-illusionistic flowers have a sprightly, charming quality we have associated in the past with traditional folk art. Each flower is portrayed frontally and in perfect symmetry. The folk quality of her style is also evident in the charming portraits of her children.

Stark creates her images in a "free-hand" manner:

> I do not use a program to create the ASCII pictures. Essentially I sit at the keyboard and type. The more I do, the faster and easier it becomes. Some pics I make come from models (usually one of my kids' toys), pictures in books and magazines, or from my imagination . . . they get faster to make . . . They usually take about 15–20 minutes each . . . a little longer for larger ones, less time for smaller ones. If I can see it in my head beforehand, they go fast. At times, I see lots of things in "ASCII" – it's at those instances that I have a creative spurt! I think playing around on the keyboard figuring out where the characters fit really helps . . .[66]

Stark has long been involved in crafts.

> I don't sew but I have crocheted, done cross-stitch and decorative embroidery. For a short time, I made girls' hair bows and sold them in small shops. It was around then that I "discovered" ASCII art. Since I've been involved with. . . ASCII art, I haven't found the time to participate in these crafts . . . I think the craft that most closely correlates to my ASCII art creations is free-hand embroidery. It allows for creativity – I hate following the lines!

> I've always had an interest in the visual arts. In junior high school and in high school, I won a few local art competitions for drawing. I seriously considered pursuing an art degree in college but decided against it. I didn't think that I would be able to support myself. I toy with the idea of going to art school. Perhaps some day I will.[67]

Stark's site was extremely popular. According to a Web visitor counter, in the two years between the end of September, 1996 and 1998, 250,000 people had visited her site. This was not the total number of "hits" but of distinct email addresses.[68] Stark's rise to prominence is especially interesting because she is a woman and a person who had nothing to do with computers professionally. Her popularity once again reflects the entrance of rank and file women into the world of ASCII art and the Net, as well as of content which is often more traditionally feminine than was characteristic of ASCII art in the past.[69]

Allen Mullen, M.D.

Allen Mullen is a pathologist in a Florida community hospital. Unlike Stark, who "hand-drew" her images, Mullen's scanned images from popular or high culture – e.g., a cartoon or children's book character or a famous painting. Then he converted the image to ASCII via a program called GIFASCII, one of a number of such conversion programs available. In answer to the question, "How much time do you spend doing this?" he wrote:

> I've had a lot of practice doing this so I've gotten pretty fast. It takes on average about 30 minutes per picture so I can usually finish off a whole set of 8–10 pictures in a free evening. The big ones take longer. The time I spend coloring pictures varies but generally adds about 10 minutes per picture. I usually have one or two free evenings a week to do frivolous things like this.[70]

Figure 5.33 is a detail from Mullen's version of Picasso's *Guernica*. We can see which symbols were used.

It is evident that Stark and Mullen worked quite differently. I concur with Stark's own characterization of her work as close to free-style embroidery. Mullen's work, in contrast, may be compared to the type of needlepoint in

Figure 5.33. Picasso's "Guernica" in ASCII form, by Allen Mullen, detail. http://www.inetw.net/~mullen.

which the pattern is pre-printed on the canvas mesh, often even dictating the colors to be used. As he himself virtually admitted, his pictures were more of a technical accomplishment than a creative act. Perhaps that is why he called them "pictures" rather than "art," and why he stopped creating new images in 1996.[71]

Beyond ASCII Art

In the late 1990s there were many attempts to go beyond the limitations of traditional ASCII art. Some were ordinary text, viewed in black and white or the reverse. Others incorporated color or animation or both. We have already seen that HTML color was sometimes used on the Web. I will present just a few selected examples of other types of innovation from the last years of the last decade of the 20th century.

"ASCII" Art on America Online

Long ago, the font in the software for America Online was set as Arial, a proportional font, which meant that members could not display regular ASCII art online. In 1999 I discovered that they were creating a kind of "pseudo-ASCII" art in Arial. Only when this art is displayed in Arial are images displayed properly. There was a separate sub-culture, mainly of young teenagers, surrounding this art on AOL, called "macros" by practitioners.[72] One group, called "ASCII Artists United" had its own channel on the EFnet on IRC. An example of this art is shown in Figure 5.34.[73]

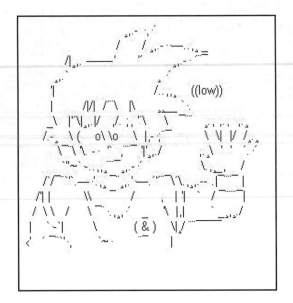

Figure 5.34. Text art on America Online.

From Static Art to Animation

A delightful series of experiments with expanding the possibilities of art from text is the creations of Pete Casso. His characters, a frog named "Frogstein" and a bird named "Birdstein," are introduced in the cartoon in Figure 5.35. The typographic simplicity of these two characters is part of their charm. Casso also created some clever animations incorporating these two ASCII creatures.

The most common type of ASCII animation found on the Web is that illustrated by three screen shots in Figure 5.36, a creation of Andreas Freise. A train pulls into the station (first screenshot); passengers debark (second screenshot); and then the train leaves the station (third screenshot).

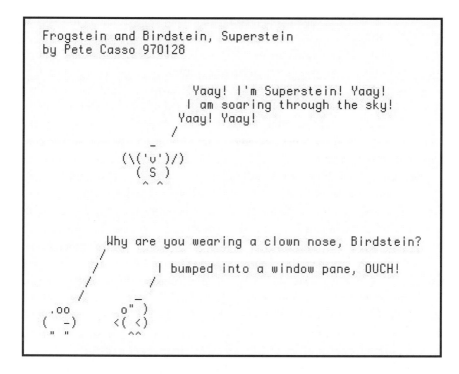

Figure 5.35. Frogstein and Birdstein, Superstein, by Pete Casso, "Pete Casso's Hilarious Website," http://www3.sympatico.ca/petecasso/.

(1)   (2)   (3)

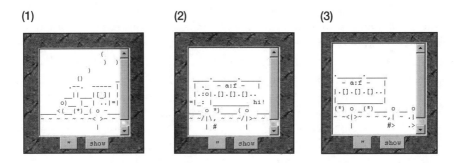

Figure 5.36. An ASCII animation by Andreas Freise, three screen captures.

ASCII and ANSI Art in the Underground Computer Art Scene

In the period between 1987 and the late 1990s, underground computer art became quite consolidated as a separate subculture. Well-organized groups of mostly males in their teens and early twenties met on their own IRC channels and established Websites of a high professional caliber, codified many aspects of their knowledge and skills, and published on the Web a series of articles about the history of this subculture.[74] Much about these groups was a direct continuation of the original spirit of hacker culture, as described in Chapter 1 – a subversive,[75] anti-establishment but not necessarily criminal stance, a love of making technology do more than it was designed to do, rampant play with language and symbols in nicknames (called "tags," as among graffiti "writers"), strong attraction to imagery from the comics, fantasy, horror and science fiction, and a predilection for sophisticated auto-ethnography.

These groups developed independent linguistic and cultural practices quite apart from mainstream groups involved in ASCII art.[76] Unlike the latter groups, they did not usually display their art on the Web; instead, they made sets of it available online in "artpacks," in downloadable zip format.. Both ASCII and ANSI[77] (colored) art continued to be of interest to them, as well as other, more advanced graphic formats that I cannot discuss here. Groups and individuals were highly competitive, yet also extremely appreciative of the work of artists they considered very talented. This aggressive, "street-style" imagery was altogether different from the art highlighted in this chapter, as well as from the "domestic" quilt-like and embroidery-like imagery we will see in Chapter 6,[78] and, perhaps, even from the earlier ANSI art done for BBSs.

In the ANSI art created in the late 1990s practitioners had developed skilled techniques to round out images, produce subtle shading, etc. The long, narrow images in Plate 5.4 remind me of *hashira-e*, Japanese pillar prints, woodblock prints made to be hung on pillars in houses (Pins 1980; 1982).[79] While the content of ANSI art and Japanese pillar prints is radically different – lurid, comics-like images full of sex, death and horror in the one case, delicate fine art images in the other – in both cases the long, narrow shape of the image creates special challenges of composition. Other ANSI images were very large, often filling the entire screen and more (Plate 5.5).

In addition to their own creative work, underground artists spent much energy developing programs to preserve and display artwork of earlier years. Images of early BBS screens like the one in Plate 5.1 were available to me because their creator had transformed them to a Web-suitable format. Similarly, Web-based viewers for animated ASCII and ANSI art performed a service in making these works accessible to all.

Interest in ASCII Art among Avant-garde Artists

Before concluding this chapter, I should also mention briefly the interest among some avant-garde artists in ASCII art in the late 1990s. A group called the "ASCII Art Ensemble" experimented with non-meaningful ASCII text for its visual and conceptual effects. They developed a JAVA player that activated a "sheet" of moving ASCII characters; as one scrolled down, this "sheet" "rained" down the screen and to the right. Vuk Cosic, one member of the group, also developed an ASCII portrait camera, which when activated, produced an instant portrait of the person in ASCII; it was placed in Amsterdam, Graz and Vienna, Austria, and Ljubljana. The group also produced music videos in which moving ASCII accompanied the sound. All Web pages about the group's activities displayed ASCII in glowing green pixels on a black background, approximating the "look" of ASCII before graphical environments.[80]

ASCII Art in Perpective

Like the other forms of creating pictures from writing reviewed in this chapter, ASCII art relies on certain processes in the psychology of perception for its effects. We both see and do not see the small components which make up the larger image. When viewed from the proper distance – and this distance clearly varies greatly, depending on whether we are looking at a printed page, a computer screen, a tiled wall or a mosaic mural in a church – the smaller parts merge and we mainly see the larger image.

In ASCII art, it is necessary to be able to see that the image is composed of typographic characters – sometimes, even which characters – in order to appreciate that this is not just an ordinary image, but one consisting of typographic characters which create a certain visual impression. Otherwise, the image may just as well not be composed of typographic characters at all. The role of processes of perception, and particular the concept of *gestalt* [81] in psychology (seeing a whole where an image is less than whole, preferring regular to irregular images) is discussed in further detail in Chapter 6.

In this chapter I have not been able to discuss at length the emergent social context in which this art has developed. Unfortunately, too little is known about these aspects. Nevertheless, when this overview is combined with the case study of IRC art in Chapter 6 – which does attend closely to issues of social context, as well as analyzing visual aspects of images in detail – I believe that we are led to recognize digital text-based art as an emergent folk art without physicality.

This claim raises a number of difficult issues, such as: What is folk art? What is craft? Can a form of visual expression in an intangible medium, practiced by people who cannot see each other and most likely have never met, be considered a folk art or a craft or both? These challenging issues are discussed in the final chapter, Chapter 8.

Notes

1. See http://www.youvegotmail.com/.

2. Barbara Kirshenblatt-Gimblett called to my attention the need to stress this point. The geometric nature of ASCII art is further explained in Chapter 6.

3. The address of this list is ASCIIART@lsv.uky.edu.

4. The Website of Joan Stark, a well known ASCII artist whose work I will present below, contains a useful section on the history of ASCII art; see "Joan Stark's ASCII Art Gallery," http://www.ascii-art.com.

5. The computer underground art "scene," as it is called by members, including continuing interest in ASCII art as well as ANSI art (a more elaborate form incorporating blocks of color) and other types, became highly organized in the late 1990s. See Bell (1998) and http://www.acheron.org/, as well as the brief discussion of these groups, below.

6. According to John Foust, the standard ASCII character set was formulated in 1961 but actually adopted only in 1968. See http://www.threedee.com/jcm/aaa/index.html.

7. The source of this information was the Boston Computer Museum. In 1999 it merged with the Museum of Science, Boston. See http://www.mos.org/tcm/tcm.html.

8. ASCII artists recognize that even fixed-width fonts vary in the effects they create. See Allison (1996); Thomas (1997; 1998).

9. In the material presented in Chapter 6 the choice of font does become relevant. Images often look better in Fixed Sys than in Courier New. The viewer can switch from one to the other.

10. Tiles and tile patterns are really a special case of mosaics, only in this case the individual pieces are a good deal larger and of regular shape.

11. For additional references on ancient Greek pattern poems and the history of this phenomenon, see Higgins (1987) and Hollander (1991), Introduction, p. xvii.

12. A related phenomenon is the practice of of drawing faces inside initial large letters in medieval manuscripts. Letters with a round "bowl," such as *o*, *a*, *c*, or *p*, were sometimes enhanced this way. The earliest known example is from the 8th century. Walter Cahn provided this information.

13. See, e.g., Higgins (1987); Solt (1968); Williams (1967); Drucker (1994; 1996; 1997). I am grateful to Andrew Belsey, a practitioner of typewriter art as well as an academic, for presenting me with a gift of this rare, out of print book.

14. A fascinating Website called "UBU Visual/Concrete/Sound Poetry" presents the work of major figures past and present, including Apollinaire and Solt, and is well worth a visit. See http://www.ubu.com/.

15. See Kac's Website, http://www.ekac.org/.

16. The Bauhaus was a very influential design movement in Germany in the 1920s that had a lasting impact on 20th-century design. See Erlich (1991) and the discussion of Bauhaus typography in Chapter 7.

17. Effects created by moving the angle of the paper in the carriage are not available in teletype or ASCII art. Stacey's work may be viewed in Riddell (1975, frontispiece)

and online at Joan Stark's ASCII Art Gallery, pages on the history of ASCII art, http://www.ascii-art.com/.

18. Cited by Mark Frauenfelder in a Wired News article, "The ASCII Artists" (Frauenfelder 1997), archived at http://www.wired.com/news/news/wiredview/story/6346.htm.

19. This citation is from the biography Stark supplied on her Website; URL in footnote 4.

20. See Grabar (1992); Schimmel (1990); Gaur (1994).

21. See also Heller (1994) for a rich survey of various forms of play with typography by professionals.

22. In contrast, typewriter art tends to be recognizable as such – the old-fashioned-looking typeface and the rough or blurred contours of the letters give this away. For details on how RTTY art was made, see Royer (1970); Green (1978).

23. There were other competing codes, but Baudot was the most widely used.

24. For further information on this code, see "The Baudot Code Set," http://telecom.tbi.net/baudot.html.

25. Personal email from John Sheetz, former Director of Public Displays at Bell Laboratories, who owns a collection of over 2000 RTTY images, August 19, 1999.

26. See Green (1978), Figure 12-2. Green's article is also available at http://www.rtty.com. Green's name does not appear in the chapter, though he compiled the manual in which this chapter appeared.

27. A yellowing printed version of this image was given to me by Bryan Meadan, a Hebrew University student formerly from the United States. It had been printed on paper manufactured by a Canadian firm, and had hung on his grandmother's wall until she died at age 90 in 1998. At first I thought it was an early ASCII computer image, but realized that it was an RTTY image when Green's (1978) chapter on RTTY art, including this image, became available on the Web in September 1999.

28. Note that Larsson's "signature" is embedded in the last line, right side.

29. Personal email from John Sheetz, August 19, 1999. Although this art was supposedly circulated already as of the 1950s, I have not seen any images attributed to that period.

30. Don Royer and John Sheetz ran these contests for several years. This information is cited on the Website of Marc I. Leavey, M.D., another ham radio operator, http://www2.ari.net/ajr/rtty/9710rl.html.

31. Personal email from Jack Lally to Joan Stark, 2 November 1997, archived on Stark's Website.

32. I learned of this image on Joan Stark's Website.

33. Personal email from Rick Hoover to Joan Stark, 27 March 1997, archived on Stark's Website. See her Website for additional letters reconstructing the history of ASCII art.

34. See the RTTY Art Gallery, http://www.rtty.com/gallery/gallery.html. The collection was assembled by Bob Roehrig, John Foust, Tom Jennings, and John Sheetz. Another collection of images is available at http://fido.wps.com/Baudot/Bob-Roehig/.

35. Since then his collection grew to over 2000, but he did not update the classification.

36. This information was supplied in a manual for RTTY users, at http://telecom.tbi.net/baudot.html. I noted that there are some overstrikes in Figure 5.7 too.

37. I found this image on the site of the Jefferson Computer Museum. John Foust was not able to supply a date. The image of the eye is presented upside down.

38. See, e.g., "The Great ASCII Art Library," http://www.geocities.com/SouthBeach/Marina/4942/ascii.htm; Christopher Johnson's ASCII Art Collection, http://www.chris.com/ascii/; Andreas Freise's "ASCII Dictionary," http://studserv.stud.uni-hannover.de/~freise/index.html; and the links at http://www.afn.org/~afn39695/collect.htm.

39. In the mid-1970s I knew personally a father and son who ran a node of FidoNet in the Boston area from their home.

40. Personal email from Ian Wallis to Joan Stark, 18 April 1998. There are far more sites preserving general ASCII art than BBS screens.

41. This definition is from the Artpacks Archive's Introduction to the underground computer art scene, cited in Bell (1998), section on ANSI art.

42. These "blocks" are the little rectangles into which, in ordinary text, we insert typographic symbols as we type. If we leave a slot empty it appears "white" on screen; artists colored these blocks to dramatic effect.

43. To learn more about how ANSI art was created, see, if possible, the tutorials at iCE (they are not always accessible to non-members; Insane Creators Enterprises), http://www.ice.org, one of the major sites of the underground computer art scene. Readers will see that coding resembles that of IRC images, although the exact codes are different. Both are text-based forms of art.

44. Or, green or amber phosphorescent pixels on a black monitor.

45. It would be very worthwhile to carry out case studies of these newsgroups, the regulars, the history of their involvement, their social relationships, and so on. Such a study was beyond the scope of my research.

46. The URL of Stark's personal gallery is in footnote 4; the URL for these links is in footnote 36. Readers should be forewarned that in many instances, only a very few images are provided, and they are not necessarily very impressive. Moreover, some links were found to be dead as this book was completed. See Chapter 6 for an attempt to assess how many people are involved in interactive text-based art on IRC.

47. The geometric nature of text-based art is discussed in much greater detail in Chapter 6.

48. This typology does not include underground ASCII and ANSI art, which require separate research.

49. See Allison (1994; 1996); Thomas (1997; 1998); Atkins (1998).

50. This distinction is central to my analysis of IRC art in Chapter 6.

51. That is, unless we now interpret "picture" to mean "image" of any kind.

52. In the case of early ASCII art, there was little awareness of the desire or need to give credit to the artist. Many Web archives store the art with no indication of the artist's name. Thus, wherever no artist is named in these illustrations, it indicates that

I was unable to ascertain his or her name or that an email address was unavailable or invalid. Today, ASCII artists sign their names, and ASCII art fans try to identify the artists in cases where no name is given, often with little success. Joan Stark tried to help me locate several artists whose work is featured in this chapter, but again, without success. See the discussion of intellectual property in Chapter 8.

53. Veilleux's art is archived at www.afn.org/~afn39695/veilleux.htm.

54. This distinction between line style and solid style echoes earlier distinctions. Shaped poems using lines of text to fill a silhouette could be said to be in "solid style," whereas micrography used to create contours or outlines of objects is a form of "line style."

55. Another variation is images in reverse solid style; here the image itself consists of white space, contrasting with a dark background filled with typographic characters.

56. This does not work for me, even with the corrective of glasses.

57. See my discussion of "handmade" vs. program-generated images in Chapter 6.

58. Unfortunately, I cannot show any examples because of copyright limitations.

59. Other aspects of signature files were discussed in Chapter 2.

60. See, e.g., "Wicked ASCII Art," http://www.wigwam.org/Ascii/.

61. Barbara Kirshenblatt-Gimblett brought this type of ASCII art to my attention.

62. This was a partial reinstatement of the old way of viewing ASCII images as green or amber pixels on a black DOS or UNIX monitor. Some ASCII artists displayed works on the Web in a simulation of the original green, glowing display; see, e.g., the Website of Marc Schmitz, also known as "meph," at http://studenten.freepage.de/meph/.

63. See the last URL in footnote 38.

64. See Chapter 6 and my discussion of intellectual property in Chapter 8.

65. The butterflies are a light touch of animation, visible on the Website, but frozen in this screen-capture.

66. Cited from Stark's Website.

67. Personal email from Joan Stark, 27 September 1998.

68. Her Web counter reported that between June 28, 1999 and August 21, 1999 alone, over 45,000 persons had visited the site.

69. Typically masculine themes such as war and guns are absent from her site. Another indication that women were becoming increasingly involved comes from a tally of the gender of people listed in the Stark-Mullen collective gallery. Of 157 persons listed, 45, or nearly a third had female-sounding first names. Some of those listed only by gender-ambiguous nickname or initials may also have been female.

70. This passage comes from Mullen's personal FAQ file on his Website, http://www.inetw.net/~mullen.

71. Revisiting his site in August 1999, I found that it had not been updated since 1997, probably confirming that he had lost interest in this activity.

72. See http://come.to/themacrohouse. One promoter of ASCII art, at least, Christopher Johnson, went on record as quite opposed to this variant. Calling creators of AOL art "perpetrators," he argued that using a proportional font unnecessarily limits the audience for the art. These remarks are no longer on his Website.

73. Perhaps it is more neutral to call it AOL text art, since I have no desire to denigrate it.

74. See especially "Acheron.Org," http//:www.acheron.org. The original Acheron is one of the rivers in Hades, the Underworld in Greek mythology.

75. Just what these groups signaled by calling themselves "underground" was not self-evident at least from initial exploration of their sites. As far as I could tell, no overt political protest was involved, perhaps just adolescent rebelliousness. I am indebted to Oren Golan, a Ph.D. student in my fall 1999 seminar on "Virtual Culture," for this point.

76. See Lyons (1997).

77. A definition of ANSI was provided at the beginning of the section on Fidonet and Usenet newsgroups, above.

78. Avner Lehavi, a student in my "Virtual Culture" seminar, suggested this apt distinction.

79. Apparently, there were several recognized genres, including logos and these narrow, elongated images.

80. See "ASCII Art Ensemble," http://www.vuk.org/ascii/aac.html, and "Contemporary ASCII," http://www.vuk.org/ascii/.

81. See Kohler (1929); Koffka (1935); Arnheim (1954); Kreitler and Kreitler (1972), Chapter 4.

6

"Welcome to Our Beautiful World of Colors!" Art and Communication on Internet Relay Chat

This chapter presents an ethnographic study of two IRC channels in which the players communicated not by typing words, but by displaying striking text-based, visual images in real time. The players invented a form of "pixel patchwork," of "quilting in time" rather than space, that happens also to be a novel mode of communication. This art draws on, but differs from ASCII art in several important ways. Social aspects of the groups' activities were no less interesting than the visual/aesthetic ones. This research can be viewed as a case study in the anthropology of art,[1] or alternatively, as a study of a new form of folk art. Most work in the anthropology of art has examined the art of pre-literate societies.[2] Most typically, folklorists study the art of groups leading a traditional lifestyle, generally on the periphery of modern societies.[3] The groups I studied fit neither of these categories.

Unlike ethnographic or folk art of the past, this art had no tangible substance. It was created by individuals who are not only literate, but very computer-literate. Most were hobbyists newly arrived on the Internet, who had rapidly acquired impressive, sometimes virtuoso skills. The players saw themselves as creating, performing, playing[4] "art." Many explicitly called themselves "artists," and took their art seriously enough to be concerned about intellectual property rights. In warnings on channel Websites and online, players were told not to erase the signatures of artists when playing or modifying their work.[5] Novel aspects aside, this was spontaneous, grass-roots art, created and shared by people untutored in the Western fine art tradition, and with no pretension of contributing to it.

The players greeted each other at holidays and birthdays with mostly traditional imagery that we customarily associate with greeting cards. This art also had in common with paper greeting cards the theme of the "pop-up" greeting. In some types of greeting cards, a three-dimensional design "pops up" when we open them. The dialog boxes in computer programs are said to "pop up" too. Channel participants talked of displaying, collecting and working on their "popups," and a program used by many to create them was called "Popedit."[6] Sets of files designed to be played during holidays and other special occasions on *rainbow* (one of the two channels studied) were dubbed "bowpops" and "holipops," perhaps also invoking associations to "lollipops."

IRC art shared with graffiti a preoccupation with "getting up" – becoming visible, making one's mark – under sometimes difficult conditions.[7] Creating a large graffiti work on a subway train is no small feat since there is little time to work, it is illegal, and the authorities seek to erase it. In the case of IRC the difficulties were primarily technical. There is poignancy in both genres in that they are ephemeral. "Writers," as graffiti artists often call themselves, face the threat that their work will not be viewed by the public, and will disappear any time, since the authorities systematically destroy it.

IRC images are even more ephemeral than real-world graffiti: once we log off, they are gone forever. An important difference between the two genres is that graffiti artists tend to be marginal, lower-class, minority youth, mostly males, whereas the players in these channels were mostly mainstream adults, more women than men. In addition, because graffiti are usually illegal they are blatantly subversive, whereas in the present case, I shall argue later on, the medium was domesticated to affirm mainstream traditional values.

What is New in IRC Art?

Just what is new about the form of art practiced on IRC? As we saw in Chapter 5, making art with the elements of writing is not at all new. I showed that there is a very long history of making pictures with writing, by hand in earlier stages of civilization, and with typewriters and teletype machines in the more recent past. And people have been creating images with characters on the computer keyboard since the 1960s and 1970s.

Pre-WWW ASCII Art

To recapitulate material covered in Chapter 5, the earliest forms of ASCII art were non-interactive. They were viewed and exchanged asynchronously, typically in black and white, or the color of the amber or green pixels on a dark computer screen. They were sometimes printed on large fanfold paper and hung on office walls, or they were exchanged by email. Occasionally, images were created in reverse – in this case the image consists of white space, contrasting with a black, symbol-filled background. Almost without exception, images were representational "drawings" that represented some object from the real world – whether a birthday cake, an airplane, or a teddy bear.

WWW ASCII Art

We saw in Chapter 5 that migration of ASCII art to the World Wide Web did not change it dramatically. For the most part, collections simply became more accessible, stored in individual or group galleries. Most images on the Web were still in black and white, though some artists specialized in coloring, or, as they put it, "colorizing" images by others, or creating colored images themselves. Representational images of all kinds continued to dominate. We saw that the Web and Usenet newsgroups fostered the arrival and recognition of new groups of people – not only individuals close to computer science and technological development, but also ordinary people of all walks of life. The research reported in this chapter will provide further confirmation of this trend.

IRC Art

IRC art differed from the earlier art, first of all, because it was *interactive*. This was a major innovation: for the first time, images were displayed and viewed in real time. The expression "interactive digital art" is sometimes used on the Web. Thus, visitors to digital galleries are occasionally invited to submit and even to modify images. Galleries may display sequences of images, showing how the original images changed over time. This is not what I mean by interactive art. On the Web individuals interact with images, not with people. Here, *people interacted with people, via the exchange of images*, while simultaneously logged onto the same IRC channel. The players pursued this activity both for its own sake and as a vehicle for social interaction and the satisfactions of belonging to an emergent virtual community. The images were thus not only "art" but also "communication." Images were both of interest in their own right and tokens for interaction.

This form of communication also differed sharply from graphically enhanced chat via programs such as "The Palace,"[8] Worlds Away,[9] or Microsoft Chat,"[10] although, like them, it combined "saying something" with "showing something visually." In "The Palace" and "Worlds Away," individuals composed or chose a visual avatar to represent them, and their typed contributions appeared in balloons displayed against a stable graphic background. In IRC-based Microsoft Chat, formerly called "Comic Chat,"[11] players were represented by comic strip characters, either ready-made or their own creation. Their text appeared in a balloon within a separate frame, as in traditional comics. In contrast, in the present case, people displayed personally chosen visual images in which color and design were important.

This form of communication might be thought of as interactive "digital needlepoint," or, as I put it at the beginning of the chapter, as "quilting in time," with each image constituting another "patch" in the seemingly endless ribbon of images in digital quilting bees.[12] The analogy with quilting is especially apt because quilting is more often a social activity, at least in part, while needlepoint is usually done in isolation, and because images often resembled those of quilts. I will return to the latter topic later on.

A second important difference between ASCII art and IRC art is that the newer art employed brilliant color far more extensively than was possible before. Third, it employed a greatly expanded graphic "palette" – typographic characters other than those of the basic ASCII character set were used.[13] Fourth, this art was characterized by a striking shift to abstract designs containing pattern and symmetry. While representational images continued to be popular, abstract designs were probably at least as common. As in tangible folk art the world over – pottery, textiles, woodcarving, and so on – the creation of pattern by the players was largely intuitive. All of these differences will be explained and explored in greater detail, below.

Overview of the Case Study

The Channels Studied

The channels (the IRC equivalent of chat rooms) that I shall discuss were called *#mirc_colors* and *#mirc_rainbow*,[14] or *colors* and *rainbow*, for short. Both were registered[15] channels on the Undernet, one of the main networks of IRC servers. The names of both channels begin with *mirc*, which stands for the computer program "mIRC," an adaptation of the original UNIX-based IRC program for Windows 3.x and Windows 95, in which it was possible to use many colors, unlike the plain text of earlier IRC software.[16] Whereas the original idea was to enable players to customize the colors of the fonts and backgrounds on their screens while logged on to IRC, thus making a textual environment more pleasant, the players exploited the color possibilities to create striking visual images.[17]

For a period of three years beginning in May 1997, my research assistant, Tsameret Wachenhauser, and I monitored the activities of these channels. *Colors* was started in November 1996 by a woman nicknamed <elusive>[18] (Figure 6.1), who had recently moved from Florida to the Portland, Oregon area, and

Figure 6.1. <elusive>, leader of *#mirc_colors.*

became a registered channel on the Undernet in February 1997, after passing a 30-day trial period with a minimum of 10 regulars. <elusive> managed both the channel and its Website, which was begun in July 1997. She claimed that it was the first color channel on IRC, a claim I have not been able to substantiate.

Rainbow was a spin-off of *colors.* After a period of intense conflict among *colors* "ops" (operators, persons enjoying managerial privileges), three ops defected and created *rainbow* on 3 May 1997. Many *colors* regulars followed. By 30 May it too had become a registered channel. Both channels developed stable enough identities to maintain Websites related to their activities.[19]

Rainbow had two leaders. <texxy> (Figure 6.2), a male living in Texas, as his nick suggests, administered the channel for the first two years, and did programming behind the scenes. <patches>, a female, maintained the extensive Website.[20] In 1999 she and <texxy> traded responsibilities: in addition to her

Figure 6.2. <texxy>, original manager of **#*mirc_rainbow***.

work on the Website, she became owner or manager of *rainbow*, and <texxy> took over a second, "overflow" channel that had been created, #*mirc_rainbow2*, which <patches> had previously managed. (The overflow channel was used to practice playing files to be shown later on the main channel, and to give and receive help. It also became a place regulars went to chat verbally.) *Colors* and *rainbow* saw themselves as rivals for the title of "best color channel on IRC."

Visual Greetings, Virtual "Hugs"

Look again now at Plate 6.1.[21] In a sequence of visual "hellos" exchanged by three people on *rainbow* one day in October 1997, players whose nicks were <Happyone>, <M> and <az> displayed previously prepared files from repertoires stored on their computers. The images functioned as visual "speech acts." That image collections serve as a "language of communication" was made explicit by <texxy>. Asked what makes a person a regular, he replied, "A true regular is one who visits and shares the same common files as other regulars."[22]

As is typical on these channels, in the first three cases in Plate 6.1, the players had inserted at the last moment the nick of the person they wished to greet. From the *rainbow* Website I learned that <M> was a single man from south

Florida, probably in his 40s and the owner of a photography business. <Az> described herself as a 31-year-old single mother of a son, who taught preschool.

<Happyone>'s Website biography told us that she was a 61-year-old grandmother, deeply involved in Christian affairs. Her hobbies included cross-stitch embroidery, quilting and crocheting. This is a fascinating hint that this art has strong affinities with needlework and handmade textiles of all kinds. I will have more to say about involvement of the players in crafts later on.[23] This information also hints that channel activity brings together people of all ages and all walks of life.

Plate 6.1 shows that plain typed talk was rare. A brief snippet of technical talk ("found it in dcc list. . .")[24] was interleaved between images. The players occasionally complimented one another on the beauty of their images (<Pend>: "nice one M// :)"). Once again, as we saw in Chapter 3, compliments are a sure sign that a performance frame is salient. Sometimes players were complimented for the beauty of files they had created. However, since most played files[25] created by others, either they were complimented for their taste in choosing among hundreds of files,[26] or, implicitly, the compliment acknowledged the person who had created the file, even if not necessarily known by name. In many cases, people immediately asked to receive a copy of the file, a clear compliment in its own right.

This plate also illustrates the tendency to incorporate unusual typographic characters in images. The first, second, and third images all contain exotic non-standard characters, e.g., the legal "double-S" "ſ" in the first one, and the copyright symbol "©" in the third. We can see that symbols were generally repeated to create patterns, rather than being used singly.[27]

Over time, images became larger and more dramatic.[28] Sometimes players greeted a number of people at once, in a sub-genre called "multiples." Two striking examples, designed by <sher>, one of *rainbow*'s most popular artists, and by <icy2>, are shown in Plate 6.2. To enter the nicks when playing the file, one highlights selected nicks in the list of all players present at the right of the channel window.

Many images incorporated the word "hug" explicitly. The third example in Plate 6.3, by <patches>, cleverly changes colors every time it is played. The last image (originally by <elusive> of *colors*) contains a flattened-out representation of two arms reaching wide to "hug" other players, as well as six occurrences of the word "hug." It is an adaptation of an image from a large Web archive of ASCII "hugs" and "kisses," so the idea of "hugging" people virtually in this manner was not new to IRC.[29]

The "hug" motif was also prominent on the *rainbow* Website (Plate 6.4).[30] A large, all-enveloping pair of arms encircles nine little faces in a warm embrace, beneath the caption "GROUP HUG."[31] Although the arms are extended in the last image in Plate 6.3, and here they encircle the "little people," the two images are quite similar in other respects. Both are frontal, symmetrical, highly stylized renderings of arms reaching out to enclose and embrace all comers. These images nicely epitomize the conjunction of aesthetic pleasure and unconditional group acceptance and support that is characteristic of these channels.[32] Both same-sex and cross-sex pairs exchanged these virtual hugs, with no implied sexual connotation. The images embody the etymological connection between the words "closure" and "enclosure," a theme which will be developed later in this chapter. Underneath the *rainbow* Website image (Plate 6.4) is the text,

```
We love everyone here in #mirc_rainbow!!! Come join us and
enjoy the rainbow of colors :).
```

This image reminds me of the Storyteller figures of Helen Cordero, the Pueblo Indian potter.[33] Although the image is two-dimensional, and the storyteller figures are three-dimensional sculptures, themes of protection and love, enhanced by the dramatic difference in size between the protective figure and the little people, are prominent in both. In addition, in both, the figures are generalized and non-illusionistic, as is often true of folk art (Glassie 1989).

The myth-making slogan "We love everyone here in *#mirc_rainbow*!!!" deserves closer examination. The players were saying to themselves, in effect, "Let us pretend that within the protective little world that we have created online it is possible to love everyone." No one will ask, "Is it really possible to love everyone, and love them instantly and unconditionally?"

Who Were the Players?

It was extremely difficult to estimate how many players were active on these channels, or to determine who the players were in real life. As on IRC channels generally, there was high turnover, though some became loyal regulars. Weekends were busier than weekdays. There were other difficulties, as well. Still, with some effort, we can get a sense of the extent and nature of involvement in the two channels.

In a private online chat in December 1997, <elusive> claimed that as many as 4,000 individuals had visited her channel over a period of four months.[34] As this comment suggests, she invested more in counting how many different people had visited than in establishing a criterion to identify the regulars. As of August 1999, this policy had only changed somewhat.[35]

In the fall of 1997 there were entries for about 300 persons on the *colors* Website and for 104 (called "friends") on *rainbow*. These figures roughly jibed with a check we had made of all nicks appearing in sessions monitored weekly between June 11 and November 17, 1997. A total of 284 different nicks appeared in *colors* logs, and 103 for *rainbow*. Since then, participation in the two groups reversed. As of summer 1998, *rainbow* had far more persons logged on than *colors*, just about every time we logged on.[36] Often, there were only one or two persons on *colors*, or just a handful.

Thus, by summer 1999 it was fair to say that *colors* was in a state of decline, which was not reflected in its Website. Fourteen administrative ops and 30 regular ops, or a total of 44 ops were listed, along with 54 "friends."[37] The "friends" list included 10 of the ops. Among the ops were <elusive>'s partner <shortshot>, and her own daughter <tweesta>. Of the 44 non-op "friends," one was <shortshot>'s young son, and some were only "friends" in the broadest sense of a person who was thought to maintain cordial relations with the channel but was not at all active, or only came very seldom.[38] Thus, information on the Website created an impression of far greater participation than was in fact the case.

Rainbow, on the other hand, continued to flourish, despite considerable turnover among the regulars. Of 59 "friends" listed on the Website in 1999, only 26 had been listed in 1997. However, there was a much more stable core of players than appears from these figures, which appear to suggest far fewer "friends" than in the past. I learned from <patches> that the "friends" section of the extensive Website was badly in need of updating.[39] Many people aspired to become an op in order to become a member of the "in" group.[40] At my request she tallied up the number of ops, and reported that the total as of 25 August 1999 was 106.[41] Thus being an op was a far better indication of commitment to the group and of participation than merely being listed on the "friends" page.[42] Although some ops were also listed among the "friends," as on the *colors* Website, this does not, in my opinion, detract from the generalization that in the summer of 1999 *rainbow* was flourishing far more than *colors*. Later in the chapter, I will present material on social aspects of life on *rainbow* that will further underscore that, two years after its founding, this group continued to blossom both in numbers and in substance.

In both channels in 1997 nearly all the players logged on via host computers whose address ended in .com or .net.[43] This was a hint that players were not primarily members of highly educated elites affiliated with academic or other professional institutions, with access to the Net via their occupations or studies.

Research assistants and I created a database on the players' social background, including geographical location, age and sex, marital status, occupation, hobbies, and involvement with computers. We encountered many problems in this matter. It was far easier to assemble information on *rainbow* players than *colors*, since *rainbow* included short biographies of players on its Website, whereas *colors* did not.

It was possible that some *rainbow* players had distorted or misrepresented the information submitted to the Website. Nevertheless, we took it at face value, in the belief that in most cases it was reliable.[44] From logs of interaction we managed to glean additional information, enabling us to add eleven more players to the database. The result was a usable, if not entirely complete profile for *rainbow*. In July 1999 we repeated this procedure, thus enabling a comparison over a nearly two-year period.

The totals column in Table 6.1 (combining data on the two channels) shows that in 1997 most players were American, concentrated in the West, South, and Midwest. There were Canadians as well, and a sprinkling of players from a dozen or so other countries, including Mexico, Spain, India, Mauritius, Singapore, the Philippines, Australia, New Zealand, Denmark, Sweden and Norway. This distribution was quite similar for 1999; again, there were quite a few people from other countries.[45]

Table 6.1. The players on two IRC channels by geographical location, 1997 (%).

Location*	Channel		Total
	#mirc_rainbow	#mirc_colors**	
U.S. Northeast	8%	[2%]	6%
U.S. Midwest	17	[7]	13
U.S. South	22	[5]	16
U.S. West	17	[15]	16
Hawaii	1	[–]	1
Canada	7	[3]	6
Other countries	10	[13]	11
Location unknown	19	[54]	31
Total	99%	99%	100%
N	(115)	(67)	(182)

*Classification of continental U.S. regions based on Standard U.S. Census Regions.
**Note: information available for only 67 out of 300 players on #mirc_colors.

To ascertain whether persons from certain regions of the United States were under- or over-represented, I recalculated the percentages, removing non-Americans. Of the 72 Americans who had biographies on the Website in 1997, only 12 percent were from the Northeast; in 1999 it was down to 10 percent.

In 1993 20 percent of all U.S. residents resided in the Northeast.[46] Thus, it is likely that the Northeast was under-represented among players.

With respect to occupation, professionals and high-level administrators were clearly lacking in the 1997 data. Most worked in white-collar or blue-collar occupations requiring little or no higher education, or at least not academic training.[47] Only eight women described themselves as housewives; most worked outside the home, in occupations such as products distributor, supervisor of a discount warehouse, owner of a legal typing home business, assistant director of a preschool, owner of a hair salon, court reporter and transcriber. Among the men were a photographer, an auto plan superintendent, a truck driver, a pizza delivery driver, a product maintenance technician and a quality control technician at a factory. The *rainbow* group also included two farmers, a woman who raises goats and a man who owns a horse farm. This overall picture had not changed by 1999.

The leaders of the two channels all had academic or professional training, which no doubt helped them acquire leadership and administrative skills. <elusive> had been an accountant in the American Air Force for many years, and around the time she created *colors* she had moved to Oregon to live with her partner <shortshot>, who was also active on her channel. <patches> has a B.A. in music from the University of Massachusetts and was a professional flutist for a time. When I met her, she was a housewife living in Virginia, but she later moved to California and began working for a national Internet service provider. <texxy> has a bachelor's degree in public relations from the University of Texas; he works as the customer service manager of an office supply store.

In the 1997 data a little more than half the *rainbow* players were women, and a little less than half were men. In 1999 the proportion of women had risen from 54 percent to 59 percent. Thus, women were the clear majority of players. At the same time, the large number of men is just as noteworthy. It would be easy to view this activity as "feminine" involvement with "pretty pictures" and sentimental niceties, and therefore to expect few men to be involved. In particular, the world of paper greeting cards, one of the roots of the present phenomenon, is largely one managed by women (Di Leonardo 1987; Hochschild 1983).[48] Apparently, because this activity took place via machines stereotypically associated with the world of men, male players could grant themselves license to engage in aesthetic activity resembling that of women in the past (sewing, needlepoint, etc.). The anonymity of the medium may also have fostered their participation.

It is striking that this activity brought together people of all ages. While there were large concentrations of people in their twenties, thirties, forties, and fifties, I know of players who were as young as eleven and as old as seventy. Few leisure activities other than stamp collecting bring young and old together in this manner.[49] The largest single concentration was of women in their thirties. As for marital status, roughly half of those for whom information is available were married and half were divorced or single.

While only four *rainbow* 1997 players were computer professionals, twenty-eight mentioned involvement with computers as a hobby in their Website biographies. Clearly, this group broke the stereotype regarding who uses computers. Among the computer hobbyists were a female truck driver, a male chemical purchasing agent, the male product maintenance technician and two housewives. Perhaps most interesting of all, both <elusive> and <patches> came to earn money via their newly acquired computer skills. <elusive> had her own Website design company, and as mentioned earlier, <patches> worked for a national Internet service provider.

A particularly striking finding is that many players were involved in real-world crafts. Fourteen *rainbow* women in the 1997 data mentioned either a general interest in needle crafts in their biographies, or specific involvement in one or more of the following: sewing, quilting, cross-stitch embroidery, needlepoint, knitting, and crocheting. <elusive> has been involved in sewing all her life, and <patches> is a highly skilled quilter who claims to have received as much as $3,000 for commissioned quilts. Computers are now used in connection with many of these activities – <patches> had used software to design quilts.[50] In a private online chat on Christmas Day, 1997, she showed me three images she had created, based on quilt patterns. As for the men, three of them mentioned woodworking as a hobby; one woman also mentioned woodworking.[51]

Methods

Ordinarily, interaction on the channels is ephemeral, like conversation. We view an image and it is gone with the wind.[52] While one can activate the log function in IRC, at the time of this research one could save only plain, uncolored text, as in ordinary text-based interaction. Thus, logs preserved only black and white images coded for color, not how they looked when displayed online in real time. Figure 6.3 displays a simple file I created, both as coded offline and when played online. Code four colors the typographic symbols red, and code twelve produces the bright blue of the background; code 0 yields white text.[53] To enter the codes, one types control-K and then the number of the color. Larger and more complex images are often so cluttered by coding that it is nearly impossible to recognize them when viewing them offline. We used the graphics program Paint Shop Pro to capture images of individual files and of groups of them, and stored them in a database created with Image AXS Pro, a program for the cataloging and management of collections of visual images.[54] Over 3,500 images were captured and catalogued.[55]

```
■4,12**&&**&&**&&**&&**&&**&&**&&**&&**&&
■4,12&&**&&**&&**&&**&&**&&**&&**&&**&&**
■0,12            GREETINGS TO ALL       ■12,12
■4,12&&**&&**&&**&&**&&**&&**&&**&&**&&**
■4,12**&&**&&**&&**&&**&&**&&**&&**&&**&&
```

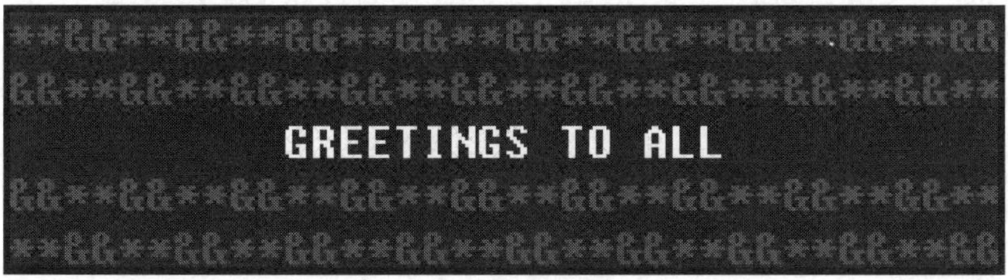

Figure 6.3. An IRC art file, offline coding and online image.

We monitored the channels in weekly sessions of 2–3 hours each, generally twice a week. During holiday periods we increased the amount of time monitored. As is evident already, we also closely examined the channel Websites and changes in their content over time. I carried out online interviews, either by email or in chat mode, with channel leaders and with many players on both channels. Finally, I met <patches> and <elusive>personally, and a research assistant conducted a telephone interview with <texxy> while visiting her family in Houston.[56]

New Features: Color, Eccentric Typography, Abstract Pattern

As we have seen, the most obvious difference between the earlier ASCII art and the art displayed on IRC is the interactive nature of the latter form. While hundreds of images shown on IRC were reworked versions of images once circulated by email or viewable on the Web,[57] thousands of images were newly created for performance online. There were three additional ways in which the newer variety differed sharply from the earlier one.

Color

A second obvious difference between the old and new art is the burst into brilliant color, made possible by the Windows version of the IRC software.[58] In Chapter 5 we saw that ASCII art on the Web was sometimes colorized,[59] and that underground ASCII artists developed their own tradition of ANSI (DOS-level colored) art, not well known to others both because of the social exclusivity of these groups and because of the technical challenge of creating and displaying it. Thus, although these earlier forms of working with color did exist before the advent of color on IRC, its use now became far more accessible to people without unusual programming skills. One needed no special programming skills to log onto mIRC and observe colored images being displayed.[60]

On IRC one could determine the color not only of each symbol in a line but of the background on which it was displayed.[61] Moreover, files could incorporate any or all of the sixteen basic Windows colors. No mixing of the sixteen colors was possible, though some colors were close enough to each other to enable one to create the illusion of depth, or three-dimensional effects, when adjacent to another. Whereas Web backgrounds have to be of a uniform color, IRC images frequently contained multicolored backgrounds, increasing the potential for complex designs. The preferred general background color was black, which contrasts sharply with a usually multicolored image. Colors seem to glow when viewed on a backlit black background, an effect that is unfortunately lost in printed color plates.

In a host of ways the players expressed their love of color. The names of the channels broadcast this, loud and clear. The word "color" was used over and over, as both noun and verb, on channel Websites and in the channels themselves. The players spoke of "learning to color." Each channel used a brilliant multicolor image as the virtual "entrance" to its Website. <elusive> designed an elaborate, multicolored castle as the opening motif for the *colors* Website (Plate 6.5). Sometimes images explicitly celebrated color verbally. In contests on *colors* people were allowed to submit images they didn't design but had only colorized.[62]

Both channels frequently incorporated the word "color" in the daily channel "topic," at the top of the channel window. Thus, the *colors* slogan for 3 May 1997 was "Welcome to *#mirc_colors*! Enjoy the show. . . A G-rated Channel!!!" On 5 May it was changed to "Welcome to *#mirc_colors*. We color your world." On 15 August 1997, the *rainbow* slogan was "Welcome to *#mirc_rainbow* . . . where the colors are bright and the people are brighter!!! Enjoy!" And on 7 November 1997, it was "The KING of color channels!!! Enjoy the show!!"

Love of color is not unique to these groups. In general, people love brilliant color because it makes them feel good. The most popular exhibit of all time at the Israel Museum was "The Joy of Color," held in 1998, the first international exhibit of the collection of Werner and Gabrielle Merzbacher of modern art.[63] Summarizing research on the psychology of color, Shulamith and Hans Kreitler wrote:

The love of color is especially prominent in childhood and in pre-literate societies, as well as in adults who undergo a loosening of conscious control due to autism, regression, or psychosis or to a poisonous delirium or a drug-induced intoxication … color [is] a factor appealing to the deeper nonrational layers of personality (Kreitler and Kreitler 1972: 54–55).

There is little conclusive empirical research on perceptions of colorfulness per se;[64] most experimental research is on the response to particular colors. Colors can evoke powerful emotions, especially bright, strongly hued colors. Red is "the most meaning-laden color," carrying both the life-enhancing associations of life and birth and those of danger and death (Kreitler and Kreitler 1972: 69). "Red is the predominant color in all tribal and peasant embroidery" (Paine 1990: 148).

In a study of the decoration of gas mask kits in Israel during the Gulf War, collaborators and I found a clear preference for bright colors among both children and adults.

In a telephone survey of 200 adult Tel Avivians in the summer of 1991, many explicitly said that they had chosen these colors and gilt materials "*še yihiye civoni*" – so that it [the kit] would be colorful. Of about two dozen persons whom we photographed while wearing a decorated or covered kit on the last day of the war, by far the majority had also chosen bright colors and otherwise eye-catching or shiny materials. (Danet et al. 1993)

Although I did not systematically study color saturation or the preference for certain colors over others in IRC images, we will see that brilliant colors prevailed and that red was very common in images.

Play with Typography: Extended ASCII Characters.

As for play with typography, with the Windows-based IRC software one could use exotic symbols from the extended ASCII character set, whose codes contain eight, rather than seven digits.[65] A selection of Windows extended ASCII characters and their codes is shown in Figure 6.4. One can see that repeating a symbol systematically has a decorative effect. In this art, typographic symbols became graphic elements-to-design-with. Apparently, the strangeness of most of these symbols to the English-based context invited artists to view them as such. Unlike color, the players rarely mentioned the subject of typography. Eventually, they came to call use of exotic characters in verbal text "fancy letters," but never used this term in connection with visual images.

```
```````` = Alt-096

{{{{{{{{ = Alt-0123

|||||||| = Alt-0124

}}}}}}}} = Alt-0125

~~~~~~~~ = Alt-0126

'''''''' = Alt-0145

'''''''' = Alt-0146

¡¡¡¡¡¡¡¡ = Alt-0161

¢¢¢¢¢¢¢¢ = Alt-0162

££££££££ = Alt-0163

¤¤¤¤¤¤¤¤ = Alt-0164

¥¥¥¥¥¥¥¥ = Alt-0165

¦¦¦¦¦¦¦¦ = Alt-0166

§§§§§§§§ = Alt-0167
```

**Figure 6.4.** A selection of extended ASCII characters and their codes.

## The Geometric Nature of Images and the Potential for Complex Designs

Like the ASCII images discussed in Chapter 5, IRC images are constructed on a grid. Thus, all art displayed in the channels is ultimately geometric in nature, even if the image appears to be a non-geometric "drawing."

> A grid is a visible or implied series of points, or axes that intersect. Grids underly the structure of all two-dimensional patterns. Grids are usually based on regular polygons: squares, equilateral triangles, and hexagon. Or they can be based on rectangles, parallelograms and rhomboids.[66]

Because images are constructed line by line in descending linear sequence, from left to right, just like ordinary text, they are, without exception, square and rectangular grids. The line-by-line nature of images, which differs sharply from that of ordinary graphic images, is also evident at the left of each image in the various illustrations: the nick of the player is repeated for each line played. Coding can yield patterns that appear to have other geometric shapes, such as a triangle or a diamond, as in the works by <twotall> and <nightrose> shown in Plate 6.6. Here, coding edges or borders "white on white" yields a file in
```

which the white of each little rectangle merges with the white ordinary background of the window in which the file is played. It is because of the geometric nature of images that many resembled patchwork quilts, rugs and needlepoint or cross-stitch embroidery. The image in Plate 6.7 is reminiscent of a quilt pattern known as "Streak of Lightning".

A comparison of this art with needlepoint illuminates several points. Needlepoint "is any counted or free stitchery worked by hand with a threaded needle on a readily countable ground."[67] In a needlepoint grid, made of loose, open-weave canvas, only one color at a time can be entered across the "mesh" between any two evenly spaced holes – one stitch, one decision (Reader's Digest, 1979: 112). While different stitches can be used to create different effects of texture, and designs may be representational or abstract, the principle remains the same.

Here, things are potentially much more complicated. The first decision is whether or not a typographic symbol will be included in a given unit; if so, then one may decide to color it as well as its background. Alternatively, one can leave the background blank, which will appear white on white. Thus, far more complex designs are possible than in needlepoint or previous forms of text-based art.[68] In practice, one does not always have to program each unit in such detail, e.g., with just a few strokes one can color an entire row solid red, or repeat a given unit of three or four typographic characters many times.

Beyond these two new features – brilliant color and extended ASCII characters – channel images were often visually quite different from earlier ASCII art. Perhaps half of those displayed or more were now abstract, rather than figurative. In short, this art was distinguished by a new preoccupation with pattern and symmetry. I turn now to a close analysis of these aspects of images.

Striving for Closure: Visual Form

I learned from interviews with players that many images took hours or even days to create.[69] Channel leaders informed me that quite a few players were "addicted," spending up to twelve or sixteen hours online everyday. Why in the world would people voluntarily spend hours at a time in a mode of communication that, although pleasant to look at, was nevertheless severely truncated and potentially so demanding in terms of preparation of images, management of one's collection, and acquisition of skills needed to play images online? To exaggerate somewhat, people never said anything to each other, or so it seemed.

My thesis is that *creating, playing and viewing images online were all means to strive for, and play with a sense of closure, completion and perfection.* I believe that cultivation of certain aspects of the form and content of images was in itself a source of great pleasure for the players. For many, if not most, aesthetic pleasure was an important reward in its own right for engaging in this activity. This is no different from individuals engaged in needlepoint or quilting, who take pleasure in seeing the design emerge and in completing it – after hours, days, perhaps even months of work. Although the aesthetic satisfactions are similar in both cases, here they were in large part inter-actionally constructed, and the sensuous satisfactions of handling yarn or cloth were absent. While for many, the social aspects of channel activity may have been just as important as the aesthetic ones, we should not under-estimate the importance of pleasure in the art for its own sake.

For some players there may have been additional sources of satisfaction in this art form. Since closure is more easily attained in this structured, protective environment than in the real world, participation may have refreshed some players, and enhanced their ability to cope with the lack of closure and satisfac-tion in their lives. As the chapter will elaborate later on, for some this activity may have been a form of escapist compensation for unsatisfying lives.[70]

The Notion of *Gestalt* and Text-based Art

The idea of closure originated in *Gestalt* psychology[71] and was elaborated by the art historian E.H. Gombrich in his (1984) study of the psychology of decorative art. Roughly, the notion of *gestalt* pertains to our tendency to perceive a stimulus as "whole" even if some portion of it is absent, or to prefer "wholes" to stimuli that are less than whole. Thus, writing primarily about primitive or ethnographic art, the Kreitlers argue:

> The art of primitive peoples consists mainly of good gestalts, characterized by simplicity, closure, regularity and symmetry . . . it is this function of the visual arts – the presentation of good gestalts – which lends meaning to the image of the artist as a god or magician who lures order out of chaos and vanquishes the formless by forms. (Kreitler and Kreitler 1972: 91–92)

IRC players conjured up order out of chaos too. Figure 6.5 identifies five strategies pertaining to visual form that players employed in the pursuit of a sense of closure.[72] These strategies pertaining to form are extensions or elabor-ations of the basic play with closure that exists even in pre-IRC forms of text-based art, which depend for their effects on processes in the psychology of perception. Thus, when viewing images, one "smoothes out the edges" of the letters and other symbols producing its outline. The better the artist, and the more skilled the choice of symbols to create the shape, the easier it is for the viewer to produce closure – to see it as a "good *gestalt*." Eventually, ASCII

(1) To create, play or view images containing pattern and symmetry.

- To create, play or view images containing purely abstract patterns.
- To create, play, or view images containing representational motifs.
- To create, play or view images containing patterns made by repeating words or names.
- To create, play or view files images contain interlace and "woven" motifs.
- To create, play or view images which are pure geometric shapes.
- To create, play or view images having borders or frames.

(2) To create, play or view images with filled spaces, whether patterned or representational.

(3) To play and view whole images displayed without interruption.

(4) To see fragmented images as if they are wholes.

(5) To play or view a sequence of images having an aspect of form in common.

Figure 6.5. Strategies for the pursuit of visual closure in the form of images.

art had become so codified that FAQ files advised newcomers which symbols to use to create seemingly smooth curves. In general, one must view the image at a sufficient distance to avoid being distracted by the graphic shape of the individual symbols.

In the IRC context, I suggest, one can pursue closure in a number of ways: by creating certain types of files offline and then performing them online; by playing or even merely viewing certain types of files displayed by others online; and by developing and cultivating categories to manage one's collection offline, much as a collector works at organizing and reorganizing his/her collection of pipes, stamps, or porcelain.[73] In the remainder of this chapter I examine the pursuit of closure in the form and content of images online.

Pattern and Symmetry

The most basic strategy for the pursuit of closure and perfection is to create, play and view files containing pattern and symmetry (strategy #1, Figure 6.5). As I will show, there are many ways to do this, and they are not necessarily mutually exclusive.

Pattern is found both in nature, as in the structure of honeycombs, leaves, and snow crystals, and in many varieties of art, particularly primitive, ethnographic or folk art,[74] and the decorative arts – wallpaper and textiles (Gombrich

1984; Phillips and Bunce 1993). Among the fine art traditions pattern is especially prominent in Muslim art (Grabar 1992).

One of Gombrich's teachers, Emanuel Loewy, had proposed that an apotropaic function could account for the purpose and origin of most if not all decorative motifs (Gombrich 1984: 257) – that is, decoration was to ward off evil. In a discussion of magical protection in traditional embroidered textiles around the world, Sheila Paine (1990) asserts that embroidered pattern, particularly geometric pattern, is "deemed effective against evil spirits," and "the force of a pattern is strengthened by doubling or repeating it" (Paine 1990: 140). For instance, among the Ainu on the island of Hokkaido, men wore decorated robes while hunting or participating in religious rituals to keep evil spirits at bay:

> Strong, web-like motifs [on robes] served to ward off evil spirits and were laid out symmetrically to protect all parts of the body evenly. Decoration was focused on the hem, upper back and front and sleeve openings to prevent evil spirits from entering at vulnerable points. (Jackson 1997: 30)

Similarly, in Palestinian embroidery, the chest panel on women's traditional dresses is the most elaborately embroidered.

> The head, neck, and chest areas are considered to be the main life centers of the body . . . they are thought to be the most vulnerable and to need protection against evil spirits, the evil eye, and bad luck. Many means of protection are used: charms, talismans, beads and other kinds of jewels, and embroidery. (Amir 1977: 13)

The creation of pattern relies on three characteristics, a unit, repetition of that unit, and a system of organization.

> A pattern can be defined as a design composed of one or more motifs, multiplied and arranged in an orderly sequence, and a single motif as a unit with which the designer composes a pattern by repeating it at regular intervals over a surface. The motif itself is not a pattern, but it is used to create patterns, which will differ according to the organization of the motif. (Phillips and Bunce 1993: 7)

Where there is pattern there is symmetry. Symmetry pertains to "the correspondence in size, form and arrangement of parts on opposite sides of a plane, line, or point" or to "regularity of form or arrangement with reference to corresponding parts."[75]

In all patterns there are four basic symmetry operations that may be performed upon a fundamental region, design or motif. Mathematicians call these rigid motions because they suggest movements without distortion of size or shape around a point, along or across a line, or to cover a plane.[76]

Mathematicians have identified 17 different kinds of symmetry, involving different combinations of the four basic symmetry operations.[77] These four basic operations are shown in Figure 6.6. First, in "translation," a unit is simply moved along a line; this type of symmetry is common in border patterns, like many of those I will examine, below. Second is "reflection," in which the unit is moved along the line but reversed. This is more popularly called bilateral or mirror symmetry. Third is "glide reflection," in which the unit is moved along a line but flipped over, 180°. Finally, in the fourth type, "rotation," the unit is both moved along the line, flipped over, and reversed.

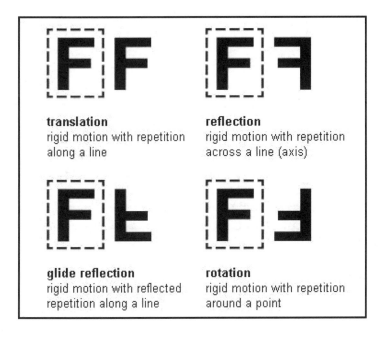

Figure 6.6. Four types of symmetry operations.

Most people are only aware of bilateral or mirror symmetry, evidently because it is most easily recognized. In this type, one half of an image mirrors the other. This type of symmetry creates a spontaneous impression of balance, harmony and order (Gombrich 1984; Kreitler and Kreitler 1972: 101–105). When an image is symmetrical, it is easier to take in details away from the central axis via peripheral vision. This was effectively demonstrated by the art historian E.H. Gombrich in the following passage:

> Take a succession of . . . signs, such as the following alternation between repeated brackets and the letter O: ((((O(((O((O(O((((O(((O((O(O. It takes a moment to see the underlying rule of diminishing numbers of brackets and to spot the redundancy. But if we do not repeat but reverse the sequence, the impression of palindromic regularity is immediate: (((O(((O((O(OO)O))O)))O)))). (Gombrich 1984: 126)

Gombrich adds,

> the role of peripheral vision in the global impression of bilateral redundancy. . . helps to explain why we rarely notice minor deviations from symmetry, unless we are set to discover them . . . Only when our attention has been drawn to . . .irregularities do we find it hard to disregard them. (Gombrich 1984: 126–129)

Bilateral Symmetry in IRC Images

Bilateral vertical symmetry is very common in channel images. The first two images in Plate 6.1 are symmetrical in this fashion, apart from the inserted words. Many images also contain bilateral horizontal symmetry: if they were folded horizontally, the bottom half would mirror the top half too. [78]

The image in Plate 6.8, by <twotall>, is especially striking. The main motif is a perfect square, containing within itself both vertical and horizontal symmetry. Also, the square is doubled to create higher-order mirror symmetry. In the richly colored world of these channels, the reduced number of colors is itself striking. In form alone the two halves of each image are identical; it is the reversal of color that provides the contrast.

Glide Reflection and Rotation

Although individual typographic symbols cannot be reversed or rotated, larger motifs can be rotated in images. However, because it is difficult to turn a motif upside down in this medium, glide reflection and rotation symmetry, the third and fourth types of symmetry operations in Figure 6.6, are extremely rare. An exception is shown in Figure 6.7, containing perfect rotation symmetry. The "W" at the chin of the upper face is as close a mirror image of the "M" for the chin in the lower one as was possible. Other than this, the image meets the definition in Figure 6.6 – "rigid motion with repetition around a point."

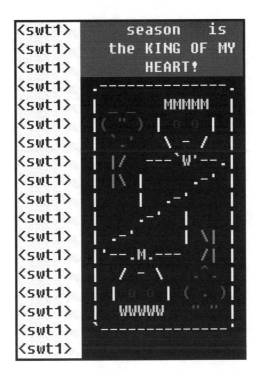

Figure 6.7. An unusual type of symmetry.

Abstract Designs

As I have pointed out, many images are abstract designs – images "devoid of an explicit object reference" (Kreitler and Kreitler 1972: 81), created with extended ASCII characters. One of the most elaborate abstract images I encountered is the work by <[blue]> in Plate 6.9. We have both vertical and horizontal bilateral symmetry, as well as diagonal symmetry both from the upper left and the upper right. There is also diagonal symmetry within each of the four squares. This pattern is created with only six extended ASCII characters, systematically arranged, and with a limited number of colors. The basic pattern contains turquoise, white, red, and blue. The border is white, and the background is black. The nickname is in regular plain text letters, in purple and pink, and is displayed a number of times, both in regular order and in reverse.

Repetition of Figurative Motifs and Words

Just as individual typographic symbols or clusters of them can be repeated, representational motifs become patterns when repeated. In the first example in Plate 6.10 typographic symbols have been used to "draw" a stylized spider. This motif is repeated six times, and is reminiscent of patterns in traditional ethnic embroidery and woven textiles (Paine 1990; Washburn and Crowe 1988). The restrictions imposed by the typographic characters result in images whose simplification and generalization resemble cross-stitch embroidery, for instance. While this type of simplification in representational images was already present in earlier forms of ASCII art – a byproduct of the constraints of the medium – its mobilization to create patterns is new to the art studied here.

Repetition of words and nicks is very prominent in images too. In the second example in Plate 6.10 the word "hello" is repeated seven times, creating a visual pattern. There is also great visual play with nicks in the corpus. The third image in Plate 6.10, an impressive creation by <windmist>, is unusually elaborate.

Interlace and "Woven" Designs

A striking form of pattern that has appeared in many magical and religious contexts in the past, and that reappears in this corpus is the interlace design. Interlace is a form of "braid" or twist in which elements are intertwined, producing a near-three-dimensional effect, as in Plate 6.11. This motif has been traced back to Neolithic pottery (Wilson 1994: 173), Islamic art and Anglo-Irish manuscript illumination. The Anglo-Saxon Lindisfarne Gospels (7th century) and the Irish Book of Kells are especially famous for using this type of motif to fill spaces (Grabar 1992; Gombrich 1984: 81–82).[79] Gombrich (1984: 263) cites Hildburgh's (1944–45) suggestion that knots, mazes, tangles and other forms of "indeterminability" are considered in folk belief to be excellent protection against evil influences. Both interlace designs in Plate 6.11 are by <sher>. A similar effect is produced in designs that simulate weaving (third example, Plate 6.11, by <joesin>).

Pure Geometric Shapes

We have seen that because text-based images are geometric, they are necessarily of a regular shape – rectangles and squares. Even if an image consists only of a "drawing" without a background, there is a rectangular grid which happens to be invisible to the eye.

Creating, playing or viewing ordinary rectangular images whose shape is made more prominent by a colored background[80] might sometimes contribute to the sense of closure. There is a small hint that this may be the case in the Kreitlers' discussion of the perception of *gestalts*:

when a pattern consists of a great number of dishomogeneous parts, varying in both form and color, an overall arrangement in the form of a rectangle is more conducive to the perception of a whole than an overall arrangement in the form of a circle or triangle. This may possibly be the reason why most paintings actually are on rectangular canvases. (Kreitler and Kreitler 1972: 93)

Creating, playing and viewing other geometric shapes, more difficult to accomplish in this medium, are also likely to contribute to the sense of closure because they too are, ideally, satisfyingly regular. We have seen that it is possible to create diamonds and triangles, with some effort (Plate 6.6).

It is even possible to create, play and view circles, though they were rather rare because they are especially difficult to accomplish in the IRC medium. Often a symbol of unity and perfection, the circle is among the most ancient known human symbols. It appeared in prehistoric rock paintings, and has been in use in ideographic systems of writing for more than 5,000 years (Liungman 1991: 274). One thinks also of the mandala:

Mandala is a Sanskrit word meaning magic circle, and its symbolism includes all concentrically arranged figures, all radial or spherical arrangements, and all circles or squares with a central point. It is one of the oldest religious symbols. . . and is found throughout the world. (Fordham, 1953, cited in Gombrich 1984: 246)

While the pursuit of closure in the present context has no necessary links with religious aspirations, the longing for wholeness, unity, coherence, is common to both secular and sacred contexts.[81] The appeal of the circle very likely has to do with the fact that it has infinite axes of symmetry. Not surprisingly, then, it appears in many folk traditions of embroidery. It is a potent symbol "of the cosmic force of the sun and moon and of the motion and rejuvenation of the wheel . . . [and] offers protection from evil spirits" (Paine 1990: 141).

Borders and Frames

Frames and borders are very common in images. The etymological connection between "closure" and "enclosure" is once again significant. Whether of solid colors or filled with repeated, usually eccentric typographic symbols, these borders are like picture frames, and what art historians say of picture frames holds true for these images too:

No matter what its appearance, the frame is always a conventional sign indicating that what it surrounds is out of the ordinary. It marks the boundary within which something "aesthetically important" takes place, something that "has no practical value." It is artificial and pure, and seeks nothing beyond its own aesthetic worth. (Traber 1995: 226)

In Ortega y Gasset's more poetic articulation:

a frame is not the wall . . . but neither is it . . . the enchanted surface of the painting. As the frontier for both regions, the frame serves to neutralize a brief strip of wall. And acting as a trampoline, it sends out attitude hurtling off to the legendary dimension of the aesthetic island. (Ortega y Gasset 1986: 24)

Incorporating a border in one's image, or playing or viewing such images is yet another variation of strategy #1 in Figure 6.9. Borders are far more common in this material than in the earlier ASCII art. Moreover, borders made with repeated patterns of extended ASCII characters are unique to IRC. These borders may have a latent magical function similar to that of traditional embroidery or other decoration on the edges of costumes. It is only a small step from saying that what is inside the border is enchanted (Ortega y Gasset) to suggest that it is protected:

. . .evil spirits likely to attack the body are kept out by decorative devices at every edge and opening. From Asia to Western Europe embroidery is commonly placed encircling the neck, along hem and cuff, around pockets and also at buttonholes. Seams are closed with decorative stitchery and certain vulnerable places carry heavy embroidery . . . Even when they cover much of the garment these areas of embroidery never intermingle but are always clearly defined. (Paine, 1990: 133)[82]

Two examples of elaborate extended ASCII borders are shown in Plate 6.12. In the first example, a file used to greet me (my nick on IRC is <doremi>), five colors are regularly alternated, and the arrangement of colors is systematically moved one space to the left as we descend the rows, in a diagonal or "diaper" effect. Note that in this case, only one extended ASCII symbol has been used in the border or frame. The inner solid-black border separating the outer, multicolored border from the inner image adds depth to the image, creating a slight illusion of three dimensions.

Note the sharp differentiation between the familiar ASCII characters inside the second image in Plate 6.12 – a romanticized horse or unicorn with flowing "mane" (originally by Joan Stark) and the exotic ones in the frame. This differentiation is very common in my corpus. The idea that the border has a latent magical effect, staving off the danger and chaos in the material world, is especially pertinent in such instances.[83]

Filling the Space

In Gombrich's formulation, framing and filling go together. They are the two, mutually interdependent principles of decorative art. Framing delimits the field or fields; filling organizes the resultant space (Gombrich 1984: 75). As in so much previous decorative art, in IRC art the framing grid and the filling motif together constitute the ornament – the image. I suggest, then, that filling a space in images is yet another way to strive for closure (strategy #2, Figure 6.5).

It might seem rather trivial to pursue closure by filling a space. In research on collecting (Danet and Katriel 1989; 1994) I was fascinated to discover that some collectors take great pleasure in doing just that. A young collector of stickers enjoyed filling the doors of her wardrobe with them. Even an adult collector, of antique books about travel to the Holy Land, took great pleasure in sitting opposite his filled shelves and contemplating how his collection filled them (Danet and Katriel 1989: 266–267).[84]

The players showed a strong preference for images with filled backgrounds and other spaces. It is possible to create or display images with no background; in this case, the background is in effect the white of the ordinary window, and images look like the first one in Plate 6.13. In fact, such images were quite rare. It is fascinating that the very image that I had chosen to illustrate the non-filled background reappeared about two years later on one of the channels, this time with a black filled background and a red frame (second example, Plate 6.13).[85]

Fragments and Wholes

Contrary to the impression readers may have gained thus far, the flow of images online was usually anything but smooth. In fact, extended uninterrupted sequences were rather rare, and screens like the unsightly one in Plate 6.14 were very common. The players called this phenomenon "picture collision." At least, in Plate 6.14 the clearly different widths of the three overlapping files help the eye make out which parts belong to which image.

There are several reasons for the frequency of "spoiled" images. First, as we saw in Chapter 3, a "plague" of life on IRC is lag – delays of seconds or minutes in the appearance on screen of one's message or the messages of others. The players complained about lag much as in real life one complains about the weather. One of the three discernible files in Plate 6.14, the one played by a person nicknamed <carman>, is a humorous file which asks "Are we lagging?"

Second, there is a problem of "flooding," which was quite acute for some time. Playing large files can cause players to be "bumped" peremptorily from a channel, leaving images only partially displayed. To some extent this can be controlled, and technical improvements increasingly allowed players to play larger files without interruption. A third problem was that the comings and goings of players were acknowledged by the software in one-line messages, often interrupting the presentation of images. Knowledgeable players could suppress the display of these by activating certain commands. However, bits of text typed by other players could not be suppressed, thus frequently interrupting the display of a file. For all these reasons it was extremely rare to view a sequence of as many as five uninterrupted images, as in Plate 6.1, especially as files became larger over time.

In short, an important strategy for the pursuit of closure was to strive to play, and manage even to view whole files without interruption (strategy #3, Figure 6.5). One particularly dramatic instance of this was the repeated efforts of <MikeChat> on *rainbow* to display a long poem on the channel.[86] Hopelessly mangled by various interruptions during two efforts to play it, the poem was finally displayed in its entirety in a third attempt during the same session.

It was a great surprise to me as I chose the illustrations for this chapter to discover that so many of the images we had saved were fragmented, perhaps as many as two-thirds. In some cases just one line of text interrupted the flow of an image, in others, many more. At first I thought of this merely as a publication problem: how to find whole images for illustrations for this book? Eventually, I came to realize that my own reactions to these ostensibly "spoiled" images were an important clue to the fascination of channel activity. Why had it taken me so long to take full account of the fact that so many images were broken up when displayed?

I believe that, like the players, I had incessantly practiced seeing fragmented images as wholes. I suggest, then, that this is yet another strategy to strive for closure (#4, Figure 6.5). Time spent in the channels is time practicing seeing *gestalts*, becoming better and better at seeing flawed images as wholes. The players rarely commented on interruptions of a line or two, and often gave each other compliments on such images, as if they had been "perfect." Players frequently apologized when their actions unintentionally interrupted others' images, another indication of the striving by all to view whole files. When only one line interrupts an image, one can quite easily look past the interruption, as in the image in Figure 6.8. Hundreds of images look like this.

Sequences of Images of Similar Form

In a group situation, not only formal characteristics of individual images, but of entire sequences of images, may contribute to the sense of closure (strategy #5, Figure 6.5). Occasionally the players spontaneously played sequences of files that were variations on the same design. In one instance, someone played a file whose design featured the word "HEY" "written" in capital letters via

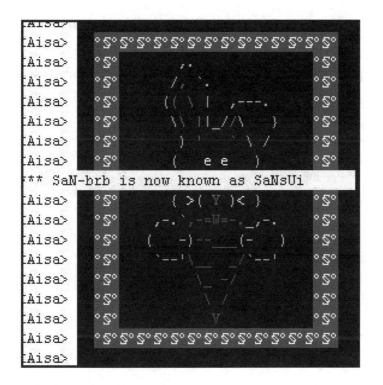

Figure 6.8. A lightly "flawed" image of a rabbit.

repetition of the # symbol. This inspired others to play the same file but in different colors. Such spontaneous "runs" are possible only if several players have the same set of variations of an image on their hard disk, and can easily call up the different versions. One must have considerable facility at the keyboard to accomplish this. Such copycat displays were partly a function of the thirst for fads in the channels. Runs of similar images resembled completing a series in stamp collecting. The individual variations "rhyme" with one another visually (Danet and Katriel 1989). But closure is constructed interactively, not by a solo player.

Striving for Closure: the Content of Images

The content of images also contributed importantly to the sense of closure. Strictly speaking, *gestalt* theory pertains only to form. I will argue that in this instance content is as pertinent as form to my hypothesis, though we must understand the concept of closure more loosely than is the case for visual form of images. It is quite striking that stereotypically male images, which were very popular in the past, e.g., of planes, tanks, guns, space vehicles, etc., were rare in this material.

The players had a strong preference for sentimental and other types of tension-reducing images of non-controversial content that reaffirms traditional values. This generalization held true for both men and women. This was the first and most common of three content-related strategies that the players pursued to strive for closure (strategy #1, Figure 6.9). Representational images conjured up a child-like, even regressive world where all was – ideally – sweetness and light, displayed in an atmosphere in which all were welcome and accepted.[87]

---

(1) To create, play, or view representational images with traditional, non-controversial themes.

(2) To create, play, or view humorous images.

(3) To create, play or view sequences of images that are variations on a substantive theme.

Figure 6. 9. Strategies for the pursuit of closure via the content of images.

Teddy Bears and Other Cute Animals

Images of teddy bears were very common. One such image is shown in Plate 6.15, adapted for IRC by <bamacutie> from a plain ASCII work by Robin Chokie. As in cartoons, children's book illustrations and toys, a normally aggressive, hulking, potentially terrifying bear has been transformed into something adorable. The appeal of teddy bears, to adults as well as children, is not difficult to grasp. Morreall and Loy analyzed the appeal of cuteness in living creatures:

> Cuteness is a group of features that evolved in mammalian infants as a way of making them attractive to adults. These "releasing stimuli". . . include a head large in relation to the body, eyes set low in the head, a large protruding forehead, round protruding cheeks, a plump rounded body shape, short thick extremities, soft body surfaces, and clumsy behavior. (Morreall and Loy 1989: 68)

The following formulation of the appeal of teddy bears, by the founder of the Teddy Bear Museum in Stratford-upon-Avon, England, focuses on almost the same features:

> A teddy bear is fundamentally different from the image of a real bear because it is in no way threatening. The vulnerable appearance of babies brings out the protective nature of adults and it is the babylike qualities of the teddy bear which distinguishes it from the bears that went before. Its face is unrealistically wide, more like the smiling round face of a baby. It has a cute little nose, bright round eyes and a compact, soft body with movable arms and legs which make it easy to cuddle. As with a baby, in comforting it we feel comforted, in loving it, we feel loved in return, but unlike a baby it makes no annoying demands on us. In the eyes of its owner, the teddy bear is dependable, trustworthy and loyal. (Brown 1997: 20)[88]

Predictably, images of other cute animals, especially bunnies (Figure 6.8), kittens, and puppies, as well as cute or cartoon-like babies and other human beings were also common. Cuteness was sometimes further enhanced by puns, as in greeting cards from the 19th century onwards, and in digital greetings on the Web. Thus, one example contained the pun, "You aRe a BeaRY GooD FRIeND!" Such puns evoke baby-talk, further giving license to a regressive state.

Hearts and Flowers

Hearts and flowers were extremely common in images too. A symbol of love and romance as well as friendship and togetherness in Western culture since the 15th century, when it first appeared in European painting,[89] the heart motif is very familiar from paper Valentines (Barth 1974; Staff 1969) and other ephemera of American popular culture. It has also been prominent in folk art, notably, that of the Pennsylvania Germans in the American context (Swank et al. 1983; Emmerling 1998). An IRC example by <joesin> is shown in Plate 6.16.

There were plenty of examples of flowers in the corpus too, especially roses, the traditional symbol of love and romance since ancient Greek times (Goody 1993).

Usually, "roses" were constructed with the @ symbol as the flower, a Net convention; often they were arranged symmetrically. An unusual, asymmetrical ASCII drawing on the rose theme is a design by <aisa>, a player from Spain, in the lower half of Plate 6.16.

Patriotism, Religious Sentiment

Another area in which IRC images reinforced traditional, conservative values and sentiments was that of religion and politics, just as has been documented for many material objects often deemed "kitsch" (Dorfles 1969; Henry 1979). While these images were not common, they did occur. Thus, on the Fourth of July many people played images containing flags (Plate 6.17). Here, conventional patriotic imagery is cleverly combined with imagery from life online. Anti-patriotic, hostile sentiment was extremely rare. A player who displayed a green and white flag with the inscriptions "The Star-Spangled Lie" and "Anarchy Lives" was promptly booted out of the channel.

Angels

Angels are a common theme in traditional greeting cards and scraps (Gordon 1984; Allen and Hoverstadt 1990) as well as in folk art (Glassie 1989). This motif occurred in IRC images too. Angels can evoke either a religious or a merely sentimental connotation. In most instances in my material, they were of the latter type, as is true of the image in Plate 6.18. Here, computer imagery is combined with the angel motif (adapted from a design by Joan Stark).

Humor

A good deal of the time communication on the channels is without irony or humor – a sentimental "love-in." But humor is also very common. After all, it is a well-known way to reduce or release tension and have fun (strategy #2, Figure 6.9). The upper image in Plate 6.19 is a visual and verbal pun on the notion "a barrel of fun." The barrel contains the word "fun" over and over, in exotic characters. Occasionally, the players poked fun at themselves and at Net culture, as in the lower example, by <nuffers>, in Plate 6.19.

Sometimes the humor of an individual file was interactively enhanced (Figure 6.10). The first image, played by <Puriel> for <Krptonite>, is a verbal and visual pun on the concept of "match." <Krptonite> responded rapidly by "throwing an ice cold bucket of water" on her. He did not type these words, but rather, located a ready-made small file of an appropriately witty nature, played it, and only then typed, "now that will take care of the match." A player must be very quick and skilled to locate and display instantly such an appropriate response.

Theme and Variations

A third content-related strategy to enhance a sense of closure is to play or view a sequence of files that are variations on a substantive theme (strategy #3, Figure 6.9). This strategy parallels strategy #5 in Figure 6.5. However, now

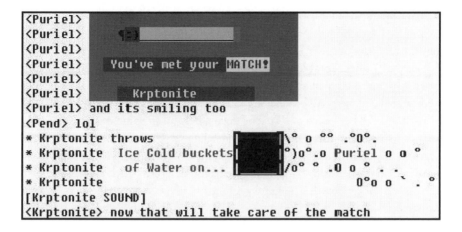

```
<Puriel>
<Puriel>       (:)
<Puriel>
<Puriel>    You've met your MATCH!
<Puriel>
<Puriel>          Krptonite
<Puriel> and its smiling too
<Pend> lol
* Krptonite throws              \°  o  °°  .°0°.
* Krptonite   Ice Cold buckets  °)o°.o Puriel o o  °
* Krptonite   of Water on...    /o°  °  .0 o  °  . .
* Krptonite                           0°o o  `  .  °
[Krptonite SOUND]
<Krptonite> now that will take care of the match
```

Figure 6.10. A humorous exchange.

content recurs, not form. For instance, one day in July 1998 a spontaneous series of three images of cows was played in sequence (Plate 6.20). The first cow image comes from earlier ASCII cow collections, adapted for IRC.[90] Note that all three images contain puns ("Don't be a COWch potato;" "MOOOOOOrning, glint;" "MOOOOOOOOOING over ya"). The items "rhyme," but here it is the associative content of the images that rhymes, rather than formal aspects.

Discussion

"Kitsch" or Folk Art?

Nearly all the representational images in the corpus contained content often labeled by cultural analysts as "kitsch."[91] We have seen that they typically dealt with non-controversial themes that readily appeal to stock emotions and reinforce traditional values, offered little or no cognitive challenge, and suppressed the unpleasant aspects of life. The lack of irony in images is also a classic feature of objects often labeled kitsch. Kitsch always means what it says, and says it literally. As Thomas Kulka (1996: 26) puts it, kitsch themes "are highly emotionally charged . . . with stock emotions that spontaneously trigger an unreflective emotional response."

> Kitsch come to support our basic sentiments and beliefs, not to disturb or question them . . . The aim of kitsch is not to create new needs or expectations, but to satisfy existing ones. Kitsch . . . breeds on universal images, the emotional charge of which appeals to everyone. (Kulka 1996: 27)

Milan Kundera's blunt formulation in *The Unbearable Lightness of Being* comes to mind: "Kitsch is the absolute denial of shit, in both the literal and the figurative senses of the word; kitsch excludes everything from its purview which is essentially unacceptable in human existence" (Kundera 1984: 248). As Saul Friedlander remarked at a 1990 symposium on kitsch, "There is no kitsch which ends with a question. All kitsch ends with a statement" (Friedlander 1990: 253).

Although the concept of "kitsch" seems helpful in some respects, in other ways it is problematic. Objects designated as kitsch are usually commercial commodities manufactured by others and merely consumed. More important, application of the term "kitsch" is class-related, a term some groups apply to the taste of others, with derogatory intention. Here, we are talking of a do-it-yourself craft activity of no tangible substance and with no monetary value. More important, it is preferable to find a formulation that is less judgmental and class-biased.

We can avoid this problem by turning instead to Henry Glassie's (1989) characterization of folk art. He finds that it is idealized, frontal, and not illusionistic. Images are of types, not individuals. People are portrayed frontally (and sometimes from the side) in a stylized, non-realistic, reductive manner. People tend to be expressionless, to stand or stare straight ahead, to be in their own world. Animals and flowers are popular themes. Animals are portrayed in a simplified, stylized manner without aggression – cute rather than threatening. The symmetry of flowers is part of their appeal. In general, there is, he reiterates, much pattern and symmetry in folk art, a point I made earlier. Folk art shows a love of brilliant color. It is an art which is "not muddy, sketchy, vague; it is bright and firm" (Glassie 1989: 165).

I propose, then, to call this art an "incipient" or "emergent" folk art. The status of this art is an issue I will debate in the concluding chapter. Suffice it to say for now that it fits enough of Glassie's criteria to be usefully characterized as a candidate for inclusion under the folk art rubric.[92]

What Is the Significance of This Art in the Players' Lives?

What significance did this art have in players' lives? For some, the pursuit of closure may have been a response to an unarticulated sense of dislocation caused by extremely rapid technological and social change. Whether the players were dislocated in this sense or not, channel activity offered them a remarkably creative, constructive way to participate in the new digital culture, and at the same time, to cultivate a sense of continuity in very unsettling times. This sense of continuity derived, first of all, from the constant display and viewing of representational images, many of which had been imported from the conventional world of commercial greeting cards, or which reinforced traditional values of belonging, mutual support, and so on.

Despite the novel use of exotic typographic symbols and many other distinctive aspects of this new medium, images also had important formal and substantive links with the art of many earlier cultures. Certain specific images were universal in appeal, or nearly so, notably, the archetypal outstretched arms welcoming players. At a deeper level, I have argued, via the quasi-magical cultivation of pattern and symmetry, the players conjured up the illusion of a safer, more protected world than the turbulent one in which they lived their physical lives.

Comparing Channel Subcultures

Totally spontaneous *communitas* cannot survive for long. It is inevitable that a complex activity that is supposed to be sustained 365 days a year, around the clock and world-wide, and that had scores of regulars, required organizational decisions and responsibilities. Both channels responded to these needs, but in different ways. Both had groups of ops committed to help run the channel, offer assistance to newcomers, teach new skills, all according to a scheduled division of labor, and held regular ops meetings to discuss problems. *Colors* even created a special channel for ops alone.

The two channels differed dramatically in leadership style and the relative emphasis placed on rules. Earlier in the chapter I pointed out briefly that <elusive>'s leadership style sometimes tended to be rather autocratic, and that former *colors* players defected to create a more democratic atmosphere in *rainbow*. There had also been disagreement over sexual content; <elusive> wanted to keep the channel suitable for children, whereas the defectors preferred a freer atmosphere. Many remained loyal to <elusive>, appreciating the sense of order that her style offered. No doubt, her years in the Air Force helped shape her preferred leadership style. One indication of her more bureaucratic approach is that she created a very elaborate hierarchy of ops with finer status distinctions than are called for by the regular IRC program.

The most striking difference between the two channels was in the attitude toward rules. There was a very strong emphasis on rules in *colors*. In an online chat with me, <elusive> remarked, "Without rules there is no organization." The main rule on the channel Website was "Have fun in *#mirc_colors*, but think of others also!!" A closer look at the Website revealed that in August, 1998, there were no less than sixteen separate rules for ops and another fifteen for all players. In effect, *colors* became a little bureaucracy! Consider the tone of the following notice, posted in a special box on the site:

MANDATORY: It is now mandatory that ALL OPS join #*mIRC_Colors_OPS* while on the channel as an active op. Thank you.

Just as in the real world one fills out a job application, to become an op one had to fill out a form on the channel Website, providing basic information and answering the question, "Please tell us about yourself and why you want to be an op for #*mirc_colors.*" Yet, <elusive> was also capable of laughing at herself—one of her creations was a file mocking her own preoccupation with rules.

The atmosphere on *rainbow* was very different. From the very beginning, the slogan on its Website has been "There is only one rule here – To have fun, fun fun!" As <texxy> put it, "*Rainbow* is about freedom and few rules . . . *Rainbow* has two official rules 1) It is just irc, have fun 2) It is your irc experience, do with it what you want."[93] Other, mostly unarticulated rules did eventually emerge to govern life on *rainbow*, and there too it became necessary to fill out a form when applying to become an op. Still, by and large, my observations confirm <texxy>'s claim. He added,

> I think the issue of freedom and few rules makes a huge difference. I think that *disorder can be fun.* . . and the channel is often at its best when everyone is trying to play stuff at once. I have often called it *controlled chaos* (italics added). The screen really moves and crash.wav is heard often, I laugh every time.[94]

Note his claim that *rainbow* people actually enjoyed picture collisions, whereas <elusive> told me that when there were 30 or more people in the channel, she made them take turns!

Another difference between the two channels was in the relative emphasis they placed on the two primary functions of channel activity. *Colors* stressed the art as individual accomplishment somewhat more. It featured monthly contests for the best art. <elusive> periodically presented shows of her own work. At the same time, I should not exaggerate – *rainbow* also increasingly recognized certain artists as talented "stars," and included examples of their work on its Website. As of spring, 1998 it also began to hold regularly scheduled shows of the work of individual artists. In 1999 a new genre of occasional planned event was added, the "challenge." For instance, the challenge for the month of January was "Fire and Ice." Individuals could submit files on this theme, which were then displayed online at a planned time. Still, on *rainbow* most files were tokens for interaction, and files were very often shared. Recall in particular the phenomenon of "holipops" and "bowpops," sets of collectively prepared files for special occasions, meant to be shared by all.

The two channels also differed in their relative emphasis on play versus art. <texxy> observed that

Colors seems to be more into the actual art. The remaining ops do not make the fancy aliases, popups, or share-files. Also, Elusive has always been txt oriented herself. Rainbow seems to be more into the fun popups or aliases. They are much quicker (hard to get a .txt file out with 40 folks on channel) and they usually communicate a message. But we also churn out incredible txt art.[95]

One expression of the more social, more playful nature of interaction on *rainbow* was the players' delight in humorous scripts, mini-programs sometimes called "talkers." Usually created by <texxy>, a virtuoso behind-the-scenes programmer, these scripts decorate typed text in a playful, even silly way. Thus, one could talk in "undies" or in "teddy bears" (Figure 6. 11). Such talkers marked or highlighted verbal communication.

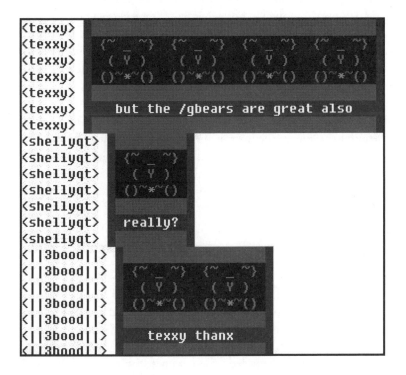

Figure 6.11. "Talking" in teddy bears, a "talker" by <texxy>.

Activities on *rainbow* had some elements in common with children's trading and collecting. In Tamar Katriel's (1991) study of Israeli children's collecting and trading activities, children collected stationery and stickers in order to trade, to be part of the group. One boy told her, "I prefer to collect things that all the kids collect because this way I can swap for things I don't have, and this is a great part of the fun" (Katriel 1991: 169). In contrast, our later research on collecting in both adults and children demonstrated that for adults the experience of collecting itself and its objects are the main goal (Danet and Katriel 1989). Like these children, *rainbow* players engaged in channel activity in order to communicate, to an extent greater than in *colors*.

I mentioned earlier that the *rainbow* crowd had a second channel, #*mirc_rainbow2*, that became a place where players went to chat, via ordinary typed text. This was yet another indication of the importance of social aspects on this channel. <elusive> did report that her second channel, #*mirc_colors_ops*, ostensibly a forum for technical discussion and ops meetings, was also a place to go to chat – but only for ops. Thus, in both channels, there was an inner circle, mainly among ops, who considered themselves friends.

RL ties slowly developed in both channels. Some people talked on the telephone, and a small number of individuals had met in real life.[96] <texxy> and <patches> became best friends, and <patches> visited <texxy> in Texas several times. <punkie1>, one of the chief ops on *colors* for a while, traveled from Pennsylvania to Oregon to visit <elusive>. In some cases, several family members were involved in the channels. Two sisters from Portland, Oregon became ops on *colors*. As noted earlier, <elusive>'s RL partner <shortshot> was a regular on *colors*, and his son also learned to create images. Moreover, <elusive>'s daughter <tweesta> was an op too. In another instance, a father and son were active on *rainbow*. A couple that met on IRC and had been active in one of the channels were married in the summer of 1998. There were several other RL romances as a result of channel participation.

Breaking Frame

Casual visitors to these channels may have had the impression that the frame of play, of a perfect miniature world without sorrow, was maintained throughout. In fact, over time one cannot keep out the real world and real-life troubles. One test of just how well the play frame can or cannot be maintained was the death of Diana, Princess of Wales, at the end of August 1997. I quickly discovered that her death "flooded" the channel frame in both cases. To my knowledge, this was the first open acknowledgment of death on the channels. The players created and played many special images to commemorate her, one of which is shown in Plate 6.21.

The death and illness of players or their relatives also changed the channel frame. When an op on *colors*, a twenty-two-year-old young woman from Quebec, died suddenly in September 1997, the others commemorated her online and on the channel Website. In a particularly interesting development, her mother, who had never even been on IRC before, became a regular and an op, all in very short order.

In June 1999 a fairly recent regular on *rainbow*, a seventeen-year-old nicknamed <b-e-n>, died of leukemia. Only a small number of players had known of his struggle. In August 1999 a tribute to <b-e-n> went up on the Website, including visual and textual tributes by several players, as well as some of <b-e-n>'s images and poems. The last poem he wrote before he died is shown in Figure 6.12.

The *rainbow* Website contained yet another remarkable tribute, to <nuffers>, a Florida student and one of the original three who had created the channel in May 1997. In the fall of 1998 <nuffers> suddenly disappeared from the channel

---

I CAN SLEEP

The sun sets slowly
and daylight fades away.
The glow of the western rim
marks the end of a tiring day.

A shadow falls gently
and cools the night air.
Night sounds ebb and fade
till I forget they are there.

Breezes blow softly
and I see now the time.
The night sings a lullaby
and chills run down my spine.

I grin so faintly
and I smile a bit too.
I think with love about
the fun we had, me and you.

My head rests lightly
and feels peace so deep.
The pillow caresses my face
And I know at last
    I can sleep. . . .
                June 1999

Figure 6.12. <b-e-n>'s last poem.

without explanation, never to return, not even answering email. She was much appreciated both as a virtual friend and as a talented artist (the "sideways" face in Plate 6.19 is her creation). The two-part tribute to her contained both files in her praise and a slide show of her own work. One of the images honoring her, by <aisa>, is shown in Plate 6.22.

What Other Needs Does This Activity Fulfill?

I have suggested that for some, this activity may have been a form of compensation or escape from unsatisfying lives. While I would certainly not like to view the channels merely as virtual "Lonely Hearts Clubs," for some players they may have performed this function. As <texxy> wrote:

> There are many irc addicts on Rainbow. It is an escape for many and I hope that Rainbow helps brighten their days. Most are just regular folks looking for something to do . . . I have run into many that have debilitating conditions. I often find folks who run support groups for various illnesses.[97]

<nuffers> had confided to me in an online interview that a fair number of players were ill or even dying in one case, handicapped, recovering from divorce, or lonely. In a later communication <texxy> added:

> there are a lot of single people looking for friendship or romance. . . As for irc being an escape, the main thing they are escaping is boredom. Most folks [sic] lives are not all that exciting and this is at least communicating with others (beats watching nothing on TV). I also think that folks are often not happy in their real lives. On irc everyone is attractive and smart (just don't ask for a .jpg).[98]

Beyond the masking of physical appearance, this mode of communication was also a boon to people who have other difficulties creating social relationships or are not very verbal. <elusive> claimed that her group had "become a special family. . . and we all stick together." When I asked her how can people be a "family" if they've never met, she replied, "You can become closer to people here than in real life. . . because there are no color. . . no racial things. . . just souls talking. . . without fear."

Should We Celebrate or Mourn This Activity?

People who distrust new technology or fear change, and those with little or no first-hand knowledge of the Internet tend to see individuals involved in the new culture as alienated, psychologically abnormal, or social misfits escaping into their computers and the Internet, instead of cultivating real-world social ties. In the view of others, the Internet "causes" alienation and harms mental health and social well-being, rather than involvement on the Internet being a response to pre-existing conditions.[99]

While a small proportion of the players may fit one or more of these descriptions, no simple generalization fits the channels. Creating, viewing and playing IRC art are potentially no less constructive and satisfying a way to spend time and enrich one's life than gardening, making a quilt, or playing bridge or chamber music. Many forms of leisure activity are time-consuming and offer an intense, "flow" experience not unlike that experienced by the players. In part the novelty of this activity is what leads observers to find it peculiar, unhealthy, even threatening. And many earlier forms of leisure are potentially as isolating as sitting before a computer, e.g., doing needlepoint alone at home instead of visiting with friends.

In this chapter I have for the most part celebrated the art of these groups and the ingenuity of the players in mobilizing quite limited resources and using them in remarkably creative, adaptive, enjoyable ways. Although by the time this book went to press, *rainbow* had long overtaken *colors* in popularity, <elusive> made an important contribution – to both channels – in initiating a framework both for the art itself and for the mode of social interaction surrounding it.[100]

On balance, I think we should congratulate the players on their success in adapting in rapid, organized fashion to the affordances and constraints of a new medium, to create a form of artistic activity that offered great pleasure and may also have met profound human needs. As a cultural phenomenon their activities offered this potential. To what extent they actually contributed to the well-being of individual players is a matter that is beyond the scope of this research.[101]

Notes

1. This research also falls under the rubric of visual anthropology and its agenda, "to analyze the properties of visual systems. . . and the conditions of their interpretation and to relate the particular systems to the complexities of the social and political processes of which they are a part" (Banks and Morphy 1997: 2). I also draw on earlier research on aesthetics and material culture – studies of play and aesthetics in collecting (Danet and Katriel 1989; 1994) and of the quasi-magical function of decoration of gas mask kits by Israelis during the Gulf War (Danet et al. 1993).

2. See, e.g., Boas (1955 [1927]); Otten (1971); Layton (1981); Coote and Shelton (1992); Eban, et al. (1990); Washburn (1983a; 1983b); Washburn and Crowe (1988). A recent reconceptualization of the field is Marcus and Myers (1995). One exception is Brian Moeran's (1997) book on a community of Japanese folk-art potters.

3. For example, Jones (1975; 1987); Pocius (1979); Briggs (1980); Bronner (1984); Babcock (1986); Babcock et al. (1986); Vlach and Bronner (1992). Glassie (1989).

4. The players speak of "playing a file," something like playing an audio or video tape.

5. See the discussion of intellectual property in Chapter 8. It is common for players to modify ASCII art images in some way e.g., to color them for display on IRC. This is considered entirely legitimate, especially if credit for the original image is given. Among needlepoint practitioners this is also considered legitimate: the American Needlepoint Guild includes among its prizes several for adaptations of designs created by others; see its Website, URL http://www.needlepoint.org/.

6. This program was created by Ole D. Nielsen.

7. See, for example, Castleman (1982); Cooper and Chalfant (1984); Chalfant and Prigoff (1987); Stewart (1987).

8. See http://www.palacetools.com/home.php3.

9. See Vzones.com, http://www.avaterra.com.

10. Microsoft chat offered the option of either text or comics mode; it integrated with either mIRC or pIRCh, the other version of IRC which can employ color (see footnote 58). Microsoft gave up the name "Comic Chat" because it gave too much priority to the comics option. See the Microsoft Chat Home Page, http://www. microsoft.com/ie/chat.

11. Microsoft also offered a dynamic, three-dimensional version of chat, called "V-Chat."

12. The analogy is most apt in connection with album quilts or friendship quilts. For instance, among the Amish in Pennsylvania, "Quilt patches are distributed to friends of the recipient . . . Each patch is signed by its maker in embroidery stitching . . . Finished blocks are then assembled and quilted, often at a quilting where many of the patchmakers are present. The finished quilt is then given to their mutual friend" (Pellman and Pellman 1984: 106). But even the quilting of ordinary quilts has an important social aspect. While patches may be prepared individually, their assembly and especially the final quilting process (sewing the top layer, filling, and bottom layer or lining together) are often done in groups. This is what is usually meant by a quilting bee. The AIDs quilt is a contemporary variation on this traditional practice.

13. Just as I speak of a "palette" of symbols, needlepoint practitioners speak of a "palette of stitches." See the American Needlepoint Guild Website, URL in footnote 5. At first the players called their art ASCII art too (as in "mIRC ASCII art"). However, eventually, they dropped this expression to refer to their own art, preferring instead to call it "color art," to differentiate it from the earlier art, even though hundreds of ASCII art images have been adapted for use in the channels. In this book I prefer the expression "IRC art," since the term "color art" would be too general for readers.

14. I have not disguised the names of the channels. The existence of Websites for the channels on the World Wide Web indicates that the players wished to be known, though not by their real names. I have also retained original nicks (nicknames in IRC parlance) of players, with channel managers' permission generally, and which are, I believe, sufficient disguise of personal identities. No email addresses of players are

provided. To preserve the ethnographic flavor of images played online, I show each image in the illustrations together with the nicks of the person who played it and the recipient. These cannot be erased without modifying the very phenomena I wish to study.

15. Registered channels earned recognition as a stable locus of interaction on an IRC network. This distinguishes them from "fly-by-night" ones, which can be created temporarily at any time.

16. These are the same colors as are available in, e.g., Microsoft *Word for Windows*. Khaled Mardam-Bey created the mIRC program. For further information on mIRC, see URL http://www.mirc.co.uk.

17. The players also occasionally used color to mark or highlight short sections of text. While this can be done on the fly, the images analyzed here are far too large and complex to be produced on the fly.

18. Following IRC practice, I render nicks just as they appear online, in angle brackets, and without a capital letter at the beginning, if that is how they are regularly presented.

19. The *rainbow* website is at http://www.mirc-rainbow.com/. The *colors* Website was located at http://www.mirc-colors.com/. In December 2000 <elusive> removed it, a probable indication that activities of this group had ceased.

20. When I met <patches> in person in January 1998, she was a housewife and a former professional musician. She later found work for a while with an Internet service provider. She also had other responsibilities for the group. She collated and edited collections of files to be distributed to players for use in the channel at holiday times, and often organized art shows and celebrations such as channel anniversaries.

21. Another screen capture of this type was shown in Plate 1.19, Chapter 1.

22. Personal email, November 1997. .

23. See the discussion of hobbies of the players in the section "Who Are the Players?" and the section on "The Geometric Basis of Images," as well as McCullough (1996).

24. "DCC" is a feature of the IRC program that enables synchronous transfer of files, while logged onto a channel.

25. "Playing a file" is the players' expression for performing or displaying an image. The connotation is something like "playing a tune." See also footnote 4.

26. Regulars acquire and store hundreds and even thousands of files. This requires considerable organizational skill, since once must be able to find and play a given file, or at least type of file, at a moment's notice.

27. These are so-called "extended ASCII" characters, which are not included in the standard set used on the Internet. See the section "Play with Typography: Extended ASCII Characters," below.

28. Generally, images grew larger over the period of the research, made possible by advances in the technology. The illustrations for this chapter were mainly documented in 1997 and 1998.

29. See the Cuddly Collection of ASCII Art, www.geocities.com/Paris/LeftBank/3839/ascii.html.

30. This image was originally created by Joan Stark, and adapted for *rainbow* by <diedra>. Many IRC players download Stark's images and color them for display in the channels. She herself does not participate on IRC.

31. Stark did not design this image specifically for this Website. She had designed it as a motif for a sports newsletter at the request of a group of men, and had no idea how it made its way to the channel or the Website (personal email, 8 November 1997).

32. Both images contain bilateral symmetry; see the discussion of bilateral symmetry and its appeal, below.

33. See Babcock (1986); Babcock et al. (1986); Glassie (1989: 45–49).

34. Online chat with <elusive> on ICQ, 17 December 1997.

35. In practice ops are often equated with regulars. Many people aspire to become an op in order to become a member of the "in" group.

36. I asked <patches> who she considers to be a regular. In personal email on 24 August 1999, she wrote that newcomers who come to the channel just about every day for a month can be viewed as "regulars."

37. These numbers were observed on 28 August 1999.

38. For instance Joan Stark, famous on the Net for her ASCII art (see Chapter 5), was listed as a "friend," though she never participated in the channel. She was a friend only in the sense that many players admired her art, and downloaded her images. The Website also listed Khaled Mardam-Bey, creator of the mIRC program as a "friend," though he too never participated. I also knew of several other individuals who had long left the channel but who were still listed, or who participated in both channels but were far more active on *rainbow*.

39. Personal email from <patches>, 24 August 1999.

40. This was probably true on *colors* too.

41. This was slightly less than appeared on the Website on that date, indicating that ops listings were also not entirely up to date.

42. This information was useful for assessing how many were involved, but not for ascertaining who they were.

43. As I explain below, most participants were American, though there was a smattering of people from other countries.

44. We had little choice in the matter except to make do with what was available. In some cases, the information sounded so naïve as to make deception unlikely – one person gave his height and weight.

45. For 1999 we did not tabulate information on players from other countries. I have put the 1997 data on *colors* in brackets because data were available for such a small number of persons.

46. The data for 1993 come from the *Encarta Encyclopedia* (Microsoft 2000).

47. The group did include a physician, a concert pianist, a retired vice-president of a marketing research company, two accountants, a psychiatric nurse with a Ph.D. and a few undergraduate and graduate students in academic fields. But these were exceptions to the general pattern.

48. See Chapter 4.

49. See Danet and Katriel (1989) for a discussion of stamp collecting and a photograph of individuals of all ages trading stamps in the Madrid weekly stamp market.

50. See, e.g., Hilberg (1997), a book of computer-generated designs for patchwork quilts.

51. A few people on *colors* besides <elusive> also engaged in crafts.

52. Technically, images may be viewed as long as we remain in the mIRC program, even if we get disconnected. It is this fact that enabled us to capture so many images.

53. This is only a hint at how coding is done. For detailed explanations of coding, see the channel Websites and other links supplied by them.

54. There were times when these procedures proved inadequate. Sometimes a response to an image occurred only a screen or two later, making it difficult to reconstruct that the two were related. Nevertheless, we managed to document some important interactional phenomena. Only videotape could preserve the entire flow of events.

55. At first we captured many images in each session, but after three to four months we drastically reduced the amount of material saved because there were diminishing returns in saving so many.

56. While at the Smithsonian on sabbatical in Washington D.C., I traveled to northern Virginia to meet <patches>, in January 1998. I met <elusive> and <shortshot> in Portland, Oregon in October 1998.

57. Joan Stark usually signs her creations with her initials, "jgs." Those using her images on IRC do not always leave her initials in place, as she requests.

58. There are other software programs besides mIRC which enable the use of color; the main rival is pIRCh. For resources on pIRCh, see, for instance, Koach's Workshop, http://koach.com; Ariadne's Complete pIRCh Help, http://www.geocities.com/Silicon Valley/6895/index.html.

59. Some may object to the neologism "colorized." "Colored" means merely "having color," whereas "colorized" was introduced to refer to the recent phenomenon of transforming formerly black and white films into color.

60. It did require some skill to learn to play images, and certainly to create one's own. Old-timers on the channels extended a great deal of help to newcomers in this respect.

61. To the best of my understanding, this is fairly similar to ANSI art, but the "blocks" which one can color are apparently different in ANSI. See the discussion of ANSI art in Chapter 5.

62. Reproducing or modifying the work of others has a long history even in fine art. In various forms, copying has been a recognized form of artistic activity, e.g., Byzantine icons. I am indebted to Walter Cahn for this point.

63. In the last four months of the exhibit alone, 250,000 people visited it, an extraordinary number for a small country. The curator attributed the success of the exhibit to the exuberant color of the paintings as well as to their quality. In Hebrew the exhibit was called *Shixron Tsvaim*, "Color Intoxication," or more loosely, "Drunk with Color" (Gillerman 1998). See also the exhibition catalog (Rachum 1998).

64. At the least, complexities of the phenomenon prevent simple generalizations.

65. There are several methods for inserting these symbols, despite their absence on the English keyboard. With the NumLock key on, one can type Alt, and then use the numeric keypad to type 0 plus the three-digit code of the symbol; one can insert the symbol via the menu in a word-processor, or, one can learn a variety of tricks to insert large numbers of these symbols in files, e.g., by using the Popedit program or its later version, Popeplayer. One can type a whole line of a symbol, then copy and paste it over and over.

66. This citation is from the joint Website of the Textile Museum and the Math Forum at Swarthmore College. It offers an excellent, refreshingly non-technical exposition of pattern and symmetry, both in general and in relation to Oriental carpets. See http://forum.swarthmore.edu/geometry/rugs/.

67. This definition is from the Website of the American Needlepoint Guild, URL in footnote 5.

68. Another difference between this art and needlepoint, less relevant in the present context, is that in needlepoint, stitches cross units in the grid, while in the present case "stitches" fill units in the grid.

69. <elusive> told me that the castle image on the *colors* Website took her three days to create. The program called "Popedit," and the later, more sophisticated version of it, Popeplayer, made creating images much faster and more efficient, since it enables players to preview the image as they go along. It is also very easy to insert extended ASCII characters with this program.

70. I have no reason to believe that more than a minority fell into the category of escapist compensation. See the discussion at the end of the chapter.

71. This discussion of the notion of *gestalt* extends a briefer presentation in Chapter 5. See Kohler (1929); Koffka (1935); Arnheim (1954); Kreitler and Kreitler (1972), chap. 4.

72. This list of strategies is adapted from previous research on the pursuit of closure in collecting. As forms of aesthetic activity, collecting and interactive ASCII art share some features. See Danet and Katriel (1989).

73. Cf. Danet and Katriel (1989).

74. See Boas (1955 [1927]); Stevens (1984); Gombrich (1984); Hargittai and Hargittai (1994); Washburn (1983a); Washburn and Crowe (1988); Paine (1990). The preference for symmetry is not universal, however. Traditional Japanese art and culture showed a strong preference for asymmetry and irregularity (Keene 1995). In an exhibit called "Ikat: Splendid Silks of Central Asia" that toured the United States in 1997-98, next to the one textile in which the pattern was symmetrical there was a note explaining that this textile had been modified for Western tastes (Fitzgibbon 1997)!

75. These definitions come from the *Random House College Dictionary*.

76. This quotation is from the Textile Museum/Math Forum Website, URL in footnote 66.

77. Formal analysis of types of symmetry becomes far more technical than readers of this book need to know. See Stevens (1984); Hargittai and Hargittai (1994); Washburn and Crowe (1988), and the Website of the Textile Museum/Math Forum, URL in footnote 66.

78. As readers will note, many other illustrations in this chapter also contain mirror symmetry.

79. See the discussion of "Filling the Space" below.

80. Or by a border; see the next section.

81. I am grateful to Ken Friedman for calling this point to my attention.

82. See also the citations from Jackson (1997) and Amir (1977), above.

83. Images such as this, consisting of a pictorial element in the center, a filled dark field and an elaborate border, also remind me of Haitian Vodou flags. Typically worked in brilliantly colored sequins and beads on satin, velvet or rayon, these flags are powerful ritual objects meant to invoke Vodou deities. For examples, see Polk (1997); Galerie Macondo, Voodoo Flags, http://artshaitian.lm.com/Pages/flags.html; American Museum of Natural History, "Sacred Arts of Haitian Vodou," www.amnh. org/exhibitions/vodou/.

84. This person was an entomologist with a Ph.D., a high-ranking official in the World Health Organization, and a man of some sophistication.

85. Of course whether or not the background is filled may also be a function of the player's skills.

86. A special genre of files is original poems whose text is colorized, usually with ASCII and extended ASCII decorations. Over a period of months, <MikeChat> displayed many such poems.

87. In practice, the little worlds on these channels were not quite so idyllic as this sounds. The split from *colors* which led to the creation of *rainbow* is one example. But conflict and real-world troubles infiltrated in other ways too; see the Discussion below.

88. This transformation is a 20th-century phenomenon, resulting from the convergence of developments in the toy industry in Europe and the United States with Teddy Roosevelt's bear-hunting experiences at the beginning of the 20th century. In the 19th century bears were portrayed more realistically. See King (1997); Schoonmaker (1999); Brown (1997); and "Teddy Bears on the Net," http://tbonnet.com/.

89. See, e.g., a 15th-century French tapestry called "The Offering of the Heart," in Ring (1949, Figure 11), in which a young courtier presents a lady with a tiny, symmetrical red heart. There is a color version of this painting on the back of the paper cover of Michael Camille (1998), *The Medieval Art of Love*. Walter Cahn led me to this example. Liungman (1991: 231) claims that this symbol was already known in ancient Greece.

90. For a sample of "plain" ASCII cows, see Figure 5.26, Chapter 5.

91. For the voluminous literature on kitsch, see, e.g., Greenberg (1939), reprinted many times; Dorfles (1969); Broch (1969); Moles (1971); Barth (1974); Calinescu (1977); Friedlander (1984); Kulka (1996); Solomon (1991); Morreall and Loy (1989); Crick (1983); Kundera (1984); and Salmagundi (1990). Whereas these writers generally refer to manufactured objects of popular culture, I am writing about do-it-yourself cultural products, so claims about commodification are not relevant.

92. This is a much bigger issue than I can deal with here. As Glassie (1989: 129) points out, full-fledged folk art blossoms in religious societies, whereas IRC art must be seen as largely secular.

93. Memorandum from <texxy>, 28 December 1997.

94. Memorandum from <texxy>, 28 December 1997. Crash.wav is a sound file of something crashing.

95. Memorandum from <texxy>, 28 December 1997.

96. There was also, no doubt, a fair amount of private exchange of messages online, invisible to others.

97. Memorandum from <texxy>, 21 December 1997.

98. Memorandum from <texxy>, 28 December 1997.

99. This is the position taken by Kraut and colleagues (1998), in their controversial study of the effects of Internet use on a Pittsburgh neighborhood. A later survey by Norman Nie and Lutz Erbring found that the more time people spent online, the less time they spent with real-life human beings (O'Toole 2000). Research by Barry Wellman and his colleagues and by the UCLA Center for Communication Policy contests these negative views. See Wellman (1999; in press) and http://www.ccp.ucla.edu/ucla-internet-report.asp.

100. <patches> acknowledged the important contribution made by <elusive> in email to me, 13 October 2000.

101. I am distinguishing here between the cultural level of analysis and that of clinical diagnosis. As a sociologist and communication scholar, it is not my business to diagnose who on the channels was "normal" and who was not.

7

"There's More to Life than Times New Roman!" Font Frenzy

We come now to the last case study in this book, digital typefaces or fonts and the preoccupations of ordinary people with them. These preoccupations were well epitomized by a slogan on a Website called "Fontopolis"[1] in late December 1998: "There's More to Life Than Times New Roman!" Times New Roman (henceforth TNR) is the default font, or set of typographic characters, in Microsoft Windows 95 and 98, many word-processors, and Web browsers – the one that is pre-selected for use when one installs the software or boots up the computer. We will see that there was astonishing hostility toward this typeface among digital type enthusiasts.

By late 1998, interest in fonts among people without formal training in graphic design or typography had become so extensive that it was no exaggeration to call it "font frenzy." I coined this term well before encountering a Website with this very title. The manager of "Font Frenzy" declared, "Hello my name is Susie, and I'm a Fontaholic!" (Figure 7.1).[2] I wrote to Susie, a housewife and mother of three, to ask why she was so enthusiastic about fonts. This is what she said:

```
Oh becuuuuuzzzz!!!! lol The power of fonts is incredible! I
mean, they can change the whole look/atmosphere of a document,
or a web site, or a flyer/brochure. . . anything they touch is
instantly transformed! Think about, for example, what wedding
invitations would look like if the only font available was
Arial or New Times Roman!! YUCK!!! ROFL³
```

289

Susie was a member of a group called "Fonts Anon~," vocalized as "Fonts Anonymous" (Figure 7.2), a gathering place for font enthusiasts playfully based on the idea of Alcoholics Anonymous.[4]

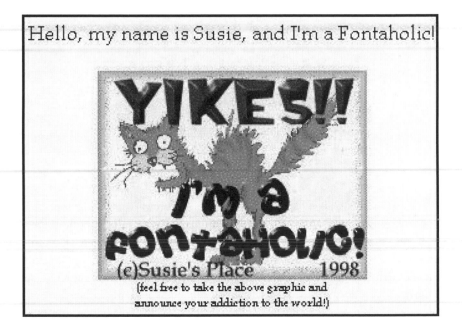

Figure 7.1. Susie, a fontaholic.

Figure 7.2. The logo of "Fonts Anon~," http://www.fontsanon.com/.

Consider also some comments by Tom Murphy, a student of computer science at Carnegie-Mellon University who designed fonts as a hobby, and displayed them on his charming, playful Website, "Divide by Zero"[5] (Figure 7.3):

The simultaneous. . . artfulness and utility of fonts intrigues
me. A font can be an aesthetic thing on its own. . . the shapes
of the letters can be a picture, tell a story. At the same
time, people can take a font and use it in ways that I never
intended, adding to its story or totally revising it. I love
that since they're digital, people can copy and share my fonts
without any cost to me. [italics added].[6]

Figure 7.3. "Divide by Zero," Tom Murphy's font Website.

An important indication of burgeoning interest in fonts was an index called "True Type Resource" (Figure 7.4). Initially started by Jami Reed because he wanted to learn HTML,[7] the index soon mushroomed. In mid-December 1998, it listed over 1,300 links organized into three main categories, freeware and shareware collections of fonts, sites displaying individuals' original font designs, and commercial organizations – "foundries" run by professional designers and distributors of others' fonts.[8] The first two categories are of primary interest here. In mid-December 1998, this index listed 354 Websites displaying personal font collections and almost the same number in which creators of fonts displayed their wares. By August 1999 the number of sites indexed had grown to over 1600, and the various categories had grown accordingly too.[9]

This chapter asks: how did it happen that lay people began to take an interest in typographic matters that were formerly the domain of professionals? In what ways did this interest differ from that of professionals, and what forms did it take? What aspects of computers and the Internet promoted this preoccupation among lay persons? Was there evidence that font frenzy had become part of popular culture? How did it challenge professional norms and practices?

Since computers became widespread, many people use the terms "font" and "typeface" interchangeably, much to the chagrin of design and typography professionals. Strictly speaking, they are not synonyms. Actually, it is helpful to distinguish between not two, but four different terms. "Typeface" refers to the stylistic features by which a character's design is recognized, hence the

Figure 7.4. The True Type Resource Index.

word "face." It is the most widely used term in the history of typography. "Character" refers to the smallest component of written language that has semantic value, to the abstract idea, rather than a specific shape – that is, to the idea of an "a" rather than a particular shape of an "a." "Glyph" pertains to "the actual shape... of a character image." For example, an italic "a" and a roman "a" are two different glyphs representing the same underlying character. Finally, narrowly defined, a "font" is

> a particular collection of characters of a typeface with unique parameters. . . . The word "font" or "fount" is derived from the word "foundry," where, originally, type was cast. It has come to mean the vehicle which holds the typeface character collection. A font can be metal, photographic film, or electronic media. (Walsh 1992–96) [10]

According to traditional terminology, each size of a typeface is a different font, strictly speaking. In the case of metal type, this is literally so – the letters of each size are a separate set of physical objects.

Typefaces come in "families." To this day, all the members of each typeface "family" share a distinctive style. [11] Thus, in Figure 7.5 we see nine different versions of a traditional typeface called Frutiger. [12] The basic version is simply "Frutiger." There are light as well as bold, and even "ultra black" variations; three are italic. We can see that this list does not exhaust all the possibilities,

292

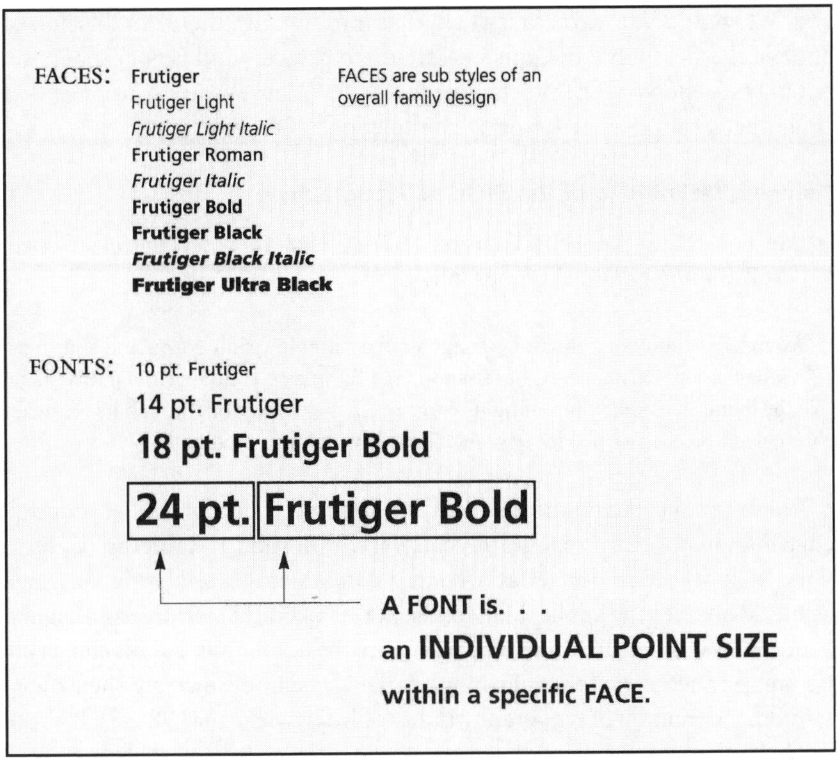

FACES: Frutiger   FACES are sub styles of an
        Frutiger Light   overall family design
        Frutiger Light Italic
        Frutiger Roman
        Frutiger Italic
        Frutiger Bold
        Frutiger Black
        Frutiger Black Italic
        Frutiger Ultra Black

FONTS: 10 pt. Frutiger

        14 pt. Frutiger

        18 pt. Frutiger Bold

        24 pt. Frutiger Bold

                    ↑   ↑
                    └──────┴──────── **A FONT is. . .**

        an **INDIVIDUAL POINT SIZE**

        within a specific **FACE**.

Figure 7.5. The Frutiger font family.

and that a font family can be quite large. Moreover, variation in the size of the typeface can create very different effects.

Despite inevitable objections of typographic and design professionals, I shall use the term "font," since lay people involved with computers widely use it. Perhaps professional typographers and graphic artists will increasingly recognize that the distinction is becoming obsolete. One design professional reluctantly acknowledged that "in the digital era, perhaps there is some ground for calling [typefaces] fonts, inasmuch as most of them are both a typeface and a font simply because there is only one version of the design."[13]

A Capsule History of Typography

To put the phenomenon of font frenzy into historical and cultural context, we need to review briefly the field of typography up until the events to be described here. We should be aware, first of all, that traditionally, there is a division of labor in the field: type designers create the typefaces, and typographers set text in type, choosing the typeface or faces they believe to appropriate either for aesthetic purposes or for practical functions of a given text.

Changing Definitions of the Field of Typography

As late as 1992, in the second edition of *The Elements of Typographic Style*, Robert Bringhurst defined typography as

> the craft of endowing human language with a durable visible form, and thus with an independent existence. Its heartwood is calligraphy – the dance, on a tiny stage, of the living, speaking hand – and its roots reach into living soil, though its branches may be hung each year with new machines. (Bringhurst 1996: 11)

While even the most radical approach to digital typography must acknowledge that, historically, typography has important roots in calligraphy, durability is obviously no longer an essential component of rendering language visible. Moreover, the applicability of the notion of craft to writing is changing, in an era in which ordinary people with fairly basic computer skills can easily use fancy or eccentric fonts in sophisticated ways, or even create their own.

Another definition of typography is that of Ruari McLean (1980: 8): "'Typography' is the art, or skill, of designing communication by means of the printed word." Although McLean's definition is the older of the two, it is potentially more flexible. By changing just one word, and perhaps adding another, we can bring it up to date and read it as encompassing the activities of ordinary people, online and offline:

> Typography is the art, or skill of designing communication by means of the visible, inscribed word.

My preferred definition is that of Matthew Woolman,

> TYPOGRAPHY is the art and technique of creating and composing type in order to convey a message. The term TYPE includes the design and function of alphabetic and analphabetic symbols to represent language.(Woolman 1997) [14]

Professional classifications of typefaces tend to be rather difficult to assimilate for lay persons. They often use inconsistent, unsystematic or non-transparent nomenclature. Categories point sometimes to historical context or origins, sometimes to aesthetic/visual aspects, sometimes to technology or mode of construction. For the purposes of this chapter, only two main distinctions are important, I believe – that between text and display typefaces, and between typefaces with and without serifs.[15] Display typefaces are typically used in large sizes and are meant to catch the eye, as in advertising. Text typefaces are those used in large amounts of text, and are supposed to be readable and legible, that is, to be "transparent," rather than calling attention to themselves.[16]

Figure 7.6 makes clear the difference between a serif and a sans serif typeface. Times New Roman, or TNR, as I have been calling it, has little extender feet. For instance, the letters "T","I" and "m " in the word "Times" all have little horizontal lines at the bottom. In the other typeface, Arial, there are no such extender feet.

TIMES NEW ROMAN   This is a serif typeface.

ARIAL   This is a sans serif typeface.

Figure 7.6. Times New Roman and Arial: serif versus sans serif typefaces.

The goldsmith Johannes Gutenberg is often credited with the invention of printing in the mid-15th century, but strictly speaking, it was invented in China circa 1040 AD.[17] The contribution of Gutenberg and his colleagues was the invention of cast-metal, movable types for individual letters of the alphabet.[18] Individual types were little metal objects, "rectangular castings from molten lead [each] with the shape of a letter protruding from its top" (Olmert 1992: 141). Rows of letters were arranged in matrices, and then pressed onto paper, each type leaving the imprint of the letter on the paper. Types were kept in separate cases for small letters and for large ones, hence our distinction between upper and lower case. Arranging the types to prepare a page for printing was a tedious task, but once it was done, many copies could be produced very quickly, thereby speeding up book production enormously, compared to the painstaking pace of scribal culture.

The earliest typefaces imitated scribal lettering styles, and are usually called "Blackletter."[19] In these typefaces, letters have thick shapes and distinctive diamond-shaped serifs, made originally with a broad calligraphic pen.[20] Such typefaces were developed in France, Italy and England, as well as Germany. Another variant, "Fraktur," was still used in German texts in the mid-20th century. As printing spread over the Continent, especially southward and to England, "roman" or "Humanist" types came to supercede "Blackletter," in many cases. These typefaces have upright classical letters with serifs, and graduated thick and thin strokes (Lee 1965: 80). Roman upper case "is based on Roman imperial inscriptions," whereas "lower case is a legacy of the Holy Roman Empire, the pagan empire's Christianized successor" (Bringhurst 1996: 124), and comes from manuscript typefaces. Both are often called "humanist" in typographic circles.[21]

> Like Roman inscriptional capitals, Renaissance roman lowercase letters have a modulated stroke (the width varies with direction) and a humanist axis. This means that the letters have the form produced by a broadnib pen held in the right hand in a comfortable and relaxed writing position. (Bringhurst 1996: 123)

As Johanna Drucker has pointed out, "It took nearly a century and a half before the designers of text fonts used in printing conceptualized their designs independently of the manuscript tradition" (Drucker 1995: 162).

An important trend in the history of typography is the effort to rationalize the design of letters.[22] Renaissance theorists including Geoffrey Tory and Albrecht Dürer tried to develop systematic principles for constructing letters. Again in the 18th century rational considerations predominated. Perhaps the most outstanding instance of rationalization in that period was "Romain du Roi" (the "King's Roman," designed for Louis XIV). Each letter was constructed "on a mathematical basis. Each letter was drawn on a square containing 2,304 small squares, an odd anticipation of digitized letter forms" (McLean 1980: 60).

The Bauhaus and New Rationalist Approaches

In the first half of the 20th century there was again a revival of interest in rationalist approaches to typographic design. The trend had started in the 1920s European art world, with El Lissitzky of the Constructivist movement and Herbert Bayer, Josef Albers, and Jan Tschichold of the Bauhaus, the influential German design movement (1919–33). Although typography was not originally a high priority on the agenda of the Bauhaus (Erlich 1991; Gottschall 1989), in time members of the movement became heavily involved in teaching and design regarding typography. Tschichold's 1928 book *The New Typography* (Tschichold 1998 [1928]) called for major reform: texts should be in all lower case, laid out asymmetrically on the page. He and others sought a new design climate after World War I, and rebelled against the nationalistic associations of typefaces in use in Germany and Austria, and the decorativeness that had flourished in some 19th-century and early 20th-century typefaces.[23] Although Tschichold later repudiated too strict conformity with some of his principles, Bauhaus functionalism had a major influence on later 20th-century typography and design.

One of the most distinctive contributions of Bauhaus typography, which remains important to this day, was sans serif typefaces. The first such typeface had actually been designed in England in 1816, but sans serif began to come into its own in the early 20th century when a new typeface was designed for the London Underground (McLean 1980: 64). However, it was the Bauhaus movement that gave real impetus to the design and use of such typefaces. Typefaces with serifs are usually considered more legible for continuous, extended text than typefaces without them (McLean 1980: 42).[24] Bayer also advocated use of all lower case, in titles as well as text. He and Albers aspired to create all the necessary letters, symbols and numbers from a small number of basic shapes (Lupton and Miller 1996: 58). Thus, in his design, the letters "b," "d," "p" and "q" were all the same, flipped either vertically or horizontally or both. Similarly, "h" and "y," "m" and "w," and "n" and "u" were identical pairs. Although fanatic preference for sans serif typefaces eventually dissipated, the demand for them continued. In 1957 two influential sans serif typefaces were created in Switzerland, "Univers" by Adrian Frutiger and Helvetica by Edouard Hoffman. Both are still widely used today, though not all professionals are enthusiastic about them.[25]

"Script" typefaces imitate handwriting, as the name implies. Many of them are cursive, with letters designed to flow together in partially connected fashion. We are familiar with them in formal contexts, such as wedding invitations. "Manual" typefaces having a free, spontaneous look resemble lettering with a brush or pen and are usually not suitable for text setting; they are mainly used in advertising.

The Role of Technology[26]

Technologies for the inscription of written text have undergone many major changes since the 15th century. Until the late 19th century, printing remained bound to the tedious procedures of hot metal. Each little letter had to be cast by hand. The first major improvement came with the invention of the pantograph, a punch-cutting machine, in 1884, and of the Linotype and Monotype machines for typesetting, in 1886 and 1894, respectively. The punch-cutter eliminated the need to cast every letter separately. Although using slightly different technologies, the Linotype and Monotype machines allowed for much faster setting of lines of text than had been possible before.

The next major breakthrough was photocomposition, which caught on in the 1950s. Typeface masters for composition were stored on film, and characters were projected onto photo-sensitive paper. These devices were driven by punched paper teletype tapes used to keyboard the text. Writing as late as 1980, Ruari McLean (1980: 82) called this technology "a revolution... still in progress."

The digital revolution profoundly transformed type design and typography yet again. To begin with, a process that had always been grounded in the physical world now involved only the manipulation of pixels on a computer screen. Even though today's digital fonts often look like the typefaces we have known in the past, we (laypeople as well as professionals) can manipulate them with unprecedented ease. The number of fonts and font families prolife-rated tremendously, and typographers have an enormous, even overwhelming choice at their disposal. Even amateurs can now change fonts or font size with just a click of the mouse, altering the look of a word, a heading, or an entire text, combining in the same text as many different ones as we like, and so on. Such a dizzying choice invites chaos, and at the least, challenges old norms and ways.

The Macintosh computer played a pivotal role in these developments. In the mid-1980s a graphic artist named Zuzana Licko, a Slovakian immigrant to the United States who was to become one of the central figures in *Émigré*, a leading graphic design company and publisher of *Émigré* magazine, experi-mented with the digital design of low-resolution[27] typefaces on the Macintosh (Figure 7.7). Licko and her husband and partner Rudy VanderLans later recalled:

> This was a breakthrough of some sort. Although it has always been possible to design and draw a typeface, the actual typesetting equipment one needs to set type freely is cumbersome and highly specialized equipment, usually owned and operated by typesetters and typefoundries. The Macintosh allowed you to store the data that defines the typeface and then access it through the keyboard. Now, for the first time, it was possible for any individual to design and draw a typeface and then use it without restrictions. (VanderLans and Licko 1993: 18)

The effect was revolutionary.

Fonts for the World's Languages

One of the largely unsung accomplishments of the computer revolution was the development of digital fonts for the world's languages, enabling speakers and writers of even the most exotic languages to enjoy the benefits of word-processing. In some instances, the traditional symbol set of a language was digitized, e.g., Inuit or ancient Egyptian hieroglyphics. In others, the spoken language is rendered in Roman characters. Non-alphabetic languages such as Chinese and Japanese, with their thousands of ideographs, pose special dilemmas with respect to computerization. As of December 1998, World Wide Fonts offered commercial fonts for 350 languages, generally, for both the Macintosh and Windows.[28] While some sites were commercial, others were

Figure 7.7. Digital typeface designs on the Macintosh by Zuzana Licko, 1985.

non-profit, e.g., the Yamada Language Center Font Archive at the University of Oregon,[29] where linguists could download fonts for unusual languages without charge. The utilitarian message of these sites was: "You need to be able to write in language X; we have the font you need." The utilitarian aspect of fonts is not relevant to this chapter, and I shall not discuss it further.

Playfulness in Postmodern Typography

As a result of the transition to digitization, playfulness became a distinctive feature of typography among professionals in the postmodern period. To a large extent, they were influenced by the same cultural trends and technological developments as the rest of us, and many wrote about it. In a book called *American TYPEPLAY* (Heller and Anderson 1994), Steven Heller, Senior Art Director at the New York Times and editor of AIGI Journal of Graphic Design, wrote,"The personal computer has become a canvas on which type has become the equivalent of paint. Digitization has made it possible for the tutored and untutored to play at will, indeed create art with letterforms" (Heller and Anderson 1994: 12). Another designer noted that professionals "use[d] type as if letterforms were dominoes or tiddly winks as if lines of copy were pipe cleaners or pickup sticks. They use[d] type playfully, joyously, exuberantly, with utter abandon" (Jacobs 1994: 150). Similarly, in a study of wit in graphic design called *A Smile in the Mind*, Beryl McAlhone and David Stuart observed, "For designers with expertise in typography and identity, the alphabet is a playground" (McAlhone and Stuart 1998: 80). If professionals could play, the rest of us could play too, and so we did.

A Smorgasbord of Fonts

People involved with computers and the Internet were exposed to fonts everywhere, both offline and online. First of all, computers fresh out of the box came with many fonts. The Windows 95 operating system included all the fonts listed in Figure 7.8.[30] The number of options was quite large, and the variation in font style considerable. The first four fonts were called "core" fonts by Microsoft because they could also be used on the World Wide Web. Courier New was designed as a typewriter face for IBM, and was eventually redesigned specially for the IBM Selectric. Arial was created by Robin Nicholas and Patricia Saunders and was marketed by the Monotype Corporation, one of the leading players in the world of typography. The sans serif font, Comic Sans MS, of a freer, more expressive nature, was specially created as a digital font by Microsoft, designed by Vincent Connare.[31] To these four basic fonts, Windows 95 Plus! added five others, of varying styles. This list does not include sets of ornaments – what typographers call "dingbats"[32] – or the variants of these fonts that are bold, italic, etc. With just a little effort one could install many more typefaces of various kinds.

People who were used to typewriters in the past might never have paid attention to the variety of fonts available, or realized that one could add to those already installed, unless, perhaps, they had had experience with the IBM "Selectric," which became widely used in offices in the 1960s, but was too expensive, I believe, for most homes to own one. The interchangeable "golf balls" of the IBM Selectric typewriter did offer a preview of the freedom to change typefaces that was to come with computers.[33]

There were many ways in which users added fonts to their computers, sometimes knowingly, sometimes unknowingly. One major source was software installed on one's computer. I am not referring to packages for professionals such as Adobe Acrobat or Quark Express, but rather to those aimed at the mass market of ordinary users. For instance, printers came with software that included additional fonts. Software for the creation of greeting cards and related ephemera such as banners and posters, and programs for home design of business cards all offered many fonts too, which might be installed auto-

Font*	Sample	Source
Arial**	Font Frenzy	©The Monotype Corp., plc.
Courier New**	Font Frenzy	©The Monotype Corp., plc.
Times New Roman**	Font Frenzy	©The Monotype Corp., plc.
Comic Sans MS**	Font Frenzy	©Microsoft Corp., 1995
Abadi MT Condensed Light	Font Frenzy	©The Monotype Corp., plc, 1992-94.
Book Antiqua	Font Frenzy	
Calisto MT	Font Frenzy	©The Monotype Corp., plc.
COPPERPLATE GOTHIC BOLD	FONT FRENZY	©URW Software & Type, GmbH
Lucida Handwriting Italic	Font Frenzy	©Bigelow & Holmes, Inc., 1991

Figure 7.8. The basic font set in Microsoft Windows 95.

matically or not. Thus, a program called "CreataCard Plus!" by American Greetings and Micrografx included 19 choices among 14 fonts.

A major source of fonts was specialty CD-ROM collections. These are not the expensive collections for professionals, such as Bitstream's CD-ROM of 500 fonts, which cost nearly $70 in January 1999, but rather, collections meant for a mass audience. A company called Expert Software[34] issued five CDs, entitled "2000 Fantastic Fonts," "Fonts CD!," "Funky Fonts," "Handwriting Fonts," and "Kids Fonts." They were sold in American computer stores such as Egghead, Staples, Office Depot, CompUSA and Computer City. They were generally inexpensive, costing $10 or $15 for hundreds or even thousands of fonts each, though they could be poorly assembled and sometimes offered too many look-alike fonts (moreover, certain fonts suspiciously resembled fonts designed by others). Advertising for these CDs invited people to have fun, to express some aspect of their personality, to impress others, etc.

A related trend was collections of handwriting fonts. These are not digital versions of scripts which have become codified over the centuries since medieval

Font	Sample
Calligraph421 BT	Font Frenzy
Lucida Calligraphy	Font Frenzy
Brush Script MT	Font Frenzy
Commercial Script BT	Font Frenzyy
Formal436BT	Font Frenzy
Mercurius Script MT	Font Frenzy
Signet Roundhand	Font Frenzy
Freehand591 BT	Font Frenzy
French Script MS	Font Frenzy
Park Avenue BT	Font Frenzy

Figure 7.9. Calligraphy and script fonts.

times, such as the formal script we associate with wedding invitations, or calligraphic fonts intended to look like the hand-work of professional calligraphers (Figure 7.9). Unlike the latter two, idealized categories, these are fonts which look like, or are even based on the handwriting of real, specific, 20th-century individuals.[35] Thus, two companies, ClickArt and SoftKey, marketed collections of these fonts.[36] Among the thousands of freeware and shareware fonts offered on the Web were many handwriting-like fonts (Figure 7.10).

One of the most striking developments was the availability of very easy-to-use programs to enhance fonts graphically, to stylize them in the manner of professional display fonts, as used in advertising. Thus, Expert Software marketed a program called "3-D Font Creator" to transform any two-dimensional font into a three-dimensional one." One could "shine" light on the font or apply custom colors and patterns, e.g., to make it look as if it is made of marble or wood. A compact little program to stylize short texts was "Bitstream

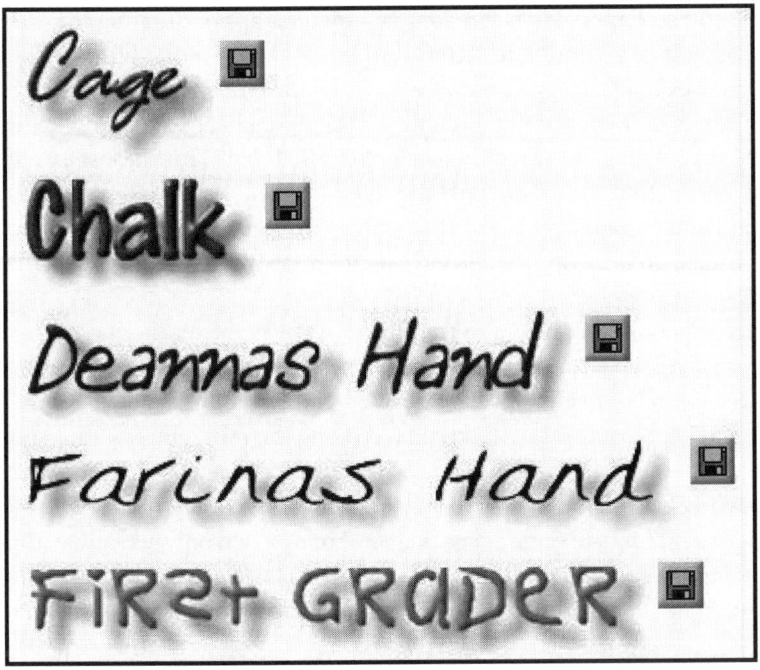

Figure 7.10. Handwriting fonts. "The Fonts Zone," http://www.geocities.com/fontszone/.

Mini-Makeup," in which the text could be displayed and colored in any of 40 different shapes. In seconds, one could add an outline, choose different types of fills, and vary a second color to be used in the fill, introduce any of eight shadow effects, rotate one's creation, and change its size, height and width.

In a program called "My Type Artist" by My Software, Inc. one could effortlessly introduce even more elaborate effects. There were 40 screens of options, each containing 25 different "looks." One entered the text to be stylized at the top, chose one of the "looks," and clicked. Instantly, one saw how the text would look with that choice. Styles available included "classic," "gothic," and "modern," and invited attention to "pattern," "effect," and "texture." This was a very inexpensive (only $20), extremely easy-to-use program. One could save one's creations, export them to other programs, and incorporate them in Websites.

A Word Art utility also came with Microsoft Word 97. In Plate 7.1 three different effects of stylizing the expression "FONT FRENZY" via Word Art are displayed, using three different fonts on my computer. In the first I chose an Art-Nouveau-like font called Yesternight, and gave it a three-dimensional, double spiral shape, which spread it in a manner approximating the arc of a circle or cylinder, colored the letters purple, and added a thin black border. In the second example, I used Glowworm, a font with a rounded, three-dimensional effect, colored the text red, and added a shadow effect seemingly "behind" the text to enhance the three-dimensional look. Finally, for the last example I chose Sci-Fi Oblique, a font with an italic-like slant,[37] colored the text green and added a secondary bluish effect which also makes the text look slightly three-dimensional, with the virtual "light" at a different angle from that in the second example.[38]

Another fascinating trend in the late 1990s was the marketing of fonts in museum shops. Here the appeal was to a better educated audience, and quite a different kind of product was marketed – fonts as a fine art form, or at least an applied art form of quality design. Among the museums where I spotted these fonts were the Metropolitan Museum of Art in New York and the Wadsworth Atheneum in Hartford, Connecticut. A company called P22 Type Foundry sold fonts in separate packages of one or two only, usually with a set of ornaments suitable for use with that font.[39] The cover of their 1998 print catalog is shown in Figure 7.11. In an old-fashioned-looking font, the text read,

Computer Fonts & Other Fine Things.

Turning to the first page, we learned:

> We are dedicated to producing quality art and computer-related products. Our goal is to revive historical materials and present them in a contemporary, relevant form. By doing so, we make great art and design accessible to every level of computer user.
>
> We work closely with museums and foundations toward the development of historically and aesthetically accurate products. Each font set is uniquely packaged with background information on its source and inspiration. (P22 Type Foundry, 1998: 3)

Many P22 fonts were associated with particular art movements – Constructivism, De Stil, the Bauhaus – or with specific artists, such as Cézanne, Leonardo da Vinci, Rodin, Michaelangelo. Fonts came in 6" square boxes attractively decorated with appropriate motifs. Even diskette labels were appropriately stylized.

One font (Figure 7.12) came in two versions, Acropolis Then and Acropolis Now (a clever pun on *Apocalypse Now*).[40] Acropolis Then was a digitized version of ancient Greek stone carving characters, and Acropolis Now was a modern version suitable for writing in English. Strictly speaking, the "old" version was superfluous. The average purchaser of this font was not likely to

Figure 7.11. Cover of the P22 Type Foundry 1998 catalog.

Figure 7.12. Acropolis Now, a font by the P22 Type Foundry.

know ancient Greek or to need the font. People were to enjoy looking at it for fun, aesthetic pleasure, as well as edification.

The short texts accompanying the image of each font box were not just advertising copy to promote sales. They gave buyers and potential buyers short lessons in the history of typography and of art more generally. The presentation of some fonts in this catalog also made claims to authenticity, even to a "pedigree." A "Bauhaus" font was accompanied by the following statement:

> The font set includes three type faces designed by Herbert Bayer, including the famous "Universal" font most commonly associated with the Bauhaus school . . . This set is authorized by the Herbert Bayer Estate. (P22 Type Foundry, 1998: 26)

Similarly, the explanation for an Albers-style font concluded, "This set was produced in conjunction with the Guggenheim Museum and the Josef and Anni Albers Foundation" (P22 Foundry, 1998: 27).[41] In contrast, inexpensive commercial CD-ROMs told consumers little about what types of fonts were included, who created them, what their historical origins were, etc.[42]

"Let's Smash the Crystal Goblet:" an Expressive Approach to Fonts

The logos of dozens of amateur font sites were carnivalesque or celebratory in nature. Both verbally and graphically, they proclaimed, "Fonts are fun!" "Fonts are wonderful!"[43] The logos in Plate 7.2 play with the "f" in the word "fonts," naming their Websites "Font Freak," "Free Font Fiesta," "Font Frenzy," and so on.[44] Another example was "Fred's Font Funhouse," included in the introduction (Figure 1.20). Note also the exuberant wordplay in expressions like "Fontalicious Zone," "Fontazm," "Fontrageous," and "Fontomania" (Plate 7.3). By December 1998 there were ten Webrings of font Websites, and the logos of several of them were similarly ecstatic. Another colorful expression of love of fonts was "The Friday Nite Type Fights." Every Friday, the manager of True Type Resource put up a list of six or more fonts and invited visitors to choose the one they liked. The allusion was, of course, to boxing.

Hostility to Times New Roman

There was vociferous hostility to Times New Roman, the typeface I mentioned at the beginning of this chapter. TNR was created in England for the London Times in 1931 (Bringhurst 1996: 97).[45] It was called Times New Roman to contrast with Times Old Roman, an earlier typeface. Its upright, straight lines and serifs hark back to lettering in ancient Roman stone inscriptions; at the same time it was meant to be "modern" and, at least according to some accounts, readable as well. One book called it "the most successful typeface of all time" (Klein et al. 1991: 172). It became a standard 20th-century typeface for use in extended printed text of all kinds, including books, magazines, reports and even advertising,[46] although it is actually best suited to narrow newspaper columns, since it is quite condensed.[47] A sample text in this typeface (Figure 7.13) is typically unremarkable. We almost don't see the graphic shape of the letters, so used are we to seeing "through" them to the meaning.

A particularly striking sign of keen interest in fonts was vociferous hostility to Times New Roman, the typeface I mentioned at the beginning of this chapter. TNR was created in England for the London Times in 1931 (Bringhurst 1996: 97). It was called Times New Roman to contrast with Times Old Roman, an earlier typeface.

Figure 7.13. A sample text in Times New Roman.

Many amateur font designers parodied or defaced TNR, Tom Murphy of Divide by Zero among them. Among his designs was Tom's New Roman (Figure 7.14), a verbal as well as visual play on Times New Roman. Asked why he disliked this font, he replied:

```
There are a number of common fonts which the internet type
community is generally sick of. TNR is a popular one to pick
on, since it's the default font in most word processors and web
browsers, and resembles most of the printed text that people
read daily. I see the careless use of TNR as a way of implicitly
saying that the way one's text looks is unimportant; ignoring
form in favor of content. . .   I've had people tell me that
they've permanently replaced their TNR with my "upgraded" Tom's
New Roman.[48]
```

Similarly, Jeff Wrench, owner of an alternative fonts Website, created a font he called Cannibal Times, "made of the dismembered remains of TNR:"[49]

```
If I dislike anything about TNR, it's just that it is so common.
. . . . It has become transparent. When a document is set in TNR
nobody notices the font at all. . . . I just don't see it as
"interesting". TNR's ubiquity, however, is what made it my
choice to deconstruct for the Cannibal Times typeface. Its
recognisability meant that it would be fairly obvious that
```

Figure 7.14. Fonts by Tom Murphy.

Cannibal Times was in fact constructed from the cut-up parts of another typeface, and not just made from arbitrary shapes or drawn from scratch. In fitting with the "cannibal" idea, my font is supposed to look rough, sharp, fierce. It is something of a "Frankenstein" font; pieces are joined unnaturally and things stick out in odd places.[50]

Ironically, both Murphy and Wrench decried TNR for being the very thing it was supposed to be!

Similarly, Peter Langdon, owner of the Website with the slogan "There's more to life than Times New Roman," told me,

```
I just wanted to say that there are many, many different and
better fonts than TNR. I find it plain, boring and ugly . I
know a lot of people who run font sites feel the same. I have
come across some people who like it because technically, it is
excellent. I don't like it on an aesthetic basis. [italics
added].51
```

Because TNR was the default font in operating systems, a new user could simply use it unthinkingly for all writing purposes without ever becoming aware of other available options. People who learned to keyboard on a typewriter were especially likely to fit this pattern. Younger people who learned to keyboard directly on a computer were likely to be aware of these possibilities and to make use of them.

On the Fonts Anon~ Website I encountered a tongue-in-cheek document called "Fontaholicism A–Z," abridged in Figure 7.15. The entries for the letters "*B*" and "*I*" are variations of the aversion to TNR. Another highlight of Fonts Anon~ was "Times New Roman Nevermore!," a delightful parody of Edgar Allen Poe's famous poem, *The Raven*. Clicking on an image of a raven, one reached the poem itself. Here are its first three stanzas:

> fingers cramping, shoulders weary,
> knowing dawn was soon upon me,
> chocolate wrappers strewn about my floor. . .
>
> Heart a-pounding, mouse poised ready,
> seeking one last site, the feeling. . . heady,
> browser window opens "Kyl's Medieval"52
> I pause to stretch my fingers sore.
>
> A-humming dirge-like tunes,
> bleary eyes perusing Runes,
> my *intent to look and not to store* [italics added],
> Only this and nothing more. . .

The key phrase is "intent to look and not to store" – fontaholics could not resist downloading fonts. There *are* objective limits to how many fonts one can store on one's computer. The limit in Windows 95 was 1000 fonts.53

You:*

(A)re extremely proud that you own the fonts for all the languages from all the Star Trek shows, Babylon 5, and more, even though you will probably never use them (unless you are giving it to a fellow fontaholic).

(B)ored with Times New Roman. . . .

(C)annot abide the default font in any word processor.

(D)ownloaded so many fonts that when you go to a pretty elementary site, you look at their small font collection and say "Got that, got that, got that. . ."

(E)nable other fontaholics by supplying them with font files and URLs if for no other reason than to enjoy their reaction.

(F)eel compelled to spend hours upon hours typing up and printing an alphabetized 'catalogue' dedicated to all the fonts and dingbats collected so far.

(G)et headaches searching for fonts, but you don't care.

(H)ave never actually *purchased* a font. (spoils the 'thrill of the hunt')

(I)gnore web sites that use Times New Roman.

(J)ump, skip, leap, hop, spring, bounce, bound or vault when you find a new font that you THINK you've not seen before.

(K)neel before saying names like Gill, Goudy or Zapf; especially in the presence of fonts.

(L)ust after just a peek at fellow fontaholics C:\windows\fonts folder.

(M)ind wanders to 'www.font.com' during serious conversations with your spouse.

(N)ever pass up a good font URL or the chance to share it with fellow fontaholics.

(O)ffer blood donations for copy of fonts folder.

(P)rovide downloadable font from your webpage so visitors will be able to view with your chosen font/s.

(Q)uit denying your addiction to fonts.

(R)egret having to delete old fonts to try new ones. (Windows only holds 500 fonts at any given time. . . . *sniff*)

(S)nicker over those poor souls that use those plain fonts on their web pages.

(T)ried to get type tatoo but couldn't commit to one font.

(U)nderestimate the power of your font addiction.

(V)iew intricate and detailed dingbats at magnification large enough to fit your screen.

(W)atching TV, you name fonts that you see in commercials and TV titles.

(X)erosis (dry eyeballs) is considered a normal part of life, and not a result of staring at a screen for hours and hours. . . and hours.

(Y)ell "I LOVE FONTS!' from the nearest rooftop.

(Z)ipup those fonts you're not using and save them in another directory for later use.

*Compiled from Fonts Anon~, http://www.fontsanon.com/.

Figure 7.15. Fontaholicism, A–Z.

I also asked the members of Fonts Anon~ about their attitudes toward TNR.[54] A man nicknamed Studio_Bob, a middle-aged nurse who designs fonts on the side, posted this reply to the Website's messageboard:

> I have nothing against TNR. If used appropriately, it can be a very nice font . . . it's overused to abuse. It's not the nicest font in the world . . .
>
> I . . .like Goudy Old Style better. It has an elegance in the serifs and points which puts TNR to shame. It looks nicer in almost every instance, and looks appropriate in almost any circumstance . . .
>
> I have maybe 50 serif fonts which are as legible and produce a more interesting result.[55]

Whereas the objections of all the people I have cited thus far were largely aesthetic, a female graphic artist nicknamed JMR related primarily to the cultural connotations of TNR:

> TNR brings to mind things dry, and somber. . . institutional cornerstones; dry quotations meant to somehow inspire and chasten; banks, Wall Street, and agents of the erudite elite . . . it lacks a certain bohemian aesthetic . . .
>
> TNR is . . .symbolic of the attempted constraints imposed by the superego, i.e. government and religious institutions, and therefore is to be rejected. It smacks of a Puritanical, as well as a bureaucratic ethic.[56]

This woman's reactions show that at least some people are able to articulate the cultural baggage of TNR as somehow symbolizing the weight of the Roman empire, or of Establishment institutions, to this day.

Actually, TNR was not the only object of such feelings. I already hinted at the hostility of some professionals to Univers and Helvetica, the Swiss type-faces.[57] At a site called "Victory Type," another famous typeface, "Bauhaus," and its designers were twice parodied, as "bauhand" and as "badhaus".[58] There is great irony in this parody too, since, as we saw, this very typeface was intended to streamline graphic design, to make it fresh and contemporary. In part then, preferences in typefaces are a matter of fashion.

Down with the Crystal Goblet

One of the most cited texts in typographic circles is a passage from an essay in Beatrice Warde's *The Crystal Goblet*:

> You have two goblets before you. One is of solid gold, wrought in the most exquisite patterns. The other is of crystal-clear glass, thin as a bubble, and as transparent. . . [an] amateur of fine vintages. . . will choose the crystal, because everything about it is calculated to reveal rather than to hide the beautiful thing which it was meant to

contain. . . . the virtues of the perfect wine glass also have a parallel in typography. (Warde 1956; cited in Lupton (1996: 55)

Warde was a British typographer and writer, and the director of publications at the Monotype Corporation, to this day one of the leading international typography companies. A slightly different rendering of Warde's concept of the transparent prose text was that of the Dutch typographer Gerard Unger, who spoke of a "disappearing act:"

> [when you read] the black printed letters dissolve in your mind like an effervescent pill in a glass of water. For a short moment, all those black signs disappear off the stage, change their outfits, and return as ideas, as representations, and sometimes even as real images. (Unger 1994: 112–113)

We can see now that hostility to TNR was a rejection of this traditional position so long cherished among typographic professionals, albeit a rejection by amateurs who didn't necessarily have to face the challenge of designing readable texts.[59] Indeed, a good deal of material presented in this chapter suggests that font fans didn't care about readability at all; they just loved the shapes of the letters.

Plate 7.4 gives some indication of the tremendous range of font styles available online for free or for very little money. The multi-colored display enhances the stylistic differences among them. Some, like Bloody, Acidic, and the ominous Nixon, convey notions of horror, fear, or destruction. Others, like Floralies, Shampoo and Paperclip, are charmingly playful.[60] There are also examples of two other styles that I will discuss below, "grunge" and Sci-Fi fonts. Another expression of enthusiasm for fonts was the practice of displaying or listing the "Top Ten" or "Top Twenty," i.e., the ten most popular fonts during any given time period, as measured by the number of persons downloading them.

Amateur Classifications

Not surprisingly, lay people usually classified fonts quite differently from professional typographers or graphic designers. Some sites didn't engage in classification at all, as indicated by the metaphors they used – a "library" or an "archive" of fonts. In many such cases fonts were simply alphabetized. Some combined alphabetization with substantive classification. Sites that appeared to emphasize quantity or all-inclusiveness over qualitative distinctions were better characterized as engaging in accumulation, rather than collecting with its fine discriminations.[61]

At a Website called "Font Empire" (Figure 7.16) categories included "Funky," "Gothic/Horror" and "Futuristic," pointing to preoccupations of youth culture. In general, the terms "funky" and "cool" were very often used in connection with fonts.[62] "Fonts@Fontasaurus" had six categories: ethnic, funky, grunge, "happy campers," medieval, and picture fonts. "Happy Campers" were fonts the person found to be amusing or to create a good mood. In picture fonts (Figure 7.17) individual letters were made of pictorial images, e.g., letters made of dance steps or typewriter keys. All these examples show that exuberant graphic shapes and the cultural associations of typefaces were of far more interest to collectors than staid, sober text fonts. They liked fonts "with attitude!"

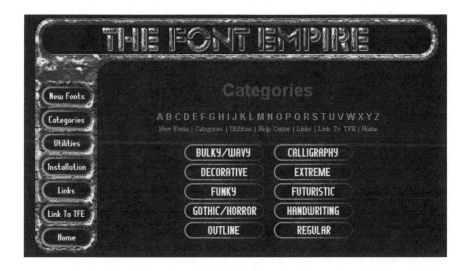

Figure 7.16. Font categories at the "Font Empire."

Collecting and Displaying Fonts

By downloading free or shareware fonts, one could create a collection of hundreds or thousands with little or no expense. Typically, fonts were stored as small zipped files that one could quickly download and install. One could aspire, in theory at least, to have all of them, or to have the biggest collection on the Web. Moreover, those who were willing to spend money could invest in the commercial sources I surveyed above, CD-ROMs and other font packages.

While very large collections required classifying fonts in some way, even if only in alphabetical order, smaller collections could be displayed online individually. Collectors invested much effort in creating handsome graphic displays. Instead of just displaying the name of the font in plain black and white,

Figure 7.17. A selection of "picture" fonts.

often they colored font names displayed in large sizes, created 3-D, shadow or other effects for them, encased them in attractive colored frames, and organized displays of multiple fonts in a pleasing manner, as in Plate 7.4. In this they were no different from collectors of dolls or antique milk bottles who enjoy arranging them in a studied manner on shelves.

While most online font collections and archives were, as far as I could tell, managed by males, reflecting the state of the Internet at the time, there were also striking sites managed by women. Thus, on "Fontain of Youth" (Plate 7.5) a woman nicknamed "Katgyrl" celebrated and displayed her font collection.[63] A note told visitors:

> My personal mission is to move all cybercitizens away from the ordinary & into the unusual & artistic. Whether it's for posting in newsgroups or sending e-mail to creating presentations for school or career, fonts are a great way of getting your

Figure 7.18. Film fonts, "Astro Grrl."

point & personality across. Well . . . ok, so basically I have a font collecting obsession & I decided to unleash it on an unsuspecting public ;-) have fun . . . !

A portion of the display at the Website of another female collector, "Astro Grrl," is shown in Figure 7.18.[64]

Some collectors specialized in particular types of fonts. Thus, at "Kyl's Medieval and Fantasy Fonts" categories were historical, foreign, runic, science fiction and fantasy.[65]

Designing Fonts

Figure 7.19 shows that even a thirteen-year-old could design and display attractive fonts. This English boy, Giles Edkins, tells us of "Anger," his very first font:

> This is the first font that I designed on the computer. It's spiky, to make it look really angry. "I am angry, annoyed, furious and generally a bit peeved." My Mum said this and I put it here because it sounds nice. Anger looks good from about 24 point upwards.[66]

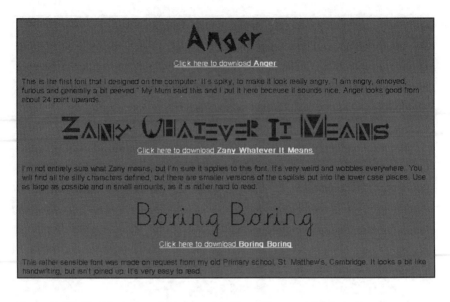

Figure 7.19. First fonts by a thirteen-year-old.

The other two fonts he designed are "Zany Whatever It Means" and "Boring Boring." Notice his use of the professional term "24 point," which refers to size, and his comments about the relative legibility of the other two fonts. Thus, teenagers were moving in on the professional type designer's "turf."

A fellow called Todd Dever whose userid is "fontdude" started "Cool Fonts Online" in 1995 (Figure 7.20). Although he had had some art classes in college,[67] he was not trained as a professional graphic artist or typographer. The title of his site immediately establishes his expressive approach.

Everything about his fonts, the manner of their presentation, and the Website design reflected a counter-cultural, even subversive approach. Note the rather "eaten-away" shapes of the fonts, their provocative names, the slang used in their descriptions, and the intentional misspelling of "scribbler." A short biography on his Website informed us that he worked in video production and played occasionally in two popular music groups. In December 1998, he offered a CD-ROM of 19 of his fonts for sale at $150. Unlike many other "guerilla designers" – to borrow an expression of Steven Heller and Anne Fink (Heller and Fink 1997) in a book called *Faces on the Edge: Type in the Digital Age*[68] – who remain part of the alternative sub-culture, Dever was eventually coopted by mainstream professionals. Two software packages by Macromedia include fonts designed by him.[69]

Tom Murphy's site, "Divide by Zero," communicated a more child-like, whimsical approach. Unlike Dever, he gave his fonts away for free. His crea-

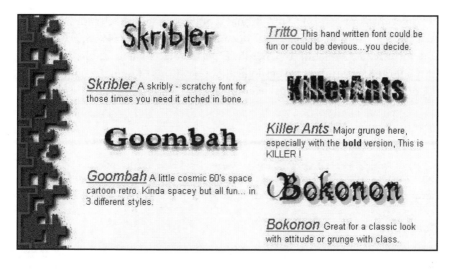

Figure 7.20. "Cool Fonts Online." Fonts by Todd Dever.

tions had names like Boring Boron, Valium, Tetanus, and Action Jackson. Playfulness was also evident in his Website logo (Figure 7.3). When I asked why he had chosen the expression "Divide by Zero," he replied,

> I wanted something that sounded sort of computery and futuristic, but more importantly, something that had the sense of breaking rules. Just as one doesn't traditionally divide by zero, I often attempt with my fonts to violate traditional type paradigms. And because it's an independent foundry and I'm just doing it for fun, I don't have to feel like I owe anybody a font that looks normal or "right"; I can divide by zero if I want. Sometimes when you reinvent the wheel, you come up with roller skates![70]

His logo also contained three of his "Tombats," small cartoon-like ornaments he designed, in this case, three whimsical faces.[71] Look again now at Murphy's creations, along with his comments about them (Figure 7.3). His scruffy-looking Prefix was meant to have a "Sci-fi" look. Germs reconstructed a style of lettering he liked to do as a kid: "each of the letters is made into a monster with sharp ravenous teeth and a glaring eye." These letters look only "mock-scary," however. Ransom is his personal version of a Ransom typeface, and mixes at least 20 different typefaces. Like Dever, Murphy too was involved in the world of popular music. He had his own band.

Sometimes opposition to traditional typography was much more extreme. At a Website called "Guerilla Type" documented in December 1998, its welcome statement read, "Welcome to Guerilla Type, the place where hundreds of years of typographical studies, psychological observations of human cognition and legibility mean less than dogs' excrement."[72]

Font Themes

Let us now have a closer look at some of the favorite categories of fonts that people collected, displayed and designed.

Cool Fonts, Funky Fonts

Again and again, I encountered the expressions "cool" fonts and "funky" fonts. We saw that Todd Dever called his site "Cool Fonts Online." One of the CD-ROMs by Expert Software contained only "Funky Fonts." A female collector called her site "Mo's Funky Fonts."[73] What did these terms mean in relation to fonts?

The origins of both terms lie in the history of jazz and its African and Black-American roots. During the 1920s jazz was dominated by "hot jazz," the brassy style of Louis Armstrong, played in stuffy, smoke-filled rooms in New Orleans. In the 1930s a different style, slow and smooth, letting in a "breath of cool, fresh air" and associated with the name of Miles Davis, became popular, and was called "cool."

According to the volume *Black Slang: A Dictionary of Afro-American Talk* (Major 1970) "cool" is

> anything favorably regarded; "cool Jazz" – style of Jazz associated with musical developments on the West Coast, usually mellow and restrained, sometimes referred to as intellectual music. A "progressive" type of Jazz which replaced the "hot Jazz" that went out of fashion. The term cool originated in Jazz, but has subsequently been used by beatniks, hippies and teenagers. (Major 1970: 40)

Actually, the term had even earlier African roots, and was assimilated into Afro-American culture to refer to self-control, being in control (Thompson 1966; 1973). In contemporary teenage culture, to be cool is not only to be in control, but also to be attractive (Danesi 1994, Chapter 2).[74] "Cool" fonts, then, are fonts that are attractive, that draw attention to themselves. By extension, cool fonts are in some way unusual, non-standard, even subversive and anti-Establishment.

In the 60s and 70s when black rhythm and blues music…was all the rage….everyone loved the soulful sound of black pop music. Something termed ' "funky" had a very cool rhythm, dance like. . . sexual. . . irresistible. You couldn't help but feel like moving and being happy when listening to that kind of music. . . .One very popular dance of the early 70s was called "the Funky Chicken" from which the term likely originated.

From the innocent hippie generation,. . . flower power, free love and drug experimentations of the 60s to the somewhat wisened age of disco in the 80s. . . this term "funky" continued to develop in it's [sic] meaning. . . Funky means cool. . . A tune with a good dance beat is funky". . . .Anything different, funny, a little shocking, freeing of the spirit, especially in terms of personal humor. . . is FUNKY.

When speaking of fonts. . . the meaning becomes even more clear. *Curly serifs are "funky." Distressed typewriter fonts can be "funky." Anything mixed up, messed up, humorous or in any way unexpected . . . . is "funky." Like all Fontaholics out there, font creators strive toward the expression of individuality. If,* in a font, some unique twist which has never been seen before creates an effect that the first time viewer of the typeface [likes, he or she] says HEY! . . . (heh heh!). . . THAT'S A FUNKY FONT. [italics added] [75]

Figure 7.21. Comments by Absinth of Fonts Anon~ about funky fonts.

I asked Absinth, the manager of Fonts Anon~ in the fall of 1998, what makes fonts funky. Her insightful comments are reproduced nearly in their entirety in Figure 7.21.

The most important clue to how the concept of "funky" evolved and how it came to be applied to fonts is the notion of "off-beat." In ordinary parlance, we understand "off-beat" to mean "unusual," "surprising," and so on. Literally, "off-beat" means just that – syncopated rhythms. Matthew Brown (1994: 484) pointed out that the off-beat is the central musicological feature of funk, a musical style drawing on African rhythm patterns which was developed in the mid to late 1960s by James Brown and the JBs, a twelve-piece group based in Georgia. In short, it seems that fonts are likely to be perceived as funky if they are non-geometric, non-linear or otherwise irregular in form, are "curvaceous," do not sit stolidly on the line, and if they are non-standard in terms of customary usage. To what extent "cool" and "funky" are perceived as synonymous in relation to fonts must await further research.

Fonts classed as funky at the "Font Empire" (Figure 7.22) all had special effects of one kind or another, thus calling attention to themselves, though the last one, with its white-on-black outline shape and conventional serifs, could easily have been dismissed as "square," in my opinion. At "Mo's Funky Fonts" "funky" font names were linguistically as well as graphically playful. HippoCritic plays with the multiple verbal resonances of "hippopotamus," "hypocritical, " and "Hippocratic," as in "Hippocratic oath." Also, Hippocritic has plump, playfully decorative elements and contours vaguely reminding us of a hippopotamus. Rhoda Dendron turns the name of a flowering shrub, "rhododendron," into a girl's name. Moreover, none of her funky fonts sit squarely and consistently on the line – the letters "dance around," or jump up and down.

Figure 7.22. Funky fonts from the "Font Empire."

Horror, the Grotesque

It is not surprising that among the lay categories often appearing on font collectors' Websites was one for "horror," "Gothic," or "medieval" fonts. I already mentioned "Kyl's Medieval and Fantasy Fonts." Beginning with "Dungeons and Dragons," computer game enthusiasts have long had a predilection for things medieval and Gothic. Inevitably, we encounter "bloody" or "dripping" fonts, and fonts with names like Dracula and Drippy Paint. Sometimes horror fonts were tongue-in-cheek, like the ones in Figure 7.23. A Halloween font featured cute pumpkins and ghosts entwined in the letters and numbers. The "tombstone" fonts in Figure 7.24, called Graveyard, Headstone, and Tombstone, respectively, all enable one to type text on virtual tombstones, each letter having its very own tombstone.

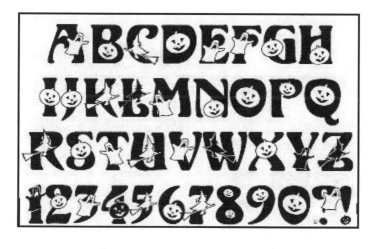

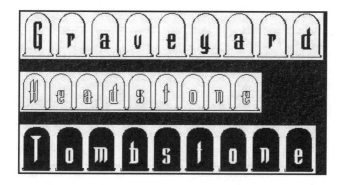

Figure 7.23. Mock horror fonts at "Fonts for Freaks," http://www.gothic.net/~tygre.

Kids' Fonts

Predictably, there were fonts that looked like, or really were representations of the writing of children. Expert Software issued an entire CD-ROM just on this theme. P22 Type Foundry, the purveyor of fine art fonts, promoted both Child's Play Regular, based on the handwriting of a real child, and Child's Play Blocks, traditional printed capital letters on bouncing blocks, as in the name of the font. Among font collectors online, Susie's Place featured Kids' Fonts prominently (Figure 7.24).

Figure 7.24. Kids' fonts at "Susie's Place".

Fantasy and Sci-Fi Fonts

Even font clearinghouses with a primarily instrumental orientation revealed a bit of playfulness. Thus, at the bottom of its list of offerings, the Font Archive at the University of Oregon, added, "And for your amusement . . . Klingon, Morse code, Romulan, and Tolkien."[76] Many more, clearly expressive font sites had offerings relating to fictitious realms or science fiction contexts too, e.g., those in Figure 7.25. "Quake" is, of course, the name of an immensely popular computer game. All of these fonts are derived from the logo of the original product to which they refer, the various Star Trek series, the films *Terminator* and *Tron*, etc.

Figure 7.25. Sci-Fi fonts at "Acid Fonts," http://members.xoom.com/scifi.htm.

Vintage Typewriter Fonts

Many free or shareware sites offered fonts that looked like the typewriter typefaces some of us remember from the 1950s-1970s. Thus, at "Old Typewriter Fonts" (Figure 7.26) fonts often look a bit washed out, to simulate the effect of a worn-out typewriter ribbon. Some are "straight" imitations of the typefaces of particular typewriters, others are parodies, like Royal Pain.

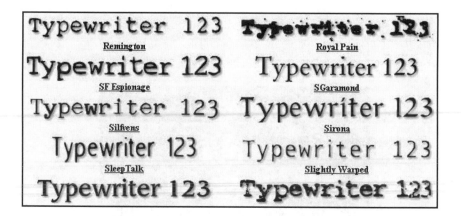

Figure 7.26. Typewriter fonts at "Old Typewriter Fonts," http://oldtype.8m.com/font4.htm.

Steven Heller and Gail Anderson (1994) noted that in the early history of the typewriter, pica and elite serif typefaces defined the look of business communication for over a century. Typewiter type was associated with personal or business writing, while other typefaces were the province of professional designers and printers. But typewriter type carried many meanings and came to be used by design professionals. Modernist designers from the 1930s saw in it a naively expressive quality similar to what Macintosh typographers saw in low-resolution dot matrix typefaces in the mid-1980s (Figure 7.7). Later, professionals used typewriter type as a form of rebellion against traditional typography (Heller and Anderson 1994: 172). The appeal of such typefaces to the public in digital form in the late 1990s was once again a form of rebellion against standardization and nostalgia for earlier times.[77]

From Hacker ASCII to Hacker Fonts

As technologies change and develop, eccentricities in their use change too. At the beginning of the book I gave an example of eccentric typography from the opening portion of "The Hacker Brothers Newsletter" (Figure 1.12). This text was, for the most part, in ordinary ASCII with bizarre substitutions and spellings, and with capital letters in unexpected places. It exploited the possibilities for eccentricity then available. Thus, the expression "The elite hacker Bible" was rendered as

```
The elE3T hax0r b1Ble.
```

Along with capital letters in unexpected places, we saw substitution of "3" for an "e" in the eccentrically spelled "eleet," and of the number "1" for "i" in "Bible." The expected "ck" in hacker is replaced with "x." In Chapter 5, I showed that underground computer artists who create ASCII and ANSI works were still using these conventions in the late 1990s to constitute and demarcate their in-group culture.

With the advent of Windows, the possibilities for eccentricity increased, and hackers and others were quick to exploit them. For instance, they gave bizarre names to "scripts," short programs that could be added to mIRC, the basic version of the IRC software for Windows.[78] Here are two examples:

```
7tH §p|-|ê(r)é
«Ðä KïffëR SçRíÞt»
```

Translated into plain English, they are "Seventh Sphere" and "Da Killer Script." The first expression substitutes § for ordinary "s," and the "registered" symbol (r) for ordinary "r," etc. In the second expression the symbol for pounds sterling "£" is used instead of the ordinary letter "l," "c" with a cedilla, "ç," normally used in French and Portuguese, instead of regular "c," among others, and "Ð," pronounced "eth," an upper-case letter in Icelandic and Anglo-Saxon.[79]

As with so many practices originated by hackers, in time these eccentricities were adopted by ordinary folks, and could be sighted occasionally in typed verbal interaction on IRC. In Chapter 6 we mainly encountered use of extended ASCII characters as abstract symbols-to-design-with, in decorative patterns or in frames for ASCII "drawings." More rarely, these characters were also used for short verbal messages in images. In the IRC channels I studied, this type of eccentric typography had been domesticated; it no longer conveyed subversiveness or hostility.

Once it became possible to design one's own fonts, full-fledged hacker fonts began to appear. Thus, in Times_Hackers (Figure 7.27), a parody of TNR (creator unknown), exotic characters has been substituted in every instance for the ordinary ones of plain English prose – the $ sign is substituted for regular "s," and the symbol for pounds sterling – £ – for ordinary "l." In another font

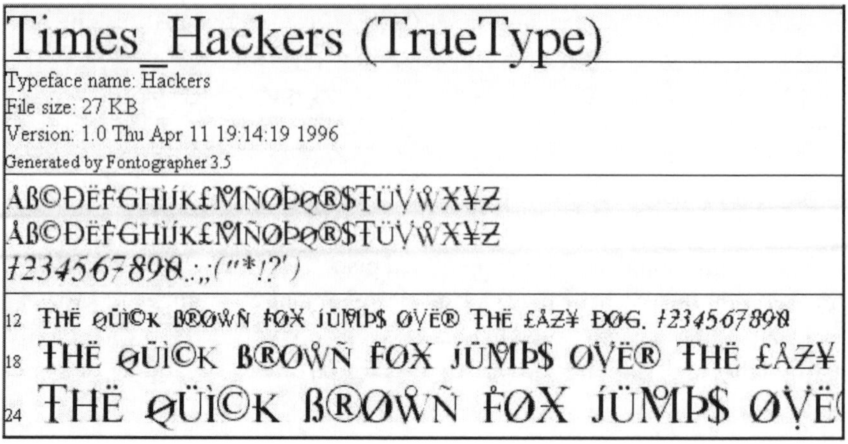

Times_Hackers (TrueType)

Typeface name: Hackers
File size: 27 KB
Version: 1.0 Thu Apr 11 19:14:19 1996
Generated by Fontographer 3.5

ΛBⒸÐËƑGHⅠJKⱢMÑØÞⓆⓇ$ƬÜⅤⱲҲ¥Ƶ
ΛBⒸÐËƑGHⅠJKⱢMÑØÞⓆⓇ$ƬÜⅤⱲҲ¥Ƶ
1234567890.:,;("*!?')

12 ƬHË �QÜⒸK BⓇØⱲÑ ƑØҲ JÜMⱣ$ ØⅤËⓇ ƬHË ⱢÅƵ¥ ÐØG. 1234567890
18 ƬHË �QÜⒸK BⓇØⱲÑ ƑØҲ JÜMⱣ$ ØⅤËⓇ ƬHË ⱢÅƵ¥
24 ƬHË �QÜⒸK BⓇØⱲÑ ƑØҲ JÜMⱣ$ ØⅤË

Figure 7.27. "Times_Hackers," a hacker font.

called "Anarchy Mono" the numeral "6" is used instead of a lowercase "b", the "@" symbol is used for the lowercase "a". Typing the "z" key produces a backwards "5 ," and so on.[80] Figure 7.28 shows what prose text in intentionally scruffy-looking Hacker Argot by andi jones looks like."[81]

"Grunge" and "Graffiti" Fonts

Of all the phenomena documented in this chapter, perhaps the most striking are "grunge" fonts. Grunge typefaces intentionally look distressed, irregular, "eaten-away."[82] Sometimes they resemble text typed with a worn-out type-writer ribbon, and may also introduce an element of randomness in the realization of letters.

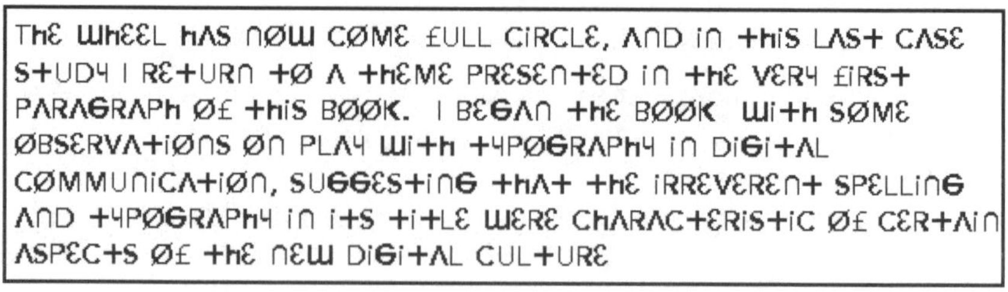

ThE WhEEL hAS nØW CØME £ULL CIRCLE, ΛnD in +hiS LAS+ CASE
S+UDY I RE+URn +Ø Λ +hEME PRESEn+ED in +hE VERY £IRS+
PARAGRAPh Ø£ +hiS BØØK. I BEGΛn +hE BØØK Wi+h SØME
ØBSERVA+iØnS Øn PLAY Wi+h +YPØGRAPhY in DiGi+AL
CØMMUniCA+iØn, SUGGES+inG +hA+ +hE iRREVEREn+ SPELLinG
ΛnD +YPØGRAPhY in i+S +i+LE WERE ChARAC+ERiS+iC Ø£ CER+Λin
ASPEC+S Ø£ +hE nEW DiGi+AL CUL+URE

Figure 7.28. A sample text in "Hacker Argot," by andijones/angelwerks/channel zero! type foundry, 1998.

Often [these fonts] look as if they have been copied on a copy machine with a low toner; the thicks-and-thins are in unconventional places; parts are missing; sometimes sans serif and serif are combined in the same character, or caps and lower case; or the strokes in the letterforms are inconsistent and awkward . . . many look as if a three-year-old drew the letters with her left hand. (Williams 1996: 9)

The names of these fonts are themselves irreverent, e.g., puckfont,[83] with its invitation to a tongue twister, 200proofmoonshine remix, and the blunt Piss Off the Professor, designed by Gregory Maronek (Figure 7.29). Except for the latter font, none is meant to resemble anyone's handwriting.

The text below Piss Off the Professor reads "Piss off your professor by using this font for extra-long reports and essays." It is barely legible, probably one of the least legible fonts discussed in this chapter. As we have seen, legibility is often a relative matter, and the legibility of individual letters may depend on the immediate context in which they are presented. To be fair, many of the fonts presented here were not intended as text fonts, in any case. But such a font is not legible in any context. Whether any student ever submitted a paper to a professor in this font is anyone's guess. But then, most likely, many of these fonts were created simply for the joy of creating and looking at them. Who actually used them and for what purpose was secondary to many designers. With our knowledge of hostility to TNR, we can also now make sense of the label Radioactive Roman in Figure 7.29, yet another attack on TNR.[84]

Contrary to what some readers may think, grunge fonts and other aspects of the grunge "look" were not introduced by amateur or guerilla designers.[85] Between 1987 and 1990 Edward Fella, an influential professional typographer

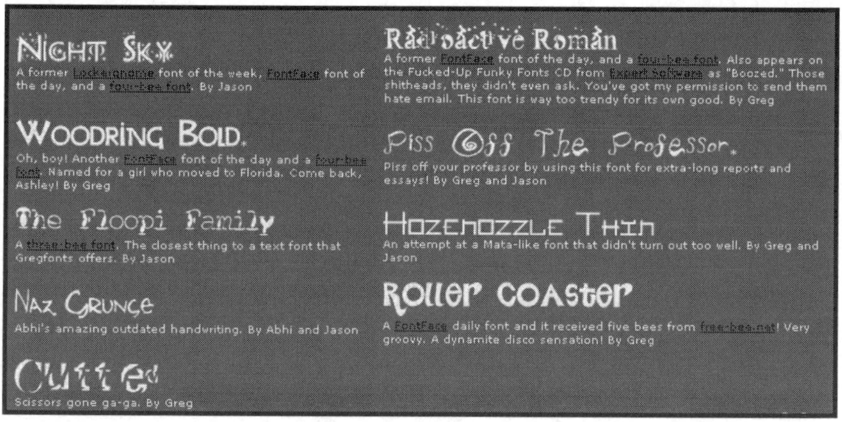

Figure 7.29. "Grunge" fonts at "Gregoryfonts."

and commercial artist, designed posters for a Detroit gallery that featured "damaged and defective forms-from third-generation photocopies to broken pieces of transfer type" (Lupton and Miller 1996: 60). Barry Deck, whose mentor was Fella at the California Institute of the Arts, designed a font called "Template Gothic" in 1990; it has since become ubiquitous (Figure 7.30). *Emigré* marketed this font with the following blurb:

> Template Gothic is Barry Deck's homage to the vernacular. "There was a sign in the laundromat where I do my laundry," Deck explains, "The sign was done with lettering templates and it was exquisite. It had obviously been done by someone who was totally naive. A few months ago, it was replaced with a plastic sign painted by a skilled sign painter. I asked them if I could have the old sign, and they gladly handed it over to me" . . . Deck was thus inspired to design a face that looked as if it had suffered the distortive ravages of photomechanical reproduction . . . Template Gothic . . . reflects Deck's interest in type that is not perfect; type that reflects more truly the imperfect language of an imperfect world, inhabited by imperfect beings.[86]

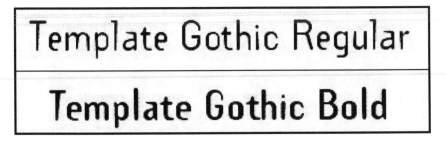

Figure 7.30. "Template Gothic," by Barry Deck, http://www.oven.com/.

In my brief discussion of postmodern typography earlier, I stressed its playful aspects. Another face of postmodernism is irony – critical detachment. Motivated by more than mere naive expressivity, Deck's typefaces invite the reader to approach the content of the message critically, in the belief that too-perfect type creates the illusion of perfection in content (Cooper 1995). Two other young professionals who became famous for grunge designs were Just van Rossum and Erik van Blokland. Their Beowulf was supposed to produce a smooth, rounded off look, but turned out irregular; moreover, it incorporates a random element: every time it is printed, "spikes" appear in different places (Spiekermann 1995).[87]

Grunge fonts bore some resemblance to graffiti scrawled on walls and subway trains. As we have seen, many of their creators were intentionally subversive of Establishment public space, offline or online, and the kinds of inscribed messages usually considered acceptable there. There were also fonts that were the digital equivalent of graffiti writing style, with names like Graffity Treat, Brooklyn Kid, Jungle Bold, and Urban Scrawl, some reflecting the urban origin of subway and wall graffiti around the world (Chalfant and Prigoff 1987; Cooper and Chalfant 1984).

A major difference between grunge and graffiti fonts and real-world graffiti is that the latter are a form of unique, one-time performance, under difficult conditions – usually on the fly in the middle of the night[88] – whereas fonts can be created at leisure, and then put online at one's convenience. More important, unlike real-world graffiti, a font is only a typeface, a potential form for a message, not the message itself. Still, putting grunge and other types of subversive or offensive fonts on the Web is a kind of meta-message, something like the act of "getting up," as graffiti "writers" call it (Castleman 1982). The Web itself becomes a kind of global, digital graffiti wall. Véronique Vienne made much the same point when she wrote, "Illegible typefaces are the graffiti of cyberspace" (Vienne 1997c: 11).

Rock Fonts

Many Websites offered fonts based on the logos of popular television programs and commercial products such as food and drink (e.g., Coca-Cola), the titles of films, and so on.[89] Still more common were sites specializing in "rock fonts" or "band fonts," elaborations of the typography used on albums of various musical groups, such as the popular "Smashing Pumpkins."[90] In January 1999 fonts for 28 different groups were available for downloading on the "Fonts for Freaks" Website.[91] At "Fontanelle" one could simultaneously download the fonts for classic rock groups and order the CD at CDNow.[92]

Personal Handwriting Fonts: a Closer Look

We are all wondering, as we move into the digital era: will anything of the so-called "personal touch" survive? One expression of nostalgia for the personal touch is the phenomenon of handwriting fonts. We have seen that pre-digital typography has long included categories for script and calligraphic typefaces. Even before the advent of computers, there was some tendency to create typefaces that look hand-done, as in brush-stroke-like typefaces for advertising and greeting cards. However, digital fonts based on the handwriting of actual, specific individuals are new. Expert Software marketed its CD-ROM, "Handwriting Fonts," as follows:

300 TrueType fonts created from real handwriting samples. Give your documents the personal touch with Handwriting Fonts. . . . Send thank you letters, business memos and personal notes *with the warm touch of personal handwriting.* [italics added]

ClickART, gushed:

Fonts that look like real handwriting! When ordinary type just won't do, use a Handwritten Font to add spontaneity, impact and a personal touch to your words. Use the speed and convenience of your computer and still take advantage of the warmth and appeal of personally written words . . .

Personally, I would consider it bizarre to adopt someone else's handwriting as my preferred font, whether for prose writing, for paper letter-writing or email, and would hardly consider it "adding a personal touch." Using the handwriting of another person as "one's own" is something like wearing a stranger's clothes. Although some women do make a cult of wearing vintage clothes, this is an exception to what seems to be the rule, and I suspect that the same principle applies here.

There are many variations on this theme of the handwriting font. Thus, among the art fonts at P22 Type Foundry are those based on the handwriting of Cézanne or Leonardo da Vinci. Another, particularly eccentric variation was the phenomenon of "killer fonts." One could actually download fonts based on the handwriting of known murderers.[93] The site stated:

Everyone has those days where words won't begin to describe how you feel. Why not help your word do exactly what they want? What better way to let your boss know your true feelings than by resigning with the help of Charles Manson? . . . And everyone will know you mean business when Lee Harvey Oswald writes your cover letters . . .

Click on the photos to see the face and the font.

Who in the world besides eccentric, marginal individuals or groups would want to use these fonts, except perhaps as a joke? Evidently, this phenomenon was part of the larger trend towards fonts as a form of digital "graffiti."

For a fee, one could also have one's own handwriting digitized. Several companies and individuals offered this service. One sent in some samples of handwriting, sometimes writing specific words or combinations of letters, so that the font would incorporate how one links letters, and not just how individual letters are formed. Some fonts even incorporated random variation in the formation of letters, so that text would not look completely standardized.[94]

In its paper brochure one company urged:

Now you can add your own handwriting to your computer! Signature Software's Personal Font is a custom font which can reproduce your handwriting – including the exact way that you shape and connect (or don't connect) your letters . . .

With a personal Font you can join the personal impact of your own handwriting with the convenience and power of your personal computer. . . . Add a friendly handwritten P.S. note to your business correspondence. Or even write and sign your FAX-modem messages.[95]

In the course of research for this book I came across only one instance of actual use of a personalized handwriting font. Véronique Vienne, a graphic designer who took part in the debate among professionals about typography and design in the 1990s,[96] revealed:

To communicate via fax-modem with my parents in France, I ordered . . . a customized typeface that's a digitized version of my handwriting. Named Colette, after my mom, my personal font gets the job done. Although she knows I didn't scribble a note to her, my mother reads my electronic messages with something that resembles pleasure. "The Vs and the Rs are realistic," she says. "Too bad the lines are too regular." (Vienne 1997c: 12)

Discussion

This chapter has shown that as the millennium approached, there was a remarkable explosion of interest in typography among people of all walks of life and all ages. Many people without formal training in this area became quite knowledgeable[97] about typographic design. A prominent trend was collecting fonts and displaying one's collection on the World Wide Web. In some cases individuals became proficient enough at type design to become commercially successful. Both aesthetic/visual aspects and cultural connotations of type design acquired an unprecedented importance for many lay persons. Computers and the Internet were contributing to a radical destabilization of norms, perceptions, and behavior regarding typography.

In my opinion, the material presented in this chapter under-estimates the extent of font frenzy. My information was primarily derived from extensive observations on the Web, supplemented by many visits to computer stores, and actual experience with fonts on my own computer and with software that supplied them, as well as with email and chat. I can attest from my own experience that one can easily amass hundreds of fonts, becoming in effect a font collector, without necessarily revealing evidence of this online. Obviously, one can invest much time, effort, and even money in fonts without creating a Website for one's collection. Similarly, there may be many amateur font designers who do not display their creations online.

As technologies develop, we are being given more and more opportunities to add play with fonts to our communicative repertoire. Until the mid- to late 1990s, the number and types of fonts that could be used in email and chat was extremely limited. In Chapter 2 we saw that on both the PC and the Macintosh one had to use a fixed-width font in email and chat, one in which each letter takes up exactly the same amount of space in a line. This meant that almost none of the myriad fonts discussed in this chapter could have been used. In addition, ordinarily, it was not possible to use bold, italic or underline functions.[98]

By the late 1990s, all this was changing. Email software was lifting some of these restrictions, although many people may not have been aware of this, or taken advantage of new possibilities. Thus, in Eudora 3.0 and onwards, ICQ, and Netscape Mail, one could use any of hundreds of proportional fonts, change the font at any time within a message or for different ones, modify font size, and use the bold, italic, and underline functions, and even color the text. Later versions of Eudora could even incorporate graphic images and small audio files. In the 1999 version of ICQ email, one could customize the background color. In Netscape Mail one could align text center, left or right, and use "bullets" for lists, just as in word-processing. A limitation of all these programs at that time, however, was that recipients could only view these effects if their software enabled them. As technologies become more sophisticated in the next millennium, this limitation will disappear.

The trend toward stylization was the same for chat. Thus, on ICQ, one could choose to view the dialog either interleaved as on IRC, or displayed in separate windows. ICQ enabled choice of fonts, bold, italic and underline functions, and choice of font color and background color. MIRC, the graphically rich Windows version of the IRC software, added many features too, including font color and background color. However, players could communicate only in either of two fixed-width fonts, Fixed Sys and Courier New.[99] Although we cannot know how extensively people made use of these features, is likely that tens of millions of young people were already doing so in the late 1990s.[100]

In 1992 a 15-year-old student at a Burbank, California high school filed a $50,000 claim against her school district for suspending her because her sweatshirt contained Old English style letters. School officials interpreted them as gang symbols, even though the girl had used them to mourn a murdered classmate.

> The cover of the Constitution is printed in the same lettering, the student's ACLU lawyer observed. "We thought that was the nicest looking writing. Even Disneyland uses it on some of its signs," the girl's mother . . . said . . . 'How can they object to a typeface and not the message?" (cited in Burdick, 1994: 135).[101]

For different sub-groups this typeface signaled "gang style," "authoritarian style," and "storybook style," respectively. This example suggests not only that the cultural associations of typefaces are dynamic and complex, but that these associations have become more salient among lay people because of the digital revolution.

The Appeal of Grunge Fonts

Probably the most provocative aspect of font frenzy was the preoccupation with grunge fonts. Many professionals were horrified by what they saw. What was the fascination with grunge typography? There is no simple answer, and it is likely that several factors worked together, in different combinations in different contexts.

One possibility is that grunge was perceived as simply informal. In some contexts grunge was an intentional kind of "dressing down," and therefore connoted informality and accessibility. Perhaps this helps to account for its co-optation into mainstream graphic design, which generally reflected greater informality in public life as the millennium approached.[102]

While all this may be true, I suspect that much more is at stake in many instances. First of all, there is the matter of fashion and imitation. For young people, if one's peers like and use grunge, then one is likely to pursue it too. One adopted it, collected it, or, in the case of font designers, created a grunge font because it looked new, contemporary, "with it." Third, one could create grunge fonts just because of the fun and ease of being able to do it. As Tobias Frere-Jones (1997: 16) put it, "Why be clear and legible when ANYBODY can do that now?" Fourth, for certain sub-groups grunge connoted an angry, subversive, counter-cultural orientation – *typography as social protest*.[103]

Still another reason for interest in grunge fonts may have been that they invite participation – they may require effort to decode. This possibility jibes well with the increasing interactivity of media today, and of course especially the Internet. People who identify with this position reject the idea that fonts must be instantly and easily decipherable. In its challenge to viewers to decode it, grunge typography is a little like graphic wit. A message with multiple layers or a visual twist invites the recipient to decode it. In their study of graphic wit, *Smile in the Mind*, Beryl McAlhone and David Stuart suggested that such wit offers viewers a chance to experience closure or completion by completing what is missing (McAlhone and Stuart 1998: 19–20).

Finally, yet another source of the appeal of grunge may be inferred from research on collecting. In our study of adult and child collectors, Tamar Katriel and I encountered the seeming anomaly of collecting imperfect objects. A stamp collector specializing in stamps with printing mistakes told us that he spent hours going through thousands of stamps with a magnifying glass, looking for mistakes. In our effort to understand this man and others like him, Katriel and I speculated:

> Perhaps touching stamps with mistakes is a way to be in touch with other human beings, fallible like ourselves . . . stamp collectors who hunt for mistakes may have something in common with the Franciscan priest we interviewed who especially treasured a deformed Roman glass bottle because it had collapsed when blown. (Danet and Katriel 1989: 270)

By extension, perhaps grunge had appeal because it was a rebellion against the very perfection that the computer makes possible. Not only Barry Deck, but many others, both amateur and professional, participated in this rebellion. Thus, grunge may have been a form of nostalgia for the handmade and its inevitable irregularities, and for the disappearing traces of the unique individual, in a world of simulation and artificial perfection.

Font Frenzy and Popular Culture

Many of the themes surveyed in this chapter relate to more general aspects of popular culture and youth culture. The fascination with "Sci-Fi," "horror" and "medieval" fonts was an extension of the interest among young people in science fiction, horror films, and genres grounded in medieval settings such as Tolkien's *Lord of the Rings* and computer games like "Dungeons and Dragons." The rise of grunge typography was related to two other genres of subversive or alternative popular culture, grunge music and grunge fashion (Pareles 1997; Polhemus 1994; Steele 1997). The affinities with grunge fashion, promulgated originally by mainly Seattle-based popular music groups of the late 1980s such as *Pearl Jam, Nirvana,* and *Nine-Inch Nails,* are fascinating. American grunge fashion was characterized by

> tattiness, . . . reliance on charity or thrift shops, . . . love of under/over sizing, [a] penchant for checked shirts, . . . lank hair and . . . chunky workboots. Most fundamentally, . . . Grunge is Dressing Down at its most extreme . . . [and cultivates] a general scruffiness which was not all that far removed from the equally unkempt residue left by the Hippies and the counterculture . . . Grunge represents . . . the ultimate blend of . . . styles . . . which share a common denominator of dressing down. (Polhemus 1994: 122–123)

Today, many of these practices have made their way into mainstream graphic design, seen widely in store windows and in advertisements, along with other violations of the old rules of typography. I documented several New York Times advertisements in which distressed lettering and related violations of conventional typography were featured. In one instance, a letter was turned upside down, in hacker style.

Font Frenzy and Its Implications for Professional Typography

Digitization and the entrance of lay people into the world of typography brought about tremendous ferment among design professionals. Some despised what was happening. Massimo Vignelli, a well-known Italian designer based in New York, was particularly blunt:

> In the new computer age, the proliferation of typefaces and type manipulations represents a new level of visual pollution threatening our culture. Out of thousands of typefaces, all we need are a few basic ones, and trash the rest. (From a poster for the exhibition "The Masters Series: Massimo Vignelli," February–March, 1991; cited in Keedy 1997: 30).

Others took a much more conciliatory position. In the belief that digitization is bringing about "a gain in creative invention and discovery," Rob Carter devoted an entire book to showing young designers how to exploit the potential of the new technologies (Carter 1997: 7). He argued that the best preparation for this was to gain a firm grasp of traditional principles, and reminded us that the typographic experimentation that accompanied many pre-digital 20th-century design movements also led to significant advances.

Jeffery Keedy added:

> The rigid categories applied to type design in the past do not make much sense in the digital era. Previous distinctions such as serif and sans serif are challenged by the new "semi serif" and "pseudo serif."[104] The designation of type as text or display is also too simplistic. Whereas type used to exist only in books (text faces) or occasionally on a building or sign (display) . . . today's typographer is most frequently working with in-between amounts of type . . . The categories of text and display should not be taken too literally in a multimedia and interactive environment where text is also read on television, computers, clothing, even tattoos. (Keedy 1997: 28)

Keedy argued that although digitization may result in some bad typefaces, "The digital era will be the most innovative in the history of type design" (Keedy 1997: 29).

One sign that amateur experimentation was being recognized by professionals is a volume called *Webworks Typography*, edited by Jason Mills and Daniel Donnelly (1999). Issued by a publishing house specializing in typography, this book and its accompanying CD-ROM displayed use of typography on the Web by 43 individuals and groups. Along with ITC, a well-established corporation that had had a strong pre-digital presence,[105] and smaller, independent, commercially successful type foundries often specializing in an alternative or cutting-edge "look" (e.g., T-26, *Emigré*, Chankstore) were many that had only recently become commercial, and even quite a number of self-taught, young individuals not necessarily interested in selling their fonts. I was both gratified and surprised to learn that a number of sites I had chosen to present in this chapter were featured in the book, including "Divide by Zero" and "Cool Fonts Online."

Legibility and Readability Revisited

Legibility and readability are complex, relative phenomena. There has often been a debate about them, and the debate was raging once again, as the millennium approached. Many argued that we cannot abandon requirements for legibility and readability. Thus, in Kevin Fenton's opinion:

> Typography's reliance on existing words is what distinguishes it from other disciplines within design. It assumes a text, which it attempts to interpret as richly as possible . . . Without legibility, I do not see how typography can exist as typography. It dissolves into illustration. (Fenton 1997: 32)

It is true that some digital typefaces and some instances of actual use of them showed no regard for legibility or readability. Quite the contrary, as we have seen, some typefaces made a point of being illegible. However, what is considered legible or readable is heavily influenced by context and experience.

Typographic professionals have long known that both visual and cultural context influence perceptions of type.[106] An excellent example of the importance of visual context in deciphering individual letters is "Gestalt" by Jonathan Hoefler. The design of this font itself, as well as the text in which it is displayed (Figure 7.31), bring home that individual letters may be illegible when viewed out of context, yet perfectly legible in the context of whole words or sequences of words.

Readability is also a function of objective factors such as spacing between letters, between words, and between lines. But these objective factors alone cannot account for ease or comfort of the reader either. Zuzana Licko and Rudy VanderLans of *Emigré* are known for stressing the role of experience in readers' ability to decipher a text. As VanderLans pithily put it, "People read best what they read most" (VanderLans and Licko 1993: 12). Overstating their case somewhat, this husband-wife team reminded us that today's typefaces would not have been legible or readable to medieval scribes.

Figure 7.31. "Gestalt," by Jonathan Hoefler, http://www.typography.com/.

It may be of some consolation to those who find grunge and graffiti-looking fonts offensive to learn that interest in grunge peaked in the early 1990s, and by the second half of the decade was falling out of favor. At least one type designer called grunge "dated" as early as 1994:

> Like any other trend, grunge has firmly dated itself and many are already tired of it. Like the arabesques of the 1880s and the swashes[107] of the 1970s, the contortions of the 1990s will fall out of favor, but not before showing us what the new tools can do. (Frere-Jones 1997: 18) [108]

Although grunge continued to be prominent in the work of many of those included in the Mills and Donnelly (1999) volume, others admitted to having moved on, or at least to being open to a return to fonts with straight, clean lines.

Considerations of fashion apart, this chapter has shown that, thanks to computers and the Internet, many lay people became intensely, even passionately interested in typography. These developments helped to open up a profession and a formerly restricted sphere of human activity to new influences and new possibilities. Much has been written to date about the nature and consequences of hypertext. Unlike the reader of a print book, who, ideally, sinks into an armchair and reads a book from start to finish with deep concentration, the digital reader is restless, constantly in "danger" of being distracted by the temptations of hyperlinks.[109] My analysis suggests that the preoccupation with visual form also encourages this kind of restlessness. While digital fonts are a source of great pleasure and interest for many, they are also a source of distraction from textual content. Like oral culture, then, digital culture will invest heavily in matters of style and form.[110]

Notes

1. The URL is now http://fontopolis.simplenet.net/ but the slogan is gone.

2. This site has since disappeared. Its logo, documented in January 1999, appears in Plate 7.2. A 1989 article for design professionals by Karrie Jacobs, reprinted in Bierut et al. (1994), already spoke of "type frenzy" (Jacobs 1994: 152).

3. Personal email, 19 February 1999. New Times Roman is correctly designated as Times New Roman" or as "Times Roman." "Lol" means "laughing out loud;" "ROFL" means "rolling on the floor laughing." See my discussion of abbreviations in Chapter 1.

4. The URL of Fonts Anon~ is http://www.fontsanon.com/. The owner of the Website playfully cited the use of ~ in abbreviations of Windows filenames that have more than eight characters.

5. See http://fonts.tom7.com/.

6. Personal email from Tom Murphy, 28 January 1999.

7. Personal email from Jami Reed, 18 December 1998. The index is at http://www.typesource.com/.

8. In addition, the site had categories for Macintosh fonts and for "miscellaneous" items, including two Usenet newsgroups for font enthusiasts, *comp.fonts* and *alt.binaries.fonts*.

9. Reed cautioned me that over time he became more and more selective about the sites included. Those offering only a very few fonts or fonts available in many others were not included. Thus, this index taps not general growth over time, but growth in sites with a substantial investment in fonts. Personal email, 2 September 2000. See also Chris McGregor's Internet Type Foundry Index, http://www.typeindex.com/; The Fontpool, http://www.fontpool.com/; The Font Zone, http://www.geocities.com/~fontszone.

10. These definitions all come from the *comp.fonts* FAQ, by Norman Walsh, 1992-1996. Of two newsgroups for font enthusiasts on Usenet (the other is *alt.binaries.fonts*), this one is devoted to more technical matters.

11. The notion of typeface family came into use in the early 20th century. "The proliferation of typefaces available for use in books and advertising led the American Typefounders Company to organize fonts into "type families" (Lupton and Miller 1996: 57).

12. I am indebted to Steve Renick for the example in Figure 7.5.

13. Email from Anthony Crouch, April 1999.

14. This book is a delightful parodic treatment of the challenge that digital typography poses to traditional norms and practices. It does not contain page numbers.

15. On the history of typography see Lee (1965); McLean (1980); Gray (1986); Drucker (1995); Bringhurst (1996); Tschichold (1998 [1928]); Friedl et al. (1998).

16. I will have more to say about readability and legibility later on.

17. The earliest surviving Chinese printed texts are from the 13th century (Bringhurst 1996: 119).

18. The Chinese contribution was wood-block printing, which did not lend itself to the printing of the thousands of ideograms in the Chinese language. Cf. McLean (1980: 13).

19. For further details and examples of this and other typefaces mentioned in this brief review, see McLean (1980), pp. 58–64.

20. Roman lettering on stone had serifs; these were the original serifs. To this day, "Roman" often means "typefaces with serifs" in typographic circles.

21. Bringhurst's entry for "Humanist" in his Glossary of Typographic Terms is

Humanist letterforms are letterforms originating among the humanists of the Italian Renaissance and persisting to this day. They are of two primary kinds: roman and italic, both of which derive from Roman capitals and Carolingian minuscules. Humanist letterforms show the clear trace of a broadnib pen held by a right-handed scribe. They have a modulated stroke and a humanist axis. (Bringhurst 1996: 292)

"Humanist axis" is "an oblique stroke axis reflecting the natural inclination of the writing hand" (Bringhurst 1996: 292).

22. This section draws heavily on Drucker (1995), Chapters 7 and 8.

23. I am referring to William Morris's Arts and Crafts movement with its interest in the revival of medieval motifs and cult of the handmade in the era of the machine (Drucker 1995: 243–244; Lucie-Smith 1981, Chapter 11), and to Art Nouveau style. In general, avant-garde art movements often had their parallels in the design of type.

24. Sans serif type is usually considered less legible "because . . . some of the letters are more like each other than letters that have serifs, and so the certainty of decipherment is diminished" (McLean 1980: 44).

25. In typographic circles "Swiss" often means "rational," "cold," and even "faceless." See Klein et al. (1991). Among digital fonts today, perhaps Arial is the best known sans serif font.

26. This section draws primarily on McLean (1980), Chapter 6, and Walsh (1992–96).

27. "Resolution" refers to a "measure of the detail in an image or sound. Images are measured in pixels (dots) per inch, and in the number of bits used to describe the color values (or greyscale) at each pixel" (Cotton, 1994: 174; italics in original).

28. Another site, "Font World," also custom-designs fonts and logos for other languages or special purposes. See http://www.fontworld.com/.

29. See http://babel.uoregon.edu/yamada/fonts.html.

30. I refer to Windows 95 because it was what I knew best at this time of this research, and because it was more widely used by people other than professional designers than the Macintosh operating system. Different variations of Windows 95 included a slightly different list, but these are the basic fonts.

31. These summaries come from the Microsoft typography site, http://www.microsoft.com/typography/.

32. Some fontaholics specialize in collecting dingbats.

33. Introduced in 1961, the IBM Selectric was the beginning of interest in diversification of fonts for ordinary typing. A basic set of interchangeable, sphere-shaped typing elements, each containing a different typeface, came with the typewriter, instead of a moving carriage and typebar (Beeching 1990: 127; Lupton 1993: 47).

34. See their Website, http://www.expertsoftware.com/.

35. I shall have more to say about handwriting fonts later on.

36. I also mentioned above that Expert Software issued a CD-ROM of handwriting fonts.

37. "Oblique" is often used as a synonym for "italic," though, strictly speaking, italic fonts are designed separately.

38. Creating special effects became so easy that even very young children could do it. Michelle Slatalla reported that on the very first use of a program called "Print Artist Craft Factory," her eight-year-old daughter designed three business cards, personalized note paper with her own trademark, a homework schedule, a school schedule, and a set of cocktail coasters, as well as invitations to her eighth birthday party (Slatalla 1998a). Most of these involved choice of typefaces.

39. This company also sells its fonts on its Website, http://www.p22.com/.

40. In other cases, they offered more versions. But the standard approach of offering entire font families was not followed.

41. The Bauhaus had colleges of design in Weimar, Dessau, and Berlin (Erlich 1991). In 1933 Hitler closed down the schools. Herbert Bayer had been the director of the workshop for typography and commercial design at Dessau. Albers taught typography, furniture design and glass painting, eventually heading the entire preparatory course. After the Bauhaus was closed, both emigrated to the United States (Friedl et al. 1998).

42. Was P22 charging too much? Or was Expert Software? At about $23, P22's one-font packages could appeal to impulse buyers. CD-ROMs containing hundreds of fonts for less money were the better deal for the ordinary user, even if their collections were indiscriminate.

43. Professionals could feel passionate about fonts too:

Intense as any thriller, lusty as any romance, and wanton as any book on this subject can be, this is a book about type and lettering . . . this is a book about passion; a passionate, often smoldering love affair between graphic designers and letterforms, in parts a veritable Kama Sutra of typography revealing many kinds of typographic love – from the sensual hot metal kiss to the orgasmic distortion of digital fonts. (Heller and Anderson 1994: 8)

44. The Website of a distributor of fonts to professionals and laypersons urged "You can never have too many friends, or too many fonts!" See Phil's Fonts, http://philsfonts.com/.

45. This is the traditional account of the origin of TNR, sometimes called just Times Roman, but some attribute it to an American type designer called Starling Burgess, as early as 1904. See Bringhurst (1996), p. 97. The first issue of the London Times in TNR appeared on 3 October 1932 (Friedl et al. 1998: 341).

46. According to Klein, et al. (1991: 175), "The first book set in Times appeared in 1934, and it soon turned up in magazines, mainly the USA, such as *Time, Life* and *Fortune.*" Although it became popular in books, the original typeface was intended only for newspapers. Additional variations, called Times New Roman Wide and Times New Roman Book, had been designed expressly for use in books though not necessarily used. Even Stanley Morison himself, who supervised the creation of TNR by Victor Lardent and others, is supposed to have commented that the newspaper version of the typeface was "hardly a book type." Steve Renick supplied this additional information.

47. I am indebted to Anthony Crouch for clarifying this point. Most standard accounts of the development of TNR do not reveal that the reasons for adopting it were primarily economic rather than aesthetic or functional (e.g., to promote readability). Not all professionals in book production are positively disposed to TNR. Memorandum from Anthony Crouch, April 1999.

48. Personal email from Tom Murphy, 29 January 1999.

49. See http://www.geocities.com/SoHo/1101. Yet another example is Radioactive Roman, in Figure 7.30 below.

50. Personal email from Jeff Wrench, 28 January 1999.

51. Personal email from Peter Langdon, 22 December 1998.

52. Kyl's Medieval was a Website whose full name is Kyl's Medieval and Fantasy Fonts.

53. The Fonts FAQ file for the Usenet newsgroup *alt.binaries.fonts* claimed that the limit is 900–1000; other sites mentioned 500 as the limit. A larger number can be maintained using a font manager like FontMinder (Hargrove 1997). Many people admitted to having more than this, which probably meant that they stored part of their collection, for instance, on Zip disks. Software manuals and help texts warn against having too many fonts on one's hard disk because this slows down the computer's performance.

54. Many thanks to Absinth, former manager of Fonts Anon~, for putting my query about TNR on the site's messageboard and for allowing me to become a member of the group.

55. Posting to the Fonts Anon~ messageboard, 24 December 1998.

56. Posting by JMR to the Fonts Anon~ messageboard, December 1998.

57. See footnote 25.

58. Still another example is "Badoni" by Chank Diesel, a parody of "Bodoni," typefaces associated with the late 18th-century type designer of that name; see "Chankstore," http://www.chank.com/.

59. Typographic professionals distinguish between legibility of individual symbols and readability of entire texts, and have much to say about what promotes both. See McLean (1980), pp. 41–48; Carter (1997), Chapter 1; Carter, et al. (1993), Chapter 4; Haley (1998), pp. 119–120.

60. When downloaded and used, these fonts are black on white, as usual.

61. See Danet and Katriel (1989) for a discussion of differences between accumulation and collecting.

62. See my discussion of these terms in relation to fonts, below.

63. See http://www.katgyrl.com/.

64. Her site was at http://www..dreaminfinity.com/fontgrrl/.

65. Like many others he also collected dingbats and initial caps, patterned after those used in medieval manuscripts. See http://www.geocities.com/kyls_fonts/.

66. See "Blahfonts," http://www.gwydir.demon.co.uk/giles.

67. I learned this from personal email from him, February 4, 1999.

68. Heller started out as something of a guerilla designer himself. See his article "A Youth in the Youth Culture" (Heller 1998). Heller defines a guerilla designer as one who "view[s] digital type like hand-lettering or graffiti – something ephemeral and not governed by typographic standards" (Heller 1997: 6).

69. Another indication of Dever's success is that his was the only guerilla type foundry mentioned in a New York Times article surveying typography in the digital age; see Liu (1996).

70. Personal email from Tom Murphy, January 28, 1999. Murphy's playfulness is also apparent in his userid: " ImightbeTM."

71. The term "Tombats" plays on "dingbats," as these ornaments are usually called by typographers.

72. The URL of "Guerilla Fonts" was http://www.liii.com/~artech/fonts/.

73. This site was later renamed "Mo's Font Collection," and in January 2001 was at http://www.geocities.com/Wellesley/3716/fonts1.html.

74. From cool musical style the term was extended to describe "any physically attractive, male jazz musician or aficionado" (Danesi 1994: 37).

75. See, e.g., Tamony (1980); Brown (1994). Absinth also comments that in other contexts "funky" can be negative:

Something that has been sitting in the back of your refrigerator for 6 months, only recently discovered, and having a fuzzy green growth all over it can rightfully be called "funky" as well. . . . Rotten fruit is "funky."

The comments in Figure 7.21 and this citation are both from personal email, 31 January 1999.

76. The URL of this site is in footnote 29.

77. Some of the late 1990s cultural associations to vintage typewriter type carried the same meanings as "grunge" fonts; worn-looking typewriter fonts sometimes appear under the category "grunge." See the next section on "Grunge and Graffiti Fonts," and the discussion of the appeal of grunge at the end of this chapter.

78. These programs are ways for IRC players who are skilled in programming to customize their environment and display their virtuosity. According to one player I contacted, the practice of "elite talkers" with eccentric looks arose on America Online; he claimed that these "talkers" were a way of displaying disdain for the ordinary folks on AOL. Personal email from Kombo, May, 1997. However, as I wrote in Chapter 5, I think these practices are much older. For lists of IRC scripts, see, e.g., http://www.mircscripts.com/.

79. Explanations of some of these exotic symbols come from Bringhurst (1996).

80. See the InDigest Press, http://www.geocities.com/SoHo/1101.

81. Downright aggressive use of hacker typography was part of the display left by hackers who broke into the New York Times Website in December, 1998, substituting their own material with the subversive title, "Hacking for Girlies." See http://www.antionline.com/.

82. See also Figure 7.20.

83. Even the information supplied with "puckfont" is irreverent. Instead of "Copyright, _____," it says "Schmopyright, 1996."

84. Gregory Meronek, the creator of Radioactive Roman, accused Expert Software of pirating this font on its "Funky Fonts" CD-ROM. I encountered two other travesties of TNR. One was called Porcupine Roman. The second, was the very first font created, at age 15, by Christopher Mueller, a German type designer and typographer who was included in a book on cutting-edge digital typography (Mills and Donnelly 1999: 35–37); he called it Old Roman Times. There seemed to be no end to these parodies.

85. The boundaries of "guerilla" in this context are ambiguous. An anti-establishment orientation among art school students studying typography is not very different from that of self-taught amateurs, after all.

86. This citation is from the *Emigré* Website, http://www.emigre.com.

87. Also, they digitized their own handwriting, as "JustLeftHand" and "ErikRightHand," and created a dirty-looking "typewriter" font by scanning typewriter characters, dirt and all (Spiekermann 1995).

88. See, e.g., Castleman (1982); Cooper and Chalfant (1984); Chalfant and Prigoff (1987).

89. Sometimes only a logo is offered, not a complete font. I discovered that this was so for Coca-Cola.

90. See, for instance, http://www.smashing-pumpkins.net/downloads/fonts.

91. The URL of this site is http://www.gothic.net/~tygre.

92. See http://www.cdnow.com/.

93. See http://wwwkillerfonts.com/.

94. In late 1998–99 there were a number of devices which could produce digitized text, while using a hand instrument such as a stylus or pen. More impressive than

personal digital assistants used with a stylus was the Cross Digital Crosspad, developed jointly with IBM, on which one could write as usual on an ordinary yellow pad, but with a special pen. The graphic shape of one's handwriting could be preserved and uploaded to a PC, or the notes could be transformed into word-processed text. See http://www.cross-pcg.com/.

95. The URL of Signature Software is http://www.signaturesoftware.com/.

96. She had three papers in the collection *Looking Closer 2: Critical Writings on Graphic Design* (Bierut et al. 1997), Vienne (1997a; 1997b; 1997c).

97. See, e.g., Will-Harris (1998).

98. There are some exceptions. Even in the text version of software for IRC, skilled users could introduce "reverse video," a bold-like effect, for selected words.

99. Increasingly, email and chat programs also offered other enhancements, including the use of sound.

100. A student of mine reported that this was very common in her experience with Italian chat on ICQ.

101. This incident was reported in the Los Angeles Times, Valley edition, 8 February 1992.

102. See my discussion of informality in public language and its relation to the emergent language of email in Chapter 2.

103. Anthony Crouch took a particularly grim view of grunge. He speculated that it may have been cultivated mainly by spoiled, disaffected middle-class young people rebelling at the affluent society in which they grew up but unable to offer anything constructive in return. Memorandum from Anthony Crouch, April 1999.

104. Unfortunately, he did not give any examples of these new categories.

105. ITC was founded in 1972; the full name is International Typeface Corporation (Mills and Donnelly 1999: 107).

106. I already gave an example of the influence of cultural context on the perception of type above, in the discussion of the high school student and her T-shirt. There, however, the issue was the connotations of type, whereas here one's ability to decode individual letters and words is at issue.

107. A swash is "a letterform reveling in luxury. Some swash letters carry extra flourishes; others simply occupy an abnormally large ration of space" (Bringhurst 1996: 297).

108. Frere-Jones's comments were originally published in 1994, and were reprinted in Bierut et al. (1997).

109. On the history and future of books, see, e.g., Birkerts (1994); Nunberg (1996); Danet (1997b); O'Donnell (1998); Snyder (1998).

110. Professors are already contending with the problem of student papers with beautiful fonts and graphics but sorely lacking in content. Similarly, many of us try to look beyond handsome fonts and graphics to identify meaningful content on the Web.

8

Concluding Reflections

This book has explored patterns of playful, artful communication on the Internet in the mid- to late 1990s. My case studies spanned a rather dizzying range of topics, from email to online Shakespearean parodies to digital greetings to text-based art to font frenzy. By the end of the millennium, all three of the modes studied – email, chat and the Web – had become part of the daily lives of hundreds of millions. These case studies showed that people were having a marvelous time experimenting with the new possibilities.

Normalization

The explosive growth of the Internet in the late 1990s was difficult to grasp. Synthesizing data from a number of sources, NUA Surveys claimed that as of September 2000, nearly 378 milliion people were online. Over half were in the United States and Canada, a quarter or so in Europe, a third in Asia and the Pacific, and the rest in the Middle East and Latin America.[1] In December 1999 America Online, the world's largest Internet service provider, reported over 20 million subscribers, double the number just two years earlier, with subscribers in 15 countries and in seven languages.[2] ICQ, the most popular service to track friends, family and colleagues online, reached 50 million subscribers in December 1999.[3] As this book was completed in late 2000 the total had jumped to well over 94 million. Nevertheless, with a world population of 6 billion, participation online remained the privilege of a minority.

The ninth, 1998 "GVU[4] WWW User Survey," conducted by a consortium of institutions coordinated by the Georgia Institute of Technology since 1994, reported a clear trend toward "mainstreaming" of the Web. Particularly in the United States the demographic characteristics of Web users increasingly resembled those of the general population. Nearly 39% of all users in their sample were females, indicating massive entrance of women into cyberspace. When the first survey in this series was carried out in 1994, women had been only 5% of those on the Web. One category of users even contained more females than males – users who had been online for less than a year (Georgia Tech Research Corporation 1998).

Although my research was not cast primarily to establish these trends, several studies reflected them. The studies of email (Chapter 2) and stylized written performance on IRC (Chapter 3) focused on the activities of generally highly educated elites. However, those on digital greetings (Chapter 4), text-based art (Chapters 5 and 6), and font frenzy (Chapter 7) examined activities of people from many walks of life.

In Chapter 4 I presented a bit of evidence that women were especially interested in digital greetings. Among those signing up in 1997 to be updated on developments at CardCentral.Net, fully 70% were women. This was a strong hint that women were continuing to play their traditional role of facilitator of kinship and social ties, while opening themselves up, perhaps even quite eagerly, to the idea of digital greetings.[5]

Visiting America Online's Website on Christmas Day 1999, I learned that it offered a wide range of free digital greetings as well as commercial paper ones.[6] Online as well as paper greetings included all four of the categories of what I called "life's troubles" in Chapter 4 – get well, support/encouragement, apology, and even sympathy, the category I viewed as the litmus test for normalization. At the same time, it was rather hard to find these categories on the cluttered AOL Website, compared to celebratory ones such as birthday greetings. Recall that one of my main findings in Chapter 4 had been that death was largely absent from Websites offering digital greetings. I suggested that in their fledgling state digital greetings were too playful, and that for a variety of reasons, there was a latent struggle to learn how to adapt the new medium to traditional ritual needs. Of eight digital sympathy offerings on AOL, two were tastefully animated, in my opinion.[7] These offerings strongly hinted at increasing integration of digital greetings in everyday life.[8]

Relatively early research on IRC such as Elizabeth Reid's 1991 B.A. Honors thesis (Reid, 1991; 1996a), Christopher Werry's (1996) study of linguistic and interactional features of chat on IRC, and my own analysis of the textual and typographic simulation of smoking marihuana (Ruedenberg, et al. 1995; Danet, et al. 1997; Danet, et al. 1998; Chapter 3 of this book), were all carried out in the years when young males, especially students, dominated on IRC. My studies of the Hamnet Players and of IRC art documented the entrance of very different groups in the mid- to late 1990s. The Hamnet study (Chapter 3) documented the participation of grown-ups – both men and women – with serious artistic aspirations and commitments. Stuart Harris, the founder of the group, and many of his associates had professional, semi-professional, or amateur experience in theater. Notably, women were quite well represented among those participating.

As for the IRC art channels (Chapter 6), it was striking that rank and file men, and especially women of lower-middle- and middle-class, non-professional background, concentrated in the American West, South and Southwest, were the main players. I reported in Chapter 6 that about three-fifths of the players on *#mirc_rainbow* were women, and two-fifths men. As far as I could tell, the picture was roughly the same for the second channel studied, *#mirc_colors*. Although the players were by no means a sample of IRC players generally, the social composition of these groups reflected the arrival of millions of people of moderate education online, and their remarkably rapid, self-starting integration into new forms of social and cultural activity. The range of occupations represented was very broad, from pizza-delivery driver to kindergarten teacher to housewife to salesperson, and so on. This study was also notable for documenting a quite novel form of leisure activity, whereas in many other cases the Internet is largely facilitating the pursuit of more traditional interests, such as doll collecting, gardening, or building model airplanes.

Many forms of activity on the Internet were bringing together people of all ages. In the past, informal activities had tended to be quite age-segregated. In *No Sense of Place* Joshua Meyrowitz (1985) noted that television brought adults and children together, e.g., that children were routinely exposed to content intended originally for adults only. The Internet has intensified this effect. I refer not, e.g., to the problem of children's access to pornography on the Web, an important topic but not relevant to this book, but to evidence in this book that the Internet facilitates shared activity by people of all ages. We saw that teenagers and even 11- and 12-year-olds, and people in their 60s and 70s were among the players on the IRC channels, and teenagers were sometimes accepted as ops. In Chapter 7 I took note of the font creations of a 13-year-old boy, proudly displayed on the Web, "next door" to the work of adult professionals and amateurs. Few leisure activities in the past brought children and teenagers into regular, willing contact with older people.[9] In an era when youth culture seeks in so many ways to differentiate itself from adult culture, this trend is striking, even if moderate, and bears watching in the future.

Another sign of integration of the Internet into daily life was evidence for occupational mobility among participants. Thus, <patches> of *#mirc_rainbow* had not worked for quite a few years as a professional musician, her original occupation,[10] and was at home. As a result of her intensive involvement in the channel and its Website she became so highly skilled in computer and administrative matters that she was eventually hired full-time by a major Internet service provider. The leader of the other IRC channel, <elusive>, had been an accountant in the American Air Force before her retirement. Via her involvement in the channel and its Website she developed her own Web business. Then there is the story of Absinth, the original convenor of Fonts Anon~. Trained as a classical violinist, she became a graphic artist and Webmaster, making money from her activities. So successful was she in these activities that she had to step down as convenor of Fonts Anon~.

It is especially intriguing that all these individuals are women. But there were examples of men making money from their new activities too. One of the designers of fonts whom I presented in Chapter 7, Todd Dever, was coopted by the computer establishment. Some of his fonts were included in products marketed by Macromedia, and he marketed his work online. There were many others with similar stories.

IRC Art as Incipient Folk Art and as Craft

My most extensive study of playful artistic expression by ordinary people was the one on ASCII art (Chapter 5) and the far more elaborate form of text-based art practiced on IRC (Chapter 6). IRC artists mobilized basic and extended ASCII characters to create and display multi-colored representational "drawings" or abstract designs. People created, viewed and displayed the art for the sheer pleasure of looking at it. But images also served as visual "speech acts," and had striking visual and geometric resemblances to physically based handicrafts such as embroidery, weaving, needlepoint, and quilting.

In Chapter 6 I proposed briefly that we think of IRC art as an incipient or emergent form of folk art and craft. On the face of it, this idea seems misguided. In several fundamental ways, this art differs from what is ordinarily thought of as folk art. Nevertheless, I believe that there is a case for this claim for IRC art, though not for earlier ASCII art because social aspects are much too diffuse and inchoate. It is only with fairly stable synchronous communication over time among a loyal group of regulars that conditions justify use of the term "folk" in a less than superficial sense.

Another solution might have been to call this art "popular" rather than folk." I have avoided using this term because too often it connotes the merely faddish or fashionable, or that which is characteristic of millions, whereas I shall argue below that there is analytic "bite" to the term "folk." Also, the terms "popular art" and "popular culture" have often been used to refer to artistic products of commercial interests, whereas in the present context, no monetary market is involved.

The concept of "folk art" has always been extremely troublesome even in its application to pre-digital forms of expression. Folk art falls within the wider domain of folklore, though it has been something of a step-child.[11] Consider the following definition by Robert Georges and Michael Owen Jones:

> The word folklore denotes expressive forms, processes, and behaviors (1) that we customarily learn, teach, and utilize or display during face-to-face interactions, and (2) that we judge to be traditional (a) because they are based on known precedents or models, and (b) because they serve as evidence of continuities and consistencies through time and space in human knowledge, thought, belief and feeling. (Georges and Jones 1995: 1)

In Elliot Oring's formulation, folklorists

> pursue reflections of the communal (a group or a collective), the common (the everyday rather than extraordinary), the informal (in relation to the formal and institutional), the personal (communication face-to-face), the traditional (stable over time), the aesthetic (artistic expressions), and the ideological (expressions of belief and sytems of knowledge). (Oring 1986: 17–18).

In the light of these definitions, the analomies seem egregious, indeed.

The Anomalous Nature of IRC Art

To begin with, IRC art was hardly "traditional," since it came into being only after the arrival of Windows 95 and the Windows-based version of the IRC software. Even the earlier forms of the decades preceding the IRC variety were not exactly traditional. When folklorists speak of tradition, they mean tradition that has existed for scores, even hundreds of years, and passed on from one generation to another, primarily by oral means and in direct face-to-face contact.

In contrast, IRC art is a "cutting-edge," very new high-tech phenomenon that changes and evolves constantly, as does most everything on the Internet. It might even disappear within a very few years, or at least be so transformed that one can no longer speak of it as such. Neither is this art cultivated in face-to-face interaction, handed down from generation to generation, among members of a local community living a full round of life. To the best of my knowledge, few players had met in real life or were even interested in doing so. We even saw there was quite a high rate of turnover among the players, despite the stable core of committed individuals.

A second, particularly glaring anomaly was that this art had no tangible substance. In pre-digital times the very essence of art and craft was the manipulation of tangible material – whether paint, wood, clay, or cloth – the rich appeal to the senses of its touch, texture and smell, and the joy of seeing one's creation emerge. Some of these satisfactions were well articulated by Judy Elsley with regard to quilts and quilting:

> Quilting is quiet, slow, meditative work. The quilter centers on the regular, rocking movement of the needle, feeling the subtle ridges of cotton form under her fingers. She focuses on her needle, her fingers, her thread, her breathing, and the detail of her quilt. Quilting is tactile, sensual, spiritual work. (Elsley 1996: 53)

An important consequence of the lack of physicality is that, unlike traditional folk art, there is no "market" for this art, and characteristics of tangible art such as uniqueness, rarity or provenance do not apply. This art circulates in a gift economy, rather than one of money.[12] It is fame or reputation, not monetary value that matters to artists, along with the strictly aesthetic satisfactions of creating the art.[13]

The Case for Digital Folk Art

Despite all these anomalies, I propose that we think of IRC art as an emergent or incipient form of digital folk art, in the belief that this conceptualization best fits it. Early approaches to the study of folklore focused on the preservation of traditional ethnic ways in the face of modernization (Glassie 1989). More recent approaches reformulated the field to include the expressive culture of urban groups in modern societies. Henry Glassie (1989: 34) wrote, "Today we think of folklore not as a kind of material but as a kind of action." In a particularly influential definition, Dan Ben-Amos (1972) suggested we define folklore simply as "artistic communication in small groups."[14] With its emphasis on "communication" this definition begins to sound quite appropriate. However, one would hardly characterize the groups involved in IRC art as small. We saw in Chapters 5 and 6 that many thousands have been involved in this art, even if not always as creators of it.

What, then, is my case? To begin with, popular artistic expression on the Internet is not totally incompatible with tradition. Recall that I found that the players had rapidly domesticated the medium in a manner that strikingly reinforced traditional social values of family and friendship, social acceptance and support, thus providing a sense of continuity in a time of major social and cultural change. In this respect, the players were very different both from the hackers who had created ASCII art in a subversive spirit in the early days, and the computer underground ASCII and ANSI artists of the late 1980s and 1990s (Chapter 5). Whereas I found underground art to be lurid and to feature themes of sex, violence, horror and death, the art on IRC was "sweet," decorative, heartwarming, cute, sentimental, or tension-reducing if humorous.

As for the matter of numbers, their significance seems quite different in the physical world and online. Even though thousands were involved, hardly the "small groups" intended by folklorists, this was clearly a group art rather than a solo form, such as that practiced by self-taught real-world artists working in isolation but who win social recognition, such as Grandma Moses, Simon Rodia, or Howard Finster. Such artists are often called "outsider artists" today.[15]

As John Michael Vlach (1992: 19) pointed out, "The concept of group art implies, indeed requires, that artists acquire their abilities, both manual and intellectual, at least in part from communication with others." *This fits the present case precisely.* First of all, we saw in Chapter 6 that artists were intensely involved with the group, that they were among the most prominent players. Second, teaching and learning how to play files and how to color in a group situation were very important. The groups even organized online classes, and newcomers were very much encouraged to ask ops for help – that is what ops were for. Third, some forms of the art became the focus of planned collective activities, scheduled shows. Via the art, players celebrated events such as public holidays, channel anniversaries, and individual players' birthdays. Most important of all, the art was itself communication – to experience it, whether while displaying it or viewing it, was to be in communication with others in real time. In the beginning only a small minority of individuals created the art for its own sake, and although the proportion of players creating their own art grew considerably over the years, for many players the art remained primarily a means to communicate with others. A distinction by Crease and Mann (1983: 91) cited in Dubin (1997: 39), between folk art and naive art seems particularly apt: "Folk art says 'We are,' but the works of [naive artists] cry 'I am.'"

As for the lack of face-to-face interaction, even this is not so anomalous as appears at first sight. As with so many other forms of online interaction, there was a strong sense of "co-presence" among IRC players, despite the mediated nature of communication (Biocca 1997; Lombard and Ditton 1997). This sense of "live" presence can (and does) substitute reasonably well for face-to-face relationships, although I would not argue that it can substitute entirely for an extended sense of community that emerges from a shared way of life rooted in the physical world.

Earlier in the book, I discussed the notion of "presence" in connection with performances by the Hamnet Players (Chapter 3). The factors fostering a sense of presence were not unique to contexts of virtual theater, on IRC or any other chat mode, for that matter. Like the Hamnet Players, participants on *#mirc_ rainbow* and *#mirc_colors* shared their art during "focused gatherings" (Goffman 1963) within a performance frame, coordinating their activities with great care, displaying their skill and, at least latently competing with one another, even if the atmosphere was mainly one of cooperation and mutual support. These activities took place in an atmosphere of contingency. The players lived with the problems of lag, netsplits, flooding, and potential "picture collisions."[16] Channel activity had a sense of "live" presence because of the sense of control that derives from being present in the "here-and-now."

Some might think it absurd to consider so new a phenomenon a folk art, when in the past, folk art traditions crystallized over decades and even hundreds of years. Nevertheless, my analysis reveals, I believe, that this was a highly organized cultural form, which happened to have developed with disconcerting speed. It *is* unsettling to learn that the Internet speeds up not only the exchange of individual messages, but also the evolution of complex social processes.

Formal Features of IRC Art

In Chapter 6 I reviewed the features of folk art, as discussed primarily in Henry Glassie's (1989) *The Spirit of Folk Art* and Sheila Paine's (1990) *Embroidered Textiles*. I argued that in visual form, ASCII art images, and especially images displayed on IRC, had much in common with traditional folk art. These features are summarized in Figure 8.1.

We saw that, as in traditional folk art, representational images of people in most pre-IRC and IRC art were of idealized types, not individuals, typically portrayed in frontal, non-illusionistic images, or in schematized, sideways silhouettes. Figures tended to be reductive and simplifying – to have large heads

---

"Craft" important as well as "art;" value of the handmade; demonstration of skill, virtuosity

Utilitarian as well as "art"

Idealized types, not individuals, portrayed frontally, non-illusionistically, in a reductive, simplifying manner

Love of decoration, brilliant color

Emphasis on geometric design: repetition, pattern, symmetry.

Popular themes: stylized, non-aggressive people, animals; flowers

Unambiguous, direct, clear

*Compiled mainly from Glassie (1989); Paine (1990).

Figure 8.1. Features of folk art.

and eyes, to be static rather than dynamic, often quite expressionless, seemingly frozen in their own inner world. Like more conventional folk art the world over, decorativeness and brilliant color are clearly prominent features of this art. There was an emphasis on geometric design – on repetition, pattern, and symmetry. Nearly all images were brilliantly colored; purely black and white (or greyscale) ones were extremely rare. Whether representational or abstract, images were unambiguous, direct and clear.

Representational images also resembled those of folk art in that popular themes included stylized, non-aggressive portrayals of people and animals. The absence of all aggressive connotations, even in connection with the most violent or threatening of animals, bears, dragons, dinosaurs, and wolves, was particularly noteworthy. Images of animals were cute and lovable, as in children's story-books and animated cartoons. Flowers too were portrayed in a highly stylized manner.

Readers might think that these features of the art were dictated by the limitations of the medium. To some extent this is so, because of the rigid grid underlying the art and the inability to rotate letters. It *is* quite difficult to "draw" with typographic characters. However, ASCII and ANSI art by teenagers and young men in the computer underground art scene was completely different. We saw that their art was quite the opposite in flavor and form – a complete rejection of decorativeness or cuteness, no interest in pattern, a predilection for the lurid, etc. Perhaps the one feature the two forms shared was the love of brilliant color, though the preferred use of color seemed quite different in the two cases.

Digital Text-based Art as Craft

As for craft, *prima facie*, the case for this form of expression as craft seems lost. Craft involves the demonstration of skill in the manipulation of material with one's hands and careful eye-hand coordination. Not only did this art lack physicality, but our traditional notion of the "handmade" seems totally inapplicable. Surely, a machine – the computer – has taken over the work of the hand and therefore one may no longer speak of craft.

Yet another potentially anomalous feature is the lack of utility. The prevailing view is that typical folk objects are made not as pure art objects to be purchased by collectors outside the group, but as utilitarian objects for everyday use by the group. Although this criterion has been compromised by the phenomenon of tourist art – objects made not for local consumption but for sale as souvenirs to tourists[17] – many continue to believe that the "true" or "pure" folk object is a utilitarian one for local consumption. The objects created by channel players were "useful" in the sense that they served as tokens for interaction.

However, we shouldn't make too much of this fact – sometimes non-utilitarian folk art objects are made for local consumption (Quimby and Swank 1980: 52).

The *Random House College Dictionary* defines "craft" as "skill or dexterity;" the transitive verb "to craft something" is "to make or manufacture (an object, objects, product, etc.) with skill and careful attention to detail." Henry Lucie-Smith (1981: 7) defines craft as "handwork used for making objects." He divides the history of craft into three stages: the time when everything is craft; the period from the Renaissance to the Industrial Revolution, in which craft became differentiated from fine art;[18] and the period from the Industrial Revolution to our own time, in which the craft object became separated from industrial products made by machines (Lucie-Smith 1981: 11).

Writing a mere 15 years after Lucie-Smith, Malcolm McCullough (1996) provocatively suggests that we add a new stage in the history of craft – that of digital craft. His book gave legitimacy to my intuitions about the IRC players. The invention of the computer, particularly the personal computer, has opened up new possibilities for craft, he argues. Usually the term is set in opposition to "high-technology processes in which the hand plays a diminished role" (McCullough 1996: 21). He suggests, for example, that

> In digital production, craft refers to the condition where people apply standard technological means to unanticipated or indescribable ends. Works of computer animation, geometric modeling, and spatial databases get "crafted" when experts use limited software capacities resourcefully, imaginatively, and in compensation for the inadequacies of prepackaged, hard-coded operations . . . *To craft is to care* . . . to craft implies working at a personal scale – acting locally in reaction to anonymous, globalized, industrial production. (McCullough 1996: 21–22; italics added)

Not by chance, McCullough's comments echo hackers' appreciation of virtuosity (Chapter 1). Moreover, all this applies to IRC art too, in which careful eye-hand coordination were also of paramount importance. Moreover, the players actually spoke of their creations as "handmade" when crafted step by step, rather than produced by a conversion program which takes the labor out of producing them. And Joan Stark stressed that she "drew" her art by hand, without the aid of conversion programs (Chapter 5).

As for the lack of tangibility, here I agree with John Ruskin, who, along with William Morris,[19] was an ardent critic of the effects of the Industrial Revolution, that the role of hands is more important than the material itself:

For it is not the material, but the absence of human labor, which makes the thing worthless; a piece of terra cotta, or of plaster of Paris, which has been wrought by the human hand, is worth all the stone in Carrara, cut by machinery. (Ruskin 1989 [1849], cited in McCullough 1996: 14)

Like McCullough (1996: 65), I believe it can become meaningless to ask what is truly made by hand. In nearly all forms of handwork, some kind of tool is involved.[20] What is critical is not what is or is not considered handmade, but the matter of control. "Continuous control of process is at the heart of tool usage and craft practice" (McCullough 1996: 66). The players on IRC displayed remarkable skill and control of their medium.

Intellectual Property Issues

One other feature of this art might prevent its being recognized as an emergent folk art. Starting around 1998, artists became increasingly preoccupied with issues of intellectual property – both on the Web and on IRC. Some thinkers believe that traditional folk artists are not preoccupied with originality. Thus, one of America's best known experts on folk art, Henry Glassie, claimed that true folk art is generally unsigned and anonymous, that many different people may create similar objects, though insiders can often recognize the work of individual artists or craftsmen (Glassie 1989: 184).[21] Nevertheless, objects that seem to fit the category of folk art in other respects are often signed.[22]

The Growth of Concern with Intellectual Property Issues

In the past there had been very little concern among ASCII artists and enthusiasts with recognition of originality. Among the dozens of Websites housing ASCII art collections and archives in the 1990s, few paid attention to the issue of who had created the images stored there. Most images did not include a name, initials or an email address. As readers saw in Chapter 5, quite a few of the early images I included as illustrations gave no name or email address, and thus I was unable to approach the artists for permission to use the image.

In the second half of the 1990s, some sites started paying closer attention to this matter. Thus, a site run by Lennert Stock, that displays a large collection of favorites from *alt.ascii-art* started in September 1996, includes the statement, "The copyright holder of each picture is the artist."[23] However, in the majority of cases, the artist was not named. All too often, the identity of the artist is simply unknown. In some cases, managers of archives and collections openly acknowledged their inability to give credit to the artists, and solicited help from visitors to identify specific creations.

A 1997 FAQ file for subscribers to *alt.ascii.art* urged:

If the picture contains a few letters in one corner which don't seem to be part of the picture, they're the artist's initials. DO NOT remove these initials – would you cut away the part of a Van Gogh painting containing his name?

Leaving the initials on is a small price to pay for being able to use the picture for free.

If you're going to use a picture in your signature file. . . you should really e-mail the artist (or post to the newsgroup, if you don't know their address) and ask for permission, because otherwise people may get the mistaken impression that you were the one who drew the picture. (Thomas 1997)

In the "ASCII Art FAQ Ten Commandments," enthusiasts were even urged not to post unsigned art unless one reported than one had not created it (Thomas 1998).

The art of Joan Stark[24] was extremely popular. While she was glad to share her work with others, her Website revealed much concern with copyright issues.[25] On the initial page of her site was the prominent admonition:

ASCII ARTWORK COPYRIGHTED. (c)1996–1999. Joan G. Stark. ALL RIGHTS RESERVED.

LEAVE INITIALS ON ALL ASCII ART IMAGES

PLEASE READ THE GUIDELINES FOR USING THIS ASCII ART (capital letters in the original).

Clicking on the Guidelines link, one reached the following:

Please keep in mind that even though I have posted my ASCII art on the internet, the pictures are still my property – and they follow internet copyright laws. If you would like to use some of my ASCII artwork, I ask the following three things:

* please leave my initials "jgs" on the pictures –

*please don't receive compensation for use of my artwork! Non-commercial use please! (Unless you write to me.)

*if you have a website, please consider linking to this website.

Stark even gave links to two sites offering information on copyright law.[26]

There was also much concern with copyright on the IRC channels and their Websites. For many months the *rainbow* Website contained the following admonition:

> Please remember, when you download anything here it has been made by someone at one point or another, be it ascii art, a script, or colored pictures, this is there [sic] work. Taking art or an idea and placing your name on it is wrong. Please respect all of the artists who so generously offer to share there [sic] talents with us.

In late 1999, matters escalated dramatically. <patches> had added a new section called "You be the Judge," Displaying two images, one clearly marked "The Original," by a *rainbow* artist, the other marked "The Copy," by someone from *colors* who claimed it as her own work, <patches> wrote, in an oversized font:[27]

> You be the Judge
>
> That's right, this time, you decide, did she copy, or really draw the castle on her own.
>
> She will tell you she did, but the fact remains that I believe she took the idea from seeing it and made small changes so she could call it her own. An infamous trick from the very beginning. Why I remember the time very well that she once tried to convince us that. . . she drew it, when in fact it was taken from the web with those initials removed. She didn't even start adding initials, till she was practically forced to do so.[28]

Who was right in this instance is not the issue; what is of interest is that concern with such matters was so salient to the players.

As noted in Chapter 6, it is quite common for players to modify others' images in some way, for instance, to color an originally black and white creation for display on IRC. This is considered entirely legitimate if credit for the original image is given, as Joan Stark requests.[29] But just how much must be different in order to be absolved of giving credit to the previous artist? This was unclear and was likely to continue to be a matter of negotiation. We have seen that many of Stark's works were used on IRC without acknowledging her contribution. There was a practice of embedding the name or nickname of the artist in the code behind an image, but in such cases the name would not be visible when the image was played online. I was surprised to learn that the players considered this a legitimate way of giving credit, even though it was invisible on screen.

One indication of growing social pressure to attend to these issues was a site called "Respect ASCII Artists,"[30] that sought to educate visitors about a "Respect ASCII Artists Campaign." The campaign had its own customized virtual blue ribbon. This site urged:

> When an ascii artists [sic] draws any art, that art is rightfully theirs. . . . Most Ascii artists will tag their art in some form or another. . . .
>   Anything really, not belonging to you should not be changed without prior consent of that particular artist or creator. It's just common sense and respect toward others.

Like Joan Stark, this woman includes links to sites offering information on legal aspects of copyright.

Comparison with Developments in Popular Music

In the latter half of the 1990s lawyers and legal scholars and others began to struggle with a host of difficult issues raised by digital art works for copyright law.[31] Two programs for the distribution of music files online, Napster[32] and Gnutella,[33] began to make headlines. These programs enable thousands of users to swap music files directly, downloading from each others' home computer, rather than from a centralized file server. This innovation threatened major financial interests of musicians, composers and the compact disc industry.

The young men who created Napster and Gnutella were working in much the spirit of early hacker culture. Thus, in a Time Magazine article on Shawn Fanning, the creator of Napster, Karl Garo Greenfeld's (2000) description of him fits the hacker stereotype: "awake 60 straight hours writing code," "crashing on his uncle's sofa or the floor," seeking to exploit "the transgressive power of the Internet to leap over barriers and transform our assumptions about business, content, and culture."

Whatever the outcome of the legal cases surrounding Napster and Gnutella, one thing is clear: the hacker spirit generally opposes applying traditional notions of copyright to digital creations, whereas in the present case, IRC artists and players are, once again, very traditional in their orientation, trying to cling to notions of intellectual property from print culture. In pointing to this fact I am by no means criticizing them, just putting their orientation into broader context.

Intellectual Property and Avant-garde Digital Art

In the world of avant-garde visual art there are similar struggles over intellectual property issues. The ease with which a work can be modified or transformed is a source of great concern to some. Thus, the Getty Conservation Institute organized a conference on this issue. The conference packet included "a document recommending a system that would guarantee artists 'exclusive rights' to ensure that they 'maintain control' of their work" (Ippolito 1998). It is fascinating to note that some people in the digital art world are taking quite the opposite position. Thus, in an essay called "Intellectual Property or Intellectual Paucity?" (Ippolito 1998), Jon Ippolito, a digital artist and curator of media arts at Guggenheim Soho, discussed issues of reproduction, distribution and communication with the public. Reviewing developments in digital art and parallels with conceptual art in the 1960s and 1970s, he concluded that

> Artists and arts administrators should stop wasting time trying to impose conventional copyrights on digital media. Their time would be much better spent cracking open a book on Conceptual art, where they would find solutions invented in the 1960s to problems that didn't surface till the 1990s. Maybe then they would realize that object-oriented models of intellectual property are impediments to, rather than protectors of, artistic imagination (Ippolito 1998).[34]

Fans of IRC art are not likely to develop such an ideological position.

The preoccupations of ASCII and IRC artists and and their friends and fans with matters of digital intellectual property came to the fore at a time when borderlines between ethical and legal considerations were very blurred. Viewed in the context of the developments just surveyed, one has the impression that these artists and their fans were resorting to the rhetoric of legal rights in order to create social pressure for informal social norms, not really seeking to put a legal structure in place to pursue issues of copyright. In my opinion, it is unlikely that this art will become the subject of full-fledged legal battles, because of the lack of an objective criterion of value of the art works, and perhaps also because the parties lack the financial and other resources to pursue their interests.

Although prominent concern with intellectual property among *rainbow* people appears to conflict with at least some notions of folk art, I believe that the concept of folk art best characterized the substance and the spirit of this artistic activity as this book went to press. One change that can already be discerned within the short span of three years and a half years since I began this study is decreased dependence on the ASCII art of the past, while acknowledging a debt to it. At my invitation, <patches> summed up:

> It is with a note of praise that I commend the artists of yesterday, who gave us what we have today. The[ir] ability, their creativity, the sharing of the art they so generously gave us. Had it not been for these "pioneers" we certainly would not have gotten as

far as we have today. . . . In 1996, we mostly depended upon ASCII art on the web. . . . four years later . . . many artists create there [sic] own work, without the help of ASCII art.[35]

In my own terminology, the pronounced concerrn with pattern and symmetry, along with use of brilliant color and exotic typographic characters, is what makes IRC art distinctive.

Citing the contributions of eight artists and scripters, <patches> also pointed to potential themes for future research: "We've seen the influence of tv, movies, sounds, and even cartoons come into the art."[36] The fact that zipped files of the works of 70 artists came to be stored for downloading on the *rainbow* Website argues for increased importance of the art and artists in the future, and perhaps a different mix of social and aesthetic elements in this emergent culture from the one that characterized it during the period studied.

Fonts and Intellectual Property

There was parallel concern with intellectual property issues in relation to fonts, the topic of Chapter 7. Naturally, professional type designers and typographers struggled with the consequences of digitization, since major commercial interests were at stake. Thus, a Website called "Typeright," linked to many professional and amateur font Websites, issued "The Typeright Guide to Ethical Type Design." It defined originality as:

> the degree of authorship you contribute to the typeface design. To have originated a typeface design, you must have created the design and not copied it. If, on the other hand, you set out to duplicate the style of an existing typeface, then you are creating a revival. And if your typeface is based on the outlines from another typeface then you are creating a derivative typeface (also known as "remix").[37]

The guide acknowledged that "remixing" and renaming were "gray areas," and warned against "piracy."

Since I have stressed grassroots participation on the Internet in this book, it is more pertinent to examine how amateur font designers dealt with this issue. In general, there is much similarity between their views and those expressed in relation to ASCII art. No doubt, this is in large part because of the commitment to circulating free goods (or shareware, in the case of fonts) by amateurs.

One of the amateur designers featured in Chapter 7, Tom Murphy, gave much thought to these issues (Figure 8.2). Note that he wants to be generous because he knows that "people benefit from the fact that I give them away. I

. . . I am employing a very generous license with these fonts...because *I know that people benefit from the fact that I give them away. I take enough stuff for free and it makes me feel good to know that I am 'giving back'.*

. . . You are free to download and use these fonts without my explicit permission for anything you want, except for the following:

You may NOT resell the actual font files (without my written permission and without having to give me something in return). . . .
You may not misrepresent the creator of the font (pretend you made them).
You may not adapt them to different fonts without my permission.
You may not modify the font files for subsequent redistribution.

However, you have permission to do the following:

Use them to make graphics for your home page, non-profit web page, or commerical [sic] web site.
Give them to your friends for free.
Make them available (for free) on your web page, as long as you don't pretend you made them. . . .
Use them in design work that you get paid for.
Use them in any smalltime publications or fliers or other non mass-produced literature.

Make commercial products like T-shirts or Mugs or Books using the fonts and sell them. In this case, since you are indirectly profiting off of my work, I ask that you send me one of the T-shirts or Mugs or Books free, where reasonable. . . . If it is inappropriate for you to send me one of your product, at least make an attempt to write me. . . and let me know where the font is being used. . . .

Figure 8.2. Tom Murphy's license for use of his fonts (abridged). "Divide by Zero," http://fonts.tom7.com/legal/.

take enough stuff for free and it makes me feel good to know that I am 'giving back'." People may even freely use his fonts on T-shirts and mugs and in books; all he asks is to receive an exemplar.

I too struggled with intellectual property issues as I chose the illustrations for Chapter 7. It was by no means obvious to me whether reproducing an image of a font without permission was a potential infringement on the rights of the person who designed it, or those of the person who designed the *display* in which the font was presented. Is an image of a font – as represented by its name or some other expression in the font at issue, a use of it?[38] With few exceptions (e.g., the designer of Hacker Argot, Figure 7.29), I chose to contact

Webmasters rather than font designers, on the assumption that I wasn't using the font in the sense of creating text with it, and given that, by and large, I sought to display freeware and shareware fonts, not commercial ones. Murphy's position points toward the kind of economy based on trust and cooperation that John Perry Barlow envisaged when he wrote that coercive legal sanctions were not likely to be effective in the digital world (Barlow 1994).

Issues of intellectual property in relation to text-based art and fonts are, of course, but special cases of far more general problems that digitization raises in relation to text, visual images, and sound. We see in microcosm some of the struggles between libertarian and regulatory approaches to the domestication of the Net that will no doubt continue to dominate in the early years of the 21st century.[39]

Bi-Stability of Text and Image

It is intriguing now to return to Richard Lanham's (1993) notion of the bi-stable text, discussed in Chapter 1. There, I reviewed his argument that, whereas the print text invites us to look through it to the meaning, the digital text is bi-stable: we are invited both to look through it and AT it. As we saw in Chapter 7, font enthusiasts are preoccupied with the "look" of digital typefaces. It seems clear that font frenzy is fostered by the bi-stability of digital text. Moreover, the punning and other forms of wordplay documented in Hamnet performances in Chapter 3 – the result of paying extra attention to linguistic form – flourished because of the masked identities and virtual co-presence of the participants, as well as the lingering presence of words on the screen.

Lanham's point is also relevant for my study of IRC art. I suggest that IRC art (Chapter 6) is characterized by *bi-stability of the digital image*. Because IRC art is experienced interactively, we are constantly invited both to look THROUGH the images to the communicative intent of the player displaying them, and AT the images as artistic creations.

Playfulness Revisited

In the introduction to this book, I suggested that *prima facie*, four factors, or sets of factors fostered playfulness in the new medium in the mid- to late 1990s. They were: objective features of the medium itself, and particularly its interactive, dynamic, immersive nature; hacker culture with its valorization of wit and play with symbols and typography, and a predilection for various forms of subversiveness; the "Wild West" quality of cyberspace as a new and relatively unsettled social and cultural frontier governed by few norms; and the masking of identity – the lack of cues to physical appearance, ethnic identity, gender, etc. To what extent did these factors play a role in the five studies reported in this book?

The first study, of the language of public email, was not primarily about playfulness, but about the lack of norms for public or business email in the mid-1990s, and the response to situations in which writers were presumed to juggle the constraints of traditional letter-writing norms on the one hand, and the invitation to informality of email on the other. At the same time, playfulness was a secondary theme.

In the case of email I would assign the greatest weight to the digital medium itself, its interactivity and dynamism, that invite one to write as one speaks. While hacker culture has certainly influenced the language of email generally, its effects were not striking in my corpora. With the exception of the letter from Technosmurf (Figure 2.4), the letters I analyzed were not chock-full of playful elements. Thus, although the medium invites both oralisms and playfulness, situational constraints limit it in official communication between strangers, and in situations where persons of authority can influence significant outcomes for writers.

With regard to business or public email, a fifth factor also fostered playfulness: the age and experience of the writer. In a period of normative ambiguity, people drew on their experiences – young people who had not internalized the traditional distinction between personal and business letter-writing brought expectations from face-to-face conversation to email writing style. In extreme cases, represented in this book by the letter from Technosmurf , they wrote at least in part the way they talked. It was older people, steeped in the traditions of literate culture, who experienced the latent conflicts I analyzed in Chapter 2.

All three components of playfulness, as formulated by J. Nina Lieberman (1977), spontaneity, manifest expressions of joy, and humor, were prominent in Hamnet scripts and performances. Spontaneity abounded since improvisation was at the heart of the entire enterprise, the key element that made these experiments in virtual theater exciting for the players and their audience, and for readers, later on. There was ample humor and wit in many of these improvisations, the most notable being the brilliant sequence of "ping-pong" punning during a performance of "PCbeth." Moreover, there were more explicit signs of pleasure and even joy in the material analyzed in this study than any other, probably because of the synchronous nature of the communication involved. The double masking of identity also helped liberate the players, releasing often surprising wit and play with language, the IRC software, Shakespearean texts, and so on. While few people actually typed "hehe", evidence of joy and pleasure included compliments that the players gave to one another, the typed shouts of "bravo!" and the virtual clapping at the end of performances, and the hijinks at "cast parties." Finally, as I began to suggest earlier, the persistence of words on screen in digital chat invites paying attention to, and playing with words.

In Chapter 4 my main goal was to offer a critique of digital greetings – to document and explicate the failure of the designers of these sites to deal with life's troubles. Looking back on this material now, it seems to me that the designers of these Websites had a great deal of fun. The exuberant graphics, typography, animations, and use of color in them all point to the fun designers had, experimenting with this new medium in a cultural "Wild West" where no clear norms existed to guide them.

In some respects both ASCII art and font frenzy were outgrowths of hacker culture. To make pictures from typographic symbols was to divert digital codes from their initial purposes, to convey information. The hacker spirit was less diluted in the earlier art than in the IRC variety. The virtuoso programming tricks that made ANSI possible at the DOS level for BBSs and the development of special programs to convert regular images to ASCII are both instances of making computers do more than they were originally designed to do. Also, the content of early ASCII art (and later underground ASCII art) drew on the transgresssive preoccupations of adolescent male popular culture.

With regard to IRC art, in Chapter 6 I emphasized the traditional, non-controversial nature of the imagery. But we should not forget that this art was also a subversion of the primary purpose of letters and symbols – to convey textual meaning – and was also made possible by virtuoso scripting by <texxy> and others, once again a manifestation of the original spirit of hacker culture. The masking of identity on IRC certainly also played a role in liberating players and artists to express themselves.

As for font frenzy, the dynamic flexibility of the medium made it easy for lay persons to learn to design their own fonts, often with great visual wit and humor. The playful hacker spirit found somewhat transformed expression in a love of fonts with "attitude," fonts that "danced" on the screen or visually shouted "Look at me!" At the same time, hackers would not have appreciated the love of mere decorativeness that characterized many font enthusiasts. Another hacker-like phenomenon was the insistence of many font designers and collectors on offering fonts as freeware and shareware, opting out of the possibility of making money from them. Most directly, perhaps, the hacker spirit lay behind the design of fonts extending the eccentric hacker look from plain text to a wider range of typefaces usable in word-processing (Figures 7.27, 7.28), and in the cultivation of intentionally distressed, subversive-looking grunge fonts (Figures 7.20, 7.29). Although one didn't have to fit the stereotype of a hacker to be hostile to Times New Roman, there were remnants of hacker subversiveness in the various parodies of it that I documented in Chapter 7.

A Grand "Grand Piano" on the Desktop

The main conclusion of this book is that by the end of the 20th century the computer had become a grand "grand piano," an exciting expressive instrument that opened up many new avenues for human expression and communication, for people of all walks of life without extensive formal training in programming or hardware aspects of computing. Three of the five case studies, of digital writing as playful performance (Chapter 3), ASCII art and its close cousin, IRC art (Chapters 5 and 6), and font frenzy (Chapter 7) addressed this issue directly. Moreover, the material on forms of textual and visual performance in Chapters 3 and 6 shows that the expressive potential of computers flourishes particularly when users are online.

In the introduction I spoke of the metaphor of a symphony orchestra and its conductor. I suggested that computer users are both the conductor and the players, able to call on the myriad effects at their disposal. But we have seen that they are no less the composer as well. Early designers of typewriters were quite interested in the piano keyboard as a model for how to build a typewriter. However, their interest was purely instrumental and technical.[40] I am suggesting, in contrast, that phenomenologically speaking, in the postmodern era of the Internet, using a computer came to resemble making music. As an amateur classical pianist who has been deeply involved at times in chamber music, I have been aware of the potential similarities – both physical and experiential – in playing the two keyboards – *especially when playing with others.*

The musical analogy seems apt at two levels, both at the general level of the experience of using computers and the Internet, and at the level of online communication in synchronous modes.[41] The studies in Chapter 3 elucidated some of the similarities of stylized chat to improvisational jam sessions. So attractive was the analogy to improvisational jazz, in which the players take turns elaborating in different ways on a theme, that my co-authors and I called our first publication on textual and typographic improvisation *Virtual Virtuosos: Play and Performance at the Computer Keyboard* (Ruedenberg et al. 1995).

The similarity to jazz was especially noteworthy in the sequence of "ping pong" punning during a performance of "PCbeth," a parody of Shakespeare's *Macbeth.*[42] This sequence was like what jazz musicians call "striking a groove" (Berliner 1994: 349), an unusually dramatic example of how deep concentration and involvement, in a situation of doubly masked identities and of "live" though remote co-presence, could yield remarkably creative, witty, improvisational uses of language – even when a pre-determined script was at the heart of the performance.[43]

The idea that words "onstage" could have musical qualities is of course not new. This idea was famously brought to fruition in Dylan Thomas's *Under Milk Wood, a Play for Voices* (Thomas 1954b), an account of a day in the life of a Welsh town by the sea. The play begins:

FIRST VOICE (Very softly)

To begin at the beginning:
It is Spring, moonless night in a small town, starless and bible-black, the cobblestreets silent and the hunched, courters'-and-rabbits' wood limping invisible down to the sloeblack, slow, black, crowblack, fishingboat-bobbing sea. (Thomas 1954b: 1)

As anyone who has heard recordings of this work can attest, the quality of the different individuals' voices and their mellifluous patterns of Anglo-Welsh intonation sharply contrast with one another, bringing out the unique personality and life circumstances of each. Yet, there is a unity to the work as a whole, a richly evocative mosaic of sound and sense.[44] But in performance Dylan Thomas's work is, after all, a wholly scripted and spoken one. Our concern here is with improvisational, inscribed communication among individuals remotely connected in real time – something new in the world.

As I showed in Chapter 3, Antoinette LaFarge, one of the practitioners of virtual theater whose activities were reviewed toward the end of that chapter, repeatedly drew on musical metaphors in trying to elucidate the special qualities of online text-based performance. When asked what is the peculiar charm in this seemingly limited type of performance, she wrote, "A single text of many voices sounds very different from what we normally expect of writing; closer to *cantata* than to prose" (italics added).[45] Other musical metaphors mentioned by her included "rhythm," "staccato," and "vocal counterpoint," all terms that one might use in connection with *Under Milk Wood* too.

Unbeknown to me at the time I first began thinking about the analogy between digital communication and music, Sherry Turkle was also developing it. In 1991 she published a paper entitled, "If the Computer Is a Tool, Is It More Like a Hammer or a Harpsichord?" (Turkle 1991). Turkle contrasted two aesthetics, an earlier "modernist" one, which conceived of computers as rational, efficient instruments best suited for calculations of all kinds, for "serious" work, versus a postmodern one extensively based on simulation, in which computers could become expressive, even playful instruments. As long as large mainframe computers dominated, the modernist aesthetic reigned, but with the advent of personal computers (first the Macintosh, later the IBM-compatible PC), color screens, powerful graphics, and CD-ROMs, ordinary users discovered that they could use a computer in many new and different ways, without needing to know how either the computer or the software actually worked. Incorporating portions of the hammer-harpsichord paper in her book, *Life on the Screen: Identity in the Age of the Internet*, Turkle argued:

> In the emerging culture of simulation, the computer is still a tool but less like a hammer and more like a harpsichord. You don't learn how to play a harpsichord primarily by learning a set of rules, just as you don't learn about a simulated micro-world. . . by delving into an instruction manual. In general, you learn by playful exploration. (Turkle 1995: 61).

Whereas Turkle's own book explored play with identity online, this book has explored artful play with communication itself, with the form of messages, and, in the case of font frenzy, with the very shapes of letters and typographic symbols.

It may not be chance, then, that participants in the form of interactive art practiced on IRC (Chapter 6) spoke of "playing a file," an expression that recalls "playing a tune." It is noteworthy that a number of other individuals mentioned in this book were also involved in music. Rick Sacks, yet another of those experimenting with text-based virtual theater whose activities I surveyed toward the end of Chapter 3, described himself on his Website as a "a percussionist/ composer/multimedia artist." We also saw that three individuals featured prominently in Chapter 7 were involved in music: two young people who designed their own fonts, and Absinth, former convener of Fonts Anon~. Todd Dever of "Cool Fonts Online" reported in his Website biography that he occasionally played in two popular music groups. And Tom Murphy of "Divide by Zero" had his own band. I asked him a question that ostensibly had nothing to do with music, "How do you see what you do versus what professionally trained designers and typographers do?" In his reply he drew on the musical analogy:

> I guess in my infinite naive-college-student angst, I'd liken it to the difference between commerical [sic] radio Rock Star music and independent, home-studio artists. The archetypal Rock Star has goals and requirements in addition to (or overshadowing) the music that she or he makes. The Rock Star has to make radio singles, and avoid offending people. This doesn't mean that his or her music *necessarily* suffers – some of my favorite fonts were created by famous commercial designers. The independent musician has sometimes has fewer resources, but no commitments beyond his or her art. Similarly, this doesn't mean that she or he automatically makes better music. But there is definitely more freedom.[46]

Finally, two women featured in my research were professional classical musicians by training. Absinth, the first manager of Fonts Anon~, is a professional violinist turned graphic artist and Webmaster, who told me that she found it perfectly natural to switch to the medium of the computer. And perhaps it is no coincidence that <patches>, leader of *#mirc_rainbow* (Chapter 6), is not only a highly experienced quilter but a professionally trained former flutist.

In the introduction I noted that this book is intended as a kind of "snapshot" or "time capsule" of playful, artful activity on the Internet. My five case studies are but a tiny sampling of the enormous amount of experimentation that took place on the Net in the mid- to late 1990s. The Internet will not make the world a better place, only a very different one from the one we have known. I acknowledge that there is a dark side to the Internet, that its seductive aspects can be deleterious for some, that it can be used to promulgate evil in the world, that commercialization is proceeding apace, and that not everyone will reap the benefits of the new medium. Nevertheless, this book celebrates the activities studied and the people engaged in them, and argues that computers and the Internet have great potential to enrich people's lives, a potential we only dimly perceived as a new millennium began.

However, we cannot take for granted that the playful spirit that flourished at the end of the 20th century will continue to flourish in the 21st. In the very period documented in this book, government and the forces of commercialization sought to transform an anarchic, even unregulable sphere, to use Lawrence Lessig's (1999) term, into an increasingly regulated one. Lessig's book analyzes the implications of the thesis that "code is law." It is no less apt to suggest that "code is culture" – that the programming codes that constitute and regulate the spaces in which people congregate online will shape the kinds of playfulness that are possible. Let us hope that playfulness will continue to flourish online in the 21st Century. And let us work to make sure that it does.

Notes

1. NUA Surveys were at http://www.nua.ie/surveys/how_many_online/index.html. The site does not explain what the initials NUA stand for; it is based in Ireland.

2. America Online Website, http://www.aol.com/. Accessed Christmas Day, 1999.

3. See http://www.icq.com/.

4. GVU is an abbreviation for "Graphical, Visualization, & Usability Center," the organization at George Tech that runs the surveys.

5. These figures were not updated on Collins' Website as of October 2000, and she did not answer email, so I cannot report whether any changes had taken place by the time this book was completed.

6. Greetings were offered in cooperation with American Greetings, Inc. I had much to say about the latter corporation in Chapter 4. Regarding paper cards, in this instance one paid for the card as well as for having it sent to the recipient.

7. Animation was done with a light touch. In one case, butterflies fluttered; in the other flowers moved. There was no cuteness of animated cartoons.

8. Unfortunately, I do not have comparable information for earlier years on AOL. There is evidence for eager adoption of digital greetings by large numbers of people in the late 1990s in Miller and Slater's (2000) study of Internet use among Trinidadians. A late 2000 survey by the PEW Internet and American Life Project (Horrigan 2000) found that a third of Americans online had sent holiday digital greetings.

9. In Chapter 6 I noted that stamp collecting was one such activity. In Danet and Katriel (1989) we included a photograph of the weekly stamp market in Madrid, in which hundreds of people of all ages trade stamps.

10. She had played in a professional symphony orchestra.

11. Within the fields of both folklore and the history of art, folk art has been treated as something of a stepchild. Having attended quite a few annual meetings of the American Folklore Society, I can attest that folk art sessions are rather rare. A book such as Dan Ben-Amos's *Folklore Genres* (Ben-Amos 1975) is actually only about verbal folklore. As for the status of folk art within the history of art, Walter Cahn informs me that here too, folk art is quite marginal. Note that folk artists never apply the term "folk art" to themselves; it is a term used by intellectuals and art world professionals.

12. Cf. Kollock and Smith (1999); see also Bergquist (2000). How this gift economy works and the role it plays in fostering a sense of community in the channels, especially *rainbow*, is a subject I will pursue in future research.

13. I should not overstate my case: in the world of high art, museums and individuals have begun to acquire digital artworks for a price. Tsameret Wachenhauser (personal email, October 16, 2000) informs me that

> The first piece of net artwork that was actually sold to anyone was "The World's Longest Sentence" (http://here.is/THESENTENCE) by Douglas Davis (a net/video artist). It was first sold to a New York art collector, Eugene D. Schwartz [and his wife Barbara] in Jan[uary] 1995) and later donated. . . to the Whitney Museum [of American Art in New York].

For further information see http://www.nettime.org/nettime.w3archive/200005/msg 00099.html and http://www.whitney.org/collection/internet/intro.html. Like RL folk art, perhaps IRC art and related forms may come to have monetary value too. I am well aware that my designating this art as a form of a folk art may even help this to happen.

14. For a review of the history of definitions of folk art over a period of 100 years or so, see Glassie (1989).

15. Howard Finster is an evangelical preacher in Georgia who became one of America's best known naive artists. Simon Rodia is the creator of the Watts towers. Grandma Moses is perhaps the most famous naive American artist of all time. This term was introduced by Roger Cardinal in 1972 (Cardinal 1972). John Maizels (1996)

apparently incorporates folk art within outsider art. The exhibit and catalogue by Laurent Danchin and Martine Lusardy (1999) also seem to confound the two. Most others see them as independent, quite different categories. Cf., e.g., Zug (1994); Hall and Metcalfe (1994); Bonesteel (1988). "Outsider art" generally connotes the creations of individuals for whom making art is less important than giving expression to powerful inner experience (Maizels 1996: 114). The term is most often associated with the art of the insane.

16. See the discussion of contingency, lag and netsplits in Chapter 6.

17. See e.g., Graburn (1976).

18. See Walter Cahn's (1979) study of the evolution of the concept of masterpiece for details on this process.

19. For more on Ruskin and Morris and the British and American Arts and Crafts movements, see Lucie-Smith (1981), Chapters 11 and 12; Boris (1986). Naylor (1990); Anscombe and Gere (1978); Kaplan and Cummings (1991); Lambourne (1980).

20. McCullough (1996: 65): 65) notes two rare exceptions in which the hands work directly with a material – pottery and basketweaving.

21. See Glassie (1989), pp. 184–187 and p.197.

22. For instance, two woodcarvings from Oxaca, Mexico that I purchased are both signed. Entire families are involved in the work; women and girls do the painting, and men and boys the carving (Barbash 1993). Only the carver gets to sign his name on the object. Commodification as tourist art for consumption by outsiders may foster awareness of accomplishment as a unique artist. The presence of the signature might merely signal the mediator's awareness that modern dealers and consumers expect it. My carvings were not purchased *in situ* but in a museum shop and a gallery.

23. Stock's site is "Amazing ASCII Pics," http://www.lstock.demon.nl/aap0.html.

24. She was dubbed "Queen of ASCII Art" by someone on *alt.ascii-art* in September 1998. See my discussion of her art in Chapter 5.

25. See her Website, http://www.ascii-art.com/.

26. The sites were "Internet Copyright Information," http://www.templetons.com/brad/copymyths.html, " and "Intellectual Property Law Primer for Multimedia Developers, by J. Dianne Brinson and Mark F. Radcliffe," http://www.timestream.com/stuff/neatstuff/mmlaw.html.

27. The use of the oversize font had an effect similar to that of typing in all caps – shouting to emphasize the importance of the message.

28. The page for this new section was at http://www.mirc-rainbow.com/ubthejudge/urjudge.htm. Accessed 24 December 1999.

29. Among needlepoint practitioners this is also considered legitimate: the American Needlepoint Guild includes among its prizes several for adaptations of designs created by others; see its Website, URL http://www.needlepoint.org/.

30. This site was at http://designs.multiservers.com/mIRC/respect.html.

31. See, e.g., Samuelson (1991); Jacobson (1999); Elkin-Koren (1996); and the large bibliography on copyright and the online world in the Cyberspace Law Bibliography at http://www.gseis.ucla.edu/iclp/bib4.html.

32. See http://www.napster.com and Greenfeld (2000); Heilemann (2000); Richtel (2000).

33. See http://gnutella.wego.com and "The Ultimate Gnutella Resources Site," http://www.ultimateresourcesite.com/gnutella/main.htm.

34. Some of Ippolito's collaborative digital art works can be seen at http://www.three.org.

35. Personal email from <patches>, 13 November 2000.

36. Personal email from <patches>, 13 November 2000. The playing of sound files to accompany images became increasingly important. I have not been able to address this phenomenon in the current research. Note that, although herself a quilter, <patches> ordinarily makes no reference to similarities with, or resemblances to, the textile arts I have discussed in this chapter.

37. See http://www.typeright.org/.

38. While one could take the position that if there is no mention of copyright on a Website, this is public material and can be freely reproduced without infringing on legal rights, I contacted Webmasters by email as a matter of courtesy and to be ethically forthcoming. All those contacted who replied gladly agreed. A few did not respond to my letters.

39. See Lessig (1999). Christina Spiesel brought Lessig's book to my attention.

40. Cf. Beeching (1990: 39).

41. Typographic professionals also see an analogy between type design and music. The Website of Typeright, an association concerned with copyright protection of typefaces, notes, "An original typeface design might be likened to an original song that uses a set series of notes to form a unique tune." See http://www.typeright.org/ethicsguide.html. However, the analogy is to all typefaces, including pre-digital ones.

42. See Figure 3.15 and the discussion of this sequence in Chapter 3.

43. On the notions of doubly masked identities and "presence," see Chapter 3.

44. The original BBC production with Richard Burton and an all-Welsh cast was recorded in January 1954 (Thomas 1954a).

45. Personal email from Antoinette LaFarge, 19 August 1999. A more extensive passage from this email was included in Chapter 3.

46. Personal email from Tom Murphy, 29 January 1999.

Bibliography

Abbott, L. L. (1986). Comic Art: Characteristics and Potentialities of a Narrative Medium. *Journal of Popular Culture*, 19, 155–176.

Adelswärd, V. (1988). *Styles of Success: On Impression Management as Collaborative Action in Job Interviews*. Linköping, Sweden: Linköping University.

Ahl, F. (1988). *Ars Est Caelare Artem* (Art in Puns and Anagrams Engraved). In J. Culler (Ed.), *On Puns: The Foundation of Letters* (pp. 17–43). Oxford: Basil Blackwell.

Allan, K., & Burridge, K. (1991). *Euphemism and Dysphemism*. Oxford: Oxford University Press.

Allen, A., & Hoverstadt, J. (1990). *The History of Printed Scraps*. London: New Cavendish Books.

Allison, B. (1996). ASCII Art Resources. http://www.geocities.com/SoHo/8608/aaresources.txt.

Amir, Z. (1977). *Arabesque: Decorative Needlework from the Holy Land*. New York: Van Nostrand Reinhold.

Angell, D., & Heslop, B. (1994). *The Elements of E-Mail Style*. Reading, MA: Addison-Wesley Publishing Company.

Anscombe, I., & Gere, C. (1978). *The Arts and Crafts in Britain and America*. London: Academy.

Apollinaire, G. (1918). *Calligrammes: Poèmes de la paix et de la guerre*. Paris: Mercure de France.

Argyle, K. (1996). Life After Death. In R. Shields (Ed.), *Cultures of Internet: Virtual Spaces, Real Histories, Living Bodies* (pp. 133–142). London and Los Angeles: Sage.

Arnheim, R. (1954). *Art and Visual Perception: A Psychology of the Creative Eye*. Berkeley: University of California Press.

Aronson, S. (1971). The Sociology of the Telephone. *International Journal of Comparative Sociology*, 12, 153–167.

Atkins, J. M. (1994). *Shared Threads: Quilting Together – Past and Present*. New York: Viking Studio Books in association with the Museum of American Folk Art.

Atkins, M. (1998). ASCII Art Mini-FAQ (Frequently Asked Questions). http://www.geocities.com/SoHo/7373/minifaq.htm.

Atkinson, D., & Biber, D. (1994). Register: A Review of Empirical Research. In D. Biber & E. Finegan (Eds.), *Sociolinguistic Perspectives on Register* (pp. 351–385). New York and Oxford: Oxford University Press.

Attridge, D. (1988). Unpacking the Portmanteau, or Who's Afraid of Finnegan's Wake? In J. Culler (Ed.), *On Puns: The Foundations of Letters* (pp. 140–155). Oxford: Basil Blackwell.

Austin, J. L. (1970a). *How to Do Things with Words*. Oxford: Oxford University Press.

—— (1970b). *Philosophical Papers*. Oxford: Oxford University Press.

Avrin, L. (1984). Hebrew Micrography: One Thousand Years of Art in Script. *Visible Language*, 18, 87–95.

—— (1991). *Scribes, Script and Books: The Book Arts from Antiquity to the Renaissance*. Chicago and London: American Library Association and the British Library.

Aytot, J., & Simpson, J. (1992). *Oxford Dictionary of Modern Slang*. Oxford and New York: Oxford University Press.

Babcock, B. (1986). Modeled Selves: Helen Cordero's "Little People". In V. Turner & E. M. Bruner (Eds.), *The Anthropology of Experience*. Urbana, IL: University of Illinois Press.

——, Monthan, G., & Monthan, D. (1986). *The Pueblo Storyteller: Development of a Figurative Ceramic Tradition*. Tucson, AZ: University of Arizona Press.

Bakhtin, M. (1968). *Rabelais and His World*. Cambridge, MA: M.I.T. Press.

Baldwin, B. W. (1996). *Conversations: Computer Mediated Dialogue, Multilogue, and Learning*. Unpublished Dissertation, University of North Carolina at Greensboro.

Banfield, E. (1989). *Visiting Cards and Cases*. Trowbridge, Wiltshire: Baros Books.

Banks, M., & Morphy, H. (Eds.). (1997). *Rethinking Visual Anthropology*. New Haven: Yale University Press.

Barbash, S. (1993). *Oaxacan Woodcarving: The Magic in the Trees*. San Francisco: Chronicle.

Barger, J. (1993). ASCII Art FAQ. http://www.stud.uni-hannover.de/~freise/ascii/zipped/faq_jorn.gz

Barlow, J. P. (1994). The economy of ideas: a framework for rethinking patents and copyrights in the digital age (everything you know about intellectual property is wrong). *Wired*, 2, 84–86, 88–90, 126–128, 129.

—— (1996). Crime and Puzzlement. In P. Ludlow (Ed.), *High Noon on the Electronic Frontier: Conceptual Issues in Cyberspace* (pp. 459–486). Cambridge, MA: M.I.T. Press.

Barnes, S. B. (1998). "Miss" or is that "Mis" Communication? Gender Issues in Online Discourse. Paper presented at the Annual Meeting, International Communication Association, Jerusalem, 1998.

Baron, N. S. (1998a). Letters by Phone or Speech by Other Means: the Linguistics of Email. *Language and Communication*, 18, 133–170.

—— (1998b). Writing in the Age of Email: The Impact of Ideology versus Technology. *Visible Language*, 32, 35–53.

—— (2000). *Alphabet to Email: How Written English Evolved and Where It's Heading*. New York and London: Routledge.

Barth, E. (1974). *Hearts, Cupids, and Red Roses: the Story of the Valentine Symbols*. New York: Seabury Press.

Basso, K. (1974). The Ethnography of Writing. In R. Bauman & J. Sherzer (Eds.), *Explorations in The Ethnography of Speaking* (pp. 425–432). Cambridge: Cambridge University Press.

Bateson, G. (1972). A Theory of Play and Fantasy. In G. Bateson, *Steps to An Ecology of Mind* (pp. 177–193). New York: Ballantine.

Bauman, R. (1975). Verbal Art as Performance. *American Anthropologist*, 77, 290–311.

—— (1977). *Verbal Art as Performance*. Prospect Heights, IL: Waveland Press.

—— (1992). Performance. In R. Bauman (Ed.), *Folklore, Cultural Performances, and Popular Entertainments: A Communications-Centered Handbook* (pp. 41–49). New York: Oxford University Press.

Bauman, R., & Briggs, C. L. (1990). Poetics and Performance as Critical Perspectives on Language and Social Life. *Annual Review of Anthropology*, 19, 59–88.

Bauman, R., & Sherzer, J. (Eds.). (1974). *Explorations in the Ethnography of Speaking*. Cambridge: Cambridge University Press.

—— (1989). *Explorations in the Ethnography of Speaking*. Cambridge: Cambridge University Press, 2nd ed.

Beaubien, M. P. (1996). Playing at Community: Multi-User Dungeons and Social Interaction in Cyberspace. In L. Strate, R. Jacobson & S. G. Gibson (Eds.), *Communication and Cyberspace: Social Interaction in an Electronic Environment* (pp. 179–188). Cresskill, NJ: Hampton Press.

Bechar-Israeli, H. (1995). From <Bonehead> to <Clonehead>: Nicknames, Play and Identity on Internet Relay Chat. *Journal of Computer-Mediated Communication*, 1 (2). http://jcmc.huji.ac.il/vol1/issue2 or http://www.ascusc.org/jcmc/vol1/issue2/.

Beeching, W. A. (1990). *Century of the Typewriter*. Bournemouth: British Typewriter Museum Publishing.

Belk, R. W. (1988). Possessions and the Extended Self. *Journal of Consumer Research*, 15, 265–280.

Bell, A. N. (1998). Abbreviated History of the Underground Computer Art Scene. http://www.acheron.org/.

Bellock, P. (1996). The Symptoms of Internet Addiction, *New York Times*. 1 December, 1996.

Ben-Amos, D. (1972). Toward a Definition of Folklore in Context. In A. Paredes & R. Bauman (Eds.). *Toward New Perspectives in Folklore* (pp. 3–15). Austin and London: University of Texas.

——, (Ed.) (1975). *Folklore Genres*. Austin: University of Texas.

Bergquist, M. (2000). The Power of Gifts: Negotiating Boundaries in an Online Community. Paper presented at the conference "Digital Borderlands: A Cybercultural Symposium," National Institute for Working Life, May 12–13, 2000. Norrköping, Sweden.

Berliner, P. F. (1994). *Thinking in Jazz: The Infinite Art of Improvisation*. Chicago: University of Chicago Press.

Besnier, N. (1995). *Literacy, Emotion and Authority*. Cambridge: Cambridge University Press.

Biber, D. (1988). *Variation Across Speech and Writing*. Cambridge: Cambridge University Press.

—— (1989). A Typology of English Texts. *Linguistics and Philosophy*, 27, 3–43.

Biber, D., & Finegan, E. (1988). Drift in Three English Genres from the 18th to the 20th Centuries: A Multidimensional Approach. In M. Kyto, O. Ihalainen & M. Rissanen (Eds.), *Corpus Linguistics, Hard and Soft* (pp. 83–101). Amsterdam: Rodopi.

—— (1989). Historial Drift in Three English Genres. In T. J. Walsh (Ed.), *Synchronic and Diachronic Approaches to Linguistic Variation:Georgetown University Roundtable*. Washington DC: Georgetown University Press.

——, & Finegan, E. (Eds.). (1994). *Sociolinguistic Perspectives on Register*. Oxford: Oxford University Press.

Bierut, M., Drenttel, W., Heller, S., & Holland, D. K. (Eds.). (1997). *Looking Closer 2: Critical Writings on Graphic Design*. New York: Allworth.

Bierut, M., Heller, S., Holland, D. K., & Drenttel, W. (Eds.). (1994). *Looking Closer: Critical Writings on Graphic Design*. New York: Allworth.

Billeter, J. F. (1990). *The Chinese Art of Writing*. New York: Rizzoli.

Biocca, F. (1997). The Cyborg's Dilemma: Progressive Embodiment in Virtual Environments. *Journal of Computer-Mediated Communication*, 3 (2). http://www.ascusc.org/jcmc/vol3/issue2.

Birkerts, S. (1994). *The Gutenberg Elegies: The Fate of Reading in an Electronic Age*. New York: Fawcett Columbine.

Bloom, H. (1994). *The Western Canon: The Books and School of the Ages*. New York: Harcourt Brace.

Blum-Kulka, S., Danet, B., & Gherson, R. (1985). The Language of Requesting in Israeli Society. In J. P. Forgas (Ed.), *Language and Social Situations* (pp. 113–139). New York and Berlin: Springer-Verlag.

Blum-Kulka, S., House, J., & Kasper, G. (1989). *Cross-Cultural Pragmatics: Requests and Apologies*: Ablex.

Boas, F. (1955 [1927]). *Primitive Art*. New York: Dover.

Bologh, R. W. (1979). Alienation in the Patient Role: Source of Ambivalence and Humor in Comic Get Well Cards. *Sociology of Health and Illness*, 1, 137–157.

Bolter, J. D. (1991). *Writing Space: The Computer, Hypertext, and the History of Writing*. Hillsdale, NJ: Lawrence Erlbaum.

Bonesteel, M. (1988). Outsider Art: Modernism's Parallel Aesthetic, *Maurice Legrand Lesueur Sullins: Paintings, 1970–1986* (pp. 1–2). Springfield, IL: Illinois State Museum.

Boureau, A. (1997). The Letter-writing Norm, a Medieval Invention. In R. Chartier, A. Boureau & C. Dauphin (Eds.), *Correspondence: Models of Letter-writing from the Middle Ages to the Nineteenth Century* (pp. 24–58). Princeton, NJ: Princeton University Press.

Boris, E. (1986). *Art and Labor: Ruskin, Morris, and the Craftsman Ideal in America*. Philadelphia: Temple University Press.

Brabant, S., & Mooney, L. (1989). Him, Her, or Either: Sex of Person Addressed and Interpersonal Communication. *Sex Roles*, 20, 47–58.

Bradac, J. J. (1982). A Rose by Any Other Name: Attitudinal Consequences of Lexical Variation. In E. B. Ryan & H. Giles (Eds.), *Attitudes towards Language Variation: Social and Applied Contexts* (pp. 99–115). London: Edward Arnold.

—— (1990). Language Attitudes and Impression Formation. In H. Giles & W. P. Robinson (Eds.), *Handbook of Language and Social Psychology* (pp. 387–412). Chicester and New York: Wiley.

Branscomb, A. W. (1997a). *Law on the Electronic Frontier, Part I. Journal of Computer-mediated Communication*, 2 (1). http://www.ascusc.org/jcmc/vol2/issue1 or http://jcmc.huji.ac.il/vol2/issue1.

—— (1997b). *Law on the Electronic Frontier, Part II. Journal of Computer-mediated Communication* 2 (2). http://www.ascusc.org/jcmc/vol2/issue2/ or http://jcmc.huji.ac.il/vol2/issue2/.

Brecher, K. S. (1988). *Too Sad to Sing: A Memoir with Postcards*. New York: Harcourt Brace Jovanovich.

Briggs, A. (1988). *Victorian Things*. Chicago: University of Chicago Press.

Briggs, C. (1980). *The Wood Carvers of Cordova, New Mexico: Social Dimensions of an Artistic Revival*. Knoxville, TN: University of Tennessee Press.

Briggs, C. L. (1988). *Competence in Performance: the Creativity of Tradition in Mexicano Verbal Art*. Philadelphia: University of Pennsylvania Press.

Bringhurst, R. (1996). *The Elements of Typographic Style*. Point Roberts, WA: Hartley & Marks.

Brinson, J. D., & Radcliffe, Mark F. (2000). Intellectual Property Law Primer for Multimedia Developers. http://www.timestream.com/stuff/neatstuff/mmlaw.html

Britton, J. (1982). Spectator Role and the Beginnings of Writing. In M. Nystrand (Ed.), *What Writers Know: The Language, Process, and Structure of Written Discourse* (pp. 149–169). New York: Academic Press.

Broch, H. (1969). Notes on the Problem of Kitsch. In G. Dorfles (Ed.), *Kitsch: The World of Bad Taste* (pp. 49–76). New York: Bell.

Bromberg, H. (1996). Are MUDs Communities? Identity, Belonging, and Consciousness in Virtual Worlds. In R. Shields (Ed.), *Cultures of Internet: Virtual Spaces, Real Histories, Living Bodies* (pp. 143–152). London: Sage.

Bronner, S. J. (1984). *Chain Carvers: Old Men Crafting Meaning*. Lexington: University Press of Kentucky.

Brown, M. (1997). *Edward Bear ESQ: The True Story of the Astonishing Achievements of Teddy*. New York: Stewart, Tabori & Chang.

Brown, M. P. (1994). Funk Music as Genre: Black Aesthetics, Apocalyptic Thinking and Urban Protest in Post–1965 African-American Pop. *Cultural Studies*, 8, 484–508.

Brown, R., & Ford, M. (1964). Address in American English. In D. Hymes (Ed.), *Language in Culture and Society* (pp. 234–243). New York: Harper & Row.

Brown, R., & Gilman, A. (1960). The Pronouns of Power and Solidarity. In T. A. Sebeok (Ed.), *Style in Language* (pp. 253–276). Cambridge, MA: M.I.T. Press.

Bruckman, A. (1992). Identity Workshop: Emergent Social and Psychological Phenomena in Text-Based Virtual Reality. http://www.cc.gatech.edu/fac/Amy.Bruckman/papers/index.html#IW

—— (1996a). Gender Swapping on the Internet. In P. Ludlow (Ed.), *High Noon on the Electronic Frontier: Conceptual Issues in Cyberspace* (pp. 317–326). Cambridge, MA: M.I.T. Press.

—— (1996b). Finding One's Own Space in Cyberspace. *Technology Review*, 99, 48–54.

Buday, G. (1954). *The History of the Christmas Card*. London: Rockliff.

Cacioppo, J. T., & Anderson, B. L. (1981). Greeting Cards as Data on Social Processes. *Basic and Applied Social Psychology*, 2, 115–119.

Cahn, W. (1979). *Masterpieces: Chapters on the History of an Idea*. Princeton, NJ: Princeton University Press.

Caillois, R. (1961). *Man, Play and Games*. Glencoe, IL: Free Press.

Calinescu, M. (1977). *Faces of Modernity: Avant-Garde, Decadence, Kitsch*. Bloomington, IN: Indiana University Press.

Campbell-Kelly, M., & Aspray, W. (1996). *Computer: A History of the Information Machine*. New York: Basic Books.

Canedy, D. (1997). Wish You Weren't Here: It's Been Live and Let Live Until Today, But Now the Greeting Card Wars Are Under Way. *New York Times*, 20 November 1997, pp. 1, 4.

Cardinal, R. (1972). *Outsider Art*. London: Studio Vista.

Carline, R. (1959). *Pictures in the Post: The Story of the Picture Postcard*. Bedford, England: Gordon Fraser.

Carlson, M. (1996). *Performance: A Critical Introduction*. New York and London: Routledge.

Carter, R. (1997). *Experimental Typography*. Celigny, Switzerland: RotoVision.

Carter, R., Day, B., & Meggs, P. (1993). *Typographic Design: Form and Communication*. New York: Van Nostrand.

Castleman, C. (1982). *Getting Up: Subway Graffiti in New York*. Cambridge, MA: M.I.T. Press.

Cazden, C. B. (1976). Play with Language and Meta-linguistic Awareness: One Dimension of Language Experience. In J. S. Bruner, E. Jolly & K. Sylva (Eds.), *Play – Its Role in Development and Evolution* (pp. 603–608). New York: Penguin.

Chafe, W., & Danielewicz, J. (1987). *Properties of Spoken and Written Language*. New York: Academic Press.

Chafe, W. L., & Tannen, D. (1987). The Relation between Written and Spoken Language, *Annual Review of Anthropology* (pp. 383–409).

Chalfant, H., & Prigoff, J. (1987). *Spraycan Art*. London: Thames & Hudson.

Charney, M. (1978). *Comedy High and Low: An Introduction to the Experience of Comedy*. New York: Oxford University Press.

Chartier, R., Boureau, A., & Dauphin, C. (1997). *Correspondence: Models of Letter-writing from the Middle Ages to the Nineteenth Century*. Princeton: Princeton University Press.

Chase, E. D. (1971 [1926]). *The Romance of Greeting Cards: An Historical Account of the Origin, Evolution, and Development of the Christmas Card, Valentine, and Other Forms of Engraved or Printed Greetings from the Earliest Days to the Present Time*. Detroit, MI: Tower Books.

Cherny, L. (1994). Gender Differences in Text-Based Virtual Reality, *Proceedings of the Berkeley Conference on Women and Language*.

Chevalier, J., & Gheerbrant, A. (1994). *A Dictionary of Symbols*. Oxford: Blackwell.

Chiaro, D. (1992). *The Language of Jokes: Analyzing Verbal Play*. London: Routledge.

Cho, N. (in press). Linguistic Features of Electronic Mail. In S. Herring (Ed.), *Computer-mediated Conversation*.

Cirlot, J. E. (1971). Heart. *A Dictionary of Symbols* (pp. 141–142). London: Routledge & Kegan Paul.

Clifford, J., & Marcus, G. (1986). *Writing Cultures: the Poetics and Politics of Ethnography*. Berkeley: University of California Press.

Clyne, M., Ball, M., & Neil, D. (1991). Intercultural Communication at Work in Australia: Complaints and Apologies in Turns. *Multilingua: Journal of Cross-Cultural and Inter-language Communication*, 10, 251–273.

Coats, P. (1970). *Flowers in History*. New York: Viking.

Coe, C. (1998). Defending Community: Difference and Utopia Online. *International Journal of Cultural Studies*, 1, 391–414.

Cohen, E. M. (1988). The Decoration of Medieval Hebrew Manuscripts. In L. S. Gold (Ed.), *A Sign and a Witness: 2,000 Years of Hebrew Books and Illuminated Manuscripts* (pp. 47–60). New York and Oxford: New York Public Library and Oxford University Press.

Collot, M., & Belmore, N. (1992). The Situational Features and Textual Dimensions of Electronic Language. In J. Aarts, P. de Haan, & N. Oostdijk (Eds.), *English Language Corpora: Design, Analysis and Exploitation: Papers from the Thirteenth International Conference on English Language Research on Computerized Corpora, Nijmegen 1992*. (pp. 41–55).

—— (1996). Electronic Language: A New Variety of English. In S. C. Herring (Ed.), *Computer-mediated Communication: Social, Linguistic and Cross-cultural Perspectives* (pp. 13–28). Philadelphia and Amsterdam: John Benjamins.

Constable, G. (1976). *Letters and Letter-collections*: Turnhout: Ed. Brespols.

Consumer Guide. (1979). *Miniatures*. New York: Beekman House.

Cooper, D. (1995). The Year Mozart and Sid Vicious Shared an Office in New York. *Wired*, 3, 130–133, 163–165.

Cooper, J. J. (1978). *An Illustrated Encyclopedia of Traditional Symbols*. London: Thames & Hudson.

Cooper, M., & Chalfant, H. (1984). *Subway Art*. New York: Henry Holt.

Copeland, R. (1990). The Presence of Mediation. *TDR: The Drama Review*, 34, 28–44.

Cotton, B., & Oliver, R. (1994). *The Cyberspace Lexicon: An Illustrated Dictionary of Terms from Multimedia to Virtual Reality*. London: Phaidon.

Coupland, J., & Coupland, N. (1992). "How Are You?" Negotiating Phatic Communion. *Language in Society*, 21, 207–230.

Crease, R., & Mann, C. (1983). Backyard Creators of Art That Says: "I Did It, I'm Here", *Smithsonian Magazine* (pp. 82–91).

Crick, P. (1983). Kitsch. *British Journal of Aesthetics*, 23, 48–52.

Cringely, B. (1996). *Triumph of the Nerds*. New York: Ambrose Video Publishing.

Crystal, D. (1991). *A Dictionary of Linguistics and Phonetics*. Oxford: Basil Blackwell.

Csikszentmihalyi, M. (1977). *Beyond Boredom and Anxiety*. San Franciso: Jossey Bass.

—— (1979). The Concept of Flow. In B. Sutton-Smith (Ed.), *Play and Learning*. New York: Gardner Press.

—— (1993). *The Evolving Self*. New York: HarperCollins.

—— & Csikszentmihalyi, I. (1988). *Optimal Experience*. New York: Cambridge University Press.

Culler, J. (1988). *On Puns: the Foundation of Letters*. Oxford: Basil Blackwell.

Cupach, W. R., Metts, S., & Hazleton, V. (1986). Coping with Embarrassing Predicaments: Remedial Strategies and Their Perceived Utility. *Journal of Language and Social Psychology*, 5, 181–200.

Curtis, P. (1996). MUDding: Social Phenomena in Text-based Virtual Realities. In P. Ludlow (Ed.), *High Noon on the Electronic Frontier: Conceptual Issues in Cyberspace* (pp. 347–374). Cambridge, MA: M.I.T. Press.

Danchin, L., & Lusardy, M. (1999). Art Outsider et Folk Art des Collections de Chicago (Outsider and Folk Art; The Chicago Collections). Paris: Halle Saint Pierre.

Danesi, M. (1994). *Cool: The Signs and Meanings of Adolescence*. Toronto: University of Toronto Press.

Danet, B. (1971). "The Language of Persuasion in Bureaucracy: 'Modern' and 'Traditional' Appeals to the Israel Customs Authorities". *American Sociological Review*, 36, 847–859.

—— (1973). "'Giving the Underdog a Break:' Latent Particularism among Customs Officials". In E. Katz & B. Danet (Eds.), *Bureaucracy and the Public: A Reader in Official-Client Relations* (pp. 329–337). New York: Basic Books.

—— (1980). Language in the Legal Process. *Law and Society Review*, 14, 445–504.

—— (1984). The Magic Flute: a Prosodic Analysis of Binomial Expressions in Legal Hebrew. *Text*, 4, 143–172.

—— (1985). Legal Discourse. In T. Van Dijk (Ed.), *Handbook of Discourse Analysis* (pp. 273–291). London: Academic.

—— (1990). Language and Law: an Overview of Fifteen Years of Research. In H. Giles & W. P. Robinson (Eds.), *Handbook of Language and Social Psychology* (pp. 537–559). Chichester, England: Wiley.

—— (1994). Hamming it up on the net. *Wired*, 10, October, p. 38.

—— (1997a). The @ symbol. WiredStyle, http:www.wiredstyle.com

—— (1997b). Books, Letters, Documents: the Changing Aesthetics of Texts in Late Print Culture. *Journal of Material Culture*, 2, 5–38.

—— (1997c). Speech, Writing and Performativity: An Evolutionary View of the History of Constitutive Ritual. In B.-L. Gunnarsson, P. Linell & B. Nordberg (Eds.), *The Construction of Professional Discourse* (pp. 13–41). London: Longman.

—— (1998a). Text as Mask: Gender, Play and Performance on the Internet. In S. G. Jones (Ed.), *Cybersociety 2.0: Revisiting Computer-mediated Communication and Community* (pp. 129–158). Thousand Oaks, CA & London: Sage.

—— (1998b). Flaming. In P. Bouissac (Ed.), *Encyclopedia of Semiotics* (pp. 246–247). New York and Oxford: Oxford University Press.

Danet, B., & Gurevitch, M. (1972). Presentation of Self in Appeals to Bureaucracy: An Empirical Study of Role-Specificity. *American Journal of Sociology*, 77, 1165–1190.

Danet, B., & Katriel, T. (1989). No Two Alike: Play and Aesthetics in Collecting. *Play and Culture*, 2, 253–277.

Danet, B., Loshitzky, Y., & Bechar-Israeli, H. (1993). "Masking the Mask:" An Israeli Response to the Threat of Chemical Warfare. *Visual Anthropology*, 6, 229–270.

Danet, B., Ruedenberg, L., & Rosenbaum-Tamari, Y. (1997). "Hmmm . . . Where's That Smoke Coming From?" Writing, Play and Performance on Internet Relay Chat. In F. Sudweeks, M. McLaughlin & S. Rafaeli (Eds.), *Network and Netplay: Virtual Groups on the Internet. Journal of Computer-mediated Communication*, 2 (4). http://jcmc.huji.ac.il/vol2/issue4/ or http://www.ascusc.org/jcmc/vol2/issue4/.

—— (1998). "Hmmm . . . Where's That Smoke Coming From?" Writing, Play and Performance on Internet Relay Chat. In F. Sudweeks, M. McLaughlin & S. Rafaeli (Eds.), *Network and Netplay: Virtual Groups on the Internet* (pp. 47–85). Cambridge, MA: AAAI/MIT Press.

Danet, B., & Wachenhauser, T. (1997). "Out, Out Damn Bot! Will These Channels Ne'er Be Clean?" Shakespeare Live on IRC. Unpublished paper.

Danet, B., Wachenhauser, T., Bechar-Israeli, H., Cividalli, A., & Rosenbaum-Tamari, Y. (1995). Curtain Time 20:00 GMT: Experiments in Virtual Theater on Internet Relay Chat. In B. Danet (Ed.). Play and Performance in Computer-mediated Communication *Journal of Computer-Mediated Communication*, 1 (2). http://jcmc. huji.ac.il/vol1/no2 or http://www.ascusc.org/jcmc/vol1/issue2.

Davies, E. (1987). A Contrastive Approach to the Analysis of Politeness Formulas. *Applied Linguistics*, 8, 75–88.

Davies, E. E. (1988). Public Intimacy: the Language of Valentines in the National Press. *Language and Communication*, 8, 95–107.

Davis, B. H., & Brewer, J. P. (1997). *Electronic Discourse: Linguistic Individuals in Virtual Space*. Albany, NY: State University of New York Press.

Davis, J. M. (1978). *Farce*. London: Methuen.

Demos, V., & Jache, A. (1981). When You Care Enough: An Analysis of Attitudes toward Aging in Humorous Birthday Cards. *The Gerontologist*, 21, 209–215.

Dery, M. (1993a). Flame Wars. *South Atlantic Quarterly*, 92, 559–568.

—— (1993b). Flame Wars: The Discourse of Cyberculture. *South Atlantic Quarterly*, 92.

DeVries, M. A. (1994). *The Elements of Correspondence: How to Express Yourself Clearly, Persuasively, and Eloquently in Your Personal and Business Writing*. New York: Macmillan.

Di Leonardo, M. (1987). The Female World of Cards and Holidays: Women, Families and the Work of Kinship. *Signs*, 12, 440–453.

Dibbell, J. (1996). A Rape in Cyberspace, or How an Evil Clown, a Haitian Trickster Spirit, Two Wizards, and a Cast of Dozens Turned a Database Into a Society. In P. Ludlow (Ed.), *High Noon on the Electronic Frontier: Conceptual Issues in Cyberspace* (pp. 375–396). Cambridge, MA: M.I.T. Press.

Dickel, M. H. (1995). Bent Gender: Virtual Disruptions of Gender and Sexual Identity. *EJC: Electronic Journal of Communication, 5.* http://www.cios.org.

Dillon, K. M., & Jones, B. S. (1981). Attitudes toward Aging Portrayed by Birthday Cards. *International Journal of Aging and Development,* 13, 79–84.

Dorfles, G. (1969). *Kitsch: The World of Bad Taste.* New York: Universe Books.

Drucker, J. (1994). *The Visible Word: Experimental Typography and Modern Art, 1909–1923.* Chicago: University of Chicago Press.

—— (1995). *The Alphabetic Labyrinth: the Letters in History and Imagination.* London: Thames & Hudson.

—— (1996). Experimental-Visual-Concrete: Avant-Garde Poetry Since the 1960's. *Avant Garde Critical Studies,* 10, 39–61.

—— (1997). Digital Reflections: Art and Technology. *The Art Journal.*

Dubin, S. C. (1997). The Centrality of Marginality: Naive Artists and Savvy Supporters. In V. L. Zolberg & J. M. Cherbo (Eds.), *Outsider Art: Contesting Boundaries in Contemporary Culture* (pp. 37–52). Cambridge: Cambridge University Press.

Duranti, A. (1986). Framing Discourse in a New Medium: Openings in Electronic Mail. *Quarterly Newsletter of the Laboratory of Comparative Human Cognition,* 8, 64–71.

Eban, D., Cohen, E., & Danet, B. (Eds.). (1990). *Art as a Means of Communication in Pre-Literate Societies.* Jerusalem: Israel Museum.

Eco, U. (1986). Towards a Semiological Guerilla Warfare. In U. Eco (Ed.), *Travels in Hyperreality* (pp. 135–144). New York: Harcourt Brace Jovanovich.

Edwards, V., & Sienkewicz, T. J. (1990). *Oral Cultures Past and Present: Rappin' and Homer.* Oxford: Basil Blackwell.

Eff, E. (1978). Folk Art: the Heart of America, *The Clarion* (pp. 17–35).

Eklundh, K. S. (1986). *Dialogue Processes in Computer-Mediated Communication: a Study of Letters in the COM System.* Linköping, Sweden.

Eklundh, K. S., & Macdonald, C. (1994). The Use of Quoting to Preserve Context in Electronic Mail Dialogues. *IEEE Transactions on Professional Communication,* 37, 197–202.

Elkin-Koren, N. (1996). Public/private and copyright reform in cyberspace. *Journal of Computer-mediated Communication,* 2. http://jcmc.huji.ac.il/vol2/issue2/.

Elliot, A. G. (1990). *General and Social Letter Writing.* Tadworth, Surrey, UK: Elliot Right Way Books.

Elsley, J. (1996). *Quilts as Text(iles): The Semiotics of Quilting.* New York: Peter Lang.

Emmerling , M. (1988). *American Country Hearts.* New York: Clarkson N. Potter.

Erlich, D. (1991). *The Bauhaus.* Leiscester, England: Magna.

Fenton, K. (1997). The New Typographer Muttering in Your Ear. In M. Bierut, S. Heller, D. K. Holland & W. Drenttel (Eds.), *Looking Closer 2: Critical Writings on Graphic Design* (pp. 31–33). New York: Allsworth.

Ferber, S. (1977). Micrography: A Jewish Art Form. *Journal of Jewish Art*, 3–4, 12–24.

Ferguson, C. (1964). Baby Talk in Six Languages. *American Anthropologist*, 66, 103–114.

—— (1994). Dialect, Register, and Genre: Working Assumptions about Conventionalization. In D. Biber & E. Finegan (Eds.), *Sociolinguistic Perspectives on Register* (pp. 15–30). Oxford: Oxford University Press.

—— (1977). Baby Talk as a Simplified Register. In C. E. Snow & C. Ferguson (Eds.), *Talking to Children* (pp. 209–235). Cambridge: Cambridge University Press.

—— (1983). Sports Announcer Talk. *Language in Society*, 12, 55–73.

Ferrara, K., Brunner, H., & Whittemore, G. (1991). Interactive Written Discourse as an Emergent Register. *Written Communication*, 8, 8–33.

Fielding, G., & Evered, C. (1980). The Influence of Patients' Speech upon Doctors: The Diagnostic Interview. In R. N. St. Clair & H. Giles (Eds.), *The Social and Psychological Contexts of Language* (pp. 51–72). Hillsdale, NJ: Lawrence Erlbaum.

Fitzgibbon, K. (1997). *Ikat: Silks of Central Asia*: Antique Collectors' Club.

Frauenfelder, M. (1997). The ASCII Artists. *Wired News*. http://www.wired.com/news/news/wiredview/story/6346.htm. 25 August, 1997.

Frere-Jones, T. (1997). Towards the Cause of Grunge. In M. Bierut, S. Heller, D. K. Holland & W. Drenttel (Eds.), *Looking Closer 2: Critical Writings on Graphic Design* (pp. 16–18). New York: Allsworth.

Friedl, F., Ott, N., & Stein, B. (1998). *Typography: When, Who, How*. Koln, Germany: Konemann.

Friedlander, S. (1984). *Reflections of Nazism: An Essay on Kitsch and Death*. New York: Harper & Row.

—— (1990). Kitsch and the Apocalyptic Imagination: Preface to a Symposium on Kitsch. *Salmagundi*, 85–86, 201–206.

Fruman, N. (1994). Bloom at Thermopylae. *New York Times Book Review*, October, p. 9.

Funk, J. B., & Buchman, D. (1996). Playing Violent Video and Computer Games and Adolescent Self-Concept. *Journal of Communication*, 46, 19–32.

Garcia, C. (1989). Apologizing in English: Politeness Strategies Used by Native and Non-native Speakers. *Multilingua: Journal of Cross-Cultural and Inter-language Communication*, 8, 3–20.

Gaur, A. (1994). *A History of Calligraphy*. London: The British Library.

Geffner, A. B. (1995). *How to Write Better Business Letters*. Happauge, NY: Baron's Educational Series.

Gell, A. (1992). The Technology of Enchantment and the Enchantment of Technology. In J. Coote & A. Shelton (Eds.), *Anthropology, Art and Aesthetics* (pp. 40–67). Oxford: Clarendon.

—— (1996). Vogel's Net: Traps as Artworks and Artworks as Traps. *Journal of Material Culture*, 1, 18–31.

—— (1998). *Art and Agency: An Anthropological Theory*. Oxford: Clarendon.

Georgakopoulou, A. (in press). On for Drinkies? Email Cues of Participant Alignments. In S. Herring (Ed.), *Computer-mediated Conversation*.

Georges, R. A., & Jones, M. O. (1995). *Folkloristics: An Introduction*. Bloomington and Indianapolis: Indiana University Press.

Georgia Tech Research Corporation (1998). GVU's 9th WWW User Survey. http://www.cc.gatech.edu/gvu/user_surveys/survey-1998-04/.

Gibbon, D. (1981). Idiomaticity and Functional Variation: a Case Study of International Amateur Radio Talk. *Language in Society*, 10, 21–42.

—— (1985). Context and Variation in Two-way Radio Discourse. *Discourse Processes*, 8, 395–419.

Gibson, W. (1984). *Neuromancer*. New York: Ace.

Gilbert, N., & Mulkay, M. (1984). *Opening Pandora's Box: A Sociological Analysis of Scientists' Discourse*. Cambridge: Cambridge University Press.

Giles, H., & Powesland, P. (1975). *Speech Style and Social Evaluation*. London: Academic Press.

Glassie, H. (1989). *The Spirit of Folk Art*. New York and Santa Fe: Harry N. Abrams and Museum of New Mexico.

Godin, S. (1993). *The Smiley Dictionary: Cool Things to Do with Your Keyboard*. Berkeley, CA: Peachpit Press.

Goffman, E. (1959). *Presentation of Self in Everyday Life*. Garden City: Anchor.

—— (1963). *Behavior in Public Places*. Glencoe, IL: Free Press.

—— (1967). *Interaction Ritual: Essays on Face-to-Face Behavior*. Garden City, NY: Anchor Books.

—— (1974). *Frame Analysis: An Essay on the Organization of Experience*. New York: Harper & Row.

Goldberg, I. (1996). Are You Suffering From Internet Addiction Disorder? http://avocado/pc/helsinki.fi/~janne/ikg/.

Gombrich, E. (1984). *The Sense of Order: A Study in the Psychology of Decorative Art*. London: Phaidon.

Goody, J. (1986). *The Logic of Writing and the Organization of Society*. Cambridge: Cambridge University Press.

—— (1987). *The Interface Between the Written and the Oral*. Cambridge: Cambridge University Preess.

—— (1993). *The Culture of Flowers*. Cambridge: Cambridge University Press.

Goody, J., & Watt, I. (1963). The Consequences of Literacy. *Comparative Studies in Society and History*, 5.

Gordon, A. (1984). *Scraps*. Jerusalem: Israel Museum.

Gordon, B. (1986). The Souvenir: Messenger of the Extraordinary. *Journal of Popular Culture*, 20, 135–146.

Gottschall, E. M. (1989). *Typographic Communications Today*. Cambridge, MA: M.I.T. Press.

Grabar, O. (1992). *The Mediation of Ornament*. Princeton: Princeton University Press.

Graburn, N. H. H. (1976). *Ethnic and Tourist Arts: Cultural Expressions From the Fourth World*. Berkeley: University of California Press.

Gray, N. (1986). *A History of Lettering*. London: Phaidon.

Green, M. (1986). *Zen and the Art of the Macintosh: Discoveries on the Path to Computer Enlightenment*. Philadelphia: Running Press.

Green, W. (1978). RTTY Art. In W. Green (Ed.), *The New RTTY Handbook*. Peterborough, New Hampshire: 73, Inc.

Greenberg, C. (1939). Avant-Garde and Kitsch. *Partisan Review*, 6, 3–21.

Greenfeld, K. T. (2000). Meet the Napster, *Time*. 2 October, 2000. http://www.time.com/time/magazine/article/0,9171,1101001002-55730.00.html

Greeting Card Association. (1997). GCA Industry Fact Sheet. World Wide Web. http://www.greetingcard.org/gca/facts.htm.

Griffiths, M. (1997). Computer Game Playing in Early Adolescence. *Youth and Society*, 29, 223–237.

Griffiths, M. D., & Hunt, N. (1998). Dependence on Computer Games by Adolescents. *Psychological Reports*, 82, 475–480.

Grotowski, J. (1968). *Towards a Poor Theatre*. New York: Simon & Schuster.

Gumperz, J., & Hymes, D. (Eds.) (1972). *Directions in Sociolinguistics: the Ethnography of Communication*. New York: Holt, Rinehart and Winston.

Gundlach, R. A. (1982). Children as Writers: The Beginnings of Learning to Write. In M. Nystrand (Ed.), *What Writers Know: The Language, Process, and Structure of Written Discourse* (pp. 129–148). New York: Academic Press.

Gusfield, J. (1976). The Literary Rhetoric of Science: Comedy and Pathos in Drinking Driver Research. *American Sociological Review*, 41, 16–34.

Gustafsson, M. (1974). The Phonetic Length of the Members of Presentday Binomials TT. *Neuphilologische Mitteilungen*, 4, 663–677.

—— (1975). *Binomial Expressions in Present-Day English*. Turku: Turun Yliopisto.

—— (1976). The Frequency and "Frozenness" of Some English Binomials. *Neuphilologische Mitteilungen*, 4, 623–637.

Hafner, K., & Lyon, M. (1996). *Where Wizards Stay Up Late: The Origins of the Internet*. New York: Simon & Schuster.

Hafner, K., & Markoff, J. (1991). *Cyberpunk: Outlaws and Hackers on the Computer Frontier*. New York: Simon and Schuster.

Hale, C. (1996). *Wired Style: Principles of English Usage in the Digital Age*. San Francisco: Hardwired.

Hale, C. L. (1987). A Comparison of Accounts: When Is a Failure a Failure? *Journal of Language and Social Psychology*, 6, 117–132.

Haley, A. (1998). *Type: Hot Designers Make Cool Fonts*. Gloucester, MA: Rockport Publishers.

Hall, M. D., & Metcalf, E. W., Jr. (Eds.) (1994). *The Artist Outsider: Creativity and the Boundaries of Culture*. Washington D.C.: The Smithsonian Press.

Hallmark Corporation (1997). Annual Report. http://www.hallmark.com.

Hamburger, J. F. (1997). *Nuns as Artists: The Visual Culture of a Medieval Convent*. Berkeley: University of California Press.

Handelman, D. (1976). Play and Ritual: Complementary Frames of Meta-Communication. In A. J. Chapman & H. Foot (Eds.), *It's a Funny Thing, Humour* (pp. 185–192). London: Pergamon.

Hanff, H. (1990). *84, Charing Cross Road*. New York: Penguin.

Hargittai, I., & Hargittai, M. (1994). *Symmetry: A Unifying Concept*. Bolinas, CA: Shelter Publications.

Hargrove, B. (1997). Usenet Newsgroup *alt.binaries.fonts* Frequently Asked Questions File. World Wide Web (not available).

Haraway, D. J. (1997). *Modest.Witness@Second.Millenium.FemaleMan_Meets_Onco Mouse:Feminism and Technoscience*. New York and London: Routledge

Harris, S. (1994). Much Ado about IRC. *Online Access*, 9, 28–32.

—— (1995a). *The IRC Survival Guide: Talk to the World on Internet Relay Chat.* Addison-Wesley: Reading, MA.

—— (1995b). Virtual Reality Drama, *Cyberlife!* (pp. 497–520). Indianapolis, IN: Sams.

Havelock, E. A. (1982). *The Literate Revolution in Greece and Its Cultural Consequences*. Princeton: Princeton University Press.

—— (1986). *The Muse Learns to Write: Reflections on Orality and Literacy from Antiquity to the Present*. New Haven: Yale University Press.

Hawley, M. (1997). Introduction. In R. Silvers, with Michael Hawley (Ed.), *Photomosaics* (pp. x–xii). New York: Henry Holt.

Haworth, E. (1990). *Roses*. London: Garamond.

Headlam, B. (1999). Art on the Head of a Microchip. *New York Times*. Circuits. 4 March 1999.

Healy, D. (1997). Cyberspace and Place: The Internet as Middle Landscape on the Electronic Frontier. In D. Porter (Ed.), *Internet Culture* (pp. 54–68). New York and London: Routledge.

Heath, S. B. (1983). *Ways with Words: Language, Life and Work in Communities and Classrooms*. Cambridge: Cambridge University Press.

Heilemann, J. (2000). David Boies: The Wired Interview, *Wired*. 8 (10). http://www.wired.com/wired/archive/8.10/boies.html.

Heim, M. (1987). *Electric Language: A Philosophical Study of Word Processing*. New Haven: Yale University Press.

Heller, S. (1997). Introduction. In S. Heller & A. Fink (Eds.), *Faces on the Edge: Type in the Digital Age* (pp. 2–8). New York: Van Nostrand Reinhold.

—— (1998). A Youth in the Youth Culture. No longer available online.

Heller, S., & Anderson, G. (1994). *American Typeplay*. Glen Cove, NY: PBC International.

Heller, S., & Fink, A. (1997). *Faces on the Edge: Type in the Digital Age*. New York: Van Nostrand Reinhold.

Herring, S. (Ed.). (in press). *Computer-mediated Conversation*.

Herrnstein-Smith, B. (1968). *Poetic Closure: A Study of How Poems End*. Chicago: University of Chicago Press.

—— (1978). *On the Margins of Discourse: The Relation of Literature to Language*. Chicago: University of Chicago Press.

Hibbitts, B. J. (1992). "Coming to Our Senses": Communication and Legal Expression in Performance Cultures. *Emory Law Journal*, 41, 873–960.

—— (1995). Making Motions: The Embodiment of Law in Gesture. *Journal of Contemporary Legal Issues*, 6, 51–81.

Hiemstra, G. (1982). *Teleconferencing, Concern for Face, and Organizational Culture*. Beverly Hills, CA: Sage.

Higgins, D. (1987). *Pattern Poetry*. Albany, NY: State University of New York Press.

Hilberg, B. (1997). *The Patchwork Planner: 350 Original Designs for Traditional Patchwork*. Brunel: David and Charles.

Hildburgh, W. L. (1944–45). Indeterminability and Confusion as Apotropaic Element in Italy and in Spain. *Folklore*, 56, 134–149.

Hill, C. R. (1969). Christmas Card Selections as Unobtrusive Measures. *Journalism Quarterly*, 46, 511–514.

Hillier, B. (1982). *Greetings from Christmas Past*. London: Herbert Press.

Hiltz, S. R., & Turoff, M. (1978). *The Network Nation: Human Communication via Computer*. Reading, MA: Addison-Wesley.

—— (1993). *The Network Nation: Human Communication via Computer*. 2nd ed. Cambridge, MA: M.I.T. Press.

Hochschild, A. R. (1983). *The Managed Heart*. Berkeley: University of California Press.

Hollander, J. (1991). *Types of Shape*. New Haven, CT: Yale University Press.

Holmes, J. (1989). Sex Differences and Apologies: One Aspect of Communicative Competence. *Applied Linguistics*, 10, 194–213.

—— (1990). Apologies in New Zealand English. *Language in Society*, 19, 155–199.

—— (1993). New Zealand Women Are Good to Talk To: An Analysis of Politeness Strategies in Interaction. *Journal of Pragmatics*, 20, 91–116.

Honigmann, J. (1977). The Masked Face. *Ethos*, 5, 263–280.

Horowitz, R. B., & Barchilon, M. (1994). Stylistic Guidelines for E-Mail. *IEEE Transactions on Professional Communication*, 37, 207–212.

Horrigan, J. (2000). *The Holidays Online: Emails and E-greetings Outpace E-Commerce*. Washington, DC: PEW Internet and American Life Project, 31 December 2000. http://www.pewinternet.org/reports/toc.asp?Report=29.

House, J., & Vollmer, H. J. (1988). Speech Act Performance in German: on Realizing the Speech Acts of Requesting and Apologizing. *Linguistische Berichte*, 114, 114–133.

Hughes, G. (1991). *Swearing: A Social History of Foul Language, Oaths and Profanity in English*. Oxford: Basil Blackwell.

Huizinga, J. (1955). *Homo Ludens: A Study of the Play Element in Culture*. Boston: Beacon.

Hussey, S. S. (1992). *The Literary Language of Shakespeare*. London and New York: Longman.

Hutcheon, L. (1985). *A Theory of Parody: The Teachings of Twentieth-Century Art Forms*. London: Methuen.

Hutsko, J. (1999). Programs That Can Redecorate Your Computer Screen. *New York Times*. 14 October 1999, p. G11.

Hymes, D. (Ed.) (1964). *Language in Culture and Society: a Reader in Linguistics and Anthropology*. New York: Harper and Row.

Inge, M. T. (1990). *Comics as Culture*. Jackson and London: University Press of Mississippi.

Ippolito, J. (1998). Intellectual Property or Intellectual Paucity? Nettime archive. http://www.nettime.org/nettime.w3archive/199809/msg00012.html.

Ito, M. (1997). Virtually Embodied: the Reality of Fantasy in a Multi-User Dungeon. In D. Porter (Ed.), *Internet Culture* (pp. 87–109). New York & London: Routledge.

Jackson, A. (1997). *Japanese Country Textiles*. London: Victoria and Albert Museum.

Jacobs, K. (1994). On Typishness: This is My Theory, My Theory is Wrong. In M. Bierut, W. Drenttel, S. Heller & D. K. Holland (Eds.), *Looking Closer: Critical Writings on Graphic Design* (pp. 149–152). New York: Allworth Press.

Jacobson, D. (1996). Contexts and Cues in Cyberspace: the Pragmatics of Naming in Text-based Virtual Realities. *Journal of Anthropological Research*, 52, 461–479.

—— (1999). Doing Social Research in Cyberspace. *Field Methods*, 11, 127–145.

Jakobson, R. (1960). Concluding Statement: Linguistics and Poetics. In T. Sebeok (Ed.), *Style in Language* (pp. 350–377). Cambridge, MA: M.I.T. Press.

Johansen, R., Vallee, J., & Spangler, K. (1979). *Electronic Meetings: Technical Alternatives and Social Choices*. Reading, MA: Addison-Wesley.

Johnson, S. K. (1971). The Christmas Card Syndrome. *New York Times Magazine*, 38–39.

Jones, M. O. (1975). *The Handmade Object and Its Maker*. Berkeley: University of California Press.

—— (1987). *Exploring Folk Art: Twenty Years of Thought on Craft, Work, and Aesthetics*. Ann Arbor, MI: UMI Research Press.

Jones, S. G. (Ed.) (1997). *Virtual Culture: Identity and Communication in Cybersociety*. London, Thousand Oaks and New Delhi: Sage.

Kac, E. (Ed.) (1996). *New Media Poetry: Poetic Innovation and New Technologies*. Special issue, *Visible Language*, 30.

Kalcik, S. (1985). Women's Handles and the Performance of Identity in the CB Community. In R. Jordan & S. Kalcik (Eds.), *Women's Folklore, Women's Culture* (pp. 99–108). Philadelphia: University of Pennsylvania Press.

Kalin, R. (1982). The Social Significance of Speech in Medical, Legal and Occupational Settings. In E. B. Ryan & H. Giles (Eds.), *Attitudes towards Language Variation: Social and Applied Contexts* (pp. 148–163). London: Edward Arnold.

Kalin, R., & Rayko, D. (1980). The Social Significance of Speech in the Job Interview. In R. N. St. Clair & H. Giles (Eds.), *The Social and Psychological Contexts of Language* (pp. 39–50). Hillsdale, NJ: Lawrence Erlbaum.

Kaplan, W., & Cummings, E. (1991). *The Arts and Crafts Movement*. London: Thames & Hudson.

Katriel, T. (1991). *Hahlafot*: Rules and Strategies in Israeli Children's Swapping Exchanges. In T. Katriel, *Communal Webs: Communication and Culture in Contemporary Israel*. Albany, NY: State University of New York Press.

Kaufman, L. (1999). "Excite@Home to Acquire Bluemountain." *New York Times* 26 October 1999.

Keedy, J. (1997). The Rules of Typography According to (Crackpots) Experts. In M. Bierut, W. Drenttel, S. Heller & D. K. Holland (Eds.), *Looking Closer 2: Critical Writings on Graphic Design* (pp. 27–31). New York: Allsworth.

Keenan, S. K. (1993). Investigating Deaf Students' Apologies: An Exploratory Study. *Applied Linguistics*, 14, 364–385.

Keene, D. (1995). Japanese Aesthetics. In N. G. Hume (Ed.), *Japanese Aesthetics and Culture: A Reader* (pp. 27–42). Albany, NY: State University of New York Press.

Kelley, T. (1998). "A Small Card Maker Finds Itself Atop the Web." *New York Times*. 4 June 1998.

—— (1999). "In E-Mail, Many Ways to Say Goodbye." *New York Times*. 22 July 1999.

Kelly, H. A. (1986). *Chaucer and the Cult of St. Valentine*. Leiden: E.J. Brill.

Kendall, L. (1996). MUDder? I Hardly Know 'Er! Adventures of a Feminist MUDder. In L. Cherny & E. R. Weise (Eds.), *Wired Women* (pp. 207–223). Seattle, WA: Seal Press.

—— (1998). Meaning and Identity in "Cyberspace:" the Performance of Gender, Class and Race Online. *Symbolic Interaction*, 21.

Kiesler, S. (Ed.). (1997). *Culture of the Internet*. Hillsdale, NJ: Lawrence Erlbaum.

Kiesler, S., Siegel, J., & McGuire, T. W. (1984). Social Psychological Aspects of Computer-Mediated Communication. *American Psychologist*, 39, 1123–1134.

King, C. (1997). *The Century of the Teddy Bear*. Woodbridge, Suffolk: Antique Collectors Club.

Kintner, E. (Ed.). (1969). *The Letters of Robert Browning and Elizabeth Barrett Browning*. Cambridge, MA: Belknap Press, Harvard University Press.

Kirshenblatt-Gimblett, B. (Ed.). (1976). *Speech Play: Research and Resources for the Study of Linguistic Creativity*. Philadelphia: University of Pennsylvania Press.

—— (1996). The Electronic Vernacular. In G. Marcus (Ed.), *Connected: Engagements with Media at Century's End* (pp. 21–65). Chicago: University of Chicago Press.

Klein, M., Schwemer-Scheddin, Y., & Spiekermann, E. (1991). The Faceless Typeface. In M. Klein, Y. Schwemer-Scheddin & E. Spiekermann (Eds.), *Type and Typographers* (pp. 116–120). London: Architecture and Design Press.

Koffka, K. (1935). *Principles of Gestalt Psychology*. New York: Harcourt Brace.

Kohler, W. (1929). *Gestalt Psychology*. New York: Liveright.

Kollock, P. (1999). The Economies of Online Co-operation. In M. A. Smith & P. Kollock (Eds.), *Communities in Cyberspace* (pp. 220–239). New York & London: Routledge.

Kozinn, A. (1997). "Attuning Classical Music to the Eye as Well as the Ear." *New York Times*. 24 September 1997.

Kraut, R., Patterson, M., Lundmark, V., Kiesler, S., Mukopadhyay, T., & Scherlis, W. (1998). Internet Paradox: A Social Technology That Reduces Social Involvement and Psychological Well-being? *American Psychologist*, 53, 1017–1031.

Kreitler, H., & Kreitler, S. (1972). *Psychology of the Arts*. Durham, NC: University of North Carolina Press.

Kulka, T. (1996). *Kitsch and Art*. University Park, PA: Pennsylvania State University Press.

Kundera, M. (1984). *The Unbearable Lightness of Being*. New York: Harper & Row.

Kunz, P. R., & Woolcott, M. (1976). Season's Greetings: From My Status to Yours. *Social Science Research*, 5, 269–278.

LaFarge, A. (1995). A World Exhilarating and Wrong: Theatrical Improvisation on the Internet. *Leonardo*, 28, 415–422.

—— (1996). The Plaintext Players. http://yin.arts.uci.edu/~players/.

—— (1997). Did Anyone Bring a Word or an Ax: Toward an ID Theater. World Wide Web. Paper presented at the College Art Association, February, 1997. No longer available online.

Lakoff, R. T. (1982). Some of My Favorite Writers are Literate: The Mingling of Oral and Literate Strategies in Written Communication. In D. Tannen (Ed.), *Spoken and Written Language: Exploring Orality and Literacy* (pp. 239–260). Norwood, NJ: Ablex.

Lambourne, L. (1980). *Utopian Craftsmen: the Arts and Crafts Movement from the Cotswolds to Chicago.* London: Astragal.

Landow, G. P. (1992). *Hyper Text: The Convergence of Contemporary Literary Theory and Technology.* Baltimore: Johns Hopkins University Press.

Lanham, R. A. (1993). *The Electronic Word: Democracy, Technology, and the Arts.* Chicago: University of Chicago Press.

Latour, B., & Woolgar, S. (1986). *Laboratory Life: the Construction of Scientific Facts.* Princeton University Press: Princeton, NJ.

Laurel, B. (1991). *Computers as Theatre.* Reading, MA: Addison-Wesley.

Laver, J. (1974). Communicative Functions of Phatic Communion. In A. Kendon, R. M. Harris & M. R. Key (Eds.), *The Organization of Behavior in Face-to-Face Interaction* (pp. 215–238). The Hague: Mouton.

Laver, R. (1981). Linguistic Routines and Politeness in Greeting and Parting. In F. Coulmas (Ed.), *Conversational Routine* (pp. 289–304). The Hague: Mouton.

Layton, R. (1981). *The Anthropology of Art.* St. Albans, Herts and London: Granada.

Lea, M. (Ed.) (1992). *Contexts of Computer-mediated Communication.* Hemel Hempstead, Hertfordshire: Harvester Wheatsheaf.

Lee, J. Y. (1996). Charting the Codes of Cyberspace: A Rhetoric of Electronic Mail. In L. Strate, R. Jacobson & S. B. Gibson (Eds.), *Communication and Cyberspace: Social Interacton in an Electronic Environment* (pp. 275–296). Cresskill, NJ: Hampton Press.

Lee, M. (1965). *Book Making: The Illustrated Guide to Design and Production.* New York: R.R. Bowker.

Lee, R. W. (1952). *A History of Valentines.* Wellesley Hills, MA: Lee Publications.

Leech, G. (1969). *A Linguistic Guide to English Poetry.* London: Longman.

Leslie, J. (1993). Technology: MUDroom. *Atlantic Monthly,* 272, 28–34.

—— (1994). *Mail Bonding. Wired,* 2, 3, 42, 44–48.

Lessig, L. (2000). *Code and Other Laws of Cyberspace.* New York: Basic Books.

Levine, L. W. (1988). *Highbrow Lowbrow: the Emergence of Cultural Hierarchy in America.* Cambridge, MA: Harvard University Press.

Levy, S. (1984). *Hackers: Heroes of the Computer Revolution.* Garden City, NY: Doubleday.

Lieberman, J. N. (1977). *Playfulness: Its Relation to Imagination and Creativity.* New York: Academic Press.

Lind, E. A., & O'Barr, W. M. (1979). The Social Significance of Speech in the Courtroom. In H. Giles & R. N. St. Clair (Eds.), *Language and Social Psychology* (pp. 66–87). Oxford: Basil Blackwell.

Lindeborg, R. A. (1993). The Irresistible Electronic Message of the 1990s: A Case Study. *IEEE Transactions on Professional Communication*, 36, 152–157.

Lipsett, L. O. (1997). *Remember Me: Women and Their Friendship Quilts*. Lincolnwood, IL: Quilt Digest Press.

Liu, C. (1996). Digital Age Brings Explosion in Typeface Choices. *New York Times*. 5 August, 1996.

Liungman, C. G. (1991). *Dictionary of Symbols*. New York: W. W. Norton.

Loftus, G. R., & Loftus, E. F. (1983). *Mind at Play: the Psychology of Video Games*. New York: Basic Books.

Lombard, M., & Ditton, T. (1997). At the Heart of It All: The Concept of Telepresence. *Journal of Computer-Mediated Communication*, 3 (2). http://www.ascusc.org/jcmc/vol3/issue2 or http://jcmc.huji.ac.il/vol3/issue2.

Lovejoy, W. H. (1997). *back slash: a cyber thriller*. New York: Pinnacle.

Lucie-Smith, E. (1981). *The Story of Craft: the Craftsman's Role in Society*. Oxford: Phaidon.

Ludlow, P. (Ed.). (1996). *High Noon on the Electronic Frontier: Conceptual Issues in Cyberspace*. Cambridge, MA: M.I.T. Press.

Lupton, E. (1993). *Mechanical Brides: Woman and Machines from Home to Office*. New York: Princeton Architectural Press.

Lupton, E., & Miller, J. A. (1996). *Design, Writing, Research: Writing on Graphic Design*. New York: Princeton Architectural Press.

Lyons, D. (1997). #ansi culture. http://www.acheron.org/.

MacKinnon, R. C. (1997). Punishing the Persona: Correctional Strategies for the Virtual Offender. In S. G. Jones (Ed.), *Virtual Culture: Identity and Community in Cybersociety* (pp. 206–235). London and Thousand Oaks, CA: Sage.

Maizels, J. (1996). *Raw Creation: Outsider Art and Beyond*. London: Phaidon.

Major, C. (1970). *Black Slang: A Dictionary of Afro-American Talk*. New York: Routledge & Kegan Paul.

Malinowski, B. (1972). Phatic Communion. In J. Laver & S. Hutcheson (Eds.), *Communication in Face-to-Face Interaction* (pp. 146–152). Harmondsworth: Penguin.

Malkiel, Y. (1959). Studies in Irreversible Binomials. *Lingua*, 8, 113–160.

Mandel, T., & Van der Leun, G. (1996). *Rules of the Net: Online Operating Instructions for Human Beings*. New York: Hyperion.

Marcus, G. E., & Myers, F. R. (Eds.). (1995). *The Traffic in Culture: Refiguring Art and Anthropology*. Berkeley and Los Angeles and London: University of California Press.

Martin, J. (1997). *Miss Manners' Basic Training: Communication*. New York: Crown.

Marvin, L.-E. (1995). Spoof, Spam, Lurk and Lag: Aesthetics of Text-Based Textual Realities. *Journal of Computer-Mediated Communication*. In B. Danet (Ed.). *Language, Play and Performance in Computer-mediated Communication. Journal of Computer-Mediated Communication*, 1 (2). http://jcmc.huji.ac.il/vol1/no2.

Maynor, N. (1994). The Language of Electronic Mail: Written Speech? In G. Little & M. Montgomery (Eds.), *Centennial Usage Studies* (pp. 48–54). Tuscaloosa, University of Alabama [publications of the American Dialect Society Series].

McAlhone, B., & Stuart, D. (1998). *A Smile in the Mind: Witty Thinking in Graphic Design*. London: Phaidon.

McCullough, M. (1996). *Abstracting Craft*. Cambridge, MA: MIT Press.

McDowell, J. H. (1992). Speech Play. In R. Bauman (Ed.), *Folklore, Cultural Performances, and Popular Entertainments* (pp. 139–144). Oxford and New York: Oxford University Press.

McGee, M. (1980–81). Faith, Fantasy, and Flowers: A Content Analysis of the American Sympathy Card. *Omega*, 11, 20–32.

McLaughlin, M. L., Osborne, K. K., & Smith, C. B. (1995). Standards of conduct on Usenet. In S. Jones (Ed.), *Cybersociety: Computer- mediated communication and community* (pp. 90–111). Thousand Oaks, CA: Sage.

McLean, R. (1980). *The Thames & Hudson Manual of Typography*. London: Thames & Hudson.

McLuhan, M. (1965). *Understanding Media: the Extensions of Man*. New York: McGraw-Hill.

McRae, S. (1996). Coming Apart at the Seams: Sex, Text and the Virtual Body. In L. Cherny & E. R. Weise (Eds.), *Wired Women* (pp. 242–264). Seattle, WA: Seal Press.

—— (1997). Flesh Made Word: Sex, Text and the Virtual Body. In D. Porter (Ed.), *Internet Culture* (pp. 73–86). New York and London: Routledge.

Meer, J. (1986). What a Card. *Psychology Today*, 20, 16.

Meier, A. J. (1996). Two Cultures Mirrored in Repair Work. *Multilingua: Journal of Cross-Cultural and Inter-language Communication*, 15, 149–169.

Melbin, M. (1987). *Night as Frontier*. New York: Free Press.

Meyer, G., & Thomas, J. (1990). The Baudy World of the Byte Bandit: a Postmodernist Interpretation of the Computer Underground. In F. Schmalleger (Ed.), *Computers in Criminal Justice* (pp. 31–67). Bristol, IN: Wyndham Hall.

Meyrowitz, J. (1985). *No Sense of Place*. London: Oxford.

Microsoft Inc. (2000*). Encarta Encyclopedia*. Redmond, WA: Microsoft, Inc. CD-ROM.

Miller, D., & Slater, D. (2000). *The Internet: An Ethnographic Approach*. Oxford: Berg.

Mills, J., & Donnelly, D. (1999). *Webworks Typography*. Gloucester, MA: Rockport Publishers.

Mills, S. (1995). *Feminist Stylistics*. London and New York: Routledge.

Mitchell, W. (1995). *City of Bits: Space, Place and the Infobahn*. Cambridge, MA: M.I.T. Press.

Moeran, B. (1997). *Folk Art Potters of Japan*. Richmond, Surrey: Curzon.

Moles, A. (1971). *Le Kitsch: L'art du bonheur*. Paris: Maison Mame.

Mooney, L., & Brabant, S. (1988). Birthday Cards, Love, and Communication. *Sociology and Social Research*, 72, 106–109.

—— (1987). Deviance, Deference, and Demeanor: Birthday Cards as Ceremonial Tokens. *Deviant Behavior*, 8, 377–388.

Moore, S. F., & Myerhoff, B. G. (Eds.) (1977). *Secular Ritual*. Assen: Van Gorcum.

Moran, C., & Hawisher, G. E. (1998). The Rhetorics and Languages of Electronic Mail. In I. Snyder (Ed.), *Page to Screen: Taking Literacy into the Electronic Era* (pp. 80–101). London & New York: Routledge.

Morreall, J., & Loy, J. (1989). Kitsch and Aesthetic Education. *Journal of Aesthetic Education*, 23, 63–73.

Muir, K. (1971). *A New Companion to Shakespeare Studies*. Cambridge, NY: Cambridge Univ. Press.

Murphy, J. J. (1974). *Rhetoric in the Middle Ages: A History of Rhetorical Theory from Saint Augustine to the Renaissance*. Berkeley, CA: University of California Press.

Murray, D. E. (1991). *Conversation for Action: The Computer Terminal as Medium of Communication*. Amsterdam and Philadelphia: John Benjamins.

Murray, J. H. (1997). *Hamlet on the Holodeck: The Future of Narrative in Cyberspace*. New York: Free Press.

Myers, A. S. (1993). *Letters for All Occasions: the Classic Guide to Social and Business Correspondence*. New York: Harper.

Myers, B. L., & Copplestone, T. (Eds.). (1981). *The Macmillan Encyclopedia of Art*. London & Basingstoke: Macmillan.

Myers, D. (1990). A Q-Study of Game Player Aesthetics. *Simulation and Gaming*, 21, 375–396.

—— (1993). Time, Symbol Transformations, and Computer Games. *Play and Culture*, 5, 441–457.

Nagy-Farkas, D. (1997). *Easter Egg Surprises*. Grand Rapids, MI: Abacus.

Napoli, L. (1998). "In the E-mail Age, Paper Cards Are Booming." *New York Times*. 23 December 1998.

Nash, W. (1985). *The Language of Humour: Style and Technique in Comic Discourse*. London and New York: Longman.

Naylor, G. (1990). *The Arts and Crafts Movement: A Study of Its Sources, Ideals and Influence of Design Theory*. London: Trefoil.

Negroponte, N. (1995). *Being Digital*. Hodder and Stoughton: London.

Nilsen, A. P. (1984). Greetings and Salutations in a New Age. *Language in Society*, 13, 245–247.

Nir, L. (1998). A Site of Their Own: Gay Teenagers' Involvement in IRC and Newsgroups. Seminar paper, Dept. of Communication & Journalism, Hebrew University of Jerusalem (Hebrew).

Nunberg, G. (Ed.). (1996). *The Future of Books*. Berkeley: University of California Press.

O'Barr, W. M. (1982). *Linguistic Evidence: Language, Power, and Strategy in the Courtroom*. New York: Academic Press.

O'Donnell, J. J. (1998). *Avatars of the Word: from Papyrus to Cyberspace*. Cambridge, MA: Harvard University Press.

Olmert, M. (1992). *The Smithsonian Book of Books*. Washington, D.C.: The Smithsonian Press.

Ong, W. J. (1982). *Orality and Literacy: the Technologizing of the Word*. London: Methuen.

Oring, E. (1986). On the Concepts of Folklore. In E. Oring (Ed.), *Folk Groups and Folklore Genres: An Introduction* (pp. 1–22). Logan, UT: Utah State University Press.

——— (1992). *Jokes and their Relations*. Lexington, KY: University of Kentucky.

Ortega y Gasset, J. (1986). Meditations on the Frame. In R. Brettell & S. Starling (Eds.), *The Art of the Edge: European Frames, 1300–1900* (pp. 21–25). Chicago: Art Institute of Chicago.

Oruch, J. B. (1981). St. Valentine, Chaucer, and Spring in February. *Speculum*, 56, 534–565.

O'Toole, K. (2000). Study Takes an Early Look at the Social Consequences of Net Use, *Stanford Online Report*. 16 February, 2000. http://www.stanford.edu/dept/news/report/news/february16/internetsurvey-216.html

Otten, C. M. (Ed.). (1971). *Anthropology & Art: Readings in Cross-Cultural Aesthetics*. Austin and London: University of Texas Press.

Paine, S. (1990). *Embroidered Textiles: Traditional Patterns from Five Continents*. London: Thames & Hudson.

Palmer, J. (1994). *Taking Humour Seriously*. London and New York: Routledge.

Paolillo, J. (1999). The Virtual Speech Community. *Journal of Computer-mediated Communication*, 4. http://jcmc.huji.ac.il/vol4/issue4/ or http://www.ascuc.org/jcmc/vol4/issue4/.

Papson, S. (1986). From Symbolic Exchange to Bureaucratic Discourse: the Hallmark Greeting Card. *Theory, Culture and Society*, 3, 99–111.

Pareles, J. (1997). "Stitching Grunge From Borrowed Riffs." *New York Times*. 16 April 1997.

Partridge, E. (1968). *Shakespeare's Bawdy*. London: Routledge & Kegan Paul.

Peesch, R. (1982). *The Ornament in European Folk Art*. New York: Alpine Fine Arts.

Pellman, R., & Pellman, K. (1984). *The World of Amish Quilts*. Intercourse, PA: Good Books.

Philipsen, G., & Huspek, M. (1991). A Bibliography of Sociolinguistic Studies of Personal Address. *Anthropological Linguistics*, 27, 94–101.

Phillips, P., & Bunce, G. (1993). *Repeat Patterns: a Manual for Designers, Artists and Architects*. Thames & Hudson: London.

Pins, J. (1980). *The Pins Collection: Chinese and Japanese Paintings and Prints*. Jerusalem: Israel Museum.

——— (1982). *The Japanese Pillar Print: Hashira-e*. London: Robert G. Sawers.

Pocius, G. I. (1979). *Textile Traditions of Eastern Newfoundland*. Ottawa: National Museum of Canada.

Polhemus, T. (1994). *Street Style*. London: Thames & Hudson.

Polk, P. A. (1997). *Haitian Vodou Flags*. Jackson, MS: University Press of Mississippi.

Porter, D. (Ed.). (1997). *Internet Culture*. New York and London: Routledge.

Porter, J. E. (1993). E-Mail and Variables of Rhetorical Form. *The Bulletin of the Association for Business Communication*, 56, 41–42.

Powers, J. (1997). *IRC and Online Chat*. Grand Rapids, MI: Abacus.

Quimby, I. M. G., & Swank, S. T. (Eds.). (1980). *Perspectives on American Folk Art*. New York: Norton.

Quittner, J., & Slatalla, M. (1995). *Masters of Deception: The Gang That Ruled Cyberspace*. New York: HarperCollins.

Rafaeli, S. (1988). Interactivity: from New Media to Communication. In R. B. Pawkins, J. M. Wiemann & S. Pingree (Eds.), *Advancing Communication Science: Merging Mass and Interpersonal Processes. Sage Annual Reviews of Communication Research Vol. 16* (pp. 110–133). Beverly Hills, CA: Sage.

Rafaeli, S., & Sudweeks, F. (1997). Networked Interactivity. In F. Sudweeks, M. McLaughlin & S. Rafaeli (Eds.), *Network and Netplay: Virtual Groups on the Internet.* http://jcmc.huji.ac.il/vol2/issue4/ or http://www.ascusc.org/jcmc/vol2/issue4/.

—— (1998). Networked Interactivity. In F. Sudweeks, M. McLaughlin & S. Rafaeli (Eds.), *Network and Netplay: Virtual Groups on the Internet* (pp. 173–190). Menlo Park, CA and Cambridge, MA: AAAI Press and M.I.T. Press.

Raymond, E. S. (1996). *The New Hackers' Dictionary.* Cambridge, MA: M.I.T. Press. 3rd ed.

Reader's Digest. (1979). *Reader's Guide Complete Guide to Needlework.* Pleasantville, NY and Montreal: The Reader's Digest Association.

Redford, B. (1986). *The Converse of the Pen: Acts of Intimacy in the Eighteenth-century Familiar Letter.* Chicago: University of Chicago Press.

—— (1993). Beyond Talking on Paper. *University of Chicago Magazine,* August, pp. 27–31.

Reid, E. (1991). *Electropolis: Communication and Community on Internet Relay Chat.* B.A. Honors thesis, University of Melbourne. http://people.we.mediaone.net/elizrs/work.html.

—— (1994). *Cultural Formations in Text-based Virtual Realities.* Unpublished M.A. Thesis, University of Melbourne.

—— (1995). Virtual Worlds: Culture and Imagination. In S. G. Jones (Ed.), *Cybersociety: Computer-Mediated Communication and Community* (pp. 164–183). Thousand Oaks, CA: Sage.

—— (1996a). Communication and Community on Internet Relay Chat: Constructing Communities. In P. Ludlow (Ed.), *High Noon on the Electronic Frontier: Conceptual Issues in Cyberspace* (pp. 397–412). Cambridge, MA: M.I.T. Press.

—— (1996b). Text-based Virtual Realities: Identity and the Cyborg Body. In P. Ludlow (Ed.), *High Noon on the Electronic Frontier: Conceptual Issues in Cyberspace* (pp. 327–346). Cambridge, MA: M.I.T. Press.

Rheingold, H. (1993). *The Virtual Community: Homesteading on the Electronic Frontier.* Reading, MA: Addison-Wesley.

Rice, R. E., & Love, G. (1987). Electronic Emotion: Socioemotional Content in a Computer-Mediated Communication Network. *Communication Research,* 14, 85–108.

Rice, R. P. (1997). An Analysis of Stylistic Variables in Electronic Mail. *Journal of Business and Technical Communication,* 11, 5–23.

Richtel, M. (2000). "Napster Case: Hard Queries on Copyrights." *New York Times.* 3 October 2000.

Riddell, A. (1975). *Typewriter Art.* London: London Magazine Editions.

Ring, G. (1949). *A Century of French Painting 1400–1500.* London: Phaidon.

Roach, S. (1986). The Kinship Quilt: an Ethnographic Semiotic Analysis of a Quilting Bee. In R. Jordan & S. C. Kalcik (Eds.), *Women's Folklore, Women's Culture.* Philadelphia: University of Pennsylvania Press.

Robacker, E. F., & Robacker, A. (1968). The Far from Lonely Heart. *Pennsylvania Folklife,* 17, 2–7.

Rodino, M. (1998). Breaking Out of Binaries: Reconceptualizing Gender and Its Relationship to Language in Computer-mediated Communication. *Journal of Computer-Mediated Communication,* 3. http://jcmc.huji.ac.il/vol3/issue3/ or http://www.ascusc.org/jcmc/vol3/issue3/.

Rolfe, B. (1977). *Behind the Mask.* Oakland, CA: Persona Books.

Romaine, S. (1994). On the Creation and Expansion of Registers: Sports Reporting in tok Pisin. In D. Biber & E. Finegan (Eds.), *Sociolinguistic Perspectives on Register* (pp. 59–81). Oxford and New York: Oxford University Press.

Rose, D. (1994). *Minding Your Cyber-Manners on the Internet.* Indianapolis: Alpha.

Rosentswieg, G. (1995). *Type Faces.* New York: Madison Square Press.

Royer, D. (1970). RTTY Art Made Easy. *RTTY Journal.*

Ruedenberg, L., Danet, B., & Rosenbaum-Tamari, Y. (1995). Virtual Virtuosos: Play and Performance at the Computer Keyboard. *EJC: Electronic Journal of Communication,* 5. http://www.cios.org.

Ruskin, J. (1989 [1849]). *The Seven Lamps of Architecture.* New York: Dover.

Ryan, D. B. (1982). *Picture Postcards in the United States, 1893–1918.* New York: C. N. Potter.

Ryan, E. B., & Giles, H. (1982). *Attitudes Towards Language Variation: Social and Applied Contexts.* London: Edward Arnold.

Salmagundi (1990). *On Kitsch: A Symposium,* Special issue, *Salmagundi,* Winter-Spring 1990 (pp. 197–313).

Samuelson, P. (1991). Digital Media and the Law. *Communications of the ACM,* 34, 23–29.

Santino, J. (1994). *All Around the Year: Holidays and Celebrations in American Life.* Urbana, IL: University of Illinois Press.

—— (1996). *New Old Fashioned Ways: Holidays and Popular Culture.* Nashville: University of Tennessee Press.

Saville-Troike, M. (1989). *The Ethnography of Communication: An Introduction.* Oxford and New York: Basil Blackwell.

Schaefermeyer, M. J., & Sewell, E. H., Jr. (1988). Communicating by Electronic Mail. *American Behavioral Scientist,* 32, 112–123.

Schechner, R. (1985). *Between Theater and Anthropology.* Philadelphia: University of Pennsylvania Press.

—— (1988). Playing. *Play and Culture,* 1, 3–19.

—— (1993). *The Future of Ritual: Writings on Culture and Performance.* New York & London: Routledge.

Schimmel, A. (1990). *Calligraphy and Islamic Culture.* London: Tauris.

Schmidt, L. E. (1995). *Consumer Rites: The Buying and Selling of American Holidays.* Princeton, NJ: Princeton University Press.

Schoonmaker, P. N. (1999). *A Collector's History of the Teddy Bear*: Hobby House Press.

Schor, N. (1992). Cartes Postales: Representing Paris 1990. *Critical Inquiry*, 18, 188–244.

Schrum, S. (Ed.). (1998). *Theater in Cyberspace*. New York: Peter Lang.

Searle, J. R. (1979). *Expression and Meaning*. Cambridge: Cambridge University Press.

Searle-Chatterjee, M. (1993). Christmas Cards and the Construction of Social Relations in Britain Today. In D. Miller (Ed.), *Unwrapping Christmas* (pp. 176–192). Oxford: Oxford University Press.

Shaw, D. F. (1997). Gay Men and Computer Communication: A Discourse of Sex and Identity in Cyberspace. In S. G. Jones (Ed.), *Virtual Culture: Identity and Communication in Cybersociety* (pp. 133–146). Thousand Oaks, CA & London: Sage.

Shea, V. (1994). *NETiquette*. San Francisco: Albion.

Sherzer, J. (1978). Oh! That's a Pun and I Didn't Mean It. *Semiotica*, 22, 335–350.

—— (1990). *Verbal Art in San Blas: Kuna Culture Through Its Discourse*. Cambridge: Cambridge University Press.

—— (1992). Ethnography of Speaking. In R. Bauman (Ed.), *Folklore, Cultural Performances, and Popular Entertainments* (pp. 76–80). New York and Oxford: Oxford University Press.

Shields, R. (Ed.). (1996). *Cultures of Internet: Virtual Spaces, Real Histories, Living Bodies*. London: Sage.

Short, J., Williams, E., & Christie, B. (1976). *The Social Psychology of Telecommunications*. New York: John Wiley.

Shuman, A. (1986). *Storytelling Rights: the Uses of Oral and Written Texts by Urban Adolescents*. Cambridge: Cambridge University Press.

Simons, H. (1988). *Rhetoric in the Human Sciences*. London: Sage.

Sims, B. R. (1991). Electronic Mail and Writing in the Workplace. *Studies in Technical Communication*, 2, 137–155.

Sims, B. R., & Guice, S. (1992). Differences Between Business Letters from Native and Non-Native Speakers of English. *Journal of Business Communication*, 29, 23–39.

Slatalla, M. (1998a). Helpful Program for a Stubborn Girl. *New York Times*. Circuits, 31 December 1998.

—— (1998b). Turning Desktops into Theme Parks. *New York Times*. 4 June, 1998.

Slater, D. R. (1998). Trading Sexpics on IRC: Embodiment and Authenticity on the Internet. *Body and Society*, 4, 91–117.

—— (2000). Making Things Real: Ethics and Order on the Internet. *Theory, Culture and Society*.

Smith, M., & Kollock, P. (Eds.). (1998). *Communities in Cyberspace: New Forms of Social Interaction and Organization*. New York & London: Routledge.

Snyder, I. (Ed.). (1998). *Page to Screen: Taking Literacy into the Electronic Era*. London & New York: Routledge.

Solomon, R. C. (1991). On Kitsch and Sentimentality. *Journal of Aesthetics and Art Criticism*, 49, 1–14.

Solt, M. E. (1968). *Concrete Poetry: a World View*. Bloomington, IN: Indian University Press.

Spaeight, G. (1990). *The History of the English Puppet Theatre*. London: Robert Hale.

Spiekermann, E. (1995). LettError: Just van Rossum and Erik van Blokland Would Be Rich and Famous if Everyone Who Used Their Typefaces Paid For Them. *Wired*, 3 (7) , 146–147.

Spinuzzi, C. (1994). A Different Kind of Forum: Rethinking Rhetorical Strategies for Electronic Text Media. *IEEE Transactions on Professional Communication*, 37, 213–217.

Spooner, M., & Yancey, K. (1996). Postings on a Genre of Email. *College Composition and Communication*, 47, 252–278.

Staff, F. (1966). *The Picture Postcard and Its Origins*. London: Lutterworth.

—— (1969). *The Valentine and Its Origins*. London: Lutterworth.

—— (1992). *The Penny Post 1680–1918*. Cambridge: Lutterworth.

Stam, R. (1989). *Subversive Pleasures: Bakhtin, Cultural Criticism, and Film*. Baltimore, MD: Johns Hopkins University Press.

Steele, V. (1997). *Fifty Years of Fashion: From New Look to Now*. New Haven, CT: Yale University Press.

Stern, E. S. (1988). *The Very Best From Hallmark: Greeting Cards Through the Years*. Abrams: New York.

Stevens, P. S. (1984). *Handbook of Regular Patterns: An Introduction to Symmetry in Two Dimensions*. Cambridge, MA: M.I.T. Press.

Stewart, S. (1978). *Nonsense: Aspects of Intertextuality in Folklore and Literature*. Baltimore: Johns Hopkins University Press.

—— (1984). *On Longing: Narratives of the Miniature, the Gigantic, the Souvenir, the Collection*. Baltimore & London: Johns Hopkins University Press.

—— (1987). *Ceci tuera cela*: Graffiti as Crime and as Art. In J. Fekete (Ed.), *Life After Postmodernism: Essays on Value and Culture* (pp. 161–180). New York: St. Martin's Press.

Stivale, C. J. (1997). Spam: Heteroglossia and Harassment in Cyberspace. In D. Porter (Ed.), *Internet Culture* (pp. 133–144). New York and London: Routledge.

Stone, A. R. (1996). *The War of Desire and Technology at the Close of the Mechanical Age*. Cambridge, MA: MIT Press.

Strate, L. (1996). Cybertime. In L. Strate, R. Jacobson & S. B. Gibson (Eds.), *Communication and Cyberspace: Social Interaction in an Electronic Environment* (pp. 351–377). Cresskill, NJ: Hampton Press.

Street, B. V. (1984). *Literacy in Theory and Practice*. Cambridge: Cambridge University Press.

—— (Ed.). (1993). *Cross-cultural Approaches to Literacy*. Cambridge: Cambridge University Press.

Sudnow, D. (1983). *Pilgrim in the Micro-World*. New York: Warner.

Suler, J. (1996–97). Do Boys Just Wanna Have Fun? Male Gender Switching in Cyberspace (and How to Detect It). http://www.rider.edu/users/suler/psycyber/genderswap.html.

—— (1999a). Computer and Cyberspace Addiction. http://www.rider.edu/users/suler/psycyber/cybaddict.html.

—— (1999b). Life at the Palace: A Cyberpsychology Case Study. http://www.rider.edu/users/suler/psycyber/palacestudy.html.

Suszczynska, M. (1994). A Study in Intercultural Pragmatics: Apology. *Studies in Applied Linguistics*, 10, 111–122.

Sutton-Smith, B. (1997). *The Ambiguity of Play*. Cambridge, MA: Harvard University Press.

——, & Kelly-Byrne, D. (1984). The Idealization of Play. In P. K. Smith (Ed.), *Play in Animals and Humans*. New York: Blackwell.

Swank, S. T. W., Forman, B. M., Sommer, F. H., Schwind, A. P., Weiser, F., S., Fennimore, D. H., & Swan, S. B. (1983). *Arts of the Pennsylvania Germans*. New York: W.W. Norton.

Tamony, P. (1980). Funky. *American Speech: A Quarterly of Linguistic Usage*, 55, 210–213.

Tannen, D. (Ed.). (1982). *Spoken and Written Language: Exploring Orality and Literacy*. Norwood, NJ: Ablex.

Tannen, D. (1999). "Memo to Gore: Express Yourself!" *New York Times*. 11 October 1999, p. A19.

Tapscott, D. (1997). *Growing Up Digital: the Rise of the Net Generation*. New York: McGraw-Hill.

Test, G. A. (1991). *Satire: Spirit and Art*. Tampa, FL: University of South Florida Press.

Thomas, D. (1954a). *Under Milk Wood*. London: Decca Record Co., Ltd. and the BBC (recording).

—— (1954b). *Under Milk Wood, a Play for Voices*. New York: New Directions.

Thomas, M. (1997). Welcome to the ASCII-Art Newgroups. http://members.tripod.com/~tissue_2/faq.html (version 1.0.3).

—— (1998). Welcome to ASCII Art. http://www.geocities.com/SoHo/7373/faq.htm#faq. (version 2.0).

Thompsen, P. A. (1996). What's Fueling the Flames in Cyberspace? A Social Influence Model. In L. Strate, R. Jacobson & S. Gibson (Eds.), *Communication and Cyberspace: Social Interaction in an Electronic Environment* (pp. 297–315). Cresskill, NJ: Hampton Press.

Thompson, R. F. (1966). An Aesthetic of the Cool: West African Dance. *African Forum*, 2.

—— (1973). Aesthetic of the Cool. *African Arts*, 7, 41–3, 64–67, 89–91.

Tomkins, S. S. (1980). Affect as Amplification: Some Modifications in Theory. In R. Plutchik & H. Kellerman (Eds.), *Emotion: Theory, Research, and Experience*. NY: Academic Books.

Traber, C. (1995). In Perfect Harmony? Escaping the Frame in the Early 20th Century. In E. Mendgen (Ed.), *In Perfect Harmony: Picture and Frame 1850–1920* (pp. 222–247). Seattle: University of Washington Press.

Tschichold, J. (1998 [1928]). *The New Typography: A Handbook for Modern Designers*. Berkeley: University of California Press.

Turkle, S. (1984). *The Second Self: Computers and the Human Spirit.* New York: Simon & Schuster.

—— (1991). If the Computer is a Tool, Is It More Like a Hammer or More Like a Harpsichord? *The Phi Kappa Phi Journal,* 71.

—— (1995). *Life on the Screen: Identity in the Age of the Internet.* New York, NY: Simon & Schuster.

Turner, V. (1969). *The Ritual Process: Structure and Anti-Structure.* Chicago: Aldine.

—— (1974). From Liminal to Liminoid: An Essay in Comparative Symbology. *Rice University Studies,* 60, 53–92.

—— (1986a). *The Anthropology of Performance.* New York: PAJ Publications.

—— (1986b). *Carnaval in Rio: Dionysian Drama in an Industrializing Society.* New York: PAJ Publications.

—— (1986c). Performing Ethnography. In R. Schechner (Ed.), *The Anthropology of Performance.* New York: PAJ Publications.

Uhlirova, L. (1994). E-mail as a New Subvariety of Medium and Its Effects upon the Message. In S. Cmerjrkova & F. Sticha (Eds.), *The Syntax of Sentence and Text: A Festschrift for Frantisek Danes* (pp. 273–282). Amsterdam: John Benjamins.

Unger, G. (1994). Legible? In M. Bierut, S. Heller, D. K. Holland & W. Drenttel (Eds.), *Looking Closer: Critical Writings on Graphic Design* (pp. 108–114). New York: Allsworth.

van Dijk, T. (Ed.) (1985). *Discourse and Literature.* Amsterdam and Philadelphia: John Benjamins.

VanderLans, R., & Licko, Z. (1993). *Emigré (The Book): Graphic Design into the Digital Realm.* New York: Van Nostrand Reinhold.

Vienne, V. (1997a). Designers and Visibility: Design – Not Biology – Is Destiny. In M. Bierut, W. Drenttel, S. Heller & D. K. Holland (Eds.), *Looking Closer 2: Critical Writings on Graphic Design* (pp. 131–135). New York: Allsworth.

—— (1997b). Designing Beauty: From the Outrageous to the Sublime. In M. Bierut, W. Drenttel, S. Heller & D. K. Holland (Eds.), *Looking Closer 2: Critical Writings on Graphic Design* (pp. 40–42). New York: Allsworth.

—— (1997c). Soup of the Day. In M. Bierut, W. Drenttel, S. Heller & D. K. Holland (Eds.), *Looking Closer 2: Critical Writings on Graphic Design* (pp. 9–15). New York: Allworth.

Vlach, J. M. (1992). "Properly Speaking:" The Need for Plain Talk about Folk Art. In J. M. Vlach & S. J. Bronner (Eds.), *Folk Art and Art Worlds* (pp. 13–26). Logan, UT: Utah State University Press.

Vlach, J. M., & Bronner, S. J. (Eds.). (1992). *Folk Art and Art Worlds.* Logan, UT: Utah State University Press.

von Gwinner, S. (1988). *The History of the Patchwork Quilt: Origins, Traditions and Symbols of a Textile Art.* West Chester, PA: Schiffer.

Walsh, N. (1992–96). The Comp.fonts FAQ. http://nwalsh.com/comp.fonts/FAQ/index.html.

Walther, J. B. (1992). Interpersonal Effects in Computer-mediated Interaction: A Relational Perspective. *Communication Research,* 19, 52–90.

Warde, B. (1956). *The Crystal Goblet: Sixteen Essays on Typography*. Cleveland, OH: World Publishing.

Washburn, D. K. (Ed.). (1983a). *Structure and Cognition in Art*. Cambridge: Cambridge University Press.

—— (1983b). Toward a Theory of Structural Style in Art. In D. K. Washburn (Ed.), *Structure and Cognition in Art* (pp. 1–7). Cambridge: Cambridge University Press.

Washburn, D. K., & Crowe, D. W. (1988). *Symmetries of Culture: Theory and Practice of Plane Pattern Analysis*. Seattle and London: University of Washington Press.

Wellman, B. (1999). From Little Boxes to Loosely-Bounded Networks: The Privatization and Domestication of Community. In J. Abu-Lughod (Ed.), *Sociology for the Twenty-First Century: Continuities and Cutting Edges* (pp. 94–114). Chicago: University of Chicago Press.

Wellman, B., & Potter, S. (in press). *Networks in the Global Village*. Boulder, CO: Westview.

Welters, L. (Ed.). (1999). *Folk Dress in Europe and Anatolia: Beliefs about Protection and Fertility*. Oxford: Berg.

Werry, C. C. (1996). Linguistic and Interactional Features of Internet Relay Chat. In S. C. Herring (Ed.), *Computer-mediated Communication: Linguistic, Social and Cross-cultural Perspectives* (pp. 47–64). Philadelphia and Amsterdam: John Benjamins.

Weygandt, C. (1954). Hearts and Flowers from Pennsylvania. *Antiques*, 65, 146–147.

Wilkins, H. (1991). Computer Talk: Long-Distance Conversations by Computer. *Written Communication*, 8, 56–77.

Will-Harris, D. (1998). Seven Stages of Type Appreciation. http://www.webreview.com/1998/09_25/designers/09_25_98_1.shtml.

Williams, E. (Ed.). (1967). *Anthology of Concrete Poetry*. New York: Something Else Press.

Williams, R. (1996). *Blip in the Continuum: A Celebration of Grunge Typography!* Berkeley: Peachpit Press.

Willoughby, M. (1994). *A History of Postcards: a Pictorial Record from the Turn of the Century to the Present Day*. London: Studio Editions.

Wilson, E. (1994). *Ornament, 8,000 Years: An Illustrated Handbook of Motifs*. London: Thames & Hudson.

Wolfe, T. (1965). *Kandy Kolored Tangerine-Flake Streamline Baby*. New York: Farrar, Straus & Giroux.

—— (1979). *The Right Stuff*. New York: Bantam.

Woods, A. S., & Delisle, R. G. (1978). The Treatment of Death in Sympathy Cards. In C. Winick (Ed.), *Deviance and Mass Media* (pp. 95–103). Beverly Hills, CA: Sage.

Woolman, M. (1997). *A Type Detective Story: Episode One: The Crime Scene*. Crans, Switzerland: RotoVision SA.

Yabsley, S. (1984). *Texas Quilts, Texas Women*. TX: Texas A & M University.

Yates, J. (1989a). *Control Through Communication*. Baltimore, MD: Johns Hopkins University Press.

—— (1989b). The Emergence of the Memo as a Managerial Genre. *Management Communication Quarterly*, 2, 485–510.

Yates, J., & Orlikowski, W. (1993). Knee-jerk Anti-LOOPism and Other Email Phenomena: Oral, Written, and Electronic Patterns ini Computer-Mediated Communication. Working Paper #150. Cambridge, MA: Center for Coordination Science, Sloan School of Management, M.I.T.

Yates, J., & Orlikowski, W. J. (1992). Genres of Organizational Communication: A Structurational Approach to Studying Communication and Media. *Academy of Management Review*, 17, 299–326.

Yates, S. J. (1996). Oral and Written Linguistic Aspects of Computer Conferencing. In S. C. Herring (Ed.), *Computer-mediated Communication: Linguistic, Social and Cross-cultural Perspectives* (pp. 29–46). Philadelphia and Amsterdam: John Benjamins.

Yli-Jokipii, H. (1996). An Approach to Contrasting Languages and Cultures in the Corporate Context: Finnish, British, and American Business Letters and Telefax Messages. *Multilingua: Journal of Cross-Cultural and Inter-language Communication*, 15, 305–327.

Young, K. S. (1998). *Caught in the Net: How to Recognize the Signs of Internet Addiction – and a Winning Strategy for Recovery*. New York: Wiley.

Zegart, T. (1994). *Quilts: An American Heritage*. New York: Smithmark.

Zug, C. G. (1994). Folk Art and Outsider Art: A Folklorist's Perspective. In M. D. Hall & E. W. Metcalf, Jr. (Eds.), *The Artist Outsider: Creativity and the Boundaries of Culture* (pp. 145–160). Washington DC: The Smithsonian Press.

Subject Index

Names Index

3-D Font Creator, 302

Abbott, Lawrence L., 46n46, 105
Adelswärd, Viveka, 64
Ahl, Frederick, 146
Albers, Anni, 306
Albers, Josef, 198, 296, 297, 306, 340n41
Allan, Keith, 154n38
Allen, Alistair, 272
Allison, Bob, 196, 218, 236n8, 238n49
American Folklore Society, 369n11
American Greetings Corporation, 49n100,
    170, 175, 178, 182, 188n6, 190n36,
    191n40, 191n41, 301, 369n6
American Needlepoint Guild, 282n13,
    286n67, 370n29
America Online, 187, 346, 369n8
American Standard Code for Information
    Interchange, 49n102
Amir, Ziva, 287n82
Anderson, Barbara L., 190n32
Anderson, Gail, 299, 324, 341n43
Angell, David, 54, 60–63, 96n25, 96n28,
    98n58
Anscombe, I., 370n19
Apollinaire, Guillaume, 198, 236n14
Argyle, Katie, 45n24
Armstrong, Louis, 318
Arnheim, Rudolf, 240n81, 286n71
Aronson, S., 147
ASCII, *see* American Standard Code for
    Information Interchange, *and* ASCII
    characters *in the Subject Index*
Aspray, William, 44n19, 194, 195
ATHEMOO, 150–151, 156n67
Atkins, Martin, 238n49
Atkinson, Dwight, 99n71
Attridge, Derek, 146
Austin, J. L., 190n30, 190n31

Avrin, Leila, 202
Aytot, John, 155n43

Babcock, Barbara, 282n3, 284n33
Baktin, Mikhail M., 8, 45n24, 141, 144,
    155n57, 156n59
Baldwin, Beth W., 95n20
Banfield, Edwin, 161, 166, 190n29
Banks, Marcus, 281
Barbash, Shepard, 370n22
Barchilon, Marian, 95n20
Barger, John, 200, 201
Barlow, John Perry, 27, 30
Barnes, Susan B., 49n88
Baron, Naomi, 63, 88, 90, 92, 96n20, 99n74
Barth, Edna, 271, 287n91
Basso, Keith, 45n30
Bateson, Gregory, 8, 17, 102
Baudot code, 203, 237n24
Bauhaus movement, 198, 236n16, 296, 297,
    340n41
Bauman, Richard, 45n28, 45n29, 105, 113,
    153n13
Bayer, Herbert, 296, 340n41
Beaubien, Michael P., 49n91
Bechar-Israeli, Haya, 48n84, 49n92
Beeching, Wilfred A., 340n33, 371n40
Belk, Russell, 24
Bell, Andrew, 195, 236n5, 238n41
Bellock, Pam, 47n66
Belmore, Nancy, 49n96, 95n20
Belsey, Andrew, 199, 236n13
Ben-Amos, Dan, 350, 369n11
Bergquist, M., 369n12
Berliner, P.F., 105, 107, 154n30, 365
Besnier, Niko, 45n30
Biber, Douglas, 45n31, 85, 87, 91, 99n71,
    99n73
Bierut, Michael, 344n96, 344n108